LABORATORIES
OF AUTOCRACY

LABORATORIES OF AUTOCRACY

A Wake-Up Call from Behind the Lines

DAVID PEPPER

St. Helena Press
Cincinnati, Ohio

Laboratories of Autocracy:
A Wake-Up Call from Behind the Lines

Published by St. Helena Press

Library of Congress Control Number: 2021946505

ISBN (paperback): 9781662919572
eISBN: 9781662919589

"At what point then is the approach of danger to be expected? I answer, if it ever reach us, it must spring up amongst us. It cannot come from abroad. If destruction be our lot, we must ourselves be its author and finisher. As a nation of freemen, we must live through all time, or die by suicide."

—Abraham Lincoln

"[T]he first, the grandest, and most decisive act of judgment which the Statesman and General exercises is rightly to understand . . . the War in which he engages."

—Carl von Clausewitz

Introduction

I T WAS A traffic jam only Chris Christie could admire.

The cars began backing up in early October 2020, on both sides of the Norwood Lateral, one of two major East-West highways crossing Greater Cincinnati. The backups peaked late in the afternoon, but they had nothing to do with the drive home from work—most people were still not commuting downtown due to COVID. Nor was there a problem with the highway itself. No construction. No sudden spate of accidents.

No. It was something else.

The cars were jamming up the Lateral because they were all converging on the same exit halfway between Interstate 71 and Interstate 75, entering the city of Norwood. Once off the exit, the long, single-file line of cars waited at a stoplight, turned left on green, inched across the top of the highway, snaked around another gradual left, made a sharp right at a stop sign, then *another* right, past Sheriff's deputies guiding traffic, and then into the packed parking lot of the Hamilton County Board of Elections.

Yes, these were all voters. The traffic jam was composed mostly of cars lining up to drop off ballots at the *sole* voter drop box location in a county of more than 800,000 people. The others in line were there to park, then vote in person.

Even though some of those driving had been in their cars 30, 40 or even 50 minutes to get to the point where the traffic jammed up, they were the lucky ones. For those who use public transportation, some would ride multiple buses almost 90 minutes, *each way*, to get themselves to that drop box in Norwood.[1]

And these Hamilton County voters were not alone. Ohioans waited in traffic jams like this in multiple cities and counties across the state.[2] In other counties, they would have to sit on buses for up to two hours each way.[3]

And all this needless driving and braking and waiting—and waiting again if you were there to vote in person—occurred because of one decision, by one man, who had been warned that this exact scenario would take place.

For months, local elections officials and advocates (myself included) had pushed Ohio's secretary of state to allow multiple voter drop boxes around the state so that voters could cast their ballots safely in the pandemic, and without mail delays that were snagging the Ohio postal system. Other states were adding voter drop boxes for these reasons, and they were proving very popular with voters.[4] They had never been controversial before.

The first-term secretary of state, Frank LaRose, fought back. He initially said he, too, wanted more drop boxes, but had no power to add them. Only the state legislature could add drop boxes, he insisted with zero legal backing.[5] It was clear someone was pressuring him not to add them. But then he went on a legal losing streak that would rival Rudy Giuliani's legal woes a few months hence. Every court that looked at LaRose's argument concluded he was wrong. Judges of all political stripes found that he could add as many drop boxes as he wanted, wherever he wanted.[6]

Finally empowered to add them, and with some election

boards planning new drop box locations, he still refused. He banned all drop boxes except those located at a *single site* for each county—the same lone site where voters of that county cast their ballots early in-person.[7] Compare that to places like Denver[8] or Seattle,[9] where there were dozens of drop boxes in just those cities alone.

With this arbitrary decision, LaRose didn't just defeat the purpose of drop boxes, he guaranteed a month of traffic jams. Like Governor Christie, but for voting.

Think about it—LaRose required drop boxes to be located at the same (and only) location where voters also vote early, in-person. Each day, thousands of voters already converged on these sites—driving, parking, then standing in line to vote inside (late in the campaign, they wait hours to vote this way). Usually, a single road leads to these sites—two at best. Now LaRose threw the only voter drop box of a county on top of that same congestion. Mayors and other local officials had warned him what would result. So, within days of the beginning of early voting, the traffic nightmare began, backing up for miles in some places. In Summit County (Akron), LaRose's home county, the videos of long car lines winding through city streets went viral.[10] LaRose later tried to fire an election official in Summit County, citing the traffic jams as one reason, but the Ohio Supreme Court rejected his argument, saying *he* was to blame.[11]

Bottom line: at the time, it was clearly a horrible decision, and one that earned harsh criticism across both Ohio and the nation. In hindsight, it looked even worse.

Now, fast forward six months to 2021.

Ohio's new legislature is in session in Columbus, and one of the items on its busy agenda is a new voting bill.

These lawmakers all watched the debate over drop boxes and traffic jams. They saw the letters from mayors and elections officials, and the predictable results of LaRose's ban. Some of these lawmakers no doubt witnessed the congestion in person. As politicians, they would've seen the polling that 76% of Ohio voters support more drop boxes.[12]

These are the people who have the power to overrule LaRose's terrible decision. With the benefit of hindsight, they can act on the painful lesson from months before.

So, what do they do?

They propose a law *locking in the ban on more drop boxes* for all future elections.[13]

That's right, one drop box location per county, permanently— and only at the one location where early, in-person voting already draws thousands. Guaranteed congestion, now cemented into law for all future secretaries of state. For all future voters.

That's "voting reform" in Ohio in the year 2021. One of the changes, at least.

That's Ohio's statehouse at work. They *liked* the congestion. They *want* voters to endure it from now on.

But Ohio is not alone. With Ohio politicians pushing for this permanent dropbox ban as this book goes to print, states like Georgia and Iowa were so impressed by LaRose's traffic jams, they had already passed laws doing the same thing.[14]

* * *

As 2021 arrived in America, a starting gun was fired across the country.

A race among states began, in a deeply disturbing direction.

On voting rights, like Ohio, statehouses across the country jammed through voter suppression bills with ruthless efficiency and at breakneck speed. Dozens of them.[15] Many bills bore remarkable similarities to one another, while few addressed legitimate voting issues from the prior election. As with drop boxes, most were wholly disconnected from what voters in these states actually want to see happen. In some cases, so-called "reforms" dramatically defied the popular will of that state.

Beyond attacks on voters, these same statehouses rushed through changes to the inner workings of elections—the back-end procedures after votes have been cast.[16] How votes are counted. Who counts them. Who oversees the counting. Who certifies the outcomes. How outcomes can be challenged and overturned. In some cases, they shifted power to high-level and partisan (likely Republican) officials and away from local boards that traditionally benefit from checks and balances and professional guidance. In other states, certain powers were moved from Democratic to Republican officials,[17] or back to the Republican legislature.[18] Given the shenanigans from the prior November and December, during which Trump supporters around the country plumbed, unsuccessfully, for ways to overturn election results on wholly unfounded conspiracy theories, these types of changes are ominous indeed.

The sprint also encompasses rigging the next decade of elections—better known as "gerrymandering." As this book goes to print, statehouses across the country are gearing up to redraw the legislative and Congressional lines for the next decade, and in most states, this will lead to districts that are even more rigged than the egregiously undemocratic districts these states endured from 2011-2020. The new districts will mean that any casual observer will be able to foretell the outcome of 99% of the thousands of legislative elections—state and federal—that will occur over the next decade. And the proportion of legislative districts occupied by the two parties will dramatically misrepresent the proportion of people in the states who voted for candidates of each party. Just as it was from 2011-2020, extreme gerrymandering alone makes it hard to shoe-horn America's state-level politics over the coming decade into any definition of a healthy democratic system.

Statehouses also rushed through other "reforms" undermining core elements of democratic governance. Around the country, parallel bills passed imposing the risk of criminal penalties for peaceful protests while removing liability for those who injure protesters.[19] No coincidence, protests became a central point of political organizing and voter registration throughout 2020. In other states, legislators altered judicial elections and courts' jurisdiction over various matters. Their clear intent was to weaken any independent judicial check-and-balance vis-à-vis their own future legislative actions, as well as over election disputes.[20] While other states passed laws empowering individual citizens to become vigilantes on issues from abortion to election observation, another attempt to circumvent the traditional court process.

The onslaught has been so fierce, it's been easy for everyday Americans, seeking a political respite after the end of the Trump presidency or seeking normalcy amid a roiling pandemic, to lose sight of what's happening. And too often, commentators place all that's happening into the box of "voting rights," attacks on which we've seen for years. Still others attribute all these attacks to Donald Trump's "Big Lie" (i.e., that he actually won the 2020 election). But when you pull back the lens, and observe how broad and aggressive the onslaught truly is, we are witnessing something much bigger. Much deeper. It's a coordinated, nation-wide weaponization of statehouses to undermine American democracy itself. And where it could lead heading into 2022, then 2024—even permanently—is downright frightening.

Importantly, there's a reason why these attacks on democracy are happening at the state level—and happening so efficiently and effectively there. It's been building for a while now. And this is the core of the story that most newspapers, commentators and even well-regarded authors have still not pinpointed or analyzed. This isn't about Trump or "The Big Lie," although both make it worse.

To paraphrase the old Clinton mantra, "It's the statehouses, stupid."

* * *

In a 1932 dissent, Justice Louis Brandeis famously coined the metaphor of states as **laboratories of democracy**: "It is one of the happy accidents of the federal system that a single courageous state may, if its citizens choose, serve as a laboratory, and try novel social and economic experiments without risk to the rest of the country."[21] Ever since, Brandeis's phrase has been shorthand for one of the core benefits of federalism.

Since our founding, Brandeis's vision has, at times, played out as he hoped. Under progressive leadership, Wisconsin pushed for workers' rights, instituted direct primaries, protected the state's forests, and broke up large corporations, all models for progressive changes to come nationally.[22] As wild as Louisiana's Huey Long was, some of his approaches became forerunners to FDR's New Deal programs. Even Mitt Romney's approach to health care as governor of Massachusetts provided a model President Obama adopted nationally in the Affordable Care Act. And momentum from states played a domino-like role in bringing same-sex marriage to the country. Laboratories of democracy indeed.

But that's not the full story. A clear-eyed look at American history also reveals a less sanguine view of states' influence over time. Before the Civil War, again in the late 1800s, and on and off again in the 1900s, states and state legislatures played a pernicious role. In the early 1800s, state after state in both the north and south added racial restrictions as to who could vote, often mimicking one another. And after slavery was abolished, states were the collective source of the laws known as "Jim Crow" that discriminated so brutally against Black Americans. Because those laws emerged at the state level, they were far more deeply enmeshed into the fabric of the nation, holding America back for close to a century.

Conversely, some of the most important moments in our country's history have been federal efforts to protect citizens *from* state governments' worst instincts and actions. That was the whole point of the post-Civil War Amendments. And that protection lay at the heart of the civil rights legislation of the 1960s and 70s, which provided a bulwark for a generation.

But the bad news is . . . they're back. State legislatures are now assuming a renewed, dangerous role that harkens back to those darkest of eras. And, for a number of reasons, they have become deeply entrenched—nearly unstoppable—in the destructive role they are now playing. To turn Brandeis's metaphor on its head, state legislatures across our country have become ever more aggressive and effective **Laboratories of Autocracy**. When I use the term autocracy, I'm not suggesting that they have reached that endpoint yet. Or that it is necessarily their aim. But this book will show that legislatures have steadily created the precise conditions that have degenerated into autocracies and authoritarian regimes time and again, including one model that is gaining momentum in the world today. And their pace is accelerating.

This didn't happen overnight.

In recent decades, *state legislatures have atrophied as broadly representative bodies and become easily captive to narrow interests.* In the past decade, like laboratories, they have engaged in numerous "dry runs" of extreme and anti-democratic measures—dabbling in a variety of anti-democratic laws, learning from one another, sharing their work, testing the courts, assessing outcomes. Along the way, these legislatures have discovered that as extreme and broadly unpopular as their agendas may be, they face no accountability for pursuing them—a critical lesson they have internalized for the future. They can go further and further, and it doesn't matter.

And this isn't happenstance. A number of well-organized and well-funded organizations swooped in to coordinate these efforts—converting previously diffuse, part-time and low-profile governmental bodies into a unified, relentless force.

Add it all up, and 2021 comprises the culmination of it all—where all of these factors are converging to unleash extremist legislatures as a robust, integrated front attacking core democratic principles and protections. Together, they have enough power to overrun the more moderating and representative forces of statewide and local elected officials (of both parties), as well as the federal government. In the same way that Southern statehouses ushered in the end of reconstruction in the late 1800s, the early 2020s see them threatening the heart of American democracy on multiple fronts, and nationwide.

Far more than the antics of wild-eyed politicians like Marjorie Taylor Greene or Jim Jordan—and yes, even bigger than Donald Trump's "Big Lie"—these laboratories of autocracy are the most corrosive danger America faces. And if unaddressed, the risks they impose on democracy only intensify as we approach 2022 and 2024. The ultimate danger is that these statehouses calcify into permanent undemocratic structures, forever immune from popular will, constantly damaging the common good while ripping apart American democracy itself. And just as Jim Crow outlasted Andrew Johnson by a century, they threaten to carry out this destructive role long after Trump, Jordan and Greene are mere memories.

* * *

As has been the case in many areas over the generations, Ohio's recent story—a downward spiral into political sclerosis and extremism, along with increasing attacks on democracy—is the story of many states.

And from my unique perch in Ohio politics, I've had a front-row seat to all of it. Heck, I'm the one who sued Frank LaRose to add more drop boxes and videotaped the Norwood traffic jam to try to get his terrible decision reversed. So, the book's **initial chapter** will present an up-close look at the rapid decline of politics and public outcomes in the Buckeye State. Since Ohio has long been a quintessential bellwether state, our story presents both a wake-up call and a case study of what's happening nationally. If this can happen in a state that elected Obama twice, it can happen most anywhere. And understanding the details of a single state makes clear how deeply corrosive what's happening is once expanded across the country.

Chapters Two through **Five** explore all that got us to this point, drawing on events from the dramatic descent of Ohio and other states into corrupt and extremist politics to reveal the root causes of the problem in America's statehouses. A combination of issues such as extreme gerrymandering, the unknown/distant nature of so much statehouse work, the anonymity of so many officeholders, term limits, and the unappreciated, robust power of statehouses has created cesspools of dysfunction, corruption and extremism. In most states, this has resulted in a deeply dysfunctional incentive system. There are few incentives for politicians at the statehouse level to seek broader, favorable public outcomes for everyday voters on the issues that matter to them. But there are strong incentives to serve the interests of big money or power, and the extreme wing of the party. And that out-of-whack incentive system has created an enormous weakness in governance in state after state.

Chapter Six outlines how, in more recent years, some well-funded corporations and institutions identified this weakness as their golden opportunity, swooping in to harness broken statehouses as sources of power and profits on a national scale. In pursuit of a top-down vision of so-called "economic liberty" that aspires for minimal government involvement, they've weaponized state capitals on a wide variety of issues from climate change, to education, to worker rights. **Chapter Seven** explains how, captured by money and trappings of power, statehouses became champions for unpopular causes benefitting well-placed interest groups—running roughshod over local governments that better reflected the will of citizens, or end-running national efforts on those same issues. But because of anti-democratic aspects of statehouses that have strengthened with time, these statehouses can push such efforts immune from popular will, even as their policies fail miserably as a matter of the common good. Little known politicians who would've been ousted from office at a local level for taking on unpopular or failed measures get re-elected at the statehouse again and again without breaking a sweat. Their success in ramming through these extreme, unpopular measures with no accountability served as a dry run for today and the future, spinning off countless lessons and "best practices."

Chapter Eight explains how this dynamic dovetailed directly into growing attacks on democracy itself, which accelerated following Obama's win in 2008 and the GOP take-over of many statehouses in 2010. Across the country, many legislatures rolled back voter protections that had become

PART I

CHAPTER 1

Ohio, Ohio, Ohio: A Bellwether for Good and Bad

As I ARRIVED at college, some folks detected a slight twang.

"Are you from the Midwest?" they'd ask.

"I'm from Ohio," I'd reply.

"Right, so you're from the Midwest."

"No," I'd correct them. "I'm from Ohio."

I was not being cute, or argumentative. I meant it.

The Midwest was a bunch of smaller states further west and north. Yes, in the Big Ten. But colder. More plains and farms. Where they make milk and cheese.

Iowa and Wisconsin for sure. Fine states.

Not Ohio.

In my mind, the great state of Ohio stood on its own. Alone and strong. As our slogan so perfectly captured—"the heart of it all."

Even geographically, the term Midwest didn't compute. Ohio's footprint spanned both east and south, not just westward. To paraphrase Sarah Palin, we can see Kentucky from our house.

We were bigger than those Midwest states. We didn't have just one major city, but a host of them, and countless mid-sized cities to go with them. Each with its own unique story and character.

We had a richer history than those other states too. More presidents than any state but Virginia—even a few good ones. Supreme Court Justices and historic cabinet members, from William Howard Taft to Salmon Chase. Speaking of Chase, a passionate abolitionist, Ohio was the end-point of the Underground Railroad, meaning Ohio represented freedom for countless escaping slaves, scanning for candles in windows up and down the mighty Ohio. Ulysses Grant, William Sherman and countless leading figures who saved the Union came from Ohio. The author of the Fourteenth Amendment . . . abolitionist John Bingham, who represented Eastern Ohio in Congress.

And so many other national figures, non-political ones, hailed from Ohio. Heroes like John Glenn and Neil Armstrong. Writers like Toni Morrison and Harriet Beecher Stowe. Actors like Clark Gable and Dean Martin. Directors like Steven Spielberg. Icons like Roy Rogers and Annie Oakley. Coaches like Lou Holtz. History makers and barrier breakers like the Wright Brothers, Thomas Edison and Jesse Owens. Ohioans all.

"No. I'm from Ohio."

I said the words knowing we were an industrial powerhouse. We made cars and car parts, second only to Michigan. We were a national leader in corn and soybeans; coal, iron and steel—heck, we're where Rockefeller got his start. When it came to major companies and products, blue chip names could be found all over Ohio. Barney Kroger, from Cincinnati, opened his first grocery store here, and the company is still headquartered here. William Procter and James Gamble joined together to make candles, then soap, in Cincinnati; Procter & Gamble is still based here. Henry Sherwin and Edward Williams partnered up to mix paint in Cleveland around the same time; still there. Similar stories brought Dana and the National Cash Register Company (and its "mechanical money drawer") to Dayton, Goodyear to Akron, Marathon to Findlay, and later, The Limited to Columbus. Beyond the biggest names, Ohioans in town after town made products the whole nation and world enjoyed—every car part imaginable made across the state, from Mansfield to Springfield to Youngstown; glass in Toledo; shoelaces out of Portsmouth; dishware from Lancaster; Hoover vacuums in North Canton; Whirlpool washing machines in Clyde; Airstream RVs in Jackson Center; and NFL footballs (the ones in the actual games) out of Ada. As Willard Scott reminded us on every Today Show, Smuckers made its jellies out of Orville.

You name it, Ohio made it, and in many cases—the airplane, the cash register, Teflon, the vacuum cleaner or the light bulb— Ohioans invented it. And our rail and highway networks and Ohio River barges and Lake Erie ships brought these goods to market over the world. It didn't hurt that we're 600 miles—a day's drive—from 60% of the nation's population.[23]

Economically, data confirmed we were the heart of it all. Over the last 50 years, Ohio's economy was in the nation's top seven as measured by GDP—fifth in the 1960s and 70s, sixth in 1980, then seventh since.[24] Even higher—fourth—when it came to manufacturing.[25] If Ohio were its own country, its economy would generally be in the top 20 in the world. A global industrial powerhouse.

And we led the world in other ways. Ohio boasted hubs in aerospace, scientific and other research, and national defense. In the Cleveland Clinic, we had among the finest medical institutions in the world, but our medical and bioscience expertise spanned statewide, with Cincinnati Children's Hospital and Ohio State's medical facilities among them. Speaking of Ohio State, Ohio boasts colleges and universities galore. Not just *The* Ohio State University, but other major state schools as well—Cincinnati, OU. But so many more. Oberlin. Kenyon. Denison. Wesleyan. College of Wooster. Miami. Dayton. Ohio: a state *not* in New England with small liberal arts schools drawing students from across the country.

And of course, being from Cincinnati, in my mind we were the state of the Big Red Machine—America's first professional baseball team. But Ohio was also synonymous with great football, where high school rivalry games (Canton-Massilon, Xavier-Elder) generated crowds the size of college games. And great Ohio natives, both from small towns and big cities, dominated professional football—Roger Staubach, Cris Carter, Jack Lambert, Larry Csonka, Alan Page, Dan Dierdorf. More recently, Charles Woodson, Orlando Pace and Chris Spielman. Basketball, you ask? LeBron and Stephen Curry aren't just both from Ohio. They were born in the same hospital in Akron!

"No. I'm from Ohio."

All that size and might and diversity also made Ohio more politically central than most other states. Again, the heart of it all. But it was far more than size that made that the case.

We were the state whose combination of big cities and small towns and farmland approximated the mix found in the nation more than any other state. And within those big cities and small towns, we enjoyed a wide tapestry of ethnic and minority groups from across the world that also approximated the wonderful diversity of America. Italians and Irish in Youngstown. Cleveland and other metropolitan areas drawing generations of immigrants from around the world. Eastern

Europeans in the Northeast, spanning across the bottom of Lake Erie to Toledo. Irish and Germans in Southwest Ohio. A large chunk of Appalachia. A sizeable Black population, many of whom never left after escaping slavery, followed by another wave travelling north in the great migration of the 1900s. Together, our demographics arguably represented the nation better than any other state.[26] As John Glenn used to say, if you shrunk America down to 11 million people, you'd get Ohio.

Combine that representativeness with Ohio's large haul of electoral college votes, and Ohio was the state that picked presidents. First, because if you won the state that best mimicked the makeup of the country, odds were that you had what it took to win over that country. And second, because often, our large tranche of electoral college votes put you over the top.

And most importantly, that delicate balance of big city, small town, suburban and rural—and that demographic diversity—also meant one other thing. We were a swing state. A good candidate from either party could win Ohio, so our votes were actually up for grabs. A state that voted for Nixon twice then voted for Carter. A state that voted for Reagan twice and then Bush then voted for Clinton. Ohio elected W. twice then Obama twice. So, one reason Ohio really mattered for the presidency is because candidates from either party could win or lose here, and in a close national race, that would make all the difference.[27] And only a few states actually played that role.

But that closeness also impacted who won *other* races statewide, and how. And it set the tone for the broader politics of Ohio. Winning Ohio was complicated. It took work to cobble together the coalitions needed to win a majority of Ohio's wide diversity of voters. Beyond the many regions and overall diversity, no single city dominated—not long ago, you had to appeal to eight cities of 100,000 or more, and more than 50 of 10,000 or more.[28] That's work! Democrats who won had to be authentic figures who won over independents and some Republicans through that authenticity—leaders like John Glenn and Howard Metzenbaum. And Republicans who won generally did so with some patina of moderation to earn support from all the voters they needed. For the same reason, we often had a mix in government. A Democratic legislature balanced out a Republican governor. Or the opposite. Or a Democratic-leaning Supreme Court provided a check on Republican leadership elsewhere. So, when it came to Ohio politics, you thought moderate. Common sense. Maybe even boring. Nothing crazy on either side, because the population wouldn't put up with crazy or extreme for long. Things would balance out.

"No," I'd reply. "I'm from Ohio."

I meant it, not to make a point, but because it was my natural reaction. That's just how we thought of ourselves. Not part of some group of states. But "the heart of it all."

Which only was reinforced by what usually came next.

A smile. Familiarity. Then—

"Ohhhh . . . .my grandmother grew up in Ohio."

"My dad's from Cleveland."

"My mom's from Toledo.'

"Oh, we go home and visit my relatives there often. Cedar Point is so much fun!"

"I grew up a Reds fan because my dad's a Reds fan. He grew up in Dayton."

You learned quickly as an Ohioan on the East Coast that everyone had some Ohio connection. Which also made Ohio feel more central.

"The heart of it all."

O-H! How Things Have Changed

If, at my upcoming 30th reunion, someone suggested Ohio was in the Midwest, I'd still resist.

I'd still list many of the strengths I used to brag about back then that set us apart. (There's a reason my law school classmates named me "Most Likely to Be President . . . of the Cincinnati Board of Tourism.")

We're still one of the biggest economies in the nation. Seventh in GDP. Between Saudi Arabia and the Netherlands.

At 11.7 million people, we're still seventh in population. Pretty darn big.

Of course, we've faced tough times economically. But that's true of many states, the industrial ones especially. We've been buffeted by global competition, technology and other challenges. Some of the big blue chip companies remain: Procter & Gamble, Sherwin Williams, Kroger, all are still here. Other big names are gone: NCR pulled out of Dayton; Chiquita left Cincinnati.

But the real loss is slightly below those biggest of names.

Remember those one-company or one-factory towns that shipped products everywhere? Portsmouth's shoelaces and Lancaster's kitchenware? So many of those are gone, or a shell of what they were.[29] While lots of auto manufacturing remains, many plants have closed, moving overseas and decimating Ohio towns. Steel has risen and fallen—but more of the latter—while coal is dying a steady death. The biggest employers in those towns are now the city or county government itself, the school system, or a local hospital; good jobs, but not sectors that grow the pie, bringing in revenue from outside. Many of those lost manufacturing jobs (700,000 lost between 1970 and 2015)[30] have been replaced by lower paying service jobs—and those service jobs have themselves been on a downward trajectory, from a Main Street hardware store to a regional Walmart. (In 2018, Walmart was Ohio's largest employer).[31] Sadly, many of those jobs haven't been replaced at all, and many of those towns have shrunk as a result, with young people moving either to the bigger Ohio cities, or out of state completely. Still, although they've hit hard here, many of those challenges and shocks to the system aren't unique to Ohio. The root causes are national and global in scope.

But if I were being more transparent, the conversation would turn in a new direction. To the things that are going wrong specifically in Ohio, driven by dynamics *within* Ohio.

Decline Everywhere You Measure It

There are recent trends that don't just evince average decline, mirroring national trends, but where the trajectory plunges far more steeply. Beneath a surface-level picture of latent natural strengths amid modest decline—driven by national/global challenges—is a far bleaker story. One of dramatic decline in core areas, propelling a self-reinforcing downward spiral.

Here are some of the data that tell that story:

- **People leaving**: Ohio's population growth slowed to a snail's pace in recent decades, now well below states in the south and west, and worse than even our neighboring states. A growth rate of 2.3% between 2011 and 2020 ranked us 48th in the nation.[32] The relative decline is best reflected in our number of electoral college votes, or House seats in Congress. We had 25 seats after 1960. That number now stands at fifteen for the 2020s. Make no mistake, this isn't a fertility issue. Fewer people are choosing to move here, and native Ohioans are moving away at an alarming rate. Ohio routinely ranks in the top ten states in the country for the percentage of people leaving for other states,[33] primarily looking for jobs. Many of those leaving are young, so Ohio's population is also getting older.[34] A few metropolitan pockets—greater Columbus and greater Cincinnati—are seeing some growth, but vast swaths of Ohio are cratering in size.

- **Less educated**: despite its strong base of higher education institutions, Ohio now ranks in the bottom third (35th) in terms of the educational attainment of its people.[35] A public primary/secondary education system that ranked fifth in the nation as recently as 2010 has plummeted, now mired in the 20s year after year, below the national average.[36] Rankings consistently place us below average when it comes to high school graduation rates.[37] Ohio is a national leader in one major educational category: our population shoulders among the greatest load of student debt in the nation— sometimes ranking first.[38]

- **Health**: despite national- and world-class health care institutions, Ohio routinely ranks as one of the least healthy states in the nation. In 2021, the nonpartisan Health Policy Institute of Ohio ranked Ohio 47th in the nation in terms of its health value (we pay more for poorer health), on par with sub-40 rankings over the past decade.[39] Why so low?

  □ Drug overdose deaths: Ohio ranked 4th highest in the nation (we were first in 2019[40])

  □ Infant mortality: 9th

- ▫ Premature death: 11th

- ▫ Heart disease mortality: 9th

- ▫ Life expectancy: 9th (2019)[41]

- ▫ Toxic pollutants: 3rd

- ▫ Air quality: 5th worst

- **Poverty**: despite strong core assets, Ohioans are struggling economically. With Cleveland (ranked first) and Cincinnati (sixth), we are the only state with two cities in the top ten poorest major cities in the country.[42] But the struggles go beyond our major urban centers. Smaller cities and towns suffer even higher poverty rates—with Youngstown, East Cleveland, Warren, Fostoria and Cambridge all poorer than Cleveland itself.[43] Child poverty rates top 50% in each of those cities, but also in Trotwood, Ashtabula and Canton. More than a third of the children live in poverty in 38 Ohio cities.[44] Ohioans now make almost ten percent less than the average American, a number that has fallen as the number of higher-paying manufacturing jobs in Ohio has plummeted.[45] In 2018, "six of Ohio's 10 most common jobs paid so little that a typical full-time worker would earn less than $26,000 and need food assistance to feed a family of three."[46]

I could go on.

But having pored over the data for years, my rule of thumb is, *if you can measure it, Ohio lags the country in it.* And too many key measurements are plummeting each year. For Black Ohioans especially, the numbers are markedly worse. From health to education to economic well-being, outcomes trail the rest of the state.[47] No datapoint is more stark than the fact that Black babies in Ohio are three times more likely to die in infancy than White babies.[48]

And the problems only compound on themselves. When a state like Ohio fails so miserably at critical responsibilities, the consequences of those failures drive other failures. For example, the state's sky-high student debt chases young people away, and holds back our economy as in-state graduates enter the work force already strapped and spending less. And lower graduation rates keep the best employers from creating jobs here. And downward we go from there.

A snowball tumbling downhill, growing ever bigger as it rolls.

Broken Politics, Broken Government

These poor public outcomes have come during an era of deep atrophy in Ohio politics and government.

Back when I was in college, I would never have described Ohio as a state with extremist politics. And when it came to political corruption, I would've looked down upon Illinois or New Jersey or Louisiana.

Now Ohio is right there with them. Arguably, we've taken the lead.

A *USA Today* analysis in 2021 concluded as much, ranking Ohio as the most corrupt state in the nation.[49] It's hard to argue with them. Since 2001, scandal after scandal has erupted in Columbus. The first exploded in the 2000s, when millions of state dollars were invested in rare coins foisted on state government by a well-connected donor—only going public after those coins could not be found.[50] A far bigger scandal followed a few years later, when billions of dollars were siphoned away from public schools to for-profit and online charter schools championed by major political donors. The results of these schools were poor to begin with, but it turns out that the largest of these for-profit schools was a scam—cooking the books to get paid millions for student attendance that never existed.[51] Then in 2018, one Ohio Speaker resigned amid an FBI investigation into pay-to-play corruption with payday lenders.[52] Two years later, months before the 2020 election, the FBI announced the biggest bribery scandal in Ohio history, involving the bailout of one of Ohio's largest energy companies.[53] In early 2021, the lobbyist at the center of that final scandal was found in a Florida park with a bullet in his head while wearing a blue "DeWine for Governor" T-shirt (Mike DeWine is the incumbent governor here).[54] When I say Jersey has nothing on us, that's what I'm talkin' about.

At the same time corruption has exploded here, Ohio's politics have veered away from their past balance and moderation. Oddly, this is occurring even as the state still has relative balance when it comes to party affiliation. Trump did well here, of course, but so did Obama. In 2018, 50% of the state's voters voted for a Republican for the statehouse, while 49% voted for a Democrat. 52% of Ohioans voted for a Republican for Congress in that same year; 47%, a Democrat. A Republican won the governorship in 2018 by four points; a Democrat won the Senate seat by close to seven. Yes, some of the old Democratic strongholds in small towns and eastern Ohio have become more Republican. But large and growing suburbs—the prior base of Ohio's moderate GOP—have become more Democratic, a trend Trumpism accelerated. So, on the surface, the breakdown along party lines remains close to even, with a slight rightward tilt that has existed for decades.

But watching the state's political activity in recent decades, you wouldn't know it.

A legislature in a state that voted for Obama twice, and voted 50%-49% Republican/Democrat for the statehouse in 2018,[55] legislates like a deep red state. Year after year, name the issue, and extreme policies spew from Columbus that you'd expect in only the most conservative states in the nation. Policies that don't come close to reflecting the mainstream sentiment of the Ohio electorate.

Just a few examples on hot-button issues:

Guns are now allowed in Ohio day cares, bars (as long as you don't drink in those *bars)*, sports establishments, shopping malls, airports and other places. The legislature added concealed carry fifteen years ago, requiring fourteen days of firearms training; then reduced that to eight days of classes; and a new bill would remove the need for training entirely. Within a year of a mass shooting in Dayton, amid demands of frustrated citizens to "do something," the only gun reform the legislature passed was a form of "stand your ground"—broadening the defense of shooting someone to include not just your home or car, but any place you have a legal right to be.[56]

The legislature advocates new ways to ban **abortion** every few months. A 20-week ban was enacted. Then a six-week ban was passed. Then an outright ban was proposed. Polls show that amid the flurry of all these bills, some believe abortion is simply not legal in the state.[57] The number of clinics in the state halved after the statehouse passed a bill requiring clinics to sign transfer agreements with hospitals, knowing full well few hospitals would do so.[58] In 2020, the legislature passed a law requiring that women who undergo surgical abortions must either cremate or bury their fetus, making their decision beforehand. Then, amid the pandemic, they passed a law banning abortion-related services via telemedicine.

Ohio still allows people to be fired due to their **sexual orientation** even after the state lost its battle at the U.S. Supreme Court in the *Obergefell* case, which enshrined marriage equality nationally. And even after *Obergefell* opened up same-sex couples' ability to adopt, the Ohio legislature refuses to update the language of Ohio law to reflect that. The wording, they insist, must still say "husband and wife." In 2021, Ohio added a law that doctors could refuse to treat LBTGQ Ohioans for so-called "moral" reasons.

And amid the pandemic, the legislature in the state which is home to the Cleveland Clinic launched an all-out war on a science-based response. Despite a Republican governor advocating the opposite, statehouse politicians were among the first in the nation to attack testing, masks, vaccines and other measures to keep Ohioans safe. Even as the state's health director, appointed by that Republican governor, earned stratospheric approval ratings from Ohioans, the legislature personally attacked her repeatedly (spurring armed men to protest outside her home), and she ultimately resigned. They rushed through legislation stripping the governor's and her ability to issue emergency health orders—amid an *emergency*. The governor vetoed the bill, but the GOP supermajority overrode the veto. When the vaccine rollout began in 2021, GOP legislators invited anti-vaxxers to testify on the risks of the vaccines—one witness went viral when she claimed the vaccines were making people magnetic. Not their personalities, mind you, but their actual, physical bodies. Another nurse stuck a metal key against her chest and neck to prove the case—apparently, she wasn't vaccinated enough because it kept falling from her neck.[59]

As one might imagine, those behind all this extremism

comprise quite the cast of characters. Ohio Congressman Jim Jordan may be famous for his tantrums and antics on Capitol Hill. His nonsense stands out there. But he'd face stiff competition to stand out amid his old comrades at the Ohio legislature.

One house member from the eastern suburbs of Cincinnati not only tried to impeach the Republican governor for his efforts to battle COVID, but wrote a bill requiring a specific surgical procedure to correct an ectopic pregnancy (which threatens a mother's life), as opposed to terminating the pregnancy to save the mother's life. Only one problem: obstetricians explained the procedure was physiologically impossible. (Oh, that legislator is not a doctor, but he said he came across his mandated procedure in a 1917 medical journal.)[60]

Another statehouse member justified his war against masks in Biblical terms: "We are all created in the image and likeness of God. That image is seen the most by our face . . . That's the image of God right there, and I want to see it in my brothers and sisters."[61] He also attacked vaccines and testing.

We have a state senator from the northern suburbs of Columbus (blessed with some of the state's best public schools) who declared that "public education is socialism."[62] And we have a state senator from Lima who speculated during the COVID crisis that "colored people" were more susceptible to COVID because they "do not wash their hands as well as other groups."[63]

These aren't just back benchers, by the way.

The guy who thinks public education is socialism? He *chairs* the Ohio Senate's Education Committee.

The guy who speculated about Black Ohioans not washing their hands? He's not only a doctor, which should scare all of us. He *chairs* the senate's Health Committee. He was handed that role *after* his comments.

One long-time statehouse member was investigated by the FBI for money laundering, but was term limited while the investigation was still pending. He ran again a few years later, got himself reelected, and was promptly investigated again. This time, he was indicted after the FBI caught him on tape allegedly undertaking the largest bribery scandal in Ohio history. The man's name was Larry Householder, and *he was serving as Ohio's Speaker on both occasions*, the state's single most powerful political figure. He stepped into the Speakership after another Speaker had stepped aside due to an entirely different FBI investigation.

To put it mildly, the state that gave the world John Glenn and Neil Armstrong and Toni Morrison is not sending its best to state politics. And amid those who arrive in Ohio's capital, the best are not rising to be the leaders of the two branches of the legislature. And by the way, all these people *always* get reelected, unless they're indicted. And sometimes, not even that stops them.

Importantly, those paying attention to Ohio's statehouse—and one of the problems we'll explore in this book is that too few do—understand that there is a connection between the political atrophy in Columbus and the anemic public outcomes described above. These aren't parallel, unrelated tracks. There's direct causation between the corrupt and extreme politics of the statehouse and poor public outcomes.

Remember, Ohio still has strong natural, public and private assets. The Lake and the Ohio River and the natural resources and the manufacturing base and all those national caliber institutions are all still here. We're still a day's drive to most of the country's population. If state government exhibited basic competence and effectiveness, you'd expect public outcomes to reflect those natural and private strengths. But in Ohio, despite strengths that are *superior* to the average state, our outcomes are worse than the average state on issue after issue.

So, you can't blame the natural strengths of Ohio for the decline. And there's not some innate weakness in the people of Ohio leading to the poor outcomes.

If you're failing at everything, something is more deeply wrong than an errant policy or two.

Broken government lies at the heart of it all.

Bottom line: Ohio finds itself on a downward spiral. Its public outcomes are dropping across the board. But its political system, with its calcified corruption and extremism, does nothing to alter that fall. And those poor outcomes only engender the type of deterioration—more population loss, especially of young people; poorer education; etc.—that only enhances the political prospects of those in power.

The downward spiral only continues.

So how does a state with Ohio's storied history, a history of moderation, and an electorate in 2018 that still voted 50%-49%, tumble down this deep hole of extremism, corruption and decline?

It's a painful story, and I'll tell it over the course of the book.

But here's a hint: while the quality of our governors and other statewide officials has varied over the years, the heart of the problem is the state legislature, which we call our General Assembly. The 99-person house and the 33-person senate are where the action is. They set the tone for everything else. And they have enough power and sway to force the hands of statewide officials while exerting major influence over both the funding and policies of local government.

For a host of reasons which we'll explore from Chapters Two

through Five, the Ohio General Assembly is a fundamentally broken institution. And it has become a deeply undemocratic institution. Those afflictions don't just drive down public outcomes in Ohio but also carry dramatic consequences beyond the state when it comes to democracy itself.

The Biggest Problem? It's Not Just Ohio

At my theoretical reunion, if asked about my home state, I wouldn't bother reciting these depressing developments. Not the type of conversation you'd want to have catching up with an old friend over a beer. And I wouldn't want to risk my Cincinnati Board of Tourism title. But it would be in the back of my mind if they asked about Ohio.

A college student on a campus today, out of state like I was, would likely not bring any of this up either. But for too many, judging from the numbers cited above, it will be the reason why they never return after graduating.

A truly sad and sobering story for the Buckeye State, right?

But here's the thing. It's not the full story. We need to take one more step back.

The final step.

At my theoretical reunion, if I were to explain how broken things were in the great state of Ohio, the person with whom I was having the conversation would, as often as not, have one reply.

"Wow. That sounds just like my state."

If I was speaking to a friend from Georgia, or Wisconsin, or Missouri, and they were watching their state capital closely, they would say that. And they'd be right.

Alabama, or Florida, or Texas. Same response.

Out West—Arizona, Montana, or Wyoming. Same answer.

Iowa, Louisiana, Michigan. Similar story.

When you take a step back and scan the country, the dynamics afflicting Ohio's statehouse and broader body politic aren't unique. They're playing out in state after state.

Sure, some public outcomes may be better in some places, worse in others, for a variety of reasons.

But the fundamental problem of broken government and broken democracy looks the same. Cesspools of corruption and dysfunction. Extreme policies way out of step with the popular will of these states. Lack of results combined with lack of accountability. And an unrelenting focus on cementing an anti-democratic bulwark into place to allow all that work to continue with no end in sight. Absolute immunity from political consequences. And like Ohio's did in 2021, all of these legislatures kicked off the year with a wave of assaults on basic notions of democracy for the future.

Just as the collapse in Ohio is disconcerting, this trend across our country is profoundly disturbing. Plunging health, increased poverty and extremism that is out of touch with the mainstream are all deeply problematic as a matter of the common good, and America's competitiveness.

But at this moment in our nation's history, following the Trump presidency, January 6, and the dangers of the Big Lie, the state of America's statehouses has made them especially dangerous.

Dangerous to democracy itself—their own, and America's writ large.

In the coming chapters, I will explain how a fundamental breakdown in democracy has taken place at statehouses in Ohio and elsewhere, and how this has converted these state legislatures into nearly unstoppable "laboratories of autocracy." If unaddressed, they threaten the heart of American democracy in the near- and long-term.

But in addition to alarming readers to this reality, I'll

also present an agenda of how this perilous direction can be reversed.

It won't be easy, but it's essential.

And there are clear and practical examples where wins have already occurred and can be repeated.

Even in the great state of Ohio.

CHAPTER 2

With Great Power Comes Great Anonymity

THE MEETING WAS at Westwood Town Hall, on Cincinnati's West Side. It was 2005, a few years before the recession. But foreclosures were creeping up, so that was the topic of the meeting several city councilmembers were there to address.

I was one of them.

Maybe 50 or 60 residents gathered in the audience to listen to us. We were up on a raised platform, four or so of my colleagues seated in a row. We passed the mic back and forth, each earnestly talking about the need to address foreclosures, and steps we were taking. Truthfully, Cincinnati City Hall's purview would've been pretty limited in battling the growing crisis, but that didn't stop us from waxing on for some time.

After our comments, we took questions from the audience. And amid those questions, one hand shot up with more determination than the others.

I knew him right away. It was Steve Driehaus, the state representative from the west side of town—a seat he'd won after a tough race in a competitive district (some actually existed back then).

Someone called on Steve.

"Hey guys, can I take a moment to describe the bill in the statehouse I'm working on?"

Sure, we thought. Steve's a good guy. He's not on the podium with us, and like other state reps, doesn't get the attention we councilmembers get in the media. So, let's toss him a political bone and let him talk for a bit. Impress these people.

Steve—who went on to be a member of Congress—talked for the next ten minutes. And what he explained to that audience had far more relevance and potential to solve the foreclosure problem than anything those of us on the stage had offered.

I remember that moment because knowing what I know today, it's a perfect symbol of an essential problem of state politics. In districts across states like Ohio, removed from state capitals, there's a yawning gap between the understanding of how statehouses work—and even basic awareness of the names of elected state reps and senators—and the robust power those legislatures and legislators wield.

Let's think about that town hall again.

Whoever organized it thought to invite members of city council to address the issue. And I don't blame that organizer—when it comes to politicians in the area, members of city council are the ones you see the most. They're in the paper and on television weekly, at least. Radio, too. Every council committee meeting and full council meeting airs live on local cable television—and more people watch than people might ever expect. (When I knocked on doors, I was often told I didn't look as "big" as I did on TV. I never knew if that was good or bad). When councilmembers run for office, some raise enough money to run TV ads for weeks, at a time when no other politicians are up for election. And they're usually the ones invited to address issues in town halls and forums like the one in Westwood, or go to groundbreakings for projects they helped fund, etc.

Whoever organized the meeting didn't think to invite Steve at all—*the* person solely responsible for representing that part of the state in the 99-district statehouse (councilmembers, on the other hand, don't have districts). I can assure you Steve wasn't to blame for the snub—he's a highly intelligent guy, fluent in policy and well-spoken. Clearly not shy. And, as we learned, Steve was leading the way in Columbus on a bill that would do far more on foreclosures than anything that City Hall could do. But Steve had to invite himself to the forum, sit in the audience, listen to *us*, then raise his hand and get called on to share his work.

Why no invite for Steve? Because outside of his election, almost nothing Steve did got any attention in his district. Hardly a newspaper story. Definitely no television coverage. His work in Columbus is 100 miles away but might as well be 1,000. It would take fifteen years *after* that forum before the statehouse would even begin airing many of their hearings on public access, allowing folks across Ohio to see for themselves what they were doing.

To make matters worse, not even the politicians knew what Steve was up to. Not one member of council on that stage looked out at Steve's raised hand and thought: "Sheesh, Steve should be sitting on this podium with us." And none of us would've ever thought: "Steve should be sitting on this podium *more than* we should be. He not only knows more about foreclosures, but the statehouse actually can do far more about them than we can." And none of us had a clue he was actually leading an effort to pass a bill on the growing crisis. When Steve raised his hand, letting him say a few words from within the crowd was just us being politically polite. Let a fellow pol have a few moments.

But in hindsight, Steve *should've* been on that stage. His legislative work was more important than anything we were working on, or that we said. Maybe one or two council members should've been with him to give a City perspective, but the rest belonged in the audience, learning from him and taking notes on how they could help.

This seems like a small story. But it's not. It's a big one. I don't want to over-project, but my guess is the essence of that scene plays out over and over again throughout Ohio, and throughout the country.

Too few people, including those in politics, understand the immense power—the potential for both good and ill—in our nation's statehouses. For a variety of reasons, state reps and senators and what they work on are hardly known back home in their own communities. Sure, fellow partisans in their communities might know them. We work to help elect them, and we see one another at political functions. But as a matter of broad name recognition or understanding of the role, statehouse pols are among the least known of any officials in politics.

And that's a problem.

More specifically, the dramatic disconnect between power and awareness lies at the heart of the deep dysfunction described in Chapter One and through the rest of the book. And to add a little more dramatic flair to it, if the average voter *doesn't* know or care what state reps do and can do, but *insiders and interests know exactly what they do and can do,* that's dangerous. And a huge vulnerability to the common good. And extended into a worst-case scenario (which has transpired over the past decade), to democracy itself.

I'm going to dig into why statehouses fall so far below the radar, a weakness that has left them vulnerable to their slide in anti-democratic directions. But first, I'll give a rapid-fire review of the unappreciated power Steve Driehaus and his successors wield. Why they should at certain moments, and on certain issues, be a flashing red light on any political radar, as opposed to below it.

*   *   *

The Wide, Deep Power of State Legislatures

Don't let the TV ads fool you.

Governors and members of Congress dominate the airwaves during election season. Meanwhile, you only receive a late mailer or two from your state rep—maybe some cheaply produced digital and cable ads in the final weeks. While a winning governor might have her victory speech aired live on television, a state rep is lucky if her win slides by on the results ticker below. But what that imbalance of ads and coverage doesn't tell you is that the heart of state government rests with that legislative candidate whom you hardly hear from, or about.

Let's take a look at Ohio as an example. It's not subtle—while Article I of the Ohio Constitution lays out a Bill of Rights, the first Article that follows grants power to the Ohio legislature. And when Ohio's founders, suspicious of centralized authority in an executive,[64] wrote Article II back in 1803, they went all in, establishing the bicameral General Assembly as *by far* the strongest part of Ohio government. Beyond broad legislative power, legislators could serve unlimited number of terms and make executive as well as judicial appointments; Ohio's governor had neither appointment authority nor a veto over legislation. Compared to the powerful legislature, the governor "was a figurehead."[65]

Since Ohio's founding, two new constitutions and various amendments added term limits (eight years for both house and senate members), gave the governor a veto, and removed the power of appointment of executive officeholders and judges from the General Assembly, instead granting that power to the governor, or the people via elections.[66] But a hard-nosed look at the structure and functioning of government makes it clear that the legislature remains the strongest player in Ohio politics. Across the country, the same largely holds true. A few states have granted governors more power over budgeting, but for the most part, state legislatures are in the driver's seat.

The core function of the legislature is to set the state's budget every year or two years. Ohio's Constitution makes clear that "[n]o money shall be drawn from the state treasury, except in pursuance of a specific appropriation, made by law."[67] *Made by law,* meaning, approved by the legislature. Now, of course, a governor proposes and signs that budget. But without the legislature's approval, the governor and every other aspect of Ohio government simply can't function. And if it has a supermajority, with the power to override the governor's veto, the legislature essentially drives the budget from the start. He proposes it, they pass whatever they want, and if he vetoes it, they override it—it's *their* budget.

And to give a sense of what that means, let's look at the biggest items in state budgets. In Ohio's budget, similar to most states, the biggest ticket items are Medicaid (49.3% in the 2022/23 budget) and primary and secondary education (21.8%), followed by higher education (7.3%), corrections and the criminal justice system (7.3%), health and human services (4.5%), and other items, including support for local government, economic development, transportation, environmental protection, natural resources/parks and other items.[68] That's a hefty portfolio of key issues.

Beyond the power of setting the budget, the General Assembly establishes state law and policy on virtually every major issue impacting the day-to-day lives of residents, commerce, and affairs of government at all levels. From the criminal justice system (criminal law is largely a state matter), to taxation, to regulation of businesses, to health care, the legislature is in the driver's seat. And if they have a veto-proof supermajority, no one else is even in the car.

Federal Government?

"Ok. I get it," you're saying. "The statehouse is important. But not as important as the federal government."

Yes and no.

Of course, there are functions the federal government performs that states don't. The military. Foreign policy. All sorts of federal programs and entitlements and support to Americans. Aid that flows back to the states and local governments and schools. All critical, of course.

But back in the states, much of the federal funding passes to local communities and citizens *by way* of state government. About a third of Ohio's budget is federal money passing through, largely for health care but also other items.[69] Much of those funds have strings and mandates attached. But large streams of federal money leave wide discretion for states to determine how to spend. And statehouses can also decide whether or not to accept those dollars in the first place. Want to benefit from the Affordable Care Act's expansion of Medicaid? Better call your state rep to make sure it happens in your state.

Local Government?

"Well, what about local government?" you ask. "Don't they have their own powers? Ohio has 88 counties with their own commissions and governments. Cities too. Mayors and commissioners are always are on the news talking about their work."

As a former county commissioner, I can assure you county governments do a lot of good. I enjoyed my time at Hamilton County, and felt good about the public service I was able to do. But in Ohio and most states, counties are formally an administrative arm of the state. Counties don't write their own laws, but must operate within the defined powers granted to them by . . . the state legislature. They have discretion over the size of certain tax and fee rates—they can add levies as well—and then they have discretion on how to spend that mix of revenue on a menu of key services (courts, corrections, social services, etc.). But the lion's share of what is funded by counties is governed by state mandates through state law. And the broader framework in which they do all their work is governed by state law. Note: "state law" translates into "the state legislature is in charge."

"Well, what about cities? Don't they have their own charters and laws? Their own budgets?"

Good question. And a more complicated answer.

In Ohio and other states, many cities do have their own charters, or constitutions. And municipalities indeed set their own separate budgets to pay for services they provide, which are funded via a mix of revenue streams set by City Hall (but again confined by what state law allows). And, unlike counties, they also enjoy certain powers of self-government known as "home-rule." Specifically, the Ohio Constitution allows municipalities "to exercise all powers of local self-government and to adopt and enforce within their limits such local police, sanitary and other similar regulations, as are not in conflict with general laws."[70]

But that final phrase—"are not in conflict with general laws"—adds the rub. In recent decades, the Ohio General Assembly has taken a highly expansive view of when it can overrule local laws because they conflict with state laws. Sounds like some arcane legal debate, right? Not quite. Unless you consider issues like the minimum wage, gun safety, or the environment to be arcane.

Here's how it works. Let's say an Ohio city passes its own law increasing the minimum wage within its boundaries. If the state disagrees, the state can swoop in and pass a law saying cities *can't* raise the minimum wage within only their boundaries—that only the state can pass a minimum wage at the level it desires (much lower than the city's proposed level). Because the city's wage level conflicts with the state's, the city's law would be void. This has happened again and again: the General Assembly has issued statewide regulations trumping local ordinances, and the courts have backed them up. So, while cities can pass their own ordinances, and can define misdemeanor crimes within their jurisdiction, the state can trump much of that work.

Other Statewide Elected Officials?

"But I barely know these people. What do the state officials I see on all those TV ads do? You know, big shots like governor, secretary of state and attorney general? Aren't they in charge??"

Yes, governors and the others lead very important offices, with major responsibilities. But again, so much of what they do is subject to the legislature.

First, the General Assembly writes the laws that define the scope of each office's powers, as well as the laws that each of these offices must follow and enforce. Those statewide officials must operate within the ambit provided by those laws. In some cases, when there is an open-endedness in the law, a statewide official may have discretion to act in ways not precisely described by state law—but just as with cities above, if the legislature is not pleased, it can enact new laws forbidding that very action. And they do exactly that.

Second, the General Assembly sets the budget for each of these officials. Each must come before the legislature every budget cycle and present her or his plans and goals. And, except for the governor (who can veto the budget), the other officials have no recourse at all to the budget the legislature grants them. They simply must accept it.

So, not only does the legislature have direct control over many aspects of these offices, but the realpolitik of a state capital is that all this control gives legislatures *leverage* over these officeholders in so many other ways. Remember this for later.

Power over Elections

Importantly, legislatures wield especially hefty power when it comes to the heart of both our federal- and state-level democracies: they establish almost the entire framework of how elections are run. And unlike other powers the state grants legislatures, this power is enshrined in Article I of the United States Constitution itself, which provides: "The Times, Places and Manner of holding Elections for Senators and Representatives, shall be prescribed in each State by the Legislature thereof[.]"[71]

Just some examples of what this means. Outside of the Constitutionally-mandated November federal election date, the legislature sets the dates of elections. This means legislatures establish the broader window of voting—whether or not voters can vote early, for how long, and how. They can enhance or limit voting in all sorts of other ways.

Yes, in states like Ohio, a secretary of state has some discretion in managing an election within that broader legal framework, issuing directives to guide local elections officials across the state. But again, if the legislature is not pleased by a directive, it can override it by passing a new law. (For example, with the legislature's new drop box law, all future secretaries of state would be barred from adding drop boxes).

And of course, those legislators set the secretary of state's budget. So, they can condition those funds on their whims—as they did when they made clear in 2020 that the secretary of state could not use funds they allocated to pre-pay postage for absentee ballots.

There's one area where state legislatures also possess unique power—and that is the role reserved for them when it comes to *electing presidents.* Back to the Constitution, which says: "Each State shall appoint, in such Manner as the Legislature thereof may direct, a Number of Electors, equal to the whole Number of Senators and Representatives to which the State may be entitled in the Congress . . . ."[72]

And which entity determines how each state "appoints" those electors?

The governor? Nope.

The secretary of state? Nope.

The attorney general? Nope.

The state legislature? Bingo!

So, not only do state legislatures lay out the time, place and manner of every election in their state—with the power to overrule the secretary of state's discretion whenever they want— they actually determine how a state chooses its presidential electors. Most simply apportion all electors to the winner of the popular vote in that state, while Maine and Nebraska do it by Congressional district. But it's the decision of the legislature that determines it.

Drawing Legislative Districts

There's another pivotal area of democracy where state legislatures play the central role. Every ten years, the boundaries that make up the districts of the U.S. House of Representatives must be redrawn to accommodate the new population totals of each state. It's a multi-step process. First, at the beginning of each decade, the Census counts and announces the total population of each state. Second, a federal formula in the Constitution *apportions* the number of House districts that each state will have for the coming decade. But where the rubber really hits the road is step three—drawing the districts themselves. And that responsibility falls back on the states.

And how do states do this? Most commonly, through their legislatures. To be clear, Supreme Court decisions and other federal laws add some legal restrictions to the process. But it ultimately falls back on state legislatures to shape equal-sized districts that comprise the allocated number of seats for the decade. As they say in politics, they draw the district map. Even after a wave of reforms to this process, state legislatures still control the process in the vast majority of states.

Then there is the parallel issue of drawing the district lines for the state legislatures *themselves*, also done every decade. Sounds like a recipe for trouble to have state legislators drawing their own districts, right? It is. So some states have added a few wrinkles to water down such a blatant conflict of interest. But most state legislatures retain direct control in drawing their *own* lines for each decade.

Like I Said, Powerful

So, when I say that state legislatures have both broad and deep power, on issues of great import and on crucial aspects of our democracy, do you see what I mean?

They set the budget for everything. They pass laws on every topic. They have direct control or major leverage over statewide officials, and a lot of say over what happens to federal monies and policies within their state. They can overrule local governments on any number of topics.

And when it comes to democracy itself, they set the rules and construct the playing field of elections from everything to state office, to Congress, to the presidency of the United States.

That's some serious mojo.

Now here's the problem.

Too few know it.

Even fewer know who the heck most of these people are.

(And as ensuing chapters will show, too many of those who *do* know it are taking advantage of it for all the worst reasons.)

Let's take a moment to see why Steve Driehaus and his colleagues, despite an awesome array of power, get stuck sitting in the audience of meetings in their own districts.

The Anonymity of State Legislatures

Freshman year summer, back in Cincinnati to reacquire my twang, I interned for the Press Community Newspapers on Cincinnati's West Side. They had multiple community weekly papers to fill and a full-time reporter on maternity leave, so I was one busy nineteen-year old that summer. I loved every minute of it. I wrote stories (usually four or five front-page stories per weekly paper), took photos, wrote columns. Even a few obituaries, which I grew to enjoy after initial dread.

Once, my editor assigned me to do a story on a state legislator. I asked for more information about who that was and what they did. He explained it to me. And my response was: "You mean there's like a mini-Congress right here in Ohio?"

Now, I paid attention as a kid. Got good grades. Kept up with national and local politics—I even interviewed a councilmember in his City Hall office for my high school newspaper. My parents were involved in politics to some degree, both local and national. I read the paper, watched the local news, and grew up watching the Sunday shows.[73] I could've named our Congressman, governor and senators at the time. Although I didn't identify with a party, I grew more politically aware my freshman year in college. Yet I didn't know a thing about the state legislature until that summer. And even after my crash course, my summary of a state rep would've been: people with full-time jobs who, on the side, represented little districts of neighborhoods in Columbus. A "mini-Congress."

On the one hand, having now chaired a state party, it's embarrassing to admit that level of ignorance. On the other hand, my level of knowledge back then approximates what the average American knows about statehouses across the country. A Johns Hopkins poll a few years back found that fewer than 20 percent of 1,500 people surveyed could name their *own* state representative.[74] Beneath that eye-popping number were others: about half of those surveyed didn't know if their state had a one- or two-house legislature (49 have two houses—only Nebraska doesn't); more than half didn't know what part of government drew their state's district lines; and a majority didn't know if their state representative was a part-time or full-time position. Few could name the state's biggest spending item.[75]

Like I said, my lack of knowledge back at nineteen was about average.

While not apples to apples, other studies show that considerably more voters know the name of their member of Congress,[76] and a decent amount more can identify their governor.[77]

It's a cornerstone of political science that a governmental body's legitimacy hinges partly on the level of public awareness about its activity and makeup. You can't really have "consent of the governed" if you don't have the "foggiest notion" of the governed. This is something academics assess when sizing up the strength of fledgling democracies across the globe.[78] So, on that higher plane, we should be concerned about the lack of awareness about state legislatures and what that means for state politics.

But for practical purposes, this lack of awareness also comprises a central ingredient making these bodies susceptible to becoming the laboratories of autocracy they are today. So it's worth taking a moment to examine why statehouses are so overlooked in American politics.

Let's first acknowledge that people are busy managing their own lives. Many have neither the time nor the bandwidth to pay attention to politics at most levels, let alone the state capital dozens or hundreds of miles away, whose elections pass by hardly noticed. Many people don't know their governor, senator or U.S. House Member. So it makes sense that even fewer keep up with the work of state legislatures. But beyond that, there are reasons—and they are compounding—why state legislatures go especially unnoticed despite their vast powers.

For example, campaigns and elections are when politicians build up most of their notoriety. Of course, between elections, you can generate attention and media in a variety of ways—but you don't control the message, it can be mixed, or diluted, or a sliver at best. I've had many press conferences where no one showed up to hear my earth-shattering pronouncements. (Pro tip: you still do the press conference, but you talk to staff as they take pictures of you).

But when you actually campaign for office, all that money you've raised is spent shamelessly advertising yourself through every medium possible, in the most glowing light possible. As a candidate, it's in the heart of a campaign, with your full arsenal of self-promotion firing away through TV, mail and radio, that you can *feel* the recognition. Late in even a council race or county race, ads blaring away, voters would see me on the street or at a festival and recognize me—"You're David Pepper, aren't you? I see you on TV" or "you've got my vote." My first slogan was "Just Add Pepper" . . . with weeks to go, many would say the slogan back to me, gesturing with their hand as if shaking a pepper shaker, just as my ads did. And when you win, you get a day or two of great media.

Mere months later, after the ads stop airing, some humble pie is served. You may still get a double take, but much of the awareness drops. No more adding pepper. "I know you from somewhere, but I can't place it." "Aren't you the weatherman or something?" "Do you sell medical equipment at Children's Hospital?"[79] Still, even if the instant recognition fades, the lift from the campaign persists at some level over time.

These days, for a variety of reasons, almost no statehouse race or candidate enjoys that surge of attention in the first place. Many districts are simply not contested at all. Others are so one-sided that voters don't even know an election is taking place. If an incumbent has such an overwhelming advantage, neither the challenger nor that incumbent does much campaigning that truly penetrates—the challenger because of few resources, the incumbent because he or she doesn't need to be bothered.

Even when a relatively close race happens, most are ho-hum affairs lost amid higher profile races. Unlike city races, which appear on the odd-year ballot, most statehouse races come in even years. These candidates are trying to get noticed amid presidential, senate, governor, and congressional races—offices that voters understand better, and campaigns which are far better funded. Even if a statehouse candidate wants to run TV ads, running at the same time as those other races means they face more expensive rates, and are likely drowned out. And legislative districts are usually so small, it's largely a waste of money to advertise on television (outside a targeted cable television buy), because you're "overbuying" to a market far bigger than the district that votes for you. Even the types of in-person forums and debates organized for other candidates happen less with statehouse races and are rarely televised. With people generally unaware of what happens at their statehouse, interest is simply far less. And in recent years, at all levels, incumbents are skipping debates and forums because it deprives their opponents of the primary things they need: attention, and the chance to challenge those incumbents when people are actually watching. Bottom line, the vast majority of statehouse elections come and go, hardly noticed. Unlike local candidates, there isn't even a month's surge of recognition because the high-profile campaign never took place to begin with.

Without that election, the window in which state legislators will most likely gain attention is when they are *in* session, doing the actual work of budgeting and legislating. But more so than most other offices, that, too, generates limited exposure.

For most states, the legislative session occurs in a compact period of time. Most states have hard limits established by their Constitutions, laws or internal rules capping how long their sessions are. The typical statehouse meets between two and five months early each year, adjourns for the rest of that year, reconvenes early in the second year, then adjourns after several more months. In some states, there are hard dates of when that legislating ends. Indiana's legislators are done for the year at the end of April (in the odd year), and March 14 (the even year). Kentucky—March 30 and April 15. Oklahoma, Missouri and Minnesota go a little longer, wrapping up by the end of May.[80] Even the eleven states with no limits on the number of legislative days generally adjourn for the summer at the latest, rarely reconvening for much time later in the year. While sessions involve a flurry of activity, once adjourned, things quiet quickly. Legislators go back to their day jobs as lawyers, morticians, accountants, or running their farms or car dealerships (in some cases, these jobs build their name recognition more than their political work). And in the second year, they're back to running for re-election in the largely low-profile campaigns described above.

Even during session, coverage of the work is limited, and is decreasing. Especially outside the capital city, television coverage of statehouses is rare.[81] And as the newspaper business has struggled, the number of robust and dedicated statehouse bureaus has plummeted in recent decades; even those that remain are typically far smaller.[82] One 2014 study found only 164 full-time reporters covered *all 50* state capitals—three per state.[83] Cost-cutting has also diminished capacity for deep and time-consuming investigations needed to unearth complex scandals. And many papers no longer employ the old-school columnists with the history and standing to call out politicians in a way that cuts through with the public. Editorial boards have also been slashed.

Then there's a second, related problem. By and large, statehouse bureaus cover the larger stories and narratives, focusing on legislative leaders, the budget, legislation that is high-profile or controversial enough to merit coverage, and the occasional scandal. More targeted coverage of individual legislators largely comes from local newspapers back in home-towns, not statehouse bureaus. Just as I was asked to cover a state rep for my weekly community newspaper, it's these home-town and community newspapers that are more likely to feature the individual work of a community's representative. Even more than statehouse bureaus, these smaller newspapers are evaporating quickly.[84] And amid many consequences, their decline deprives readers of the most likely place where they can read about the work of the representative who actually represents them.

Finally, when I was a councilmember in Cincinnati, all of our sessions were covered live on a local cable station. Recordings of our meetings were played again and again. I was amazed how many everyday Cincinnatians told me they watched the meetings. Same thing happened when I was a county commissioner. Even our informal staff meetings were aired live, then re-aired later multiple times. Gripping television indeed—my never-ending Diet Coke refills might've been the highlight. At the federal level, C-Span provides the same service for the deliberations on the Hill, which tens of millions watch per week.

Statehouses? They're only moving in that direction. While all statehouses carry live webcasts of their work, only half air public television coverage of their meetings.[85] And even in those states, much of the work is hidden from the cameras. Only in 2019 did Ohio begin to televise its committee hearings, where the lion's share of the work is done.[86]

And building real awareness is also a function of time. In the 1990s, a movement imposing state legislative term limits swept the country, with new term limits in a dozen states.

There's been fierce debate about their overall impact,[87] but one thing is clear. As opposed to politicians who gain notoriety as a function of years of hard work in their district, many states—like Ohio—give their representatives only eight years to get known. When it comes to chairing a legislative committee—the type of work that builds even more recognition—the time is even more limited. Two years. Maybe four.

Bottom line: due to lack of high-profile elections, ever weakening press coverage and items like term limits, state representatives are hardly known in their community. And the collective work of state legislatures is hardly understood across entire states.

A college freshman's ignorance of what they are, what they do and who's in them is par for the course in America.

There's a major exception to all this, of course.

There are *some* people who do appreciate what these state legislators do.

And that, too, becomes a problem. A big one.

Read on.

CHAPTER 3

The Insiders Know: Ordering at the Statehouse Grille

I T STARTED WITH some notes on a napkin. Then another napkin. Then another.

More specifically, the napkins piled up at the West Side Waffle House in Columbus. And the man scribbling on them, William Lager, found himself dead broke after a divorce and a business gone belly up. A server at the Waffle House noticed that he'd even photocopy coffee coupons, then hand them over as if they were real, to save money on his morning caffeine fix.[88]

But on the back of those napkins, Lager wrote a business plan that would turn things around. In fact, the plan on those napkins would make him filthy rich, affording him multiple houses in Ohio and a $3.7 million home in Key West. The billion-dollar business he built became the darling of the state's movers and shakers, touching thousands upon thousands of Ohio families. He could get his calls returned by any politician in the State, from the governor on down, and Jeb Bush enlisted Lager to spread the word nationally about what he'd built.[89] He even hired the server away from the Waffle House to work for his growing empire.

Sounds like the American dream, right?

Think again. Copying those coupons was a tell.

On those napkins, Lager drew up a plan that grew into arguably the largest scam in the history of Ohio. An online, for-profit charter operation that claimed more students than any in the nation by 2015,[90] and was larger than most Ohio colleges.

From early on, problems emerged. Problem #1 was that the "school" delivered atrocious results—the worst drop-out rate of any school in the nation.[91] Problem #2 was, while his online "school" was paid thousands of dollars for each student it claimed, it turned out thousands upon thousands of kids never attended—or at least there was no proof that they did.[92] Think of them as highly lucrative ghost students. That's right, the nation's largest school wasn't taking attendance, even though the state was paying for every student *and* ghost student who Bill Lager *claimed* attended.[93]

What was the piggy bank that made Lager so rich? Big private investors? A major bank? Venture capital?

Nope.

Ohio's public schools. More precisely, the state and local dollars that Ohio taxpayers thought they were sending to educate children paid for it all. With every student Lager convinced to quit public school to attend his scam school, thousands of dollars flowed from public coffers to his private company. So, over the time that Lager's school was delivering atrocious results to his students, Ohio's already underfunded public schools were seeing precious funds ripped away.[94] And of course, they *were* taking attendance, and being held to all sorts of other standards Lager was not. Lager's scam pulled down both his own students, and those still in public schools who never fell for his heavy advertising.

The scam went on for years, totaling more than a billion dollars.

There's one other relevant fact that kept it all going. Not only did William Lager concoct one of the biggest scams in Ohio history, he also emerged as an enormous donor to the Ohio Republican Party and its politicians all that time.[95] Other Lager employees also gave richly.[96] And by far the largest amount of this largesse—around $1.4 million—supported state legislative candidates.[97] Let's call it causation.

How Lager went from napkins at a coffee house to multiple homes and a silver-plated rolodex is a long and complicated story. But at its most basic, William Lager is one person who figured out just how much power statehouse politicians in Ohio enjoy. Unfortunately, he also figured out that the incentive system in state politics is distorted, and that it doesn't take much for those politicians to use their power to work feverishly for private interests as opposed to the public good. Lager took full advantage of this unfortunate feature.

Lager's story is the worst-case scenario that should scare every American. Because the sobering reality he exposed is that Ohio's politicians were willing to sell out the state's most important function—educating its children—to support someone who lavished them with some percentage of the money generated (again, from public schools) by the scam.

And if politicians are willing to sell out a state's kids and its future all to keep a mutually beneficial gravy train going, what won't they sell out?

The answer, it turns out, is nothing.

Which presents huge opportunities for those who've figured it out. And powerful motivation to make sure those so generous with public assets stay in power.

*   *   *

A Short Drive, A World Away

When state legislators make the drive from their hometowns to their state's capital city, things change quickly. An hour or two on small roads and highways usher them into a different world entirely. And a different life.

First, from neighbors who know little about what they do, they dive into a sea of people and interests who know exactly what they do. They're surrounded by them. In all but a few states, the people and entities who live permanently in that capital, lobbying the statehouse, dwarf the number of actual lawmakers there. And the margin keeps growing.

In 2016, the Center for Public Integrity (CPI) reviewed five years of lobbyist registrations in all 50 states. They found fourteen states averaged more than ten lobbying entities per lawmaker. California (30), Florida (25) and New York (21) led the way. Ohio ranked eighth with thirteen per lawmaker, meaning well over 1,000.[98] CPI also found that lobbying activity at statehouses was on the rise, for several reasons. First, as Congress gets ever more stagnant, special interests are finding that they can serve their agenda better at the state level. Second, due to reduced journalistic coverage of statehouses, CPI also speculated that statehouse lobbying is better hidden than in DC. CPI further found that certain national entities are "scattering" lobbyist activity to dozens of states at a time to achieve nationwide goals—Uber, tobacco companies and AT&T were among the most actively expanding at the time CPI looked.[99]

Beyond the sheer number of people encircling these legislators come dramatic changes in how they're treated. No more sitting in the audiences of town hall meetings back home, waiting to get called on. Here, they're the belles of the ball. Legislators hear their praises sung over fancy meals and cocktails. Awards and honors come their way from all variety of groups, largely for legislation they support. And from driving themselves along run-down roads and county highways, some enjoy trips and dinners and nice hotels in the most luxurious destinations in the country or world.

To be clear, the technical rules vary on what gifts and meals and travel state lawmakers can accept. In some states, paying for politicians' meals is forbidden; in others, it's capped, but must be disclosed. In some states, no one can pay for a trip for you. In others, they can. But there are always exceptions to the rules. In Ohio, for example, while lobbyists can't pay for travel, political groups that lobbyists fund sure can. And there are other back doors. A legislator's or party's campaign account can pay for meals and travel, and donors and lobbyists can fill those accounts to the brim. So, one way or another, dollars flowing from all those interests allow legislators to enjoy a dramatically different life than they or their neighbors live back home.

You want an example, you say? Let me tell you a story about a once rising star in Ohio politics.

His name is Cliff Rosenberger. Cliff hailed from a small town called Clarksville, a few miles from Wilmington in Southern Ohio's Clinton County. Sadly, Wilmington has served as the epicenter of Ohio and national maladies for more than a decade. First, during the Great Recession of 2008-2009, the DHL air park that anchored the region's economy closed, taking with it thousands of jobs from communities near and far. *60 Minutes* descended on Wilmington to tell its story to the nation. A few years later, Ohio became the epicenter of the nation's opioid crisis, and Wilmington was one of the Ohio towns hit hard.

Enter Cliff Rosenberger, the quintessential local boy made good. From his town of 500 people, he graduated from high school and joined the Air National Guard while attending Wright State. He went on to work on Mitt Romney's presidential campaign and was Special Assistant to the U.S. Secretary of Interior. He ran for the statehouse in 2010 at the ripe young age of 29 and won easily. Four years later, at only 33, he was elected Speaker of the House (Ohio's youngest ever!). With a 65-34 majority, he found himself at the helm of the largest Republican supermajority since Ohio's House had shrunk to 99 members more than 50 years before. His veto-proof advantage made him more powerful than the governor.

A true star on the rise.

Until it crashed.

Once in power, Cliff was introduced to a dramatically different world than the one back in little Clarksville and struggling Clinton County. He apparently liked what he saw, partaking with gusto. In fact, you'd be hard pressed to find anyone who more enjoyed the lavish upside of Ohio legislative life.

To start, when in Columbus, Rosenberger lived in a 2,237-square-foot luxury condo in downtown Columbus. The condo belonged to a millionaire heiress and one of the Ohio Republican Party's largest donors. (She gave $1.5 million between 2010 and 2017).[100] Cliff refused to reveal how much he paid to "rent" the space, but journalists questioned whether his Speaker's salary could cover the cost of such tony digs. Apparently, one aspect of the arrangement that helped was that the heiress wasn't a stickler for timely payment—at one point, Rosenberger acknowledged he owed "back rent" for times he hadn't paid over the prior year.[101]

But even the fancy condo only kept Ohio's rising star anchored in Columbus so often, and not because he was hustling home to Clarksville to hear from his struggling constituents. No, Cliff put the frequent into frequent flyer, jetting out of state to places all over the world. Between January 2015 and February 2018, he took more than 50 trips, from LA to Key West, Las Vegas to Hawaii, to China, England and Italy.[102] With the good people of London and Paris, Ohio needing help, he was living it up in London, England and France. And these weren't quick trips squeezed in between in-state business—Rosenberger was away from Ohio for 180 days between 2016-17.[103] 111 days away in 2017 alone.[104]

Amid many exciting destinations, Clarksville's own especially enjoyed his Los Angeles visit. Charging the $3,000 bill to the Republican caucus account he controlled, Cliff stayed at the W Hotel and enjoyed fine dining at Malbec Argentinean Cuisine, Sushi of Gari Hollywood and Lawry's The Prime Rib.[105] When asked about the trip, Team Rosenberger explained his purpose was to follow-up on an Ohio business looking to close an agreement with Disney to bring a major film production studio to a suburb of Cincinnati. Why not make a phone call or send an email to inquire, the Speaker was asked. "The speaker felt that an in-person meeting was necessary in order to flush this out," his spokesman told the *Cincinnati Enquirer*.[106] And flush it out he did. It took only a single meeting for mortified Disney executives to explain that they never had any intention to move a studio to Ohio.[107]

But even more central than posh digs, trips and meals, statehouse insiders load up lawmakers like Rosenberger with one of the two[108] most important things that keep this luxuriant new life going: campaign funds. Back home in struggling Clinton County, any challenger to Cliff Rosenberger would struggle to scratch together resources to run even the most basic campaign against him. Cliff would have millions at his disposal, for both himself and his colleagues. No doubt he'd start his fund-raising by calling his heiress-landlady, but after that, he'd enjoy easy access to every interest group in Columbus, and many beyond that. They wouldn't know or care what the good people back in Clinton County needed at the statehouse. But they would know exactly what *they* wanted him to fight for there.

At the Statehouse Grille, A Savory Menu To Choose From

So, let's take a moment to run through what those deep-pocketed interests actually want for their largesse. We reviewed in the last chapter the broad powers of the legislature. But when people throw money at legislators like Cliff Rosenberger, and travel with him to all points of the globe, what are they looking for? What *exactly* can they get from statehouses in return?[109]

For some, of course, they'd like to see the general policies of the state comport with their interests or passions. A budget that keeps taxes down or allocates money in ways that satisfy their broader ideological views. And Ohio's legislature has indeed kept many big players pleased with the general direction it's taken. Ohio's version of trickle-down economics, practiced for a generation, has been to reduce state income taxes in a way that's paid off handsomely for those who make the most. And they've paid for those budget-busting tax cuts by ripping money away from local governments and schools (who then either cut spending or raise their own local tax rates) and redirecting those funds to the state. The model may be an abysmal failure, but its Ohio's status quo, and they're sticking to it!

But when it comes to the legislature, the ways in which lawmakers can help get much more specific than that, and fast.

Think of the statehouse as a restaurant—let's call it the

Statehouse Grille—where insiders know how and what to order and are willing to pay dearly. Here's a basic menu of what the lawmakers serve up:

The Appetizer: Paying for "Services"

First up on the menu, a state doles out taxpayer funds to businesses and entities who do "work" for the state or on behalf of the state. Like a business, states like Ohio and its many agencies and departments purchase goods and services in the billions of dollars—everything from accounting and legal services, to technology, to trucks, to contractors and engineering firms who fix roads and bridges. Most of these services are straightforward. Some make up a small part of a company's overall portfolio; Xerox, for example, has a division that provides numerous services for government clients. Other companies rely exclusively on government work to survive. And to be clear, most selections for this type of work won't involve the legislature at all. Depending on the type of service, they are guided by a formal bidding processes that bidders must win fair and square.

But sometimes, a nudge from the state legislature can maneuver companies into this lucrative torrent of state business, or keep a company in it once there. And that's where lobbying and political giving can make a big difference. Sometimes this "nudge" is dressed up in the high-minded language of policy. For example, when you hear about the "privatization" of previously public services, it means someone is looking to make big bucks out of taxpayer dollars. And it will too often be accompanied by major political giving at multiple levels to make it happen. Private prisons are a good national example of private companies positioning themselves to grab a big chunk of public corrections budgets.

Companies like Corrections Corporation of America have invested heavily in politicians to grow into the billion-dollar company they are today.

Of course, the most prominent Ohio example of a lucrative "government service" dressed up as policy takes us back to William Lager. What he drew on those napkins was basically a scheme to have the state pay him for the service of educating Ohio's kids at his on-line school. Helpfully, he even identified the revenue stream that would flow his way. And Ohio's legislature did exactly as he asked, diverting money that previously went to Ohio public schools for any students Lager claimed to attract. His example shows the enormous upside of getting a critical mass of statehouse politicians on your side; and it shows how, once they're in, the politically connected can continue to get paid for their "service" no matter how poor their performance. In cases like Lager's, it's not just hitting the lottery—it's a bigger payout, and you're hitting it multiple times every year, year after year. Except here, it's not luck. The legislators are spinning the wheel and stopping it on your numbers every time, so long as you give them some of the winnings so they, too, stay in power. Then they keep spinning the wheel.

Another type of state work making people a lot of money in Ohio is collecting debt for the state. In this case, the decision of who does this work isn't made by the legislature, but by the Ohio attorney general. For a generation, Ohio AGs have been notorious for raising millions from those they dole out this debt collection work to, using no competitive process to speak of.[110] The way the money flows is straightforward: private collectors pocket a percentage of the money they collect from debtors, then pass along a cut of their cut to the attorney general's campaign fund on a regular basis, who thanks them by keeping them on as collectors, year after year. Practically speaking, this means that some of the largest political donors in Ohio are (unwittingly) student, medical and tax debtors, as millions of their dollars make their way to politicians or to party accounts that then give to those politicians.

Now even though this is not a legislative function, the fact that this is orchestrated by the attorney general is highly relevant to overall corruption in Ohio. Because if you watch for long, you'll notice a pattern—it's always the FBI that cracks down on the biggest Ohio scams. Where's the policing from within the state? Well, if the chief law officer of Ohio (i.e., the attorney general) is engaged in one of the most blatant pay-to-play operations in Ohio—and everyone knows it—you'd imagine that official would be gun-shy about cracking down on pay-to-play elsewhere. And you'd be right.

As a result, pay-to-play is everywhere in Ohio, often to perform government "services." And only outside entities (i.e., the FBI) truly go after it.

First Course: A Few Goodies

Next up on the Statehouse Grille menu are the variety of valuable goodies legislators can dole out. Not because the recipients are performing a "service" for compensation, but because the entities know how to ask, and because the statehouse has the power to give. These goodies come in a variety of forms: grants, incentives, tax credits and breaks. They can be small and straightforward and make sense for all sorts of policy reasons. Or they can amount to billions and make little sense at all. It all depends on the ask, and what the legislature wants.

The largest bribery scandal in the history of Ohio, referenced in Chapter One, was essentially an enormous goody handed to one institution. There's no bigger player in Ohio politics than First Energy, out of Akron. It's one of Ohio's largest employers, and one that doles out huge amounts of money at all levels, every cycle. A few years back, First Energy had a problem—it was saddled with two ageing nuclear plants that were dragging the entire company down. The company desperately wanted the state to bail it out, but the problem was, it needed over $1 billion to get it done. That's a big ask for the state of Ohio, but perhaps inspired by Lager's success, those representing First Energy rolled up their sleeves. After the company directed more than $60 million into the hands of politicians, their campaign accounts, and other dark-money entities, the bailout passed in 2019.[111] As we see with every scam, the bailout was to be paid for by everyday Ohioans via an increase on their energy bills—whether or not they were actually a customer of First Energy. Note the trend: public assets benefiting private interests.

Now let's give credit when it's due. In case I'm leaving an impression that Ohio's legislators never worry about their own districts, there are some exceptions. Take the case of Matt Dolan, scion of the billionaire family that owns the Cleveland Indians. He's also an Ohio state senator and chair of the senate's Finance Committee. Surely, you're thinking, someone of Matt's means would feel less of a need to satisfy big donors than his colleagues, since his wealth is far greater than almost anyone giving to him. And on one occasion, when a group of residents in his district came to Matt with a concern about a local institution, Matt stepped up. He listened attentively to their issue and went so far as to add a provision into Ohio's budget just for them. Matt's amendment made it into the final budget that appeared on the governor's desk. What a legislator should do, right? True public service.

Well, the group of citizens weren't just any old residents—they were the residents of the tiny village of Hunting Valley, the single wealthiest community in the state of Ohio, and a source of major political giving at all levels. Only months before, President Trump himself had visited the village for a fundraiser. And the budget item Dolan had snuck into the state budget was a measure capping the level of property taxes Hunting Valley property owners paid to the local school district.[112] Under his amendment, homeowners only paid if they actually sent kids to the school district, which few did. No other community in Dolan's district got this special help even though they were in the same school district. Heck, no other community in the entire state of Ohio has such a deal. The school was set to lose close to $6 million—12% of its total budget—until Ohio's governor line-item vetoed Dolan's handiwork at the last minute.[113]

So bottom line, there are lots of goodies to be had if legislators are sufficiently motivated. They can get both creative and highly targeted in handing them out. And they can be really, really big.

Main Entree: Regulating Businesses

Next on the menu, the legislature also writes the laws and oversees the regulations and the regulators that impact businesses doing work in Ohio. As you can imagine, this is an intense focus of lobbying efforts. The hefty entree of the legislative meal.

No surprise, businesses work hard to ensure that their state's regulations create the best climate possible for them to succeed. The more regulated the industry, the greater the presence they have in state capitals like Columbus. So, everyone from banks to insurance companies to utilities to communications companies to nursing home operators employ a permanent team of lobbyists working on their behalf in capital cities.

Sometimes, all institutions want is the status quo, and they spend a lot of time beating back changes that might make business more difficult. Other times, they advocate that the legislature "improve" the regulatory environment for their business in some meaningful way. Once again, Ohio's legislature and its leaders have shown a willingness to step up and take actions on regulations when properly motivated.

One dramatic example occurred early in the process of the fledgling for-profit charter school industry digging its tentacles deep into state government and public school accounts. Before Lager built his empire, the largest player in the industry was a man named David Brennan, who ran a for-profit charter school empire by the name of White Hat. (Mr. Brennan, from Akron, liked wearing white cowboy hats. Go figure.). Like Lager, his schools performed terribly. But like Lager, Brennan became one of the biggest GOP contributors in the state, donating millions.[114] This is a man who got his calls returned at the highest levels. So, despite his school's glaring problems, Brennan benefited from favorable "policymaking" decisions from Columbus, which opened an ever-widening flow of funds to his web of companies.[115] Ohio became known as the "Wild, Wild West" of charter schools.[116]

At one point, Brennan and other for-profit charter school operators ran across a nagging inconvenience. Part of the initial charter school regulatory framework included an office to oversee the quality of these new schools. Which made sense, right? After all, they were all using taxpayer money and pulling money (and kids) out of public schools. The new agency, called the Legislative Office of Education Oversight, developed this annoying habit of doing its job, issuing reports raising concerns about the quality of White Hat's and other for-profit charter schools.[117] (It turns out, year after year, for-profit schools like White Hat performed worse than the public schools they were draining funds from).[118]

What was the legislative response to this oversight? In 2005, the Speaker of the House, rising star Jon Husted (35 at the time), boldly responded to LOEO's reports. He shut down the bad schools, right? No, *he shut down the Legislative Office of Education Oversight.*[119] Eliminated it. Charter school operators were highly thankful of the then-Speaker's handiwork. As Lager himself later explained on bestowing Husted the school's first honorary degree,[120] "[w]ithout Speaker Jon Husted ... the [ECOT] revolution in e-learning in Ohio may have ended."[121] Husted received $36,000 from Lager-related donors over the years, and refused to give the funds back even after the scam imploded.[122] When Lager went bankrupt amid an FBI investigation, Husted must've really paid a price, right? Nah. After a stint as secretary of state, he currently serves as lieutenant governor of the State of Ohio. (But he says he's very disappointed in Bill Lager).[123]

Another example of how hard an industry works to tilt regulations in its favor, and the largesse that can flow a politician's way for doing so, involves payday lending. This is a case of fighting to maintain a very lucrative status quo.

For years, thanks to a loophole in Ohio law, payday lenders enjoyed a more hospitable environment in Ohio than other states—specifically, they were able to charge everyday Ohioans a 591% annual average interest rate, the highest in the nation.[124] No doubt, the vast sums of money they rained upon lawmakers—almost $500,000 from payday and auto title loan companies from 2015 to 2018[125]—kept their prime position safely in place.

In 2017, prodded by some socially minded non-profits, some Ohio legislators introduced a bill to clamp down on these rates. And that's where our jet-setting rising star Cliff Rosenberger re-enters the story. The Speaker worked behind the scenes to stall the reform in committee for more than a year. While Rosenberger publicly said he wanted to reform payday lending laws, he worked feverishly behind closed doors to kill any reform.[126] At one point, Rosenberger assigned a top conservative colleague to work out a "compromise" on the legislation; when that colleague actually announced a compromise amendment, Rosenberger replaced him the next morning. No surprise, Rosenberger received a big chunk of the payday lenders' overall campaign cash—at least $54,250, with another $29,000 going to the Republican account he controlled.[127]

But these companies did far more than give him money from an arm's length. Remember all of Rosenberger's international trips? One or several representatives of the payday lending industry trying to kill the bill traveled *with him* to China, France and London.[128] In London, the son of Clarksville enjoyed reminding these lobbyists that he had the power to destroy their industry whenever he wanted to but was opting to save them.[129]

You can't help but wonder what he received in exchange for *not* destroying them and sitting on that bill all that time. Well, the FBI ultimately wondered the same thing. So much so that in 2018, it announced that it was investigating Rosenberger and the payday lending executives on those trips for extortion, bribery and violations of the Travel Act. Rosenberger resigned shortly thereafter, and the investigation continues today. Weeks after Rosenberger left office, now that all of Ohio was watching, an amended version of the payday lending reform passed the house and senate and was signed by the governor. Amazing what the FBI and some rare sunshine can do to move things forward in Ohio!

Bottom line: the Husted and Rosenberger examples show how much the legislature can do to lighten regulatory oversight or keep a favorable climate immune from change.

"It's On Me": Kneecapping Your Competition

Before you assume that lobbying only takes place to lessen regulations on industries or entities, rest assured there are moments where Columbus insiders push hard for *active* regulation of some industries—even debilitating regulation. And that, of course, is when it involves their competitors. It's the part of the menu where you get to order for another table and send them something rotten.

Because of its manufacturing legacy and know-how, few states stand to benefit more from a transition to a green economy than Ohio. With the potential to make solar panels in Toledo (which has a long tradition of glass-making) and wind turbine parts all over the state, fully embracing new sources of energy offers an enormous opportunity for a state desperately looking for the next generation of jobs.[130] In 2007, then-Governor Ted Strickland seized this opportunity by making Ohio one of the first states to impose a robust renewable energy mandate into state law.

But other players fear the competition from these new sources of green energy. And some of them, old-line companies like First Energy and Murray Coal in Eastern Ohio, happen to be entities who throw around more money in Ohio politics than almost anyone.[131] So, at the same time that they push to subsidize their own work, these players have been equally hungry to destroy their upstart competitors.[132]

No surprise, once Republicans took over the Ohio Statehouse after 2010, they've been at war with renewables, first freezing then gutting the Strickland mandates.[133] But getting rid of a government incentive to go green apparently wasn't enough. Insiders know that a nifty regulation or two can do far more damage. So, in 2014, Ohio's legislature passed the strictest state-wide setback rule for wind farms anywhere in the nation.[134] In 2021, the statehouse was back at it, pushing through another round of "regulation" making it even harder to site wind or solar projects.

The legislation had its intended effect—Ohio now has the least wind capacity of its neighboring states.[135] And the overall effort to kneecap the renewable energy sector has worked like a charm. Despite the fact that Strickland's renewable mandate placed Ohio at the forefront early on, Ohio now ranks as the second lowest state when it comes to renewable energy generation.[136]

So, after subsidizing the old and destroying the new, here's where we are: Murray Coal is bankrupt, its CEO Bob Murray passed away in 2020, and First Energy pleaded guilty to federal bribery charges. And in the meantime, at their prodding, Ohio's statehouse has succeeded in killing the next generation of energy companies (who *weren't* asking for bailouts) from growing or coming here.

Well done, boys. Keep the spiral going.

Dessert: Overturning Local Governance

There's a final area where the statehouse can come through in a big way—in this case, the dessert is an essential part of the meal. Once major players have gotten what they need at the statewide level, they're of course eager to avoid any disruptions of that profitable status quo. And one critical way to do that is to kill off efforts by *local* governments to upend it. Here, again, state lawmakers are eager to serve.

Don't get me wrong—cities can run the gamut when it comes to quality of governance. In Ohio and elsewhere, they, too, run into corruption, mismanagement and other problems. Some local elected officials will fall for the same temptations as their statehouse colleagues—and both parties have gotten into the act. Still, it's fair to say that local officials tend to be far more responsive to the concerns of their citizens than statehouses. They're closer not only to the action, but to the people. When problems emerge—whether it's the scourge of gun violence, or poverty, or foreclosures—mayors and city council members will usually feel it first. And in many places, with statehouses and Congress stagnant, cities become the place where public servants are freer to take action. Moreover, many city-level charters also empower citizens themselves to take action through petition drives and referenda.

So, what happens in a state capital like Columbus when the locals step up to take action? If those actions offend the interests of power brokers in those capital cities, the legislators stand ready to overturn the work of those local governments, using the power I described in Chapter Two. The lawyers call it "preemption," which sounds harmless and complicated. But in the brass tacks of politics, it's not as innocent: interests are basically getting state lawmakers to block locals from addressing the very issues they've already paid the state lawmakers *not* to address.

A few examples:

In 2019 and 2020, local communities in Ohio began to ban plastic bags in order to reduce their carbon footprint. This included Cuyahoga County (Cleveland and its suburbs), for which the issue isn't just global, but local—5.5 million pounds of plastic pollute Lake Erie alone each year.[137] So what did the legislature do? It *banned* Ohio communities from banning plastic bags. Why did they step into an issue of local governance? Because the Ohio Chamber of Commerce, the Ohio Council of Retail Merchants, and the Ohio Grocers Association asked them to.[138]

For another example, let's head north to Cleveland again. As mentioned in Chapter One, Cleveland is America's poorest city. A few years ago, a group of activists and labor groups began gathering signatures to place on the Cleveland ballot a measure that would raise the minimum wage to $15 per hour. (Ohio's minimum wage was $8.10 at the time and goes up a few pennies every year). Speculation grew that similar efforts might emerge in other cities. Political insiders knew that these measures were highly popular and, if they went to the ballot, would inevitably be approved as they have elsewhere. Prodded by business interests, once again the legislature swooped in, forbidding any cities from enacting their own minimum wage levels above the state wage.[139]

And then there's the issue of gun violence. While mass shootings earn broad media coverage, it's local government that experiences these killings the most directly. After a 2017 Las Vegas shooting brought nationwide attention to the issue of bump stocks, cities across Ohio passed ordinances banning bump stocks in their communities. Those laws led to immediate lawsuits by pro-gun activists, leading to the same outcome as all such suits since the statehouse passed a gun law preemption law 2006—the cities lost.[140] Whether a city tries to ban guns from its parks, ban assault weapons,[141] sue gun companies, or keep guns out of the hands of minors, the legislature has prevented them from doing a thing about guns flooding their streets and killing their constituents. This is the case in close to 40 states.[142]

Term Limits

There's one final wrinkle that has only added to the sway of the Bill Lagers and First Energies and Cliff Rosenbergers on our statehouse politicians.

It's counter-intuitive, but that factor is term limits.

Ohio and some other states imposed limits on legislative terms in the 1990s. The whole point, advocates said, was that term limits would curtail some of the very abuses described in this Chapter. If corrupt politicians figured out how to never lose their jobs on election day, a limit on how many terms they could serve would do it for them. Fresh blood would arrive every few years, cleansing the place. And on the surface, it's hard to argue with any rule that would force the Cliff Rosenbergers and Larry Householders out of power after eight years. That's got to be a good thing.

But here's the problem. The First Energies and William Lagers and next generation of lobbyists and special interests *don't leave* after eight years (unless of course the FBI takes them down). They stay through the eight years, then another eight years, then another. And the fact that those interests are always there, ordering from that menu, while the legislators cycle in and out, has made the power dynamic far worse.

The experienced and savvy private interests serve as a welcoming committee for every session's fresh crop of new legislators, most arriving from a small town and a very-part time position as a village councilmember, township trustee, school board member or county commissioner. Many won't have been in government at all. The welcoming committee is poised to make the newcomers' entrance into this new capital city as grand as can be. And it quickly becomes clear that they're the key to filling your campaign coffers, getting you re-elected and making your life better in all sorts of other ways. The Rosenberger treatment.

But on issue after issue, they also come across as the experts. State government is complicated. Being the people's representative is complicated. If you haven't been in government before, or served in a part-time local position, it takes years to figure the state out. Staff support is generally limited. Since they're permanent fixtures, the lobbyists and interests in capital cities know far more about how the state operates—the true internal plumbing—than most of the legislators they're meeting with. Heck, many are former legislators and staffers themselves.

And term limits made this mismatch even worse. Before term limits, a 20-year legislator who'd chaired a major committee for years knew as much or more about the state's finances and inner working as any lobbyist in Columbus. Now, a legislator is lucky to be named a committee chair in his or her third term, if not their fourth. Then they're out.

In the same way, term limits have also made the leaders of a party caucus far more powerful. The Husteds and the Rosenbergers and the Householders control those party accounts and dole out that money to help the others get reelected.

*   *   *

So, this is the incestuous culture of capital cities like Columbus.

Please the power brokers with what you can do for them, and you get to stay and enjoy the place. Thrive in a way you won't back home.

In Ohio, it's not just theory, or rhetoric. The above examples show that it's how the place runs, with almost no awareness among voters back at home. And it just keeps going, through thick and thin, scandal after scandal, policy failure after policy failure.

In Chapter Five, we'll look at the perverse incentives that this culture creates in statehouses like Ohio's. They form core ingredients as to how statehouses have become laboratories of autocracy.

But before we get to that, there's another major ingredient to look at.

It's a big one. And easy to understand even if hard to believe.

It's the fact that almost every legislative election in the country is pre-determined before it even starts, and regardless of who runs.

CHAPTER 4

Rigged in the Bunker: A Decade of Predetermined Elections

THEY CALLED IT the bunker.

It wasn't a real bunker, but a fancy hotel suite in downtown Columbus. Appropriately, not far from that Waffle House.[143]

Still, it was the perfect name:

First, it was well hidden. The room itself was far removed from the Ohio statehouse. And while the people laboring inside were trusted statehouse staff, they'd recently resigned, only to be re-hired as private contractors, all to keep their work secret.[144]

Second, it was indeed part of a war. Not just one party at war with another. But a war against the voters of Ohio. And against democracy.

Because in that bunker, a group of politicians and political insiders became the backroom architects of Ohio's democracy for the next decade. Big benefactors like William Lager and David Brennan and others had invested millions to make sure this group was in this room, at this moment, for their clear mission.

And from the bowels of that hotel, they rigged the next decade of elections. Through a process called gerrymandering, they carved up the map of Ohio into legislative districts in a way that pre-determined the outcome of every legislative election for the next 10 years. And they nailed it—out of 655 elections over the ensuing decade, their work in that room only failed them eight times. They batted .988!

In other rooms around the country, around the same time, insiders also rigged elections. Five cycles of them, at both the state and federal levels. In state after state. Almost every outcome, pre-determined years in advance.

What happened in that Ohio bunker and elsewhere shows the extremes some went to keep voters from having a choice in their elections, as well as to keep anyone from knowing about it until it was too late. And they were an essential foundation for what's happening in the country in 2021.

But before we enter the bunker, we need to go back a little further in time.

Because two years before, few would've believed that the people huddled in that bunker would've even been there. Or in elected office at all.

*   *   *

Storming the Bunker

It was the May 18, 2009 edition of *Time Magazine*.

A red and blue cartoon of an elephant took up most of the cover. The familiar logo of the Republican party, under the headline: "Endangered Species."[145]

The main article didn't mince words. "These days,

Republicans have the desperate aura of an endangered species. They lost Congress, then the White House . . . Polls suggest that only one-fourth of the electorate considers itself Republican, that independents are trending Democratic and that as few as five states have solid Republican pluralities. And the electorate is getting less white, less rural, less Christian--in short, less demographically Republican."[146] The article noted books appearing in bookstores with titles such as: *The Strange Death of Republican America* and *40 More Years: How the Democrats Will Rule the Next Generation.*

The article continued to pile on: "The party's ideas--about economic issues, social issues and just about everything else-- are not popular ideas . . . The party's new, Hooverish focus on austerity on the brink of another depression does not seem to fit the national mood." And then, perhaps most brutal of all: "Our two-party system encourages periodic pendulum swings, but given current trends, it's easy to imagine a third party in the U.S. At this rate, it could be the Republican Party."[147]

In Ohio, the story was similar.

Obama had just won the Buckeye State by 4.5% in November 2008. Governor Ted Strickland, who'd won by a whopping 61%-37% in 2006, was riding high after delivering Ohio. Even amid the tough economy, in April 2009, Obama enjoyed a 63% approval rating in Ohio, and Strickland stood at 56% (as a point of comparison, Trump never reached 56% approval in Ohio).[148] Even though Republicans had gerrymandered the legislature in 2001, Democrats took the Ohio House in 2008 for the first time since 1994, securing a comfortable 53-46 seat margin. If they simply held those seats in two years against the endangered party, and Strickland got re-elected in 2010, GOP gerrymandering of Ohio would finally come to an end. And as the *Time* story suggested, they were on their way.

But out of all the gloom and doom for the Republican Party, one brief sentence—a throwaway line, really—in that *Time* cover story would ultimately negate every other word:

"Of course, politics can change in a hurry."[149]

They sure did.

Beneath the surface, something was brewing. And not just the nascent Tea Party movement, which would gather steam over the summer of 2009 as the health care debate dragged out. Or Mitch McConnell's commitment to obstruct anything the new president did.

Something else.

While Democrats were celebrating the new Obama era, and giddily counting on the demographic shift that was sure to doom Republicans, a group of those Republicans was thinking ahead. And plotting. Strategically, and tactically.

They were busy targeting a particular set of elections in 2010 that would turn things around: the offices that would impact the re-districting process for the coming decade.

In most states, that meant an intense focus on state legislative races. As described in Chapter Two, legislatures are usually the entities that draw the new district maps after each census. In a few states, this also put a bullseye on an odd assortment of other elected positions that play a role in the districting process.

I would know.

I ran in one of those races.

King Coal to the Rescue

In Ohio, like most states, the legislature draws the district lines—the "maps"—for the Congressional districts. It does so by passing a bill that the governor then signs.

But to draw the *state* legislative districts, Ohio's Constitution lays out a separate process to keep the legislature from drawing its own districts. Instead of the statehouse, a small group of officials called the Apportionment Board does the work. In 2010, that Board was comprised of five officials: the governor, the secretary of state, and one representative of each party selected by the legislative leaders. Plus one other elected job, perhaps the most anonymous of all . . . .

The state auditor.

So, going into 2010, whichever party won two out of three of the statewide positions—governor, secretary of state, and auditor—would draw the lines for the state legislature.

In early 2009, Governor Strickland approached me to run for state auditor against the one Republican who'd won state-wide in 2006. At the time, I was the president of the three-member Hamilton County Commission in Ohio's third largest county. And I had shown some success winning cross-over votes. When I unseated the incumbent in 2006—I ousted the son of the inventor of the Heimlich maneuver, running with the slogan the "Heimlich Remover"—it was the first time Hamilton County had a Democratic county commission in 40 years.

I took Strickland up on his invitation and announced my candidacy in May. It was the same week as the *Time* extinction cover, so I was feeling quite heady at the time. Who wouldn't want to run against the team doomed to extinction?

Then things got even rosier when John Kasich, who was running for governor, plucked my original opponent to be his running mate. Left scrambling for a candidate, the Ohio Republican Party turned to a man named David Yost. He was an obscure prosecutor from Delaware County, who at the time was running for attorney general on an anti-spending tea party platform—even though spending in the offices he'd run had exploded during his tenure in county office.[150]

Anyway, I ran on a platform of using the auditor's office to clean up corruption and waste, while also helping governments across the state run as efficiently as possible. And I meant it. I had had a successful tenure in local government doing just that. Working across party lines, we'd stabilized a county that had been in dire straits financially when I arrived, winning awards, and shoring up our credit rating. I printed up a flyer comparing my spending record (we'd had to reduce our budget by a lot) versus Yost's big increases and passed it out at tea party booths at county fairs. The fact that they didn't care was an early sign that maybe their motivation wasn't about spending after all. Hmm.

But I also talked a lot about the Apportionment Board and the need to draw fair districts. And that was when I learned something—voters had no idea what I was talking about. Fair districting was as "insider" as insider got. The Apportionment Board even more so. Still, I insisted on bringing it up— apparently to a fault. I was once pulled aside by a long-time party leader and politely told that although we insiders knew how important districting was, the general audiences don't know or care about that part of the job. That alone seemed like a problem. Kind of like Steve Driehaus sitting in the audience of a foreclosure town hall.

By the middle of 2010, head-to-head at least, I had some momentum. I had raised more than twice the money Yost had. I would soon gain almost every newspaper endorsement, including conservative papers who endorsed Kasich. My biggest problem was that the broader environment was tough—the 2009 Tea Party brushfire had exploded into a full-on inferno by 2010. Kasich, running on a Tea Party platform back then, had ridden that wave to a lead, although Strickland would mount a furious comeback. But the good news for me was that Yost was an incredibly weak candidate.

By August, he hadn't raised enough money to run television ads in Ohio and its eight media markets. He also was awkward in the debates we had (one reason I got those endorsements), and still hardly known.

Then something strange happened.

We didn't see it until October, because fund-raising reports lag by a month. But in September, a bunch of employees of one company gave to Yost in modest increments—$20 here, $50 there, $75 here. And this was before the small-dollar online fundraising that is revolutionizing fundraising today. Even more odd was that it was a coal company . . . from a small town . . . .in Utah?!?[151] Who knew Utah American Energy was a fan of Dave Yost's prosecutorial work in Delaware County, Ohio? But they weren't his only fans. Around the same time, 26 employees gave from a number of little towns in Illinois; they worked for the American Coal Company. Over the following week, sixteen more gave from the Ohio American Energy, all hailing from small Eastern Ohio towns like Cadiz (Clark Gable's hometown), St. Clairsville, and Martins Ferry (hometown of the Niekro pitchers and kicker Lou Groza). Another 53 American Energy Corporation employees gave from a host of other small Eastern Ohio and West Virginia towns. Then ten from a company called KenAmerican in Kentucky, six from Century Mine (site of one of the worst fatal mine disasters in history) in West Virginia. And 20 from a company called Murray Energy. All these contributions were in small amounts, but combined with contributions from an assorted group of contractors and energy companies from the same towns, it totaled more than $50,000.

Again, not enough to let Yost catch me, but strange.

Now why would a coal miner in Price, Utah care who the next Ohio auditor was? Why give $25 to defeat me? I'd been to

Price once in law school but hadn't made any enemies during the visit. Did they not like my commitment to conduct more performance audits? Maybe they didn't want fair districts in Ohio. But, then again, I'd been told average folks *in Ohio* didn't care about the districting issue. Why would Utahns?

Needless to say, it was their boss who cared. Murray Energy gave it away. The companies these folks worked for were all owned by Robert Murray; the contractors no doubt performed work for his businesses. The same Murray who'd later push to kneecap new sources of energy in the legislature the auditor would help shape. Also, the Murray who'd become nationally famous when his shoddy safety practices led to a mine collapse in Utah that killed six miners and three rescuers in 2007, leading to one of the largest fines ever for unsafe practices.[152] He'd also spent years fighting coal safety regulations.[153]

Apparently, Mr. Murray cared a lot more about elections than mine safety. He cared about them so much, he was later found to be strong-arming employees to give to his favorite candidates,[154] including tracking who gave and who didn't, and punishing the latter.[155] Something tells me all those contributions that flowed to my auditor's race from Utah and Illinois came under the same duress.

Even then, what I remember thinking, naively, was, "Why would a coal company in Southern Ohio care so much about who the state auditor is?" This wasn't OSHA. The office audits Ohio governments, not private companies or mining operations.

Duh.

It was a sign. . . . I was in a close game, in the seventh or eighth inning, and with Yost on the mound, trailing, and out of gas, the big shots were warming up in the bullpen. Murray had his sights set on the legislature, which meant he needed to win the auditor's race. David Brennan of White Hat and Bill Lager gave too, with the same goal. For Lager, at least, the auditing side of the role mattered as well. In fact, Yost would later give Lager's for-profit charter school an "Excellence in Auditing" award[156]—yes, at the very time that the school was cooking the books. No surprise, Yost received additional hefty Lager contributions around the time he bestowed the award, along with the same opportunity Husted had earned years before—a chance to address the school's graduates.[157] Around that time, he also managed to make a whistleblower complaint about Lager's practices disappear.[158]

Bottom line, the big shots needed this seat because it would determine who drew the statehouse lines for the coming decade. And that would keep everything they were building going over the long run.

Still, even with those Illinois and Utah miners pitching in, Yost hadn't raised enough money for meaningful TV, or much else, by the Fall.

But then something else happened. With weeks to go, ads did begin to run across the state, pummeling me.

How?

The Republican Party itself ran them, using big bucks also provided by Brennan and others.[159] The party had already given more than $400,000 to Yost's campaign, but now they were running ads *for him* separately as well. Think of *Weekend at Bernie's,* but here the Ohio GOP was propping up one of Yost's (Bernie's) sagging shoulders while Lager, Murray and others propped up the other.

And as always, the ads were absurd.

Just for kicks, here's one: At one point when I was commissioner, Hamilton County's rock-ribbed Republican County Sheriff[160] had competed for a grant with the Department of Homeland Security to purchase a patrol boat in the Ohio River. At a time when terrorism worries were still high, DHS agreed with him that the river presented a prime target, and needed added security, so they approved his grant. One formal duty county commissioners have is to accept grants on behalf of all county officials, and then advance the funds to the relevant department. Which I did—I didn't apply for the grant, I didn't approve it, I just *accepted* it. And again, the officeholder who applied for the grant was a *Republican.* The County's most recognized Republican, in fact. Wouldn't you know it, the GOP ran ads across Ohio making it look like I used taxpayer money to buy a "yacht" for personal enjoyment, using a cartoonish image of a fancy pleasure craft, fishing rods and all. Now that doesn't sound like a very good auditor at all, does it?

Bottom line: as weak as a candidate as Yost was, the big shots knew what his race meant long term. They pulled in checks from all over the country, then swooped in and dragged him over the finish line with direct and false ads bankrolled by the party itself. He ended up winning by five points, which was a relatively close race in a terrible 2010 cycle nationwide for Democrats. Strickland lost to Kasich by two. And Lager's MVP, Jon Husted, won the secretary of state's race by twelve.

By winning two of those three races, Republicans controlled the Apportionment Board. So, from the brink of extinction in 2009, they would be scheming in the bunker only eight months later.

This may sound like a great comeback story for Republicans in Ohio, highly focused on the positions they needed to control districting, and just in the nick of time. But it actually happened everywhere.

Painting the Whole Map Red

It wasn't as if Karl Rove hid the ball. As David Daley explains so well in his must-read book *Rat-F**ked*, the former Bush guru called his shot. In March 2010, Rove boldly name-dropped his targets in a *Wall Street Journal* editorial, listing towns in Ohio, Indiana, Texas, Pennsylvania and elsewhere. "These are legislative races that will determine who redraws congressional lines after this year's census, a process that could determine which party controls upwards of 20 seats and whether many other seats will be competitive."[161] Rove pointed out that eighteen statehouses had tight margins, and eleven of them were controlled by Democrats. From there, he and his colleagues chose 107 seats in sixteen states to focus on. Win those seats, Rove explained, and lock in at least 190 safe Congressional districts. Then go win the others. (At the time, Democrats were the majority party by a whopping 257-178.)

You can read all the details in *Ratf**ked*, but Rove and an outfit called the Republican State Leadership Committee pulled it off. With $30 million raised from largely corporate and insurance interests, and savvy targeting, they flipped the New York Senate, the Pennsylvania House (erasing a 104-98 Democratic advantage), the Michigan House (erasing a 65-42 Democratic (D) advantage), along with statehouses in Wisconsin (from 50D-45R to 60R-38D), North Carolina, and Alabama.[162] And yes, they flipped the Ohio House from the 53-46 Democratic advantage to 59-40 the other way, earning Republicans their second ticket to the "bunker."[163]

In total, Republicans gained more than 700 seats nationwide, including "majorities in 10 of the 15 states scheduled to gain or lose seats under reapportionment and where the legislature controlled the new lines."[164] (i.e., where it really mattered). Of the 70 Congressional seats considered competitive at the time, "Republicans now controlled how 47 of those would be drawn, Democrats just 15."[165] In total, even better than Rove had planned, Republicans now possessed sole power to draw 193 of the 218 seats they needed to win back control of Congress.[166]

"Of course, politics can change in a hurry," *Time* had written in that throwaway caveat.

Indeed, they had. And that was just the beginning.

In the Bunker: Rigging a Decade of Elections

Which brings us to the bunker.

The bad news is that within that hotel room, they rigged Ohio legislative elections for a decade. The good news is that thanks to two heroic groups—the League of Women Voters of Ohio and Ohio Citizens Action—the machinations to keep it all a secret ultimately failed. The report issued by these groups, "The Elephant in the Room," (EITR) details the work that was done in secret, for months. You can read it yourself on-line.[167] Prepare to feel ill.

Let me start by praising the League of Women Voters (LWV). If you wanted legislative districts that represented the best democratic principles and were fair to everyone, you'd put the LWV in charge of the process. They'd also make it transparent to all, which ensures better results and no games. And basically, in the build-up to the 2011 process, that's what the Ohio LWV and other groups insisted on: transparency and a fair map based on certain nonpartisan, non-controversial criteria (like don't "split" communities needlessly between districts, don't draw crazy shapes, make politicians have to actually compete to win, and try to have the partisan breakdown of a state's districts approximate the partisan breakdown of that state).

What Ohio got instead was the opposite. Because, of course, nonpartisan and fair maps were the exact opposite of their goal.

As a reminder, in Ohio there is one process to draw the maps for Congressional districts (the legislature passes a bill), and a separate process to draw the maps for the legislature (the Apportionment Board). But both took place in the bunker.

Here's what they did:

1. Keep it Secret for Months . . .

First, it was all done in secret. Not only was all the work conducted in the private "bunker," the "joint secretaries" of the Apportionment Board were statehouse staff who (no one at the time knew) resigned from their posts from August to November, created private LLCs, and each made more than $100,000 for their four months of work (paid for by a Republican Party task force, so the payments themselves were also hidden). For one staffer, that was a six-fold increase in her pay.[168] To add to the secrecy, the group placed an outside lawyer in the middle of the deliberation, allowing them to shroud much of their work by claiming attorney-client privilege.[169]

Outside of an initial organizational meeting in early August, the Apportionment Board (which draws the statehouse lines) did not schedule a single public meeting until September 26. But beginning in July, the Board's members and legislative leaders, or their representatives, met in secret every week.[170] Both the maps for state legislative elections and Congressional elections were drawn in secret, and shared with legislative leaders (of only the GOP, even though a Democrat is a member of the Apportionment Board) in private to get their feedback. The internal schedule for the Congressional process made clear that the goal was to complete the map by mid-August, but then "hold it in the can" until the last possible moment.[171] In other words, keep it hidden from view.[172]

2. . . . Then Rush It Through

Two weeks into September, the chair of the statehouse committee with jurisdiction over the Congressional map process announced that *the following day*, they would take public testimony on their proposed map.[173] It was a bad omen that they hadn't actually introduced the map yet. That meeting happened (I was actually in attendance), they presented the map, a number of good government representatives complained, no one in the majority cared, and that committee voted to approve the map the next day. Ohioans will remember that this all came amid a statewide uproar over an anti-labor bill called Senate Bill 5, which drew attention away from this grotesque process. The room was rather quiet for the hearing I watched, given its consequences for the next ten years; while days before, a debate I'd been in over the anti-labor bill had been packed.

The full house voted to approve the map 24 hours later. Nine days after that, the Ohio Senate approved it with one slight non-substantive change, to which the house concurred immediately. Not a single change was made to the districts themselves. Five days after that, with the two privatized staff looking over each shoulder, Governor Kasich signed the bill establishing that map.[174] And with that, 80 elections—sixteen elections for the next five cycles—were rigged.

If you think the Congressional process was rushed, just wait. After not having a single public meeting between August and late September, the proposed state legislative maps were presented to the public on a Friday. The Apportionment Board formally met the next Monday to review the recommended map.[175] Just as Ohio elections would soon become, it was all kabuki theater. With each member reading from a tight script for everything he did and said,[176] the Board voted to approve the map two days later. The only changes made to the initial map came not in response to any public testimony at their meetings—which were limited—but from private requests made by legislators. And with that, close to 600 elections were rigged over the next decade, 99% going exactly as planned.

How Do You Get to 99%?

Now there are many ways to measure how rigged a legislative map is. Some like to focus on crazy shapes, like the fact that Jim Jordan's district looks like a duck quacking from near Dayton all the way to Lake Erie, or that Cincinnati is sliced in half, or that Congresswoman Marcy Kaptur would need to don scuba equipment to traverse the absurdly thin "snake on the lake" (spanning from Toledo to Cleveland) they drew to force her to run against Dennis Kucinich to eliminate one of the two.

You can also look at the results I keep mentioning—that the maps held 99% of the time. Over the decade, over more than 650 elections, only eight times did a Democratic candidate flip a gerrymandered district—seven in 2018, and one more in 2020. That's democracy, Saddam Hussein-style. And as we'll see in the next chapter, almost no races were even close.

But to show just how rigged the map was, the League of Women Voters came up with a formula to score any map based on their nonpartisan criteria. Helpfully, they also held a public competition inviting everyday Ohioans and experts to submit maps to meet those nonpartisan criteria, giving us points of comparison.

Fifty-three proposed plans were submitted for the Congressional maps. The highest score of the 53 maps, based on the criteria, was <u>222.6.</u> The tenth highest score was <u>194.7.</u> And the *lowest-performing* map submitted out of the 53 in the competition scored an <u>84.1.</u> Sounds low compared to the top scorers, doesn't it?

So how did the map drawn in secret, approved by the legislature, and signed by Kasich fare?

<u>38.5.</u>[177]

Now how can a map drawn by the politicians—the people who are paid taxpayer dollars to do this—do so abysmally worse than *any* map submitted by everyday Ohioans? Less than half the score of the *worst* map submitted?

Give them credit. It took hard work.

Crass work.

Here are a couple examples:

The map that scored 222.6 would've led to eleven districts (out of the sixteen) being competitive, because neither party would've had an advantage going in of more than 5%.

The map approved by the legislature? Not one district within 5%, and only two within 10%.

The map that scored 222.6 would've split only five counties into separate districts and would not have split a single city.

The map approved by the legislature? They split *every* major Ohio city into different districts, and 27 counties into different districts, many more than once.[178]

Looking at the whole map, the LWV bemoaned at the time: "We can already determine which party's candidate is likely to be elected in each of Ohio's 16 congressional districts for the next 10 years."[179]

And they were right.

The Big Shots Did the Work,
and Big Money Drove Some Decisions

While neither public input nor any whiff of democratic principles drove the decision-making, several influences were notable. And some surprising names directed the entire process.

The Trump era created more moderate images for Ohio Republican figures like John Kasich, John Boehner and even our scam school's first honorary graduate, Jon Husted. Kasich and Boehner have created new brands by criticizing the pro-Trump extremists in their party (I'm glad they do, by the way), including members of Congress from Ohio. Husted has always claimed to be a reformer on districting, and in 2020 was booed at a Trump rally for encouraging the audience to wear masks (kudos, Jon, for the effort). But these leaders get the opposite of kudos for 2011, when they were central to the election-rigging process.

For years to come, Kasich would bemoan the extremists in the legislature who made his tenure so difficult, and who ultimately empowered Trump himself. And his frustration was understandable—they essentially neutered him in his final six years as governor. But Kasich was both a member of the Apportionment Board, as well as the signer of the bill that established Ohio's rigged Congressional districts. Whether it was the extreme Congress or state legislature, he created the very monster he would later rail against.

Husted had spent years bemoaning gerrymandering and touted himself as a "fair districts" reformer. As he wrote in the *Washington Post* in 2014, "I am a conservative Republican, served as speaker of the Ohio House before becoming secretary of state and have been pushing to reform the way Ohio does redistricting since 2005. I believe that gerrymandering is the fractured foundation on which our legislative branch of government is built."[180] What he left out of that column, and in other appearances,[181] is that as the newly elected secretary of state in 2011, he happily participated in a secretive process that pulled off the worst gerrymander in the history of Ohio. He was in the room where it happened, but his public advocacy for reform morphed into support for the worst of election-rigging.

Finally, the central leader in Ohio's gerrymandering was then-Speaker John Boehner. As the EITR report explains, despite the high salaries paid to those privatized statehouse staffers, they were constantly taking direction from the Executive Director of "Team Boehner," and the "Redistricting Coordinator" for the NRCC. Changes that came from within the state, including from legislators themselves, had to first earn the approval of Team Boehner. The Ohio State Senate president made this point clear to two senators who wanted changes: "I am still committed to ending up with a map that Speaker Boehner fully supports, with or without votes from two memberships of leadership."[182] Translation: you're not in charge.

To make that even more clear, when one state senator requested that Clark County (the county that includes Springfield—home of John Legend), in his district, not be split in two, Team Boehner rejected the idea as "crazy" because it would have made the district less Republican.

On the other hand, Team Boehner did make changes to their map at the eleventh hour. One is particularly telling. One evening in September, after Ohio legislative leaders had signed off on the final Congressional map, Team Boehner sent an email to the privatized statehouse staffers requesting one change. The email was sent at 9:28 p.m., requesting that a "small carve out down 77 in Canton" be added to the 16th district. Eight minutes later, without even checking with Ohio's legislative leaders, the answer came back: "Yeah, sure, no problem." Team Boehner was pleased, replying five minutes later: "Thanks guys. Very important to someone important to us all."[183]

If you look at the "carve-out" that was added to the 16th, it looks like a little hook. As the EITR report points out, no one actually lives in the hook. What is it? It's both the headquarters and a major manufacturing plant of the Timken Company, one of the biggest supporters of Ohio Republicans at the state and federal level. Apparently, the company wanted to be in the 16th district. So in eight quick minutes, they got it taken care of. (Later, Jane Timken was elected chair of the Ohio Republican Party while I was the Democratic chair. When we'd appear together, she'd claim that I was overly concerned about gerrymandering. She's now running for U.S. Senate).

It Wasn't Just Ohio

Similar to those contributions from individual Utah coal miners, John Boehner's permanent presence in the bunker was a not-so-subtle clue that as bad as it was here, the process that happened in Ohio wasn't unique.

It happened everywhere.

Apparently, you don't go through all that Rove did to play good government once you get there. The secrecy of the bunker and the process inside were part of a national playbook. How do we know that? *Because they actually wrote it in the actual playbook they handed out.*

In May 2010, the Republican National Committee provided training on how to gerrymander. The theme? "Keep it secret, keep it safe."[184] That's where the Ohio staffers obtained their materials. That's where the Ohio counsel involved in the process got his training. And the trainer there would later serve as a consultant to the Ohio process, and no doubt to other states.[185] In January 2011, the Republican National Committee's "Redistricting Coordinator," presenting to a conference of state legislators, provided the same advice. He emphasized the need for secrecy throughout, encouraging the use of personal contacts and private computers while urging that legislative leaders "NEVER travel without counsel."[186] And he suggested methods of kabuki theatre, such as releasing plans to the public "to make specific points."[187] Another piece of advice he shared: "Self-interest binds, honor doesn't."[188] Inspiring stuff. But this was par for the course for this gentleman, who in the past had declared: "I define redistricting as the only legalized form of vote-stealing left in the United States today."[189] And: "Redistricting is like an election in reverse. It's a great event. Usually the voters get to pick the politicians. In redistricting, the politicians get to pick the voters."[190] Again, this is the guy *doing the training!*

All around the country, partisans returned to their capital cities armed with this election-rigging guidance. In Wisconsin, they did the work in a politically-connected private law office in an attempt to attach attorney-client privilege. Legislators could only look at the map of their own districts when they visited; they had to sign non-disclosure agreements before looking at the maps; and their public comments all followed a tight script.[191] Same story in Florida, where they got around a Constitutional amendment requiring transparency by concocting maps behind the scenes and then enlisting everyday citizens to advance them to the legislature.[192] In North Carolina, while they had formal public hearings at the statehouse, the real work took place back at state party headquarters, quarterbacked by the nation's leading gerrymandering expert.[193]

Add it all up, and 2011 led to secretive processes that rigged elections across the country. The impact would be clear within a year.

And the Maps Worked

How effective were these secretive processes? Let's just say I wish these cartographers governed as well as they rigged elections.

The best way to assess their work is to compare two years that were relatively similar—as much as that happens in politics. Conveniently, Obama won in 2008 and 2012 by close to the same margin. He lost a few states in 2012 that he won in 2008. And like Ohio, he won some states in 2012 by slightly less than he won them in 2008. But the two years provide a reasonable apples-to-apples comparison between the district maps in 2008 (many of which themselves had been gerrymandered in 2001) and those that were gerrymandered again in 2011.

Ready to compare the two?

Brace yourself.

Immediate Grip on Power

In Ohio, in 2008, Obama won Ohio 51.5%-46.9%. That year, Ohio sent ten Democrats to Congress, and eight Republicans, a breakdown that mirrored the presidential outcome. Ohio's General Assembly reflected that balance as well: 53 Democrats, 46 Republicans.

In 2012, Obama won Ohio again, 50.7%-47.7%. A little tighter. Sherrod Brown won by 6%. You'd expect around an even split among the House seats, right?

Not even close. Thanks to the work in the bunker, the 2012 Congressional delegation comprised twelve Republicans and four Democrats (Ohio had lost two seats due to weak population growth). That's right—75% of the Congressional delegation of a state that voted blue was now represented by Republicans. And remember how the map had only two districts within ten points? Well, they nailed that too. Only two races came within ten that year, and those involved previous Democratic members of Congress (i.e., well-known) trying to win in their old districts. Both lost. Those districts would never be that close again.

The statehouse? The 2008 53-46 breakdown in favor of Democrats also flipped. After 2012, Republicans controlled the statehouse 60-39! Now *that* is a map. Kasich and Husted got it done.

Other states performed in exactly the same way, blue ones included.

Obama carried Michigan in both 2008 (57%-41%) and 2012 (54%-45%). But the gerrymandered map converted an 8-7 Democratic delegation to Congress in 2008 into a 9-5 Republican delegation in 2012. A 67-43 Democratic statehouse turned into a 59-51 Republican statehouse.

Obama carried Wisconsin in both 2008 (56%-42%) and 2012 (53%-46%). But the gerrymandered map converted a 5-3 Democratic delegation to Congress into a 5-3 Republican delegation. A 52-46 Democratic statehouse turned into a 60-39 Republican statehouse.

Same story in Pennsylvania: Obama won in 2008 (54%-44%) and 2012 (52%-47%). A 12-7 Democratic delegation became a 13-5 GOP delegation. A 104-99 Democratic statehouse majority became a 110-93 GOP majority.

Obama won North Carolina in 2008 (49.7%-49.4%) then lost in 2012 (50.3%-48.3%). But the US House delegation went from 8-5 Democrats to 9-4 Republicans. The statehouse went from 68-52 Democrats to 77-43 Republicans.

I'll stop. You get the point. These are staggering numbers. Those secret mapmaking sessions worked to a tee. And while I've mentioned just a handful of states, the extreme gerrymandering took place across the country, with national impact. A Brennan Center study found that gerrymandering in half the states (and especially the more populated ones) skewed outcomes such that Republicans were over-represented in Congress by dozens of seats almost every cycle.[194] The gerrymandering was *the reason* Republicans controlled the House for most of the decade. And from Tennessee to Texas, Indiana to Iowa, Ohio to Oklahoma, gerrymandering grossly distorted representation in statehouse after statehouse (sometimes in favor of Democrats, but far more often in favor of Republicans).[195]

Staying Power for the Decade

These maps clearly had an immediate impact.

But how about long-term? As *Time* cautioned: "[P]olitics can change in a hurry."

Not here. However much politics changed around them, these maps had staying power.

Let's fast forward to 2018, the best year for Democrats of the decade, driven by former Republican suburban strongholds turning blue, driven largely by women. That shift created a wave that allowed Democrats to capture the U.S. House.

Thanks to some maps being struck down and that suburban shift, Democrats made some gains in Michigan and Pennsylvania. Ohio's Congressional delegation after the 2018 election remained 12-4, with almost no close elections (again, only two within ten points). Same with Wisconsin: 5-3. Clearly, gerrymandering saved some House Republicans from being swallowed up in the blue wave.

But for Rove and his crew, to keep the election rigging going long-term, what happened in statehouses in 2018 mattered far more. And this is where those bunkers proved even more successful.

Politics may have changed enough to crown Nancy Pelosi Speaker, but the outcomes in states hardly budged. In fact, given that this was a "blue wave" year, the maps proved impressively impregnable.

In Michigan, across the state, voters voted for Democratic statehouse candidates by a combined 52%-47% over Republican candidates. That translated into a district breakdown of 58-52— in favor of Republicans!

In Pennsylvania, even though voters opted for Democrats over Republicans 55%-44%, that translated into a 109-93 Republican advantage in the statehouse.

In Wisconsin, a 54%-45% Democratic advantage translated into a 63-36 Republican statehouse majority. Yes, that is truly absurd.

And in Ohio, voters across the state voted for Republicans 50.5%-49.5%, which translated into a 61-38 Republican supermajority.

Read those numbers again closely. They're staggering. Even in states where majorities of voters *strongly* favored Democrats to run their statehouses, the rigged maps took those votes and converted them into Republican *majorities*, and in some cases, supermajorities. One post-2018 study found that almost 60 million Americans lived in "minority rule" states.[196]

Eight years after the maps were drawn, they were able to keep a firm grip on power even when the voters voted for the opposite. A minority party locked into power no matter how the people vote, or how poorly its members perform. Hidden behind elections which offer an air of legitimacy, but whose outcomes are all pre-determined. It's a system Vladimir Putin would admire.

No surprise, since 2020 was less of a wave than 2018, those statehouses remained in Republican hands again. Bottom line: the rigged statehouse maps survived intact for the entire decade.

So, thanks to the bunker in Ohio, and similar private rooms across the country, America experienced a decade without democracy in most statehouses from 2011-2020. An entire decade with no accountability to the voters.

Personally, the ten years feel like they went by quickly. That race for state auditor doesn't feel that long ago. Nor does that hearing room where I watched them present the rigged Congressional map that sailed through in days.

But as we'll see in the next chapter, ten years without democracy turns out to be enough time to do deep and lasting damage.

CHAPTER 5

"Just Move": A Terrible Incentive Package

S IXTY MILES EAST of Cincinnati, sitting right on the Ohio River, is a small town named Manchester. Locals will proudly tell you it's the single cleanest point of the river.

The small town sits in the southwestern corner of Adams County, where my wife Alana grew up, so we spend a lot of time out there. As you wind along the hilly roads of the county, you often find yourself slowed behind an Amish horse and buggy. But you don't mind the leisurely pace because you're surrounded on both sides by a wondrous sea of corn and soybean fields, with an old farmhouse nestled in nearby.

When you arrive in Manchester itself, the idyllic scene ends abruptly. And that's when my blood boils. Almost every storefront on its Main Street is shuttered. Stately old buildings . . . empty. Hardly a soul on the street. It looks like a ghost town—depressing as hell. And all only a block from the river, which offers the town so much potential.

Manchester has struggled for some time, hit especially hard by a flood a few decades back. And then in 2016, the largest employer in the area, and largest taxpayer—Dayton Power &

Light—shut down. Jobs just evaporated and, with it, the town itself.

A few years ago, concerned citizens of Manchester approached their state senator on how to halt the decline. Mind you, this senator had voted routinely for tax cuts for those at the top, almost none of which ever "trickled down" to lift the people of Manchester. He'd voted to raid the precious local funds *from* Manchester to pay for those tax cuts. He'd voted to move money out of the strapped Manchester public schools.

Faced with the direct result of those and other statehouse policy failures, what did he tell the concerned citizens? Did he offer a new idea? Some kind of plan of action around infrastructure? Legislation to help struggling Main Streets like theirs?

No. No. And no.

What was his advice?

"You need to move."[197]

Just leave, he said.

When asked about the comment, he later confirmed it: "I did say, 'Sometimes you have to do what's best for your family.'"[198]

Yep. Just leave. It's best for your family.

Think about that. After this politician and his colleagues absolutely failed this community, with no solutions in sight, its residents don't get to say it's time for *him* to leave. Instead, he tells *them* that *they* should go elsewhere.

And for the most part, that's what happened. Manchester remains a ghost town, its population dropping below 2000 people for the first time in 90 years. And while term-limited, the senator's doing just fine—he got himself a job with the Ohio Department of Transportation.[199]

Needless to say, that conversation—that entire story—is not how representational politics is supposed to work. It's actually the opposite of how it's supposed to work. But the Manchester story is just one of many grotesque distortions to politics that arise when you have a decade without democracy.

* * *

A Decade with No Democracy: All the Wrong Incentives

A few years back, I had a heart-to-heart conversation with the leaders of the Ohio Manufacturing Association. When we arrived at the topic of the Ohio statehouse, I tried to put the problem in terms they'd understand.

If the businesses they ran operated with the same incentive structure that exists for statehouse politicians, they'd all go bankrupt quickly. Because the incentives arising from the corrupt and rigged legislature don't in any way reward delivering outcomes that serve the broader public good. As a legislator with eight short years to move up in the world, you'll do far better by helping the big donor make a mint off his for-profit school than you will helping the public schools back home in your district, where they don't know what you do anyway. More broadly, serving private interests earns you far greater rewards than the public interest. And as a politician in a rigged district, the biggest risk you face is being outflanked by an extremist in your next primary, so your incentive is to be as extreme as possible. Even if public outcomes plummet, so long as you are extreme and cater to those private interests, you and your colleagues are reelected, no sweat. And the one thing that will get you ousted from office? Working with the other party on anything. So never do that!

That's it, I told them. That's the game. And in any enterprise, such a dysfunctional set of incentives would guarantee failure— and worse—as it does for the state of Ohio.

Even more than I could capture in that meeting, a decade without actual democracy in Ohio's legislature has taught searing lessons about what happens when politics lack any accountability. When democracy doesn't really exist. And it's shown just how out of whack and dysfunctional those incentives become, and how much damage they cause.

Here are the worst of them:

No Accountability for Public Outcomes

What happened in Manchester illustrates the first consequence of a decade with no democracy—a complete lack of accountability for even the most disastrous of public outcomes. In a system where elections don't matter—where there is little awareness of what happens in the capital city and no electoral consequence for its failures—there is simply zero incentive to improve public outcomes.

Give them credit. The citizens who tracked down that state senator took a step only a tiny fraction of citizens would think to take: request a meeting with their elected senator (who most couldn't name), plead their case, and ask for answers. And *still*, he didn't even *pretend* to have answers. He told *them* to leave. That's a man with absolutely no concern about being held accountable for the failed outcome he and his colleagues are delivering for communities like Manchester.

And that's one reason you see failure across the board, and towns in the sad shape of Manchester across Ohio. It's not that a policy or two are wrong-headed. It's that the culture and structure of Ohio politics creates *no incentive* to deliver broad-based, positive public outcomes in the first place. So that's *not* the goal on issue after issue.

Take a step back.

Why should a state with the Cleveland Clinic and children's hospitals of the highest quality be ranked so low in public health access? Or ranked one of the worst in the nation in infant mortality? One reason that comes to mind: Ohio government ranks 47th in the nation in the amount it spends in public health, per capita.[200] There's just zero incentive to do more. Or better.

Why should a state with the seventh largest economy experience high poverty in city after city? Two of the ten poorest cities in the nation? One reason: the state legislature has been pushing trickle-down policies for years, including raiding cities like Manchester, Cleveland and Cincinnati of local revenue (well over $1 billion over the course of the decade)[201] in order to afford tax cuts for those at the top. There's no incentive to do better by those communities—the average voter has no idea the state has taken those funds (which, by the way, defunds local police). You can even tell them to leave their community without worry about any political reprisal.

Why should a state with so many strong colleges and universities, with the fifth best public secondary schools in the nation as recently as 2010, now rank so low in higher education attainment, while still lead the nation in student debt? Could it be because state government underfunds those colleges, forcing more of the burden on families as tuition and debt? If no one knows, and there's no accountability (they blame the college or local school board, not the statehouse), there's simply no incentive to change it.

To be clear, I still have faith that many state legislators come to their statehouses to do good by their communities, or to make a difference on issues they care about. They still view the role as public service. And I've seen many work to do that every day of every term despite countless obstacles. But over time, and across hundreds of people that cycle through over the years, the institutional incentives drive both the goals and the results of the institution as a whole, and too many (including a majority) of its participants.

So with little to no incentive to improve public outcomes, Ohio is suffering the precise results you'd expect. And just like in Manchester, across the state, people are leaving in droves. But the politicians and their broken politics stay right where they are, powerful as can be amid failure after failure.

A Powerful Incentive To Serve Private Interests

On the other hand, politicians in Columbus face a powerful incentive to satisfy the narrow, private interests reviewed in Chapter Three, and beyond (as we'll see in Chapter Six).

They get elected to the statehouse for four terms. That's eight years to garner something meaningful out of their service before finding their next step in life. The clock starts ticking right away.

Most will serve their eight years and be done. For most, the best prospects for that next step will come from that capital city as opposed to back home. From the private players who surround them. So, best to get along with them as well as you can.

Others may have aspirations beyond the initial elected post. One group tries to be lifers—jumping from the house, to the state senate, and back to the house. Some pull this off. For example, the senate leader orchestrating the 2021 districting process is the same person who, as a member of the house, rigged the maps in 2011.

Others aim higher, like Congress or statewide office.

Either way, playing the capital city game is the surest ticket to success in any of those directions. Running for Congress or statewide is a multi-million-dollar enterprise in a state like Ohio. Outside of a few big cities, the political money is largely concentrated in Columbus (or DC). To make that leap up— when you only have a few years to do it before your window of relevance closes—you've got to be in good with the powers that be. Especially, again, when the people back home have no idea what you actually do.

Just look at the trajectory of Jon Husted from young house member, to Speaker, to statewide office. He succeeded by *building* relationships with David Brennan and William Lager and Bob Murray and First Energy, not by standing up to them. And he built those relationships by doing what they wanted, when they asked. Writing the law that allowed their for-profit operations to start lapping up public education dollars. Eliminating the nagging agency that was warning about their problems. Gerrymandering the state behind closed doors despite promising reform publicly. And so on. All upside, no downside, even when it all explodes in scandal and lost public funds.

So, the decline in Ohio doesn't just result from the fact that there's no incentive to deliver positive public outcomes. It's worse. Much of that failure results directly from powerful incentives to satisfy the private interests urging policies that *undermine* the public interest. Policies that drain public assets.

The rapid decline in Ohio schools? If your politicians are willing to pull money away from more successful schools and throw that money to scams like Lager's and educational disasters like White Hat, of course your school ratings are going to fall. If leaders are willing to eliminate the agency that's trying to fix the problem, of course there's no accountability.

An economy struggling to compete in the 21st century? If

your politicians are willing to smother emerging industries—like solar and wind—in the crib because dying industries like Murray Energy tell them to, of course you're going to fall behind.

Ohio's decline is not a policy problem, because policy is not the goal anymore.

It's a pay-to-play problem. These legislators are catering to certain private interests that dominate Columbus and other state capitals, and those interests too often have their eyes on public assets they can tap into for their own gain. What the people actually want, and what would actually benefit the state, are, at best secondary; worse, wholly irrelevant; and worst of all, the exact opposite of what the private interests are demanding from government. And legislators learn quickly that serving those private goals, even at the cost of public outcomes, strengthens their grip on power.

So, in the end, the incentive to please these private interests directly correlates with failure in public outcomes.

But there are other incentives that are just as poisonous.

How to Kiss Your Career Goodbye?
Work with the Other Side

I once had the honor of attending the State of the Union Address. And it happened to be a historic one. George Bush's final SOTU. But the most famous visual from the night was not the president speaking. It was Senators Hillary Clinton and Barack Obama walking down the aisle yards apart, shaking as many hands as possible as they battled it out in that epic primary. Political theater at its best, and I watched it from the balcony behind the president's left shoulder.

You'll never guess whose guest I was.

Her name was Jean Schmidt, and she was an arch-conservative member of Congress from Ohio's Second District, which represents eastern Cincinnati all the way to Portsmouth. You might remember Jean—she earned national headlines and an SNL parody shortly after getting to Congress for scolding Congressman and Marine veteran John Murtha with the phrase: "cowards cut and run, Marines never do." And she was as conservative as it gets, often, abrasively so. Well, Jean and I ran into each other occasionally not because of politics, but because she's an intense runner, and we often finished 5Ks around the same time back then (don't let our similar speeds fool you—the difference was that she could keep running a full marathon, and I'd run out of gas after 5k).

Still, the SOTU invitation surprised me (some speculated it was because she worried I might run against her). With no intention of running against her, I happily accepted. I flew into D.C., we had dinner in the Members' Only dining room, then she excused herself early to do what she was famous for doing: grabbing the seat nearest to the aisle where the president enters the room, waiting patiently, then leaping to her feet on his arrival to get a presidential signature on her SOTU program. She'd done it every year since she'd arrived in 2005, and as southern Ohioans groaned, the animated effort amused television viewers across the country. She sought Bush's signature, as I witnessed firsthand that night from the balcony. And she snagged Obama's, which again generated media attention. ABC News once pointed out that with others also flocking to greet Obama, Jean would snag her seat six hours early to secure her prime spot.[202] In 2012, she even gave Obama a modest peck on the cheek.[203] And . . . .

. . . that peck was her demise.

From the moment she'd entered Congress, Jean had

fought off primary challengers each election. Primaries like those are rare these days, but Jean had a knack of stumbling into controversy, which drew an opponent each cycle. They'd thrown the kitchen sink at her with an assortment of attacks, but she'd always fended them off.

In 2011-12, a political neophyte named Brad Wenstrup took his turn at challenging Jean. A doctor and veteran, Brad had run for Cincinnati mayor in 2009 as a moderate Republican and lost against the incumbent. For most of the primary challenge, the perception was clearly that Jean was the more conservative of the two. Brad wouldn't commit to spending cuts and suggested that he'd sometimes disagree with the Republican caucus.[204] And by this point, Jean had even been caught on tape saying that Obama should not be president because he wasn't born in the United States (apparently, she still wanted his autograph!?).[205] Jean also outraised and outspent Brad. Late in the race, Brad did get a boost when a mysterious Super PAC dropped into the race to attack Jean on the same ethical controversies as past primaries. Still, Jean felt so confident about the win that she was in Washington the Monday night before the election.

Then, something surprising happened.

She lost.

Was it the outside Super PAC that did it? Doubtful. As *Cincinnati Magazine* wrote after doing some digging: "The ethics issues never got much attention in local media, and voters in the district didn't seem to care."[206]

No, the coup de grâce came from a different salvo. Even though he lacked funds for televisions ads,[207] Brad ran a series of radio ads arguing that arch-conservative Jean Schmidt was *not conservative enough*. Why? Simple: "The kiss."[208] The ad described her kiss of Obama at the SOTU, then suggested that the moment of bipartisan, if awkward, civility was proof that she wasn't conservative enough.[209] Voters afterward cited that attack as why they weren't comfortable with her: "Everybody had hit her about the fact of pushing people out of the way to get autographs and so forth, and I think that really hurt her in the campaign," said one voter after the fact.[210] Another agreed: "Jean lost because this standing at the aisle next to the president finally just pissed off so many people."[211] On the power of that ad, Brad eked out a close primary win and hasn't had a close election since.

All around, a pretty goofy story.

But stop and think about it for a moment. Yes, the kiss was odd. The autograph-seeking was a little much, but at least showed some level of reverence for the presidency, whoever occupied it. Like the time Chris Christie greeted President Obama following Super-storm Sandy. Small, a little awkward— but also a moment of humanity.

The fact that Jean Schmidt lost because of that moment, just as Christie heard so much grief for his, is a disturbing and cautionary tale. But, also a clear message: "You may be a birther, but you're still too tight with Obama, so you're out!" If even passing moments of symbolic bipartisanship—not even on policy, but actual human interactions—are what cost someone a career, everyone else is going to start acting pretty nuts.

And nuts are exactly what gerrymandered districts have created in Ohio and around the country. In a world of rigged districts, where you never worry about your next general election, the overwhelming risk of losing your seat comes in your next primary. And the only way you lose that primary is if someone outflanks you to the extreme, doing exactly what Wenstrup did to Schmidt. So the incentive becomes clear: as long as you toe the extreme line, whether you're a Congressman or a state legislator, you'll serve your full term and get reelected without worry. Whatever you do, don't make the mistake of displaying public civility toward anyone of the other party. And if moments of visible civility are forbidden, don't dare do anything more meaningful, such as work on actual legislation. In a gerrymandered world, that is the surest way to end your political career.

Contrast all that to the incentive if you're in a close, competitive district. I'd know—as a county commissioner, that was my existence. Hamilton County was basically 50/50 when I was there. So, I knew that for re-election, I needed independents and some Republicans to vote for me. Not only did it benefit me politically if I worked with a respected Republican officeholder on something meaningful, I *wanted* voters to know when I did so. If supporters of that official saw that we were working together, they'd perhaps consider voting for me as well. Same was true for the officials I worked with. In short, there was a real incentive to work together when possible.

But under rigged districts, there is no incentive to do so.

One person who learned this lesson well was Brad Wenstrup himself. The "aw shucks" moderate who allowed that he'd occasionally stray from his caucus never has. He adopted the Trump mantra immediately. He was a Devin Nunes acolyte on the House Intel committee. And Wenstrup was one of the House members who signed on to a Texas lawsuit against swing states contesting the 2020 election results. And whether it's health care, or infrastructure, or tax breaks at the top, he votes against all the things that struggling towns in his district (did I mention his district includes Manchester?) so desperately need. As a result, he's never had a primary, and never had a close general election. By attacking a two-second moment of surface-level bipartisanship, then eschewing bipartisanship ever since, he's secured a long and comfortable career in Congress.

Be as Partisan as Possible

But it's worse than the Schmidt and Wenstrup story.

Because not only do you risk your career if you work across party lines, there's a powerful incentive to be *as partisan as possible*. More than partisan, actually. Extreme.

Taking on extreme positions, as unpopular as they may be in the general electorate, is how you keep primary challengers from targeting you in the first place. For example, after she was caught on tape saying Obama was born elsewhere, Jean Schmidt tried to deny it. Sadly, given the attack that was coming, she'd have been better off *amplifying* it.

It's even better if certain interests align with that extreme position and support you because of it. Which is why we see occupants of these gerrymandered seats becoming ever more aggressive when it comes to taking extreme stances, and advancing legislation wholly unmoored from mainstream Ohio or American positions. Here are a few examples:

Reasonable gun safety reform is overwhelmingly popular in states like Ohio. Banning bump stocks? Supported by 70% or more of voters, including a supermajority of gun owners.[212]

Tackling climate change is broadly popular. Supported by a strong majority of Americans.[213]

Increasing the minimum wage is popular across the board[214]—even for a hike as high as $15 per hour.[215]

And in 2021, national polls show that mandating masks amid the pandemic is overwhelmingly popular.[216]

But all across Ohio, legislators are hard at work fighting *against* these highly popular positions. In a fair general election, these stances would get them thrown out of office. But in statehouses, grabbing that extreme position, and working with a powerful group to advance it, is the best way to end a future primary before it starts. And then you're in a rigged general election where victory is certain.

This dynamic is why every few weeks or months, there's a new gun bill. There's a new abortion ban. There's an attack on efforts to stem the pandemic. Many politicians go to the statehouse every day to advance the most extreme policy possible. For many, to be fair, it's who they are. But it's also good politics. It keeps them safe back in their extremely rigged district. It keeps them from being Jean Schmidt.

And even if your instinct is not to be that proactively partisan, the fact that most others are seals your fate too. Distancing yourself from the most extreme legislators, and their most extreme ideas, is the surest way to risk your seat. When the votes are called on that extreme bill, a "no" vote would draw attention. In a rigged district, you can't afford to be an R standing with a bunch of Ds. That's as bad as pecking the president on the cheek. So, the one thing *you can't do* is that. So you vote yes.

You don't want to be Jean Schmidt.

Corruption? What Corruption?

The conventional wisdom in politics is that battling corruption is a winning political strategy. And *being* corrupt is a sure-fire loser, especially if you're caught.

But in Ohio, that's no longer the case.

Over a decade of gerrymandering, with big interests helping politicians, it's become clear that there isn't even a political disincentive from engaging in egregious pay-to-play. (There may be a legal disincentive for those whose conduct is so egregious they get busted by the FBI, but not a political one).

Let's revisit the First Energy scandal. The largest bribery scandal in the state's history explodes as the 2020 election is taking place, and its quarterback was reelected with ease only months later. But it wasn't just him. There was a motion to expel that Speaker in the July 2020. Almost every member of his GOP caucus voted NOT to expel him by tabling the motion.[217] Not one of them lost his or her election. The only GOP statehouse member who lost his seat in 2020 was one who'd helped *expose* the scandal,[218] and had voted to *remove* the Speaker in that July vote.[219]

Or let's go back to Bill Lager. Over time, the politicians could see for themselves the results of Lager's scam—the worst school in the nation. They knew the money from the operation came directly out of schools in their own district, and that the Lager schools were an educational catastrophe. But they also knew, and Lager knew, that almost no voters would figure it out, let alone hold them accountable for it. And they were right.

So right, that even when the scam went belly up, and the FBI swooped in, none has ever paid a price at the polls. Again, Jon Husted raked in dollars from for-profit charter school companies, intentionally tanked the oversight of those schools, then those schools went belly up after cooking the books. The FBI was all over it. Who cared? No one. With his honorary degree in hand, Jon is now the lieutenant governor. And neither he nor any other politician has faced any accountability for being active participants in the largest scam in Ohio history. In fact, Ohio's current governor, lieutenant governor, state auditor, and attorney general *all* played active roles at key moments when Bill Lager needed their help. And all received thousands of dollars, often around the time they took those actions.[220]

In this way, corruption itself becomes calcified as a part of state politics. Even when you do it, you're fine politically. And when there's no accountability even for corruption, there's also no incentive to do anything about it, especially if you're vacuuming up gobs of money from those behind it. It's gotten so bad that politicians openly take steps to *further protect* themselves from accountability, sensing no political risk for making corruption *easier* to get away with.

Here's a concrete example: one office with jurisdiction over statehouse corruption is the Franklin County Prosecutor's Office. (Columbus is in Franklin County.) For years, the prosecutor of Franklin County was a Republican, and rarely brought corruption charges against state officeholders or legislators for even large scandals. A Democrat finally defeated that prosecutor in 2020. Finally, some accountability. Right?

Not if they can help it. In 2021, legislators put forward a bill to remove jurisdiction over their crimes from the Franklin County prosecutor and place it in their home counties.[221] This means, when in trouble, most would face a prosecutor of their own party, and potentially one as passive as the Franklin County prosecutor was for a generation.

With corruption ablaze in the state—weeks after *USA Today* ranked Ohio number one in the country—the source of the corruption wants to hand-select home court prosecutors. They do so with no worry that voters will know or care. And even if they do, their rigged districts mean the voters can't do anything about it.

That's how bad it's gotten. We'll see if it passes.

A Generation of Officeholders with No Elections

You get the point. There are numerous consequences of the extreme gerrymandering that has deprived Ohio and so many states of basic democracy for the past decade. All of them bad.

But something that's easily overlooked if you're not on the ground is the cumulative effect: there's now an *entire generation* of officeholders in the majority who've come to power, remained in power, and in some cases, risen to higher levels of power, without ever winning a contested election. A contested, general election. Some were appointed to their initial office and never faced one real election. Others, such as Brad Wenstrup, had a single moment where a narrow group of voters mattered, and that was that. The rest of his career, the voters have never been given another choice. Brad's never had to campaign again. And for Brad and so many others, that's the only politics they know.

On the flip side, there's a generation of folks who've aspired to be public servants but are locked out. Completely shut out, no matter their skills or the quality of their campaigns.

I've seen both of these patterns up close in Ohio, and they too have a profound effect on politics and incentives in the political system.

A Tale of Five Candidates

I don't say this lightly or to be cruel, but the worst candidate I have ever witnessed in action is a sitting member of Congress from Ohio. He will likely be there for as long as he wants.

I've presented a lot of data so far, but the caliber of a candidate is harder to quantify. It's more of a judgment call. "You know it when you see it." And, when you don't see it.

I've observed and trained hundreds of candidates. And believe me, the gentleman I'm thinking of—who shall not be named—was not meant to run for political office. His personal background doesn't stand out. He dropped out of two colleges, then worked for the family business that reporters would find had a history of tax problems and consumer fraud. But the truth is, many have risen from bleaker beginnings to become successful politicians and fine public servants.

No, what makes him such a poor candidate for public office was that in the campaign in which I observed him, in whatever setting he spoke, he looked like it was the last place he wanted to be. Physically, his face, his body—everything—projected misery. Discomfort. A deer facing headlights only feet away. And when someone caught up to him, and his lips unfroze to form words, this gentleman struggled to explain his most basic positions, regularly stumbling into embarrassing verbal gaffes. Which explained why he spent most of the campaign running from cameras (there are multiple videos of him actually running from them) and refusing to debate. When he finally agreed to a single debate, it was immediately clear why he'd tried so hard to avoid them. His far younger opponent ran circles around him, with one clip going viral because it captured what a mismatch it was. Never have I seen a person look more pained being in the spotlight, to the point I felt bad for him. I wanted to put my arm on his shoulder and say: "Listen, you don't *really* have to do this if you don't want to. Because if you win, you'll have to do it even more."

Apparently, he also wasn't compelling working the phones either. Even with a Yost-level surge of outside help—an entire cavalry came to Ohio, including Trump and Pence—his younger opponent dramatically outraised this man through a surge of small-dollar, online donations.

In the end, the gerrymandered district still ended up being too rigged even for this candidate to lose (although it was far closer than Boehner could've imagined back in the bunker). But even basking in the glow of victory, with the pressure off, he couldn't stick the landing. He stumbled through his victory speech, then botched the one punchline almost every American could've recited by heart. (Actually, he melded two of Trump's punchlines into one so that they made no sense): "I'm going to do everything I can to keep America great again."

I know what you're thinking. Lay off the rookie. Give people a chance to grow as candidates. Let him get a few campaigns under his belt and he'll get better.

And trust me, if that was the problem, I wouldn't bring this gentleman up. I've seen people improve dramatically with time. I was painful to watch early as well. Heck, folks from Illinois will tell you Obama struggled when he first started.

But here's the thing: this man's opponent was the inexperienced one.

This guy had served two terms in the statehouse and then two in the state senate. He'd been walking the halls of the State Capitol for a decade!

So, as I winced at the train wreck that was his every appearance, I also wondered: how the heck had this guy been in office all that time without developing the most rudimentary skills of a candidate? A little practice makes most people better. Y'know, like me and Obama.

A quick look at his electoral path gave me my answer.

In 2008, the incumbent in this man's statehouse district was term limited. So he entered the race and won the primary (well done). It was a strongly Republican district, so he went on to win the general election that year by eight points.

Welcome to the statehouse.

In 2010, he ran unopposed in the spring primary, and again unopposed in the 2010 *general* election.

Welcome back.

In 2011, a vacancy came up in the state senate district where he lives, and he was appointed to that.

Welcome to the senate.

He ran unopposed in the senate primary the next year, then won that gerrymandered district 60%-40%.

Welcome back to the senate.

In 2016, he ran unopposed in both the primary *and* the general election to get reelected.

Welcome back to the senate.

And that's it. A two-term statehouse member and two-term state senator got there by winning a single election—a primary—in 2008, where he received under 11,000 votes. Which answered my question: the reason he lacked even rudimentary campaign skills is because since that initial primary, he basically hadn't been in a real campaign. An experienced politician in the statehouse with virtually no campaign experience. And of course, that still didn't stop him. Even with his woeful skills on full display, he won another gerrymandered district, this one for Congress. And unless something dramatic happens, he will be a member of the U.S. House for the rest of his career.

This, my friends, is the career path of a successful politician in a world of rigged elections. Appointments, unopposed elections, maybe a primary at some point (which, depending on the community or district, can indeed be true elections). But some don't even face that primary. And you're wielding supermajority power or sitting in Congress without ever having had to win a competitive general election or having had to win over a legitimate swing voter, let alone talk to a voter of the other party. For many of this generation, the path through politics has been akin to a series of appointments and re-appointments that arise from within their political party. They've barely encountered everyday voters because there's been no need to.

Now let me describe four other candidates who ran in Ohio around the same time as this gentleman:

The first, who went by the call sign "Toro," was on one of her first training missions in an F-14 Tomcat when the towers went down on 9/11. She went on to fly F-14s, F-16s and F-18s, not as the pilot, but as the naval flight officer in the second seat. Think "Goose," not "Maverick." Which meant that in the air, she did the navigating and communicating while running air-to-air radar and intercepts with other aircraft and guiding precision bombs. And on the ship, she managed a team of enlisted sailors. Speaking of ships, over her naval service, she landed on the Eisenhower, Theodore Roosevelt, Harry S. Truman and Ronald Reagan, and her combat duties included missions in Iraq and Bosnia Herzegovina. After her service, Toro went on to become a successful aviation lawyer. When she speaks now—about any topic—you hear and feel her seriousness, professionalism and technical expertise in every word. But when someone says or does something that dishonors a core principle of our democracy, or service, you feel the seething anger of someone who put her life on the line to defend those principles.

The second candidate was also an aviator. He flew EP-3 Signals Intelligence aircraft and was a Combat Reconnaissance Mission commander. Most of his missions were classified, but general targets of his work included China, Russia, North Korea, along with deployments in the Middle East. After that service, he went to Yale Law School. And after Yale, he co-founded Project Rubicon, an organization that deploys American veterans worldwide to deliver humanitarian assistance and disaster relief. Amid all types of emergency assignments, he delivered a few babies along the way. His rolodex from that work includes everyone from General Stanley McChrystal to former army Chief of Staff George Casey.

The third is the granddaughter of an Alabama sharecropper who left school at age six to support his family, then at eighteen, moved to Middletown, Ohio to work in the steel plant there. He ultimately settled in

Dayton. *She* graduated from Dayton public schools and Xavier University, the first in her family to earn a four-year degree. After volunteering for the Obama campaign, she went on to work at the White House and on Capitol Hill for two U.S. Senators, where she was also elected president of the Senate Black Legislative Staff Caucus. At nights, she attended Georgetown Law School to earn her law degree.

The fourth grew up in poverty in Newark (not New Jersey, but Ohio, and hometown of Wayne Newton). She overcame tough circumstances to attend Ohio State, where she graduated as valedictorian. Number one from a class of thousands. She also went on to law school at Yale, pulled down a prestigious clerkship on the federal court of appeals, then moved to Cleveland to become a successful health care lawyer. A column she wrote for the *Washington Post*[222] describing her rise from Appalachian roots—a progressive counter to JD Vance—was one of the most shared from the *Post* that year.

I'm happy to name these four: meet Hillary O'Connor Mueri, Ken Harbaugh, Desiree Tims, and Betsy Rader. Like our other candidate, each of these four Ohioans ran for Congress. Ken and Betsy ran in 2018, Desiree and Hillary in 2020. I've seen each give powerful speeches, and campaign fearlessly in both blue and red parts of their districts. Without much outside help, each hustled to raise impressive sums of support against their incumbent opponents. Each of their opponents was too afraid to debate them. (That didn't stop Ken from confronting his opponent face-to-face to demand a debate—Bob Gibbs ran way). But when all was said and done, each lost by double digits in their terribly gerrymandered districts. Betsy lost by 10%, Desiree by 16%, Ken lost by 17%, Toro by 20%.

Betsy picked up and ran again in 2020, for state senator. Her opponent was directly caught up in the First Energy bribery scandal. He testified in favor of the corrupt bill using a script sent to him by First Energy, all while taking contributions from First Energy executives and its PAC. Betsy lost again, this time 60%-40%.

So, while the unnamed man will spend the rest of his life in Congress, my guess is none of these four immensely talented people will ever run for office again (I hope I'm wrong). They have many options beyond volunteering to be cannon fodder in rigged elections.

The lesson of these five candidates couldn't be more clear. On the one hand, gerrymandering rewards extremism and props up folks with the flimsiest of political skills by way of an insider path to office that eschews contested elections. On the other, it creates a massive disincentive for some of the best and brightest servant-leaders from stepping up to run at all. It cuts off at the knees candidates like Toro and Ken and Betsy and Desiree with the most impressive forms of public service already under their belt and natural talent, political and otherwise. And it only gets worse with time.

I was sometimes challenged as party chair: you blame gerrymandering, but statewide offices aren't gerrymandered. What about those? It's a good question, and the phenomenon I just described helps answer it. Gerrymandering doesn't make winning statewide elections impossible (as it did for Ken, Betsy, Hillary and Desiree seeking seats in Congress), but it makes the path to those statewide offices a far greater leap. Ohio is a huge state. Multiple media markets, etc. Unless you're John Glenn (and even he lost the first time), it takes years to get known on a statewide level. If you look at most successful statewide leaders in Ohio, they arise via a multi-step path. And the middle step has been key for most: Congress, or perhaps being a leader in the statehouse. John Kasich, Sherrod Brown, Ted Strickland, Mike DeWine, John Gilligan, and others. These leaders all had enough time in office, both in Congress and other positions, to build their brand and hone their skills, travel their district and the state, etc.

Gerrymandering artificially cuts off those middle-tier opportunities. So, most Democrats who run for statewide office now do so from a much lower tier of the political ladder, and start out far less known as a result. Many have been phenomenal candidates. But they are hobbled from the outset because gerrymandering cuts off the more traditional path that political figures a generation before had available to them.

Or let me put it this way. A two-term Congresswoman Hillary "Toro" Mueri would be one hell of a candidate for governor or senator. But gerrymandering means she can't ever be that Member of Congress in the first place, even though jobs she's already done have taken far more skill, guts and expertise. Heck, with all she brought to the table, Betsy Rader—Ohio State's valedictorian with a story as gripping as JD Vance's— had no chance of being a state senator against someone caught up in the largest bribery scandal in Ohio history.

Bottom line: gerrymandering rewards an inner-party, insider path that has little to do with public service and forecloses opportunities for folks with skills to be phenomenal public servants—including many who've already served in far more impressive and courageous ways.

A Rigged Supermajority

I'll repeat the reality once again so it sinks in: Extreme gerrymandering has empowered an entire generation of statehouse majorities who've never had to win a general election on anything close to a level playing field. If they've had to win a contested election at all. I'm not talking about a fraction of politicians. Or half. I'm talking about *almost every member* of the current majorities. An entire generation of them.

Here's some data bearing that out in Ohio. Let's consider the elections from 2012-2020, a "generation," which makes sense given eight-year term limits. Here's what democracy looked like in the entire decade, over five election cycles:

Seventeen of Ohio's 99 districts averaged GOP margins of victory of 50% points or better—meaning a 75%-25% win or more.[223] Many went uncontested, with either no opponents or write-in opponents (who at best get 5%). We're back to Saddam Hussein-level blowouts.

The next 21 seats averaged GOP margins of victory of 30% or better—meaning 65%-35% wins or better.

The next twelve seats averaged GOP margins of victory of 20% or better—better than 60%-40%. Still blowouts.

That's 50 seats right there. Not just a legislative majority. But an outright majority who, for a decade, averaged a blow-out win. A guaranteed majority—rigged in the bunker in August and September of 2011—without even breaking a sweat. Essentially reappointed every two years.

The next five seats averaged double-digit wins or better the whole decade. Still not close. That's now 55 seats where the mappers in the bunker guaranteed double-digit victories.

In a few seats, some Democratic incumbents held on for a few cycles. But once they cycled out due to term limits, those seats also turned into blowouts. That's led to seven more seats that have averaged double-digit winning margins since the Democratic incumbent lost or was term limited.

Sixty-two seats, out of 99. Not just winning, but *averaging* double-digit wins for an entire decade.

To be sure, due both to the need for majority-minority districts, as well as to the extreme gerrymandering, there are also a number of safe Democratic seats in the Ohio legislature—packing Democratic voters together has become an essential ingredient to creating that supermajority of safe Republican districts. This is true around the country. But make no false equivalencies here. First, there will always be some number of safe districts in any system of fair districts—a majority or supermajority of them is the problem. Second, majority-minority districts have played a critical role in combating the under-representation of Black Ohioans and Americans in legislatures. But unlike most "packed" GOP districts, sprawled across multiple unconnected communities, these more safe Democratic districts are by and large compact, and represent a commonality of interest—often coming from a single city, with members who are quite well known, who usually emerge from fiercely contested primaries to secure their seat. (And even when those primaries become contests between moderates and progressives, which side prevails is far less predictable). And mired in the minority in the statehouse, these legislators are less often (with some exceptions) wined and dined by the Lagers and Brennans of the world because their votes aren't needed. How do we know the incentives are generally different? Because from health care to gun safety to economic issues, these legislators generally advocate for laws and reforms that reflect the broad majority of the populace. Because in fighting *for* voting rights and other key elements of democratic governance, they align *with* the elements of a robust democracy, not against them. And because these legislators generally didn't push to be drawn into districts that are far more gerrymandered than needed to achieve majority-minority districts. In Ohio, in fact, whether at the federal level or state level, Democrats who didn't ask for overly safe districts have been among the loudest voices to *end* election rigging across the state, even if it makes their own path more challenging.

That's altogether different from the rigged supermajority leading the Ohio legislature after averaging double-digit wins for an entire decade. Anyway, let's look at what impact a gerrymandered generation has on the culture of the place. It goes way beyond those five candidates. It gets to the heart of democracy itself.

Living in Fear . . . Of Democracy

A quick story will make the point.

The heart of county government is the county courthouse, and the judges that serve in that courthouse. So as a commissioner, I got to know the judges as best I could on a personal level. Lunches, breakfasts, etc. I built good relationships with most, including across party lines. As much as any official in public service, judges impact individual lives, one case at a time. And most I've encountered approach that task with dedication and professionalism.

But in the process of getting to know some of these judges, one conversation stuck with me. Late 2007. One judge I met with referenced a big day that was coming up that she and other colleagues were getting ready to celebrate. But they were still a little tense as that big day approached.

Election Day? No. That was almost a year away.

Filing day.

She and other judges were waiting nervously to see if anyone was going to file to run against them for the next November's election. But at the moment, it looked like most of them would be spared an opponent. They were eagerly awaiting the deadline, getting ready to celebrate another six-year term.

Ten of them celebrated at 5 p.m. on filing day. The deadline passing, with no opponent, was their political Super Bowl. Their re-appointment to the bench. Six more years without worrying about an election. A job well done, they told one another.

One reason I never forgot the conversation was how different it was from my experience. For me, having run for City Council twice, mayor, then county commissioner, I had *always* been in an election. That's how it worked. You run. You wage a tough campaign. You win if all works out well. You serve. And, by the way, the election is fun! Knocking on doors. Forums. Parades. Festivals. And I *loved* a good debate— *those* were the Super Bowl. Plus, you never felt closer to your constituents than after a summer of knocking on doors and shaking hands at festivals. (So much so, I'd do it in the "off-year" just to stay in touch).

This judge was getting ready to celebrate the *lack* of an election. And I sensed that for her, it was a sign that she was doing a good job if she didn't draw an opponent. But I also recall something else: the look in her eyes as she asked if I knew if an opponent might file. It wasn't casual. It was worry. Fear.

I loved the process. She *feared* the process.

When you think about that judge's view of a potential election, and her own path, it actually makes sense. If you've been in office without having to win an election in some time (and county Democrats had not been challenging most Republican judges back then), or when you've simply been appointed then re-elected without worry, you *fear* an actual contested election. You haven't done it in years— maybe you've never done it. Your campaign infrastructure no longer exists, if it ever existed. Which means you have to build a campaign organization from scratch, and if you fail, you lose your power. You lose your job. For many, you lose your identity. And for the Cliff Rosenbergers of the world, you lose the incredible life that public office has bestowed upon you.

On a deeper level, if you've spent your entire political career succeeding without a real election, you have no connection to the very process of campaigning. The source of your success never came from the people in the first place. And if the biggest risk to staying in power is a real election you have never actually encountered, let alone succeeded in, for many, at least, there's not a heck of a lot of incentive to create the very condition you fear the most.

Gerrymandered Politicians Will Fail in a World of Robust Democracy . . . and Know It

But there's one more thing.

Something that wouldn't have applied to that judge, but would to most currently in power in the Ohio statehouse.

If you've spent your entire political career in a world without elections and being as extreme as possible because that's how you succeed in that world, the political record you've amassed would guarantee a blowout loss if you ever faced a contested general election. Not only because your political skills are as weak as that unnamed candidate's. But because everything you did to succeed in the rigged political world is the opposite of what you would need to do to win a close race. You'd never make it in that new world. You're a fish washed up on the beach, tide receding, and you won't last long.

Now think of an entire generation having lived and succeeded in that rigged world. A supermajority of the Ohio legislature, in fact. All doomed in a world of non-rigged elections.

Let's go back to a few of the characters from Chapter One to home in closely at members of this gerrymandered generation. Let's see just how doomed they'd be.

Recall the state representative who opposed masks because he said they obstructed the face of God. His name is Nino Vitale, and here's his career. Ohio's 85th district opened up in 2014 due to term limits, and Nino entered the primary, winning with 54% of the vote. Those 7,000 votes would be the only ones that mattered for the rest of his career (to date at least). He won the general election with no opposition. In 2016, he won the general election with no opposition. In 2018, he faced an opponent—a high school senior, who worked his tail off and showed true courage. Still, Nino won with more than 70% of the vote. In 2020, he upped the number to 91% of the vote, facing only a write-in candidate. In total, this district has been the least close of any of Ohio's 99 over the past decade. So, no surprise, Nino is not someone who appreciates the majesty of the democratic process. (Although impressively, without facing any elections, he was found guilty of three counts of election fraud.)[224]

Along the way, here are some of the positions Nino's taken. As I mentioned, he attacked the wearing of masks amid the pandemic,[225] told people not to get *tested* for COVID-19 as it exploded across Ohio,[226] attacked Ohio's health director as an "unelected globalist" (no one thought to ask him about his own election bona fides), and supported the effort to impeach the Republican governor. He referred to the GOP governor, Husted the LG, and the health director as the "Trio of Terror." But rest assured, his toxic positions go well beyond his response to the pandemic. He railed against helping those in poverty by saying "a little hunger in the belly or being a little cold on some really cold days is a good incentive for me to get up, go to work and provide for my 5 boys and wife."[227] When faced with a resolution declaring racism to be a public health crisis, he declared that he was "darker" than most members of the Ohio Legislative Black Caucus.[228] And when he got an "F" rating from Equality Ohio, he went on a homophobic rant. Now how do we know all these things this man has said? Some public records request to dig up his secret stash of controversial musings? Nope. He basically posts them on social media all the time. He *wants them* out there.

On legislative issues, by the way, this guy is the chair of Ohio's Energy and Natural Resources Committee, and is convinced that hedge funds are buying up newspapers to run negative stories about the coal industry.[229] Bills he sponsors include the Pastor Protection Act (protecting pastors from being forced to perform same-sex marriages), a bill declaring Ohio a Second Amendment Sanctuary State, a bill establishing legislative oversight over the governor's health orders, a bill voiding health orders requiring face coverings, a bill loosening "knife regulations," a bill banning the teaching of "divisive concepts," and a bill declaring gun possession as "life-sustaining" during the use of emergency powers to suppress riots, mobs, or potential riots or mob.[230] Oh, and he voted against making cock-fighting a felony.[231]

Now, future aspirants in rigged districts, *this* is how you avoid a primary! One position after the next, all toxic and out of the mainstream as can be. No bipartisan kisses from this guy—heck, the Republican governor is running away from him. In a gerrymandered world, Nino Vitale's extremist antics are the perfect way to guarantee the election-less path he's enjoyed. A proactive shield against all right-wing comers.

But throw Nino Vitale into a true democratic process, in a relatively close district, and his career would be over. A record perfect for rigged elections would turn into kryptonite in a world of fair elections and real democracy. He'd likely lose even in a district that was relatively close but leaned Republican. He probably wouldn't run.

In case you think I'm just picking on the guy from the least competitive district, let's look at a few more. Take John Becker, the man eager to force doctors to perform impossible surgeries on women at risk of death based on his reading of a 1917 medical journal. He won his initial race by 37% in 2012. He won by more than 50% in 2014. 2016 was a 45% victory. 2018 was a 33% win. (This ranks 26th in the least competitive district average for a decade). Becker only faced a primary in his first re-election, then never again.

How has Becker avoided any real risks to his career? Let's just say he made sure no one would ever outflank him to his right from the moment he arrived (actually, from long before). Out of the gate, he proposed legislation to allow all state employees to take guns to work, including in the statehouse itself, while prohibiting law enforcement from melting down confiscated weapons: "It literally brings a tear to my eye, because some of them are very nice weapons."[232]

And while Becker didn't legislate all his publicly espoused views, like his colleague Nino, he spent a lot of time putting them out there. While they pre-dated his time in office, Becker uploaded years of political musings to his website, including ideas such as expelling Massachusetts from the country because it sanctioned same-sex marriage, comparing same-sex marriage to "polygamy, incest and bestiality," and establishing "condom-free zones" around schools.[233] His self-titled "Becker Doctrine," hanging out right there on his website, muses[234] that: Ohio should nullify its membership in the United States to become a "free and fully autonomous state," (while maintaining a partnership with the US for purposes of the military and foreign affairs); that the federal government, which he calls Frankenstein's Monster, is a "cancer;" all case law should be deemed "advisory" since the legislature writes the law; and that the 14th Amendment should not be recognized (oh yeah, neither should the 16th or 17th). John dismisses the concern that this all appears like Civil-War style secession with rhetorical flourish: "To argue that the so-called Civil War settled the issue of secession is to argue that 'might makes right.'"[235] Yes, Ulysses Grant, who was born only miles from this guy's district, might want to have a word.

Finally, Becker's public views also stray to the personal. He once let us all know that his daughter's fiancé was visiting for an upcoming weekend. He was so enthusiastic, he posted a photo in anticipation of the visit, along with this sweet welcome note for all to see: "I'm looking forward to my daughter and her fiancé visiting this weekend. Her room is on the right and the guest bed room is on the left. You can see where dad will be sleeping. And yes, that is a 12-gauge shotgun propped in the corner." (I can confirm, a shotgun is indeed leaning against the corner above dad's sleeping bag and pillow, between the two bedroom doors).[236]

By the way, in his re-election campaign, this man was endorsed by the following groups: the National Federation of Independent Business, the Ohio Chamber of Commerce, the Ohio Society of CPAs, the Ohio State Medical Association and the Cincinnati Area Board of REALTORS. Apparently, accountants, among others, are okay with all this. He was also named a 2018 Ohio Farm Bureau "Friend of Agriculture."

These views all allowed Becker to avoid a primary entirely in two of his three re-election bids, from which he then cruised to easy wins over some hard-working Democratic candidates. But do you think all this would fare well in a district anywhere close to evenly drawn? You betcha it wouldn't.

One more.

Andrew Brenner, the education committee chair who thinks public education is socialism. In 2010, he won a crowded primary by getting 24.4% of the vote—like the others, those 4,203 votes basically made his career. He won that general election 70%-30%. In 2012 (in a new, gerrymandered district), 2014 and 2016, he was elected by 24.92%, 35.88% and 30.5%. By the way, in the grand scheme of Ohio's statehouse, a 23%-margin average places this district as one of the closer ones. If Vitale had the least close district, Brenner's district was 48th.

Did this cause Brenner to moderate, or was he still angling to avoid a primary? You can be the judge, but the "socialism" comments about public education—accompanied by a hammer and sickle and a call to "privatize everything"[237]—provide a subtle hint. The year after those comments went viral, he compared Planned Parenthood to Nazis,[238] pushed to eliminate pesky requirements like firearms training or certification for a concealed carry license, while fighting for the essential requirement of cursive handwriting. Oh, and Brenner's largest contributor? Bill Lager.[239]

These views were conservative enough not only to avoid primaries in two of his three re-election bids, but to mop the floor of his primary opponent for Ohio senator in 2018, where he now sits. Our public school hater is back to leading on education—he chairs the primary and secondary education committee—and is back to comparing things and people to Nazis. On Holocaust Remembrance Day, he pledged "he would not allow the Jewish Ohio Department of Health director to turn Ohio into Nazi Germany."[240]

But that 2018 senate run did send a warning signal his way—that perhaps his toxic politics might not fare so well in anything resembling a close district. Even in a gerrymandered senate district (the margin was 22.2% in 2014), he won by only

2.7% in 2018. You think he's eager to have more fair districts come 2022?

The point is, in state after state, we have a generation of political figures whose own participation in the democratic process has been minimal to none. The Nino Vitales, Andrew Brenners, and Jon Beckers have hardly faced the voters. No one in leadership has. They're not there because they succeeded through any semblance of a robust democratic process. They won a few thousand votes to start, then their path essentially avoided voters from that point on—in part because they took proactive steps to avoid any primary challenge.

Like that judge, a true, robust democratic process scares the hell out of them. And should. Everything they've done to succeed in a world of rigged districts would guarantee failure in a world of competitive districts. They'd still blog their outlandish views, but from home as private citizens, not as taxpayer-funded representatives of the state of Ohio.

But there's one difference between that judge and these statehouse members. They are the people who write the rules of our elections. And/or have leverage over those who do. Meanwhile, they know that real elections are a mortal threat to their existence in politics.

How do you think that's going to turn out?

A Repeat Loop

In closing this chapter, let's review the incentives and disincentives created by the corrupt and rigged world of statehouses:

There is no incentive to achieve public outcomes.

There's a strong incentive to do the bidding of private players whose mission is often at odds with public outcomes.

There is no incentive to work across party lines.

There's an overwhelming incentive to be as partisan as possible.

There is little to no incentive to stand up against corruption. So long as you're careful, there's an incentive to go along with it.

There is little incentive to fight for robust democracy and fair elections, but a major incentive—self-preservation, and maintaining the only political world you've known—to fight against them.

You see why I told those manufacturers they'd all go bankrupt if their managers and workers faced this set of incentives?

But I want to highlight one final point. And that is that these incentives don't work in isolation. They are self-reinforcing.

Given the dramatic failures of government, the corruption, and the extremism that is well beyond what Ohioans support, the lack of real democracy becomes an essential ingredient to keep it all going. Without real elections, there's no check on the poor performance of those in power. There's no check on the fact that these politicians are pushing agendas that are way out of the mainstream, or amount to legal or illegal bribery.

In fact, the two variables ratchet up together. The more the legislature seals itself off from any accountability, the more extreme they get—and *can* get—and the further the outcomes *can* fall, without any diminution whatsoever on their grasp on power. But the more those outcomes plummet, the more everything is about serving private interests or the extremes of one party, the more essential it becomes to avoid real democracy.

Extremism. Poor public performance. Corruption. Election rigging. They all go together, reinforcing one another.

Or to go back to one of our politicians: Andrew Brenner needs *more* gerrymandering to keep doing what he's doing.

As he saw with his close race in 2018, he desperately needs less democracy.

PART II

I KNOW WHAT YOU'RE thinking.

Woe is Ohio. What a sad tale about a once great state.

If that was the end of the story, the truth is, I wouldn't have written this book. Because this book is not about Ohio.

Ohio, as usual, is a bellwether. This book is about the country.

Ohio's politics and public outcomes are in a downward spiral because of a confluence of a specific set of factors: unknown politicians with a lot of power but a tenuous connection to democracy; private interests camped out all around them, seeking gains they know how to get; rigged elections; a toxic mix of perverse incentives; and so on. And here's the bad news for those who don't live in Ohio—those same factors exist in the majority of state capitols in the nation.

In Chapter Four, I described the processes, similar to that in Ohio's "bunker," which occurred around the country in 2011. Go back to Karl Rove's list of targets—in those states, the same rigged results were achieved. And for most, the same downward spiral has ensued. Just like Ohio, in state after state—mostly red ones—there's a generation of political majorities equally removed from democracy as Ohio's. There's a similar set of twisted, perverse incentives that reward serving private, often corrupt, ends while undermining public outcomes. And all the problems you'd expect to come with that are erupting in state after state.

Don't believe me? Take ten minutes. Look at your own districts. Research your own statehouse's election results for the last decade. Then google the words "corruption" and your state, or nearby ones. Look at the extremism in your statehouse. The retrograde policy and poor outcomes. Look at Rove's list of targets. Search the same terms for those states. You'll get the same results.

The depressing and infuriating Ohio story is happening in too many states. Because, as you'd expect, the same toxic brew of incentives causes the same results wherever they exist. Like clockwork.

Corruption? Lack of accountability due to gerrymandering and the other factors described above make it endemic, regardless of who's doing the election rigging. In the East, look at New York[241] and Rhode Island.[242] Midwest, look at Missouri,[243] Illinois,[244] and Michigan.[245] In the South, look at Alabama,[246] Florida,[247] North Carolina,[248] South Carolina,[249] and Texas.[250] Out West, check out Arizona[251] and California.[252] *Governing* took a quick look at a succession of arrests of statehouse Speakers (Alabama, South Carolina, New York, and Rhode Island) and concluded a major cause was that while "powerful, [] they receive comparatively little media attention."[253] And a study of state-level corruption by Harvard assessed the level of what researchers categorized as "legal" and "illegal" corruption in each state. While various states rose and fell over the years, one conclusion was clear: state legislatures scored far higher in terms of corruption than state executive and judiciary branches.[254]

But the states gerrymandered in 2011 to rig elections for Republicans were more than just corrupt. Like Ohio, they marched steadily to the extreme right all decade, on issue after issue. Not just your traditional "deep-red" states in the South and West, but also in the Midwest and upper South.[255] Heading into the 2020 election, the website fivethirtyeight.com looked at the trend and concluded that the pace of extremism was accelerating:

> The more extreme the Republican Party has become, the more moderates have opted out or just been passed over. The more moderates have opted out or been passed over, the more extreme the party has become. And the more the Republican Party recedes to just elected officials in solidly conservative states and districts, the more they define the party.[256]

By decade's end—fueled by right-wing media, Trumpism, far-right groups, and the pandemic—countless legislators now occupy the true fringe of right-wing extremism. Nino and Andrew and Jon are part of a new, nationwide generation of extremists, not protesting outside the statehouses, but legislating from within:

> a growing number of GOP lawmakers at the state level are doubling down on their radical viewpoints, dangerous conspiracy theories, and association with paramilitary militias and other violent extremist groups. For every Marjorie Taylor Greene (R-Ga.) currently in Congress, there are dozens of more like her at the state level—and with close ties with right-wing extremist groups.[257]

Pennsylvania's a perfect example, a traditionally blue state that was horribly gerrymandered in 2011. As bad as Ohio. Recall that even after 2018, when Keystone State voters chose Democrats by ten points for the statehouse, Republicans still controlled the statehouse 110-93.

What has the impact in Pennsylvania been?

A generation of politicians with no democracy advanced the familiar litany of right-wing legislation, on everything from abortion[258] to guns[259] to energy.[260] Rancorous division and dysfunction, leading one paper to speculate whether 2015 was "the worst political year in Pennsylvania history."[261] And corruption on an Ohioan scale. The leaders of each party's caucus both went to jail . . . so bipartisan in their criminality that they now share a cell![262] And at least a dozen legislators were indicted for violating the law over the decade.

The extremism and bad behavior also infected numerous members of Pennsylvania's Congressional delegation.[263] But perhaps the most interesting thing about Pennsylvania occurred in 2018. And it proves the point that the generation of politicians from the world of rigged elections wouldn't survive in a world of real elections. . . . and they know it more than anyone.

In 2018, the state supreme court struck down Pennsylvania's Congressional map. Recall that it was a 13-5 Republican map after 2012. It stayed that way through the next two cycles, with almost every race a blow-out for the incumbent. A special election in 2017 saw a Democrat pick up one of those seats, but other than that, the maps held.

Then came a state court decision in early 2018 striking down the rigged Congressional map, and new districts drawn in the way the League of Women Voters would draw them.[264] What happened under the new lines? A map that had been at 13-5 after 2016 went to 9-9 in the November 2018 election.

Maybe most telling? Three of the Republican incumbents didn't seek reelection in the fairer districts. For different reasons, they *knew* they couldn't survive politics in a non-gerrymandered world.

So, yes, the woes of Ohio's corrupt and rigged legislature

turn out to be a national phenomenon. Which alone sounds terrible.

But I'm about to make it worse.

If you're this far in, *you* now appreciate how weak these statehouses have become. How broken they are. How vulnerable they are to poisonous influences. But how much power they wield.

You're in on the secret.

Now what if someone was in on this secret years ago? Before everyone else. Someone with a clear agenda of what they wanted done. A national agenda, but an unpopular one. Someone who knew statehouses were the perfect place to push forward that agenda when no other level of government would or could do so for long.

Imagine a Bill Lager, but with hundreds of napkins laying out a national game-plan about far more than one get-rich-quick scheme by robbing schools of funds.

Think of all the damage that person or entity could do. Weaponizing all of these statehouses at once, to serve certain ends, knowing that the cast of characters in statehouse after statehouse has every reason to serve private interests and no incentive to serve either public outcomes or deeper democratic interests or their voters back home who hardly know them. That would be dangerous, wouldn't it? Really, really dangerous.

And here's the problem.

It already happened.

CHAPTER 6

Weaponizing Statehouses into a National Force

S AD TO SAY, I drive by and through Ohio towns like Manchester all the time.

Struggling.

Dying.

So many desperately looking for their place in the tough 21st century economy. Too few finding it.

These communities need a lift if they are going to compete and thrive. And not just a facelift. But a lift in every way. Better education. Quality health care. Paved roads. Upgraded bridges and flood walls. Hope . . . especially for future generations.

One critical lifeline they need—especially in this modern economy, where digital dominates—is high-speed broadband. Without it, these towns are just not on the 21st century map.

In 2021, countless Ohio communities still lack the broadband capacity it takes to be relevant. Vast swaths of the state remain without broadband at all, and too many other parts have substandard capacity. It's not only small towns. Cleveland, Youngstown, and Dayton rank among the least connected cities in the nation—with, respectively, 30.7%,

22.4%, and 20.47% of their citizens still lacking any broadband connection.[265] Not only does this cut residents off from global commerce, education and opportunity, but it keeps new businesses from moving in. And entrepreneurial local residents starting new businesses will likely go elsewhere. The timing also couldn't be worse. A surge in telecommuting amid the 2020 pandemic opens up a fresh opportunity for communities to draw in new residents, but it's wasted without access.

Laudably, in his 2021 budget, Ohio's governor proposed a $250 million investment in broadband improvements for rural Ohio. Common sense, right? And of course, since a big portion of the members of the statehouse represent these rural communities, such a wise investment would breeze through, right?

You've read this book long enough to know the answer is not so simple.

First, the Ohio senate responded by zeroing out the proposed broadband investment in exchange for more income tax cuts at the high end[266]—cuts that would only amount to a few dollars a year per person in the rural communities so desperate for that broadband.[267] The senate president explained that Ohio couldn't afford both those tax cuts and the broadband investment, so they of course axed the broadband. It was a fitting trade-off—paying for tax cuts at the high end by cutting broadband for the Manchesters of Ohio perfectly captures the state's priorities over the last decade.

But that was just the jab of the one-two broadband punch. The upper cut that followed showed that the attack on rural broadband was not about balancing the budget at all. In a separate bill, the senate outlawed any municipality from building its own broadband network (or partnering with the private sector to do so) in areas where a private company provides some level of broadband access. And the bill set that threshold of private service at such a low level, it eliminated 98% of communities from offering municipal broadband, including 30 communities who *already did so* (many to support their own public safety and emergency services).[268] Since this bill had nothing to do with tax cuts, the senate president unveiled a new defense: he suggested that Ohioans in these communities don't know how to use computers or the internet. "They still have to have a piece of equipment of some kind—a computer, iPad, whatever it may be—they have to know how to use it. They have to know what happens when it doesn't work."[269] (Yes, in a world of rigged elections, you can insult your own constituents as your excuse for undermining them, and no one holds you accountable.)

Now why would state senators hamstring the very communities they represent from competing in the 21st century?

Think back to Chapter Three, where the likes of Murray Coal and First Energy order from the "It's On Me" part of the Statehouse Grille menu, using the legislature to "regulate" their competition into extinction. Then recall that menu's dessert, blocking local government from solving problems the statehouse won't solve. This law combines the two.

Even if they're in no hurry to invest in broadband throughout the state, big private players are clearly not interested in allowing others—private or public—to pick up the slack in their absence. Someday, they may get to these areas, and when they finally make their move, they don't want to have to compete with anyone who got there first. How convenient that those elected to represent these communities are willing to kneecap any competition, on their behalf, until they get there. (Yes, this is a perfect example of the incentive to work against the public good).

But an interesting thing happened as Ohio reporters looked into the origins of this bill. Even though it's both lengthy and complex, the language emerged without any public discussion. The *Akron Beacon Journal* went on a hunt to find the sponsor, but no legislator would take ownership.[270] Then cleveland. com called the two largest broadband providers in Ohio— AT&T and Charter Communications. AT&T claimed they had nothing to do with the change, and Charter said it had "no position" on the funding cut (without mentioning the municipal broadband ban.)[271]

Miraculous! An immaculately conceived bill, right here in Ohio.

But more digging reveals that the origins of this law are not in Ohio at all.

There are nineteen states around the country with similar regulations on the books.[272] Most arrived via a flurry of legislation from 2002-2004, while North Carolina added a similar ban in 2011. Ohio's senate was vying to make the Buckeye State number 20.

What do these bills do? Basically, they all make it somewhere between difficult to impossible for municipalities to provide their own broadband. How? By prohibiting public broadband outright, and/or adding other poison pills that make it unfeasible. Here's a sampling:[273]

- Like the Ohio Senate bill, some forbid municipalities from providing services where private services are also available (Montana, Texas). Nebraska bans them outright. Nevada bans them for communities based on a certain size. Pennsylvania has a similar ban.

- Some forbid municipalities from providing the service beyond their jurisdiction, making it far less financially viable to set up in the first place. (Alabama, North Carolina) The Ohio Senate bill also contained this provision.

- Some restrict the type of funding that can be used to support municipal broadband (North Carolina). The Ohio bill included this.

- Others impose other financial requirements and taxation provisions that hamstring any broadband efforts (North Carolina and South Carolina); and

- Some add referenda and other procedural hoops before a municipality can move forward on a broadband network (Alabama, Florida, Louisiana, Minnesota), steps that no private company has to undertake.

And how did all these laws come forward, so similar in aim and tactics, at around the same time? Did all these states copy from one another, like kids in school eyeing each other's homework?

They might have peeked a little, but they didn't need to.

They all cribbed from the same cheat sheet.

You see, a peculiar document has been floating around statehouses for almost 20 years: the "Municipal Telecommunications Private Industry Safeguards Act."[274] It offers up a smorgasbord of restrictions that states can impose to hamper municipal broadband: outright bans, procedural hurdles, financial restrictions, etc. The very ones you now see in those nineteen states and the Ohio bill. Some states picked multiple items from the menu, others opted for just one or two. But bottom line, the reason these laws look so similar is they're built from the same template.

And who generated the template?

Part II opened by suggesting that some entities long ago discovered that statehouses, when sufficiently motivated, are happy to do the bidding of private interests. The entity behind this document, and hundreds like it, was arguably the first to figure that out. And for decades, it's been perfecting an approach to take full advantage of its early and keen insight.

The document was written and disseminated by the American Legislative Exchange Council (ALEC), and the title of that anti-broadband document sums up the organization's agenda on everything. It's not called the "Closing the Digital Divide" Act. Or the "Letting Rural Communities Compete in the 21st Century" Act. It's the "Municipal Telecommunications Private Industry Safeguards Act," laying out multiple ways that public officials can "safeguard" private industries from public efforts to enhance digital capacity. And just as with the broadband example, ALEC has been ghostwriting laws to protect private interests at the expense of the public interest for years.

* * *

ALEC: Weaponizing Statehouses as Champions of the Private over the Public

Others have told the story of ALEC's origins, operation and influence, so I won't re-invent the wheel here.[275] But let me explain enough to show how its work dovetails into the downward trajectory of statehouses across the country.

The short history is that ALEC emerged in the 1970s to wage conservative battles at the state level, starting with opposition to abortion and the Equal Rights Amendment, then shifting into business and regulatory matters.[276] ALEC's membership and activities grew, then ebbed, then grew again, largely under the radar for its first several decades. It gained more national recognition after the 2010 GOP election wave empowered so many legislatures—and governors—to implement its handiwork, which they did rapidly. Alarmed by the flurry of activity and boosted by a major leak from the inside, enterprising journalists and activists exposed far more details about ALEC in 2011.

The group is funded largely by corporations and private interest groups that make up their "members," from the Koch Brothers network and a who's who of major corporations and trade groups, including pharmaceutical, telecom, oil and gas, and other companies. Their membership dues and other contributions buy these private players seats at the table (not a metaphor, literally, seats at actual tables) with the other crucial half of the organization's membership: state legislators. And not just a few legislators. But thousands of them, from every corner of the country. In 2011, the number stood at more than 2,000, between 25% to 33% of all legislators in the country,[277] including many leaders of their respective state bodies.[278] While the group claims to be nonpartisan, 90% of those members are Republican.

What does ALEC strive for, generally? It describes its broader mission as advancing "the principles of limited government, free markets and federalism."[279] Its goal is to create "efficient, effective and accountable government that puts the people in control." And its policies aim to "reduce the cost of everyday life and ensure economic freedom." The conjoining of private and public interests is central to its cause: "Job creators and state legislators alike come to ALEC to offer important policy perspectives to ensure economic security and opportunity in their communities."[280] ALEC even touts that the states it works with comprise "America's fifty laboratories of democracy."[281]

"Limited government." "Free markets." "Economic freedom." "Efficiency." Standard rhetoric. But what do the words mean in practice. Helpfully, ALEC sheds light on this in a highly specific way. Annually, it ranks states based on what it considers their economic "outlook."[282] They call it the ALEC-Laffer ranking, named after Arthur Laffer (yes, he's from Ohio too, but also an economist famous for a theory of trickle-down economics that has never worked despite countless attempts). And the way ALEC/Laffer tabulates its rankings is instructive. Here are a few examples of how a state fares well, or poorly, under its scoring system (like golf, the lower the number, the better):

- If a state doesn't have a certain type of tax (income, property, sales, estate), it gets ranked first in that category. If it has the highest rate of that tax, it gets a 50. So, in the ALEC view, the state with the best economic outlook would be the one with no taxes. (Ask the state of Kansas how that turned out when Sam Brownback worked hard to implement that vision. Hint: it was really bad.[283])

- If a state does have an income tax, the more progressive the tax is, the lower it ranks. So, if a multi-millionaire pays the same percentage income tax as a minimum wage worker, as in South Dakota, the state gets an "attaboy" with the best score possible—a one. If the state requires those who make more to pay a higher percentage of their income in taxes, its ranking suffers.

- If a state has laws imposing hard caps on its spending, its ranking improves. If it doesn't, its ranking falls. Never mind that such laws have been disastrous when attempted, and rejected again and again by voters.[284]

- States lose points if they have more workers in the public sector. More cops, firefighters, teachers, nurses, professors? Sorry, that'll cost some points. Lay them off? Congrats—a state's prospects just rose. This also means that if a state shifts public jobs, like corrections officers, to the private sector (such as ALEC member Corrections Corporations of America), or lays off public teachers to support for-profit virtual schools or private vouchers, it rises in ALEC's ranking.

- If a state has lifted its minimum wage above the federal wage, ALEC docks its ranking. The higher the wage, the worse. But the closer a state gets to the federal minimum wage of $7.25 per hour, the higher its ranking. Think about that: ALEC considers a baseline wage of $15,000 a year to be a strong indicator of a state's economic "outlook."

- And consistent with that low-wage preference, if a state has a law on the books that guts collective bargaining (misleadingly known as "right to work" laws), you get rewarded with a one; if you don't have that law, you get hammered with a 50. So, failing to attack unions leaves a mark.

Bottom line: in ALEC's view, gutting the public sector while attacking workers and wages is how a state positions itself for economic success. No taxes, and to the extent you have them, regressive taxes, are keys to prosperity. So, ALEC sets out to create these conditions in states around the country. (Note: consistent with Arthur Laffer's own predictive (lack of) success over 40 years, the "economic prospect" ranking of a state often conflicts with the actual economic performance of that state, even using ALEC's own numbers. Take the state of Washington. Due to a high minimum wage, the absence of a "right to work" law, above-average public employment, and other factors, ALEC ranked Washington between 35 and 40 in terms of its economic prospects over seven years. Yet in 2021, its actual performance was third best in the nation according to ALEC itself, with the second highest GDP growth in the nation over the prior decade.[285] On the flip side, Wyoming scored in the top ten in terms of its economic prospects almost every year of ALEC's rankings, including second in 2020. But its actual performance in 2021 was 44th.[286] Go figure.)

So that's the ALEC vision for state success, however poorly it actually predicts success. How does it make that vision a reality? It's not registered as a lobbyist, as lobbyists in capital cities or D.C. are. It's not a corporation, but a non-profit, so the money it raises from corporations is tax-deductible. It doesn't dole out political contributions, although it raises a lot of money from those that do. It's been labeled a "dating service" between private companies and public officials happy to do their bidding, but that sounds so innocent, and falsely implies monogamy.

You've likely heard of a puppy mill. Perhaps the best description used for ALEC is a "bill-mill," where corporations and politicians conspire together to generate reams of so-called "model" legislation just like that template on how to destroy municipal broadband. Legislators then introduce that prefabricated legislation back in statehouses when the time is right—again, as they did with the broadband ban in Ohio.[287] In 2011, *Governing Magazine* estimated that more than 1,000 ALEC-generated bills emerged in statehouses around the country, with about 20% becoming law.[288] A separate article put the average number of bills introduced a year at 1,500.[289]

It's a safe bet that more residents of states know who their state legislator is than know what ALEC is. So how does ALEC manage to get so many laws introduced and passed with so few knowing? To give credit where credit is due, ALEC's leadership developed a keen understanding of the incentives and temptations that exist in state legislatures, and how to take full advantage of them. Attentive readers will even recognize a number of features from Part One of this book.

First, forget a single "bunker." Most of ALEC's work takes place through meetings in multiple "bunkers" several times a year. But in ALEC's case, the hotel conference rooms are far from the state capitals of the participating legislators. Once in those bunkers, ALEC utilizes a formal committee/"task force" process to draft its laws. Each task force comprises both public officials and representatives of private corporations and trade groups, and is co-chaired by one of each. Through these task forces, the group churns out law after law that satisfies both the legislators and the private representatives around the table. Their work is put up for a vote, with the public officials and corporate representatives each enjoying an equal vote.[290] In case the power dynamic isn't already clear, the private co-chair has an absolute veto on each task force's proposals[291]—meaning nothing goes forward without the private sector sign-off.

Even though the laws drafted in these rooms often end up becoming real laws in states across the country—and the process mirrors a public legislative process—the distant bunker approach is one of many ways ALEC ensures secrecy. ALEC also keeps its large membership a secret.[292] It keeps hidden the materials that go into drafting its "model laws," and urges members not to take photos or copies of draft materials.[293] Until the surge of attention and that huge leak of documents (the leaker was from Ohio, by the way) blew the doors open in 2011, it kept its "model laws" secret as well. And it still keeps the actual doors of its task force meetings closed. Reporters and advocates who've tried to observe the law-making sessions in action have been escorted away—just ask the *Washington Post*'s Dana Milbank, who was "quickly regurgitated from the belly of the beast" by security.[294] Or the *Arizona Republic* reporter who tried but failed to crash the party several years later.[295] The ALEC process also imports its secrecy home to the states of its member-legislators. As with that broadband law, its bills often emerge out of the blue, without any public discussion, and no one acknowledging authorship. Even statehouse colleagues often don't know of the origin of ALEC-generated laws they are asked to vote on.[296] And this also allows major players in the ALEC process to deny any involvement when an ALEC-generated law sparks inconvenient controversy in a state; for example, AT&T denied knowledge or support of the Ohio broadband bill[297] even though it was actively part of ALEC's telecom and other work.[298]

Beyond the basic process itself, ALEC slathers on other accoutrements to maximize success. ALEC's meetings don't involve field trips to struggling communities so these lawmakers can best understand their needs (i.e. like more broadband) and what legislation will help. No, these trips are to first-class destinations: Orlando. Salt Lake City. New Orleans. Scottsdale. San Diego. Austin. Denver. All places that would excite wannabe-jet setters like Cliff Rosenberger more than driving back home.

Even better, the lawmakers don't pay for the jaunts. As *Governing* noted: "Not only do legislators often find their attendance at ALEC meetings paid for through corporate "scholarships," but once they arrive, they are wined and dined and golf-coursed by the group's private-sector members."[299] Those 'scholarships' and other legislators' travel expenditures totaled around $4 million between 2006 and 2011 alone, funded by pharmaceutical companies, AT&T, Verizon, and others.[300] And what do these scholarships pay for? Air fare, hotel rooms for families, meals, drinks, baseball games, golf, and the like.[301]

Then throw in another crucial step. While ALEC itself doesn't give political contributions to its countless legislative members, those funding ALEC are happy to. Between 1990 and 2011, *Governing* found that ALEC corporate members gave approximately $200 million to state level candidates and another $85 million to state parties.[302] The incentive is clear: keep ALEC happy, and you raise a lot more money than you can back in Clarksville or Manchester.

ALEC also understands that many legislators are new to state government—or new to government entirely—and usually there for short stints. Most have little experience in the subjects on which they make decisions, and their staffs are small. So, the organization brings its own research and "experts" to the table to help educate the legislators. As is the case back in state capitals, the private players are the experts, and they're definitely not term limited. The term "scholarship" itself underscores who's being educated, and who's doing the educating. And in grant proposals, ALEC suggested that most state legislators "lack the staff and resources to be truly informed on all these issues."[303] But that educating goes beyond the task force meetings themselves. ALEC experts will parachute into states once its members present legislation back in state capitals. What many don't reveal publicly is that they served as private members of the ALEC task force that wrote the model law for which they're testifying. *USA Today* uncovered one asbestos defense lawyer who testified as an "expert" in 13 different states, but never revealed he was part of the ALEC task force that wrote the bills helping his corporate clients' cause.[304]

Take a step back and think about the tab for active ALEC members. (Not the legislators, whose annual dues are $100 for two years and get so much paid for,[305] but the private side). They pay annual membership dues—starting at between $12,000 and $25,000, and far higher depending on what access they get.[306] They pay $5,000 more to sit on a task force, which secures them a vote equal to a legislator.[307] They make contributions to ALEC legislator-members around the country. And together, they dole out millions more in "scholarships" to fly thousands of politicians to nice cities, stay in fancy hotels and gorge on fine meals. They then shepherd those politicians into closed-door conference rooms they're also paying for and entering.

What is all this buying them? In reality?

A seat at the same table as those legislators. Not simply access. Not just to give their opinion. But a coveted spot at the table to actually "write" laws together—as if everyone at the table was elected to do so—and with rules that give them at least an equal say (along with a veto).

They are *legislating*. Not just those elected officials. But the private donors themselves. And they've flown legislators in from all over the country to get them in that room so they can legislate *together*, as equals.

If you're offended by the way the Ohio GOP privatized statehouse staff in the Ohio "bunker," ALEC has done that on steroids. They've privatized the legislative process itself, and their private members have purchased themselves a vote equal to elected officials in that process.

It's like those old ads from Mastercard:

Membership: $20,000
A Task Force Vote: $5,000
Scholarships: millions
Being a private legislator: priceless!

No surprise, the end result of this privatized process makes the Statehouse Grille from Chapter Three look like a cheap deli. The menu of "model" ALEC legislation is far longer— pages and pages at the fanciest restaurant in town. And it includes mostly a la carte items, where the private interests and legislators cook up the perfect meal back in the kitchen. When they're done, they jointly serve it across the entire nation.

The list of task forces shows you the breadth of ALEC's agenda: Communications and Technology; Commerce, Insurance and Economic Development; Energy Environment and Agriculture; Health and Human Services; Tax and Fiscal Policy; and others. Together, they generate hundreds of laws a year like the one attacking public broadband. We'll review a few in later chapters, but the common theme is that these bills aggressively advance the interests of private players at the expense of the public good. None of them has anything to do with the people of Manchester or Urbana or Clarksville. Sadly, the elected representatives of many of these communities are the very ALEC members whose participation directly undermines their communities' interests.

Bottom line: we have a national organization, funded by major private corporations, that has privatized the state legislative process. And it's juiced that process to entice state legislators from across the country to be part of it all. Oh, and as we saw with Washington State and Wyoming, the baseline vision it's striving for doesn't have any bearing on how a state actually performs, at least when measured by broad public outcomes. Arguably, the opposite.

What could go wrong?

ALEC in States

Let's look at how this all plays out in practical terms, in one state. In one year.

Let's start with . . . .hmmm.

Ok.

We'll go with Ohio.

In 2011, Ohio led the nation in the most corporate money raised to fund ALEC scholarships.[308] Not a good sign. (As Chapter One made clear, outside of college football, Ohio lately seems to lead in all the wrong categories, like student debt, corruption, the opioid crisis, and now even this.)

The man responsible for that top ranking was a state rep from near Urbana—Nino Vitale's predecessor, in fact—named John Adams. No relation. But a name clearly destined for political greatness, including majority whip in the Ohio legislature. Even more important, Adams also served as Ohio's ALEC legislative co-chair. And I say more important because to chair the state for ALEC, Adams would've taken an oath declaring that "I will act with care and loyalty and put the interests of the organization first."[309] Think about that. The whip of the Ohio House committed that his "first" priority is serving the interests of ALEC. Oh, and this includes a duty to advance ALEC legislation back in your statehouse.

And putting ALEC first he did. He traveled to six ALEC events in 2009 and 2010 and served as a member of the Tax and Fiscal Policy Task Force.[310] His banner proposal as a legislator was to eliminate Ohio's income tax outright—now *that* would have moved Ohio up in the ALEC rankings (while also bankrupting the state, see Kansas) but never happened. And Adams and his top legislative aide impressed ALEC enough to be crowned ALEC State "Legislator of the Year" in 2010, and ALEC "Volunteer of the Year" in 2011, respectively.[311] Oh, and ALEC members sent $28,135 his way between 2006 and 2011.[312] Not that he needed the money—he ran unopposed in two of his three re-elections and won the other one 75%-25%.

Being ALEC state chair also meant Adams shouldered the duty to raise that scholarship money allowing fellow legislators to partake in the ALEC process. Given Ohio's top ranking, Adams clearly worked hard at that, raising dollars from the usual suspects among Ohio companies and lobbyists.[313]

And Adams led a sizeable Ohio ALEC delegation—57 members of the statehouse and state senate (all but one were Republicans).[314] Those 56 represented 68% of the Republicans in the Ohio Senate or House in the 2011-2012 term. And multiple Ohio representatives served across eight ALEC task forces (there were nine at the time). Remember the state senator who told those frustrated Manchester residents to move? Yes, an ALEC member. How about the one who proposed axing rural and municipal broadband in part because rural voters can't figure out the internet? You got it. ALEC too. Of course, Rosenberger couldn't resist, even before he was Speaker.

And how did all that Buckeye participation translate back in Ohio? After the 2011 surge of attention outed much of ALEC's work, a coalition of groups compared Ohio bills to ALEC model bills. They found 33 bills that were introduced in the Ohio legislature in 2011 alone that were "identical to or contain[ed] elements from 64 different ALEC 'model' proposals."[315] Nine of those went on to become law, all sponsored or co-sponsored by multiple ALEC members. The bills ran the gamut, including attacking collective bargaining rights of public employees; imposing a strict new photo ID requirement for voting; expanding private prisons; undermining injured consumers' rights in court; pushing private vouchers for education; hampering unions' participation in construction projects; undermining states' participation in the then-new Affordable Care Act; and stepping up immigration enforcement.[316]

Although some of these flew under the radar, others exploded into high-profile controversies. The anti-labor law, known as Senate Bill 5, passed along party lines after sparking an inferno of protest, rancor and debate; and it ultimately generated a statewide referendum that led to a crushing repeal by the voters. The strict voter ID law passed the Ohio House amid a fiery debate;[317] it didn't make it through the senate, but a broader series of voter suppression bills ultimately did, generating lawsuits, protests and a successful petition drive. Ohio expanded private prisons, leading to one problem after the next since. In sum, ALEC's handiwork didn't comprise small or niche issues. The ALEC agenda drove some of the most important agenda items and debates in Ohio politics in 2011 and after. Yet almost no one knew it came from an outside organization—I was in the middle of those fights, and I had no idea.

But once again, even with all of John Adams' hard work, Ohio didn't stand out at the time.

Wisconsin also went through a wild political ride in 2011 and after, and ALEC was right in the middle of it.[318] Wisconsin's ALEC co-chair was Scott Fitzgerald, the senate majority leader at the time. He was succeeded as state chair by Robin Vos, who would rise to become Wisconsin's House Speaker (and often traveled with Cliff Rosenberger overseas[319]). Forty-eight other Wisconsin public officials were ALEC members then, and Governor Scott Walker had been an active member himself as a state representative. In the 2011-2012 legislative cycle, 32 Wisconsin bills or budget items tracked closely with ALEC model laws, and 21 passed.[320] These laws included a form of the "stand your ground" law that let George Zimmerman off the hook for killing Trayvon Martin; the same health care bill that passed in Ohio; a voter ID law similar to the Ohio law; "tort reform" bills hampering the rights of injured victims; and others. The infamous anti-union Wisconsin Act 10, like Ohio's anti-labor law, incorporated a number of ALEC provisions.[321]

In Iowa, leadership enrolled every member of the Iowa House as an ALEC member unless they opted out (which Democrats did later).[322] Every member of the Arizona GOP statehouse leadership was an ALEC member in 2013, along with more than half of the legislature overall. Research linked dozens of these two states' laws back to ALEC model laws.[323] A joint look at Missouri and Kansas found 120 current or former legislators as ALEC members, and identified 58 and 24 laws in the two states, respectively, with ALEC origins.[324] Similar groups found the same thing in Michigan (at least 26 members)[325], Florida (60 legislators)[326], Texas[327], and Lousiana.[328] And multiple laws generated by ALEC became law in those states. These laws dealt with a wide variety of issues, but usually pursued the same themes: attacking the expansion of health care; undermining voter rights; tightening immigration enforcement; attacking unions and collective bargaining; squeezing the public sector by cutting spending, taxes and regulations; and undermining the rights of consumers and injury victims in court. Oh, and privatizing as much as possible, starting with schools.

ALEC's Lesson: "It's the Statehouses, Stupid"

So, for two decades, an organization has privatized the legislative process at a national scale, advancing its work through statehouses around the country. Far more than any bill in Congress or action by Donald Trump, ALEC's structure and process forged enormous change in state after state. We'll review some of those in the next chapter, along with important lessons learned along the way.

But the most important lesson ALEC taught was that its formula worked. ALEC showed what could be achieved by taking advantage of the institutional weaknesses of state legislatures and the personal and political interests of their members. These politicians proved to be the perfect marks to bring into the ALEC fold, and the perfect partners to achieve ALEC's ends. Why? Remember Chapter Two: great power, great anonymity. Remember Chapter Three, and all the ways statehouses can help. Statehouses wield robust power on a wide variety of issues, and their members seem more adept at ramming through bills than those who walk the halls of Congress, where so little happens. They also prove to be an ideal access point to stop unfriendly efforts at the federal (i.e. attacks on health care) and local (ie. attacks on spending, unions and broadband) levels.

No surprise, with that lesson in full view, others joined the statehouse smorgasbord. A group called the State Policy Network (SPN) emerged alongside ALEC, taking off especially in the last fifteen years. Funded by many of the same donors and corporations as ALEC, the SPN functions as an umbrella organization for conservative, state-based "think-thanks." SPN and these state-based affiliates churn out report after report advocating the same policy agenda as ALEC: privatizing education, beating back environmental regulations, regressive taxes, attacks on workers, and repealing the minimum wage.

Its proposals often become the foundation of policies that advance through the ALEC model legislative process and out to the states.[329] But when SPN advocates for these proposals on the back end, it often does so through that web of state-level think tanks—with names such as Ohio's Buckeye Institute, Pelican Institute (Louisiana), Show-Me Institute (Missouri) and Commonwealth Foundation (Pennsylvania). Even though these groups' funds largely come from the same deep-pocketed supporters as SPN, the approach (and those nifty names) leave the impression that the research and advocacy are emerging from within the state. And these state-based institutes go well beyond research, offering up and then lobbying for their own model bills for their legislatures to pass.

To amplify it and ALEC's work, and taking advantage of the weakened media within states, SPN also began disseminating its message through a faux-news operation. As Jane Mayer explains, through "bureaus" in 40 states, so-called "reporters" filed stories for their own national wire service and Web sites."[330] But what appeared as news and investigative watchdog work was actually repackaged research by SPN and priority initiatives of ALEC.

Alongside SPN's state-level research and policy support, the Koch Brothers' Americans for Prosperity (AFP) provides "grassroots" support across states to advocate for its pro-corporate policies. Most Americans first witnessed AFP through the Tea Party movement it propped up to stop the Affordable Care Act. But within a few years, as the group CREW documented, Americans for Prosperity increasingly prioritized state-level advocacy over federal work. And they expanded from propping up "grassroots" rallies into direct lobbying. Why? From Tennessee to North Carolina to New Hampshire, AFP state leaders explained that they could get more done at the state level, and that states have a tendency to use each other's laws as models to adopt.[331] And in most states, a relatively small amount of lobbying expenditures (versus in Congress) go a long way—allowing AFP to be "the big fish in a lot of little ponds."[332] In 2014, for example, AFP spent six times more than any other group lobbying the Kansas statehouse.[333]

AFP has not been shy about its state-level success: "It's been frustrating in Washington. We've lost some tough battles. But at the state level, I would argue, it's been a once-in-a-generation moment of free-market policy victories."[334] And nothing breeds success like success. AFP tripled its number of state-level lobbyists between 2011 and 2015, with registered lobbyists in 29 states by 2015.[335]

No surprise, as mentioned in Chapter Three, individual corporations are setting up shop in far more states than they used to. In 2016, the Center for Public Integrity and *USA Today* looked across all states and found that 22 corporations had lobbying operations in all 50 states (none had 50 a decade before), 67 in 40 or more states, and more than 100 in 33 states.[336] Some were non-profits such as AARP and the American Heart Association, but most were large corporate interests, including pharmaceuticals (21 companies), insurance (thirteen), telecom/cable (nine) and alcohol and tobacco (eight). The NRA was in all 50 states, and the Corrections Corporation of America was in 33.

Ask why, and you get the same answer as you do from AFP. You get Chapters Two and Three of this book:

> "Not a lot is happening in Washington," said Lee Drutman a senior fellow and lobbying expert at New America, a Washington-based think tank, and author of The Business of America is Lobbying. "If you're stymied at the federal level, you start looking to the states."

State-by-state lobbying on controversial issues may also be less visible than similar efforts in Washington, especially in light of widespread staff cuts among reporters covering statehouse news.[337]

And the numbers back them up. On average, statehouses together pass more than 128,000 bills per year—nearly 25 times what goes through Congress.[338] That's a lot of action to get in on, and a lot of opportunity.

So, the lesson is clear for those paying attention: whether you're ALEC, Americans for Prosperity, the NRA, or an individual corporation, statehouses are the place to get your national agenda implemented. But that is just the primary lesson. The experience of pushing thousands of bills through rigged legislatures over the last decade, via ALEC and other institutions, has taught much more.

To return to Brandeis, these statehouses have truly served as laboratories in recent decades. Not serving democracy, but other goals. They're always experimenting. Always learning. Always improving. Figuring out when to advance. When to retreat. And how to get the most achieved with the least blowback.

Two decades have created a roadmap of how best to succeed in statehouses. As well as which pitfalls to avoid.

And these lessons provided a foundation for what we're facing today.

CHAPTER 7

Laboratories at Work: A Decade of Dry Runs

I T WAS AN Ohio rout as ugly as some of the worst Bengals losses I've witnessed. And I've seen some bad Bengals losses. As in Wisconsin, the 2011 law attacking collective bargaining in Ohio known as Senate Bill 5 whipped up immediate backlash, generating enormous protests in Columbus and across the state. For those of us who testified, the roar of a crowd carried through even the closed, thick doors of the committee room. Thousands were seated or standing in the statehouse rotunda, and our comments were being played through a live audio feed there; they were reacting as we spoke, so loudly we could hear it. (I also testified against the bill at the house committee, chaired by . . . the guy who told those Manchester residents to move).

Despite the opposition, the bill raced through the house and senate. To their credit, some Republicans voted against it in each chamber. Still, Kasich signed the bill on March 31, 2011, less than three months into his first term. He would soon regret doing so.

In Ohio, citizens can repeal laws through the petition and

referendum process. To place a law on the ballot for repeal, you have 90 days to collect and file the required number of valid signatures. In 2011, those opposed to Senate Bill 5 had to gather 230,000 signatures by early July. No small task.

On June 29, repeal supporters marched boxes of signed petitions to the offices of Ohio's secretary of state, celebrating it as an actual parade. Why the festivities? Because the coalition turned in just shy of 1.3 million signatures, a state record. All collected in less than 90 days. The campaign to repeal the law never looked back. Despite tens of millions spent by John Kasich and corporate allies to defeat the repeal effort, the repeal won 61% to 39%. In Ohio, that is an absolute shellacking. To put that in perspective, John Kasich became governor of Ohio with less than 1.9 million votes. Votes cast to repeal his signature anti-labor law totaled over 2.2 million—in an odd-numbered year, when turnout is typically down.

And the repeal effort won *everywhere*.

Ohio has 88 counties. In 2008, Obama won 22 of them, a high-water mark that hasn't been reached since by a Democrat; he'd win 17 in 2012. The measure repealing Senate Bill 5 won in *83 of Ohio's 88 counties.* In most, it wasn't even close. Rural, suburban, urban; Republican or Democratic. Didn't matter. Rural Adams County voted against Obama 61%-37%; it voted to repeal Senate Bill 5 by an even greater margin (66% to 34%). Jim Jordan's and Nino Vitale's home county is Champaign County—it voted against Obama 59%-39%, but voted to repeal Senate Bill 5 58%-42%. And Ohio's southern tip, Lawrence County, voted against Obama 57%-42%. But the repeal effort won 75%-25%. Again, an absolute shellacking.

There were many lessons to draw from the repeal of Senate Bill 5 (Kasich never again directly attacked collective bargaining, for one), but there was one immediate consequence: almost every sitting Republican state representative had cast a dangerously toxic vote—deeply unpopular even in their own backyard. Most had fought for it until the bitter end, insulting everyday Ohioans with a tone-deaf campaign, only to be routed on election day. *And* . . . almost all of them were up for reelection in just one year. As one columnist speculated: Senate Bill 5's defeat meant its "sponsors could also become history—at 2012's election."[339]

I remember thinking . . . what an opportunity! Finally, accountability for legislative votes far outside not just Ohio's mainstream, but the mainstream within politicians' own districts. And unlike most statehouse issues, this had exploded into headlines and newscasts across the state for months. As high profile as Ohio statehouse politics ever got. And in hindsight, the perfect chance to show the ALECs of the world that when they bring a piece of toxic legislation back to states like Ohio, and try to ram it through, those who carry their water will pay a price.

A year later, the lesson was indeed taught. And learned.

But not the one you'd expect.

Of the 53 statehouse members who voted for the most nuclear piece of legislation in a generation, 41 sought re-election to the house.

40 of them won.

And they didn't just win, they hardly broke a sweat. The average margin of victory across all 41 of those districts topped 24 points (62%-38%), powered by 22 races that were decided by 60%-40% or better. The next ten races were decided by ten points or better. Only four races of the 41 were within five points, and of the 41 legislators who cast votes for SB5, only one lost. Barely. And that district swung back two years later.

In the four counties that make up the corner of Northwest Ohio which abuts Michigan and Indiana, Senate Bill 5 lost by about 57%-43%. The man who represented that district and voted for SB5? He was re-elected 68%-32%.

In the counties around Springfield, Ohio, Senate Bill 5 lost by about 59%-41%. Total blowout. The state rep for the area who voted for it? Re-elected 65%-35%.

The counties of Eastern Ohio have deep labor roots, explaining why some Democrats held statehouse and Congressional seats there in recent history. No surprise, counties up and down the Ohio River near Marietta voted to repeal Senate Bill 5 by a whopping 65% to 35%. Surely, the area rep who voted for Senate Bill 5 would be held accountable. His race was closer than most, but even he got re-elected by more than five points. His two wins that followed would be by 14% and 24%.

Four of the pro-SB5 house members actually sought a promotion—running for the state senate. All four won easily—two were uncontested, two won by 20%. One GOP house member who voted *against* SB5 ran for the state senate; he won, but by the closest margin (sixteen points) of his colleagues.

So, after all the votes were in, the first go-around of the decade's new districts taught a lesson as clear as day. Not about accountability, but the lack of it. One year after Senate Bill 5, it was as if no one had done anything controversial at all.

And remember, Senate Bill 5 was the worst-case scenario. The usual anonymity of the statehouse was shattered, from live coverage of the legislators casting their votes in the spring to the final vote of the people in November. Ads were everywhere. Debates televised. And the issue was throttled. Despite all of that, all but one candidate got reelected. And most without a moment of worry.

The lesson: even in the perfect storm of public blowback for a toxic vote, legislators will sail through. They are untouchable.

If your agenda is pushing through deeply unpopular legislation, *that* is one heck of a lesson for the future. But just the first of many.

*   *   *

Decades of Dry Runs

The onslaught by statehouses over recent decades appears overwhelming. The sheer number of issues. The aggressiveness of the laws. The breadth of the topics, including:

- undermining efforts to tackle climate change and enhance new energy sources;
- privatizing education;
- undermining the Affordable Care Act and Medicaid expansion;
- loosening gun laws;
- attacking reproductive rights;
- undermining legal rights of consumers and injured plaintiffs;
- attacking organized labor and collective bargaining; and
- slashing spending and taxes, especially for corporations and those who make the most.

Someone not paying close attention would assume this all came through a steady, well-planned march forward. But that's not how it happened. Along the way, as the Ohio labor fight shows, movement happened in fits and starts. Some efforts met with success, others failed. And each push—each success or failure—taught those pursuing these laws something important. Why did one state fail and another succeed? What was the response to one variant of the law in one state, versus another variant elsewhere?

Here are some of the other key lessons learned:

Lesson 1:
"Do Something"? Nah. Popularity Doesn't Matter

Thirty-two seconds.

That's all it took to end nine lives.

In 32 seconds, Dayton's Oregon District went from a joyous gathering of hundreds of young people to the site of America's latest massacre. Nine dead and 26 injured. And thank God some attentive police officers ended the massacre in 32 seconds—taking out the shooter with 30 rounds—or far more would've lost their lives.

The shooter turned out to be a 24-year old who had been sending off warning signs for years. Doubly tragic, one of the victims was his younger sister.

Within days, in what has become the all-too-familiar response to these shootings, Ohio's governor came to mourn the victims, no doubt prepared to share his "thoughts and prayers." But as he spoke, one of the frustrated bar owners shouted out two words of his own: "Do Something." That simple command struck such a chord with the large crowd, they started chanting it: "Do Something! Do Something!" The chants grew so loud, no one could hear what the governor was saying. Either they didn't care, or they'd heard it all before.

But those chanted words echoed way beyond Dayton, sparking calls and rallies to "Do Something" around the state. Within a week, the governor himself promised he would, indeed, "do something."

But he never did.

Ohio never did.

The governor ultimately rolled out a handful of "reforms" that were lambasted by gun reform groups as anemic at best, and fig leaves for real reform at worst. But not even those do-nothing measures went anywhere. A year after the Dayton shooting, the only bills with any momentum on guns were those further loosening gun restrictions.[340] And in the end, the governor signed a bill making things *worse*,[341] all while the statehouse refused to grant his reforms a single hearing. That's surely not what the crowd back in Dayton meant when they urged him to do something.

There's a tragic irony in this story. And there's a reason that the spontaneous chants of those Daytonians caught on. Politically speaking, when those in the crowd called on the politicians to "do something," they perfectly captured the feelings of a supermajority of Ohioans. Those at the statehouse? The officials whose actual job it is to represent their voters? In opposing any reforms, they're the ones who don't at all represent the average Ohioan. They're fighting for a small minority of Ohioans, including in their own districts.

You'd never know it, but in Ohio and elsewhere, one thing that almost every citizen agrees on is that we need common sense gun safety laws to address violence afflicting both our large cities and small towns. Take a look at any poll—public or private—and the results are staggering. Here are just a few examples from Ohio:

In 2013, 90% of Ohioans—and 86% of gun owners—said they supported universal background checks.[342] Six years later, the same year as the Dayton shooting, the same pollster asked again. The answer? 90% of Ohioans—and 87% of gun owners—supported universal background checks.[343] But even that most basic change couldn't make it through the statehouse *after* Dayton. The governor's proposal after the massacre was a diluted background check bill—adding "voluntary" background checks, whatever that means. Even that went nowhere. So, of course Democrats' more robust background check bill never moved.

The other major element debated after Dayton was a "red flag" law, which disallows gun ownership when a person, like that shooter, shows signs of extreme risk of harming themselves or others. 74% of Ohioans (including 69% of Republicans and 61% of Trump supporters) support such an "extreme risk" law.[344] Yet again, DeWine's diluted version of a "red flag" law went nowhere in the statehouse. Not even a hearing.

Now what changes do Ohioans *not* support? More than 60% of Ohioans oppose loosening the Ohio's concealed carry laws.[345] After Dayton, *that* is one bill Republicans are eager to move forward, eliminating outright the need for a license at all.[346]

These polling numbers for gun reform are similar to others across the country. Yet like Ohio, statehouses have defied them over the past fifteen years, doing the polar opposite of what majorities or supermajorities want. Adding guns in bars? Americans oppose 69%-18%.[347] Guns on college campuses? Oppose, 64%-23%. In restaurants? 52%-33%. Yet like Ohio, state after state has added these locations as legal places to carry guns. Nancy Kaffer at the *Detroit Free Press* summed up the situation in most states:

> Here's what most Michiganders want: No guns in schools, daycare centers or churches. That's the clear result of public polling conducted in the state and in the region.
>
> What the Legislature delivers: Bill after bill aimed at expanding access to firearms, increasing the number

of places guns can be carried, either in the open or concealed, enhancing the ease with which firearms can be transported, and gutting local governments' ability to make decisions about when and where guns may be carried.[348]

This trend isn't limited to gun policy. A central lesson from the major state legislative advances across the country is that the vast majority of the ideas aren't supported by the majority of voters. They don't need to be popular to succeed. In fact, they can be deeply unpopular. Even if things turn south, like SB5, the politicians ultimately make it through just fine.

Take a look at every issue listed above. On every item, the majority or super-majority of Americans disagree with the position that has been advanced in statehouses.[349] But that hasn't stopped statehouses from plunging forward on all of them:

- Strong majorities believe in climate change and want to see something done about it.

- Strong majorities support collective bargaining.

- Strong majorities support increasing the minimum wage.

- Strong majorities support Medicaid expansion, and, over time, the Affordable Care Act.

- Strong majorities support reproductive rights.

So one key lesson at statehouses: the popularity or lack of popularity of ideas is irrelevant. In fact, if an idea is *not* popular—if it defies the broad will of the people—the statehouses of this country are clearly the place to make it happen. The anonymity of statehouse members, and the gerrymandering that protects them, means they can take on unpopular causes without risk. They can get away with far more, politically speaking, than other levels of government can. So, they can set far more aggressive goals to begin with and keep pursuing them over time when officials at other levels might get cold feet or actually face the wrath of voters.

And the fact that they can do this arises as a central feature making these statehouses so valuable to those interested in advancing unpopular, even fringe, ideas. But of course, that's true only as long as they *remain* places where unpopular ideas can sail through.

Lesson 2: Keep the Donors Out of the Spotlight

On the evening of February 26, 2012, George Zimmerman—a neighborhood watch leader of his gated community in Sanford, Florida—called 911, reporting that a "guy" in a gray hoodie was walking around the neighborhood, "up to no good." A short while later, Zimmerman shot and killed seventeen-year old Trayvon Martin. The killing, the decision by prosecutors not to initially charge Zimmerman, and his eventual acquittal for second-degree murder, sparked understandable national outrage. The wave of recriminations from the murder washed far and wide. And one institution that took a direct hit was ALEC.

Prosecutors initially chose not to charge Zimmerman because Florida law granted Zimmerman the right to "stand his ground" and use force if he feared for his life.[350] That concept also became a part of the ultimate instruction the Florida judge read to the jury at Zimmerman's trial for second-degree murder: Zimmerman, the judge instructed, had no duty to retreat from the confrontation with Trayvon Martin, but had "the right to stand his ground and meet force with force, including deadly force, if he reasonably believed that it was necessary to do so to prevent death or great bodily harm to himself."[351] One juror explained after the trial that this language of "standing your ground" had been a factor the jury had weighed.[352]

Prior to 2005, such an instruction would *not* have been read. Instead, the judge would have told the jury that Zimmerman "had a duty to retreat by using 'every reasonable means.'"[353] But in 2005, Florida became the first state in the nation to add "stand your ground" language to its criminal statutes. By 2012, 24 states had added the same law to their books.[354]

Why?

ALEC.

Months after Governor Jeb Bush signed the Florida language into law, ALEC's Criminal Justice Task Force—whose private sector chair was an executive at Wal-Mart[355]—unanimously voted to approve the Florida language as a model ALEC bill for the country. How do we know this happened despite the secrecy of these meetings? Because the NRA's chief lobbyist touted it in a press release, taking credit for the model bill's adoption.[356] The task force and ALEC's members got to work, successfully disseminating the language throughout the country.[357]

Then, seven years later, Zimmerman killed Trayvon Martin and ALEC's model law helped get him off. This also occurred right as the media and activists were already sniffing out ALEC's behind-the-scenes involvement in voting and other controversial bills. So as journalists scrutinized the Florida law that allowed Zimmerman to kill Martin with no accountability, they quickly homed in on the role that ALEC had played in spreading the "shoot first" law everywhere. Story after story connected ALEC, state legislators, the NRA, and corporations like Wal-Mart to the Trayvon Martin killing.[358]

What happened next followed two tracks.

On the one hand, as in so many other cases, the public officials hardly blinked. They've continued to expand "Stand your Ground" across the country. The law is now on the books in 30 states, and the duty to retreat has been removed from eight other states.[359] Even after Dayton, the Ohio legislature passed an expanded "Stand Your Ground" law. That was the bill the governor signed after having promised to "do something."[360]

But the second track took the opposite direction. After the Trayvon Martin murder, a civil rights organization called Color of Change went to company after company—all members of ALEC—demanding that they leave the organization. Other groups such as Common Cause joined them.[361] And it worked. More than 60 private sector members left ALEC, or allowed their memberships to expire, including Walmart, Coca-Cola, McDonald's, Pepsi, Kraft, Wendy's and others, as well as non-profits such as the Gates Foundation.[362] At about 28% of its corporate membership,[363] these departures hit ALEC hard financially. The backlash got so fierce, ALEC disbanded the task force that had spread "Stand Your Ground" around the country.[364] It also removed "Stand Your Ground" as one of its model bills.[365]

So, while the legislators themselves remain impregnable to public opinion, it turns out the corporations are far more sensitive to the backlash if their fingerprints (or money) are tied to controversy. Needless to say, this means secrecy and lack of transparency are key, especially for companies that rely on a broad consumer base or have public employee pensions or unions as large institutional investors.[366]

But for an organization like the NRA, a separate lesson was also learned: who needs ALEC? Even with the task force most aligned with its agenda disbanded, the NRA—having set up shop in all 50 states—kept plugging away successfully. Even if Walmart or other corporations get cold feet, the politicians will still move forward. The ALEC model works even without ALEC.

Lesson 3: Legislators Can Overrun Statewide Officials

What happened after Dayton also exemplifies another important lesson. When there is a disagreement between state legislatures and statewide officials, the statehouse members usually prevail in the end. Their control of the legislative and committee agendas, their ability to veto items, and their control of other aspects of governance (the budget), give them strong leverage to get the results they seek.

Lesson 4: Over Time, 20% is a Win; But the Other 80% Is Key

In Chapter Six, I shared the datapoint that ALEC successfully passed about 20% of the laws its members introduced in America's statehouses.

When all was said and done, the Ohio Senate bill gutting municipal broadband was *not* one of those 20%. In 2021 at least. It was pulled from the budget at the last minute. The original proposal supporting broadband was restored.

Per Lesson 2, the attack on broadband became a textbook example of what ALEC and its members do <u>not</u> want, if they can help it. Attention. Controversy. The bill exploded publicly from the outset—in part because it was terribly timed, unveiled just as a broader national discussion began on the need for rural broadband. Legislators ducked quickly, orphaning the bill from the outset. Reporters hunted down AT&T and Charter Communications to see what they knew, no doubt sending alarm bells through their public relations departments. Then the senate president stuck his foot in his mouth trying to explain it, only drawing more unwanted attention. Local officials from across the spectrum decried it in multiple newspapers, and major Capitol Square organizations—such as the Ohio Municipal League, the County Commissioner Association of Ohio, Ohio school districts, and others—made killing it a top budget priority. So just as it appeared out of the blue, the bill vanished. Forgotten almost as quickly.

As the Trayvon Martin example makes clear, ALEC and others have learned that when something generates too much heat, *especially for its private members,* cut bait. And that's what happened at the last minute here as well. The bill came and went, tossed so quickly that the name ALEC didn't appear in a single story in Ohio papers. The connection of AT&T back to ALEC was never made. As one legislator asked in a tweet a few days after: 'So did we ever find out which Senator was behind that municipal broadband killer amendment?"[367]

No, we didn't.

No harm, no foul.

Next.

And that "next" came immediately. With rural broadband dominating the *public* budget fight, other items in that same budget didn't get nearly the attention. And some of those, too, came right out of the ALEC playbook. For example, the Ohio House and Senate dramatically expanded private school vouchers, and also expanded tax credits for the provision of private school vouchers across the state. Unlike broadband, not a lot of papers focused on this. So, language mirroring ALEC model bills passed with little controversy. Also left intact was the provision adding more tax cuts. Specifically, the legislature combined the two highest tax brackets into one—the lower one—leading to a hefty tax cut for the wealthiest Ohioans and a more regressive income tax overall. Little was made of this either. Heck, Ohio may even move up a notch or two in its ALEC/Laffer ranking due to this step alone.

And while the budget got all the attention that day, Ohio legislators served up more orders from the Statehouse Grille late that evening. In addition to some troublesome new voting rules, they enacted a new round of regulations hampering wind and solar farms,[368] and enacted the final version of the ban on local plastic bag bans/fees.[369] All in all, a pretty good day for ALEC, First Energy, Murray Coal and others who stalk the statehouse from near and far.

And this late frenzy highlighted another lesson learned over the prior decade: order everything at once. To get 20% or more through, you need the other 80% thrown into the churn. *Let's call it the 80/20 strategy.* If some bills draw all the attention and need to be sacrificed, others sail through largely unnoticed. The press can only cover so much, after all. Those fighting back can only focus on so much.

Now widen the strategy across the entire country. 80/20 is especially powerful when pressing similar legislation across multiple states, and when playing a long game. As Columbia political scientist Alexander Hertel-Fernandez explains: "the model of multistate lobbying means that groups get many bites at the same apple. [Groups] can afford to lose some battles as long as they still succeed in other states":

> With more opportunities to win, groups like ALEC have pursued fairly ambitious proposals, knowing full well that some of those bills would have no chance of adoption in most states. But some states would take the most extreme versions of their proposals, creating a precedent [] to build on in subsequent legislative battles.

In this way, the range of the possible slowly expands over time.[370]

Win a battle over one aspect of an issue in one state, win another aspect elsewhere, and before you know it, you have "models" in place all over the country to build from. Not ALEC models—but actual state laws. And then you keep building from there.

80/20, from coast to coast, results in countless wins and ever-growing momentum.

Lesson 5: Through Success and Failure, Always Learning

One of the most powerful ads that ran in the 2011 Ohio Senate Bill 5 (anti-labor) fight featured a Cincinnati great-grandmother, Marlene Quinn, whose great-granddaughter local firefighters had saved from a burning home. To keep fire units at full strength, she urged viewers to vote for repealing the bill. It "can mean the difference between life and death," she said.[371] Other ads on the repeal side featured a non-stop parade of firefighters and police officers talking about how the law would risk Ohio communities' safety. And articles on Senate Bill 5 delved into how it might affect fire staffing, safety equipment, the number of officers in patrol cars, and other safety matters.[372] As one long-time columnist wrote, cops and firefighters became the "poster children" of the entire campaign.[373] It was a powerful argument from compelling messengers—so powerful, proponents of the bill felt the need to parrot the safety argument. That same columnist wrote: "Based on the 'vote no' ads, and the GOP's attempts to respond, you'd think that police and fire services were all that's on the table."[374] The pro-SB5 side went so far as to pirate footage of Mrs. Quinn from ads opposing the measure and twisted her words in their own ads to urge a "yes" vote on the measure: "She's right. By voting 'no' on Issue 2, our safety will be threatened."[375] The ad was so misleading, numerous television stations pulled it.

Oops.

That pretty much sums up the desperate effort to save the doomed anti-union bill.

On almost the same timetable, up in Madison, the equivalent to Senate Bill 5 passed through Wisconsin's statehouse. Passions were just as high as in Ohio—a controversial new governor and new majority in the statehouse, protests, a packed state capital, wall-to-wall news coverage. Without a repeal mechanism in their constitution, those opposed to the measure instead tried to recall Governor Scott Walker. Like the Ohio forces, they organized well, gathering more than 900,000 signatures to get the recall on the ballot, spent big money, and waged a fierce campaign to oust him. But unlike Ohio, they lost. In fact, it wasn't very close. Walker won by 53%-47%, more than he had in 2010.

There were many differences, of course. But one crucial one was that Walker and his allies exempted police and fire from their attack on collective bargaining.[376] That didn't stop unionized first responders from joining the coalition fighting the law,[377] and it meant Walker and the legislators couldn't claim as wide an impact as Republicans in Ohio could about Senate Bill 5 (police and fire are the biggest expenditures at the local level). But it diluted the argument Ohio repeal supporters made so powerfully in every corner of the state. In hindsight, Ohio Republicans made a "huge mistake" by including police and fire in the bill.[378] Walker avoided that mistake.

Two states. Two different bills. Two laboratories in action.

Two different outcomes. And one clear takeaway for any similar efforts going forward.

Future anti-labor pugilists took heed. In 2012, Michigan's legislature advanced a so-called "right to work law," including attacks on collective bargaining for public employees. But who'd they leave out? All 1,700 bargaining units that represent Michigan police officers and firefighters.[379] In 2015, when Governor Bruce Rauner of Illinois went after public employee pensions, he too carved out police and fire pensions.[380] Again in 2017, when Iowa pushed to weaken collective bargaining for public employees there, police and fire were exempted.[381]

It's a simple example of the cross-learning and (sometimes unwitting) experimentation that takes place as statehouses push similar laws around the country. A nip here, a tuck there—an exemption with no sound justification but political expedience—and Iowa was able to accomplish something in 2017 that Ohio failed to get done in 2011. Ohio's failure, and Wisconsin's success, illuminated the way.

And in case legislators themselves aren't equipped to seek out these lessons on their own, organizations are happy to document and disseminate them. Recall the State Policy Network from Chapter Six, which partners with state-based "think tanks" (funded by the same donors) to disseminate policy on a variety of topics to statehouses. SPN runs working groups on a variety of topics that mirror ALEC's task forces, from energy to education. With so many states moving forward at the same time in these areas—sometimes succeeding, sometimes failing—these SPN working groups and in-state partners share "best practices" and lessons learned from those state experiences.[382]

For example, SPN issued a "State Workplace Freedom" toolkit advising legislatures and their allies on how to best battle public unions. It explicitly draws on the "countless lessons learned" over the "last several years,"[383] doing so at a far more granular level than whether or not to exempt police and fire. The toolkit outlines a variety of policy proposals to combat unions, suggesting different paths depending on the situation in particular states (i.e., some measures are recommended for states with "legislative majorities and executive branches that support union reform"), and recommending ideal messaging points along the way. (It's clear they watched the failed Ohio union-busting effort in 2011, because SPN warns not to "rant against unions" or use terms such as "corrupt union bosses," "union fat cats" or "other overly negative language."[384])

But way beyond political guidance, the lessons delve into the effectiveness and regulatory viability of statehouse reforms. One SPN toolkit instructs states on how to reduce their Medicaid rolls, outlining steps such as adding work requirements, reducing eligibility, capping enrollment, adding time limits, and other steps. Throughout, they point to lessons learned in specific states on what worked and what didn't.[385] The report also cites various states' applications for federal approval on proposed Medicaid reforms—noting which were successful, and which were not.

Waging the war across all states also allows the creation of useful legal precedent. SPN's toolkits cite legal decisions upholding some states' reforms, clearing the way for other states to follow in those footsteps.[386] And after the landmark *Janus v. AFSCME* Supreme Court decision dealt a blow to public employee unions, SPN immediately disseminated guidance to states on how they could take advantage of the ruling.

The point is clear: both on their own, and supported by an active network of national and in-state organizations, statehouses have been testing reforms and learning from one another's outcomes for well over a decade. On union-busting.

On energy. On cutting taxes. On attacking abortion access and reproductive rights. On privatizing schools and corrections. You name it. Think of it as an unending series of experiments, the outcomes of which always teach all involved something new.

The value of these learnings places an even greater premium on aggressively pushing forward as many initiatives as possible. The more, the better—in individual states and nationally. If some measures fail to get enacted, or lose in court, then you learn the outer boundary of what's possible. If some win in court, or get approved by the federal government, or overcome other hurdles, you have a new "best practice" to be applied elsewhere along with precedent to support it. If some state-level reforms only make a small difference, perhaps they're not worth the fight elsewhere. If controversial ones make a profound difference, a tough fight might be justified.

And on and on and on. Always experimenting. Always pushing. Always learning.

Final Lesson: The Politicians Don't Matter

There's one final lesson, which will bring us into the attacks on democracy itself.

Warning: for the world's oldest democracy, this is a bleak one.

In the current political culture of statehouses, the individual politicians don't matter. They may not realize it, and voters may not realize it, but certain powers that be have figured it out.

The formula is simple: guarantee the election results, ensure the right combination of incentives is in place, erect strong mechanisms in the background that maximize those incentives—and the individuals who ultimately win elections in all these legislative districts don't change a thing. Which members rise to become leaders of statehouses doesn't matter all that much either. And what happens to those politicians, personally, during their years in service also doesn't matter. What matters is that the political system and culture ensure that enough of them vote the right way while they're there—that all the incentives line up.

The past decade has shown that that mission, too, has been accomplished.

Just look at Ohio.

When Cliff Rosenberger flamed out because he travelled too much with payday lenders, the next guy up grabbed the same baton and ran with it. In fact, Larry Householder ran faster. When he was booted from the Speakership because . . . well, the FBI . . . the next guy up grabbed the baton and just kept running—pushing through more tax breaks and attacks on wind and solar, among other steps.

In state after state, you'll see the same thing. The ten-year experiment could not be more conclusive: the occupants cycling through these offices respond to the same incentives in the same ways. Like clockwork, and with few exceptions, they line up to be the pawns the ecosystem designs them to be.

Political scientist Hertel-Fernandez said it best: "[t]he Kochs have never viewed individual politicians as being central, considering them to be mere 'actors' reading off the scripts provided to them."[387] Whoever gets elected doesn't matter; that they all behave in a predictable way once elected does. And several decades have affirmed that that's exactly what happens.

Look past the short-term. Beyond the day-to-day, or even year-in and year-out, drama. When it comes to outcomes, these statehouses essentially run on automatic pilot as the politicians pass through—rising, falling, or serving out their terms and returning home. After his spirited ride with ALEC, John Adams is back to operating his furniture store in Sidney,

Ohio. Rosenberger, still waiting for the FBI's investigation to close, actively travels as a private citizen, and has gotten in shape (he documents his weight loss on social media.) That Manchester state senator is plugging away at Ohio's Department of Transportation. They all played their roles and have since left the stage. Others replaced them on that stage, now advancing the same things they did. And Ohio, having adopted right-wing policy after right-wing policy, continues to sink.

Now . . . if the individual officeholders don't matter, what does matter is sustaining the broader ecosystem and its core elements. That terrible mix of incentives. The buffers that protect ALEC's "public members" from even the most unpopular actions. The anonymity back home. All the things that allow them to survive even when they are anti-majoritarian to the extreme. Even when the policies they implement generate failed outcome after failed outcome regardless of where they fall on the ALEC/Laffer scorecard.

Sustaining an ecosystem of zero accountability takes work. And amid all that failure and unpopularity, this work has only grown more important over time. It is essential for everything else.

To pull it off, statehouses across the country have been operating as laboratories in one other way, for almost just as long.

Read on.

CHAPTER 8

Laboratories of Autocracy: Warming Up

ROLAND GILBERT VOTED from the same Columbus location every year, so there was no doubt that he lived where he said he lived. His birthdate was on file at the Board of Elections. And his signature matched the signature on file at the Board.

But weeks after voting in the low-profile, 2014 midterm election, Roland learned that his vote hadn't counted.

Why? Because Roland, legally blind and in his 80s, had made a single mistake when he'd filled out the form accompanying his absentee ballot.[388] In the field where he was supposed to write his birthdate, he mistakenly wrote in the date that he was voting.

Due to that single, immaterial error, Roland's entire ballot was tossed out. And because he only learned this after the election, Roland never had the chance to correct the mistake.

A similar thing happened to Kadar Hiir, a Somali immigrant who became an American citizen in 2012 and voted in his first Ohio election in 2014.[389] Given a provisional ballot when he voted in person, he wrote the day of his birthday first, then the month—the order used in his native Somalia and most other parts of the world. But the form required that the month be written first. His ballot was tossed out.

Katherine Galko, 92, voted that year from her assisted living facility in Summit County, where an aide helped her fill out her ballot. They accidentally wrote the day of the election where four digits of her social security number belonged, so there went Katherine's vote.[390]

That same election, Elizabeth Hire had her provisional ballot tossed because she miswrote one number of her social security number.[391]

As with Roland, there was no doubt that Kadar, Elizabeth and Katherine were registered voters. They provided enough information to verify that, and their signatures matched the signatures on file. To get their absentee ballots sent to them in the first place, Roland and Katherine had sent the required information to elections officials in a prior application. The form on which they made the mistake was only sent to them *because* their first form had verified that they were validly registered voters. Still, because of errors that didn't bear in any way on their eligibility to vote, their actual ballots were thrown out.

"Those are the rules," some might say. "Tough luck."

But there's a twist. Two years earlier, Roland's and the others' votes would've counted. The rules were changed.

It was only in 2014 that the Ohio legislature amended the law to mandate that entire ballots be disqualified for even minor mistakes on forms accompanying their absentee or provisional ballots.[392] The legislature also reduced the amount of time voters could "cure" any such errors so their vote could count, and they barred elections officials from assisting voters in filling out the form.[393] As a result, in 2014, thousands of ballots were disqualified for just these type of small errors for the first time.

Data gathered from the 2014 and 2015 elections confirmed that poorer, less educated voters made these small mistakes more often, and therefore their ballots were tossed at a higher rate. Homeless voters. Voters like Roland and Katherine, elderly or with disabilities. More broadly, data showed that the new rule disqualified more ballots from large, urban counties than small counties. "[M]ore than half of the provisional and absentee votes discarded for minor errors in 2014 came from five large, Democratic-dominated urban counties."[394]

But deeper digging also revealed another problem. The new rule was being enforced differently depending on where voters lived. And not randomly. The rule was more strictly enforced in those larger, Democratic-leaning counties.[395] Officials in many smaller, Republican-dominated counties would *not* disqualify a ballot for an incorrect address or birthday, while officials in most larger, Democratic-leaning counties *would* disqualify a ballot for that same incorrect address or birthday.[396] This harkened back to the Jim Crow era, where literacy tests were selectively enforced—White voters (if they even had to take the literacy test at all) usually got a pass for errors that would rule out Black voters. Overall, the new rule meant that Ohio's minority voters were more likely to have their absentee and provisional ballots rejected due to these errors than white voters.[397]

When challenged in court, the state didn't even pretend that combating fraud was a justification for its new, strict treatment of small informational mistakes.[398] It couldn't, because the original purpose of the form in question had been simply to collect more information for "identifying and registering" voters, not to verify that a voter was registered.[399] And as part of the lawsuit, elections officials testified that they could identify which voters were registered without all the form's information. Nevertheless, the legislature in 2014 voted to punish *any* mistake made on that informational form by tossing out the entire ballot.

And with that change went Roland's ballot, and the ballots of thousands of other Ohio voters.

Bad rule, right? Infuriating.

Well, it was a mere ripple amid a tsunami of attacks on Ohio voters.

Certain voters, that is.

*   *   *

Targeting the Obama Coalition That Turned Ohio Blue

Ready . . . Aim . . .

When it came to new voting laws after 2010, the 80/20 principle introduced in Chapter Seven—that to get 20% of laws passed you push aggressively on another 80%—was unleashed to full effect throughout the country. Through waves of new and amended laws, legislatures like Ohio's snared millions of voters in a wide net. But as with that 2014 Ohio law, voters weren't impacted equally. The net was thrown in the direction of the emerging and diverse coalition that turned states like Ohio blue for Barack Obama in 2008.

As former Ohio state representative Kathleen Clyde explained to me, the GOP statehouse wasn't just reacting to the outcome at the White House level. It was also about securing their own power:

> They wanted to attack the rising American electorate that not only put Obama in office in 2008, but actually overcame a Republican gerrymander in Ohio to take the Ohio House from them from 2009 to 2011. . . . The

Republicans were livid about that, so did everything they could do to ensure that Democrats could never win the majority again.

And how do we know that coalition was the target of the new voting rules? Simple: in Ohio, at least, the legislators and their allies told us.

Black voters across Ohio found themselves at the center of the legislative bullseye. While Obama did well across the state compared to Democratic candidates before or since, what put him over the top was a surge of support in large, urban counties with sizeable Black populations. Here's how crucial the large, urban counties were in Obama's Ohio victory: with 83 out of 88 counties fully counted, McCain led Obama in 2008 by more than 200,000 votes. But throw in his vote margins in Ohio's five largest counties, Obama won the state by slightly more than 262,000 votes. Five counties swamped the other 83—the five that represent 73% of the state's Black voters.[400] In 2012, the margin of victory in Cuyahoga County alone (Cleveland and its suburbs) was the difference between victory and defeat.

Ohio Republicans couldn't hide their frustration at the difference Black voters made. One GOP election official explained: "I guess I really actually feel we shouldn't contort the voting process to accommodate the urban—read African-American— voter turnout machine."[401] As a federal judge pointed out, this was not a "slip of the tongue" somehow recorded by a hidden mic. It was a "written response to a reporter's question."[402] You can only imagine what they said in private. So, legislative target #1 after 2010 was Black voters. Mark it down.

A second core group of the winning Obama coalition was young voters. Like those large, diverse counties, young voters played a critical role in Obama's 2008 and 2012 wins in Ohio and across the country. Not only did voters under 30 show up in big numbers, they voted overwhelmingly for Obama. In 2008, the margin was 66%-32%; in 2012, it was 60%-36%. No other age bracket (30-44, 45-64, 65+) broke nearly that decisively in either election.[403] In 2012 especially, young people made the difference in key battleground states. In Ohio, "48% of voters 30 and older voted for Obama. When younger voters were included, his share of the vote increased to 50% (vs. 48% for Romney)."[404] Same thing happened in Virginia, Florida, and Pennsylvania.[405] In short, Mitt Romney would've been president were it not for young people in Ohio and elsewhere.

Ohio's college voters—more than 100,000 of whom hail from out of state—were critical. So important that in the final days of his re-election campaign, Obama toured Ohio college campuses diagonally down I-71. The last stop was at University of Cincinnati's basketball arena, the night before the election. I remember the energized crowd to this day.

So, like Black voters, these young voters drew the ire of Ohio legislators. How do we know? Well, again, they told us. In 2013, after the Obama win in Ohio, Speaker of the Ohio House Bill Batchelder questioned the involvement of college students in Ohio elections, calling their participation "peculiar": "[W]hen I first came here people who were coming in from New York or some other place could not vote in Ohio. Then there were federal court decisions and other peculiar things, so that was permitted."[406] He then minimized the knowledge and connection of these young people to the Ohio communities where they live:

How do they vote on the school levy, how do they vote on the sheriff's race, and so forth? Obviously it would be possible for people to become knowledgeable in those areas, but there's to me a significant question, about what the particular levies, what the result of having people who don't have to pay for them would do in terms of adopting those things.[407]

Even though his wife was a long-time federal judge, Batchelder apparently was unaware that the "federal court decisions" he cited prohibited the very motivation he was publicly confessing to—excluding voters based on the assumption that they are strangers to a community, know less about the issues at stake, and might therefore vote a certain way.[408] As the Supreme Court said in one of those "peculiar" cases, "[t]his is precisely the sort of argument this Court has repeatedly rejected."[409]

Finally, intersecting with their targeting of Black and young voters, the legislature placed its third primary bullseye on early voting. Ironically, Republicans had supported the expansion of early voting after endless lines and countless problems turned the 2004 Ohio election into a national debacle. Polling places were so overwhelmed that year that some Ohioans (including college students) waited until early in the morning to vote, while thousands of others simply walked away. Back then, absentee voting was thought of as mainly for senior voters (i.e., Republicans). So the bipartisan expansion of "early vote" in 2005—which opened no-excuse absentee voting to all voters while also initiating early, in-person voting—was seen as a common sense way to alleviate the election day surge that had overwhelmed polling places.

But the Obama juggernaut changed that sanguine view of early vote. His 2008 campaign urged voters to vote early, in person or by mail, and they did so at record numbers. They wisely organized "sporadic" voters—ones who might not show up on election day—to ensure they "banked" their vote early; by doing so, they grew the overall pie of voters, as opposed to simply encouraging people to vote early who were going to vote anyway. Beyond traditional door knocks and phone calls, the campaign organized rock concerts and rallies, drawing big crowds who then marched directly to early voting locations. (I spoke at a few—pro tip: never speak in between The National and Natalie Portman). Through what was called "souls to the polls," churches organized buses from churches to those same early vote locations. And many voters just showed up on their own. In the final three days of the election, more than 100,000 Ohioans voted in-person, and they were disproportionately Black and young voters in Ohio's biggest cities.[410] One study found that 19.9% of all Ohio Black voters voted early in-person, while 6.2% of White voters did the same.[411] A court that looked at the data concluded:

> Voters who chose to cast their ballots early tended to be members of different demographic groups than those who voted on election day. Early voters were "more likely than election-day voters to be women, older, and of lower income and education attainment." Data from Cuyahoga and Franklin Counties suggests that early voters were disproportionately African-American and that a large majority of early in-person votes (82% in Franklin County) were cast after hours on weekdays, on the weekend, or on the Monday before the election.[412]

Overall, more than 1.7 million Ohioans voted before election day, accounting for 29.7% of the total vote in the election.[413] Fueled by the surge in early vote, minority turnout increased in the 2008 Ohio election over prior elections.[414]

Republicans again couldn't contain their frustration. These were all parts of the "urban—read African-American—*voter turnout machine"* that that Republican official so coarsely described. Another state legislator went off in a house committee meeting: "There's that group of people who say, 'I'm only voting if someone drives me down after church on Sunday.'... Really? Is that the person we need to cater to when we're making public policy about elections?"[415]

So, based on the 2008 and 2012 elections, the legislature's target list emerged: Black voters, young voters, early voters.

And what did the legislature do to strike these targets? Let us count the ways.

...Fire

The legislature began its attack immediately after the GOP wins in 2010, its first opportunity to do something about the Obama coalition. And as they did in Chapter Seven on other issues, legislators went to war on multiple fronts.

80/20, but on one subject matter alone.

Wave 1: Attacking Early Voting

Narrowing the early vote window emerged as the legislature's immediate priority.

At the same time the Senate Bill 5 battle engulfed the state, the legislature rammed through its broad attack on early voting. While sixteen bills came forward, in one bill alone, it: slashed the early, in-person vote window from 35 days to seventeen days, including the last weekend and Monday of early vote; slashed the absentee vote (by mail) window from 35 days to 21 days; reduced hours on election day; forbid county boards of elections from proactively sending out absentee ballot applications;[416] and forbid county boards of elections from pre-paying postage on absentee ballot applications.

Eliminating the first week of early voting also scrapped what had been called "Golden Week"—a window of time where voters could both register to vote and vote at the same time. In 2008, more than 67,000 voters had voted in person that week, and almost 13,000 had registered as they did so.[417] Data showed that the "usage rate" of Golden Week by Black voters was "far higher" than white voters.[418] Again, churches and other organizations had used the unique opportunity of the week to organize same day registration/voting drives.[419]

As with Senate Bill 5, voting rights advocates fought back after the bill passed, mounting a successful petition drive that stopped it in its tracks. When faced with 300,000 signatures to repeal the bill, and fearing defeat at the polls, the legislature repealed its own law—eliminating the repeal election the petition drive should've triggered.[420] They then brought forth a watered-down bill that again eliminated the final weekend and Monday of early in-person voting. That too was ultimately struck down by a federal court. But with 100,000 disproportionally minority voters offering too plum a target to overlook, [421] they tried *again* after 2012.

After a flurry of court decisions, more laws, repackaged provisions, and new directives, the dust settled by the 2016 election. The net result was that the final weekend and Monday of early vote remained, while the first week and "Golden Week" were eliminated. Several Sunday voting days were eliminated and weekday evening hours—which had been hugely popular in 2008[422]—reduced. The new limits on local boards of elections—forbidding them from sending out absentee ballot applications and prepaying postage—remained intact. Along the way, the legislature added those stricter rules around ballot informational requirements, which a court narrowed before the 2016 election.

These new limitations on the days and hours available

for in-person, early voting play an especially pernicious role thanks to a state law that caps early vote locations to just one per county. That law means a diverse county of one million people—whose voters disproportionately use early, in-person voting—gets the same, solo early-vote location as a county with under 15,000. From the outset, that cap created a bottleneck—putting an artificial limit on the number of people who vote early over the election cycle, while guaranteeing hours-long lines each and every election cycle. And every new limitation on hours and days of early vote has only squeezed that bottleneck tighter. (LaRose's ban on multiple drop boxes was just the latest pile-on to these over-loaded locations).

In 2020, when the pandemic put a premium on vote by mail and drop boxes, the legislature added yet another obstacle. As LaRose added his ban on drop boxes, the legislature passed a law prohibiting him from pre-paying postage on absentee ballots, something that had been done all decade by secretaries of state (even after counties had been banned from doing so). The one-two punch managed to make voting by mail harder however you tried it.

Wave 2: Purging Voters

While the legislature attacked the early vote process, Ohio also pursued the most aggressive purging of voter registration rolls in the nation. As often happens in the voting arena, this was a symbiotic partnership between Jon Husted, the former house leader and state senator who rose to become secretary of state in the 2010 election, then his successor, Frank LaRose, and their former colleagues at the statehouse.

As background, states around the country all face the same challenge of how to keep their voting rolls updated. As voters move and pass away, states need to remove them from the rolls, or update their voter registrations with the most current information. It's a legitimate issue every state contends with. But in this modern age, where private companies can track our every move via our phone, and when lists are generated whenever people move or pass away, this is something states should be able to pull off, right?

Well, some do at least. Because they're actually trying.

All states use regularly generated and easily obtainable lists of people who have moved or died to keep their rolls updated. More recently, numerous states have also adopted a process called automatic voter registration (AVR). It's a system that automatically registers voters when they interact with various government agencies and provide the necessary information, and updates that data to the registration system when changes occur; voters can opt out if they want to. Get a new driver's license after moving, where you add a new address? The AVR process adds that new address to your voter registration information. As the Brennan Center explains, the system creates "a constant stream of updates between registration agencies and election officials," which both increases registration while reducing errors and bloated rolls.[423] Clean and easy.

If AVR is the 21st century best practice for cleaning your rolls, Ohio's leaders have been happy to keep riding the pony express. Ohio's legislature showed zero interest in adopting AVR between 2010-2020. Instead of modernizing, here's the process Ohio used all decade instead.

Brace yourself!

First, Ohio *does* utilize the national change of address database and Ohio health department data to update or remove voters from the rolls who have moved or passed away. These updates occur regularly and are both standard and uncontroversial. Like all other states.

But Ohio also uses a parallel procedure to remove voters. It's innocently called the "supplemental process," but the more accurate short-hand term is "use it or lose it." If voters don't participate in the voting process over several elections, they ultimately are knocked off the rolls. Here are the basics: if a voter does not vote in two years (two consecutive elections) or participate in other ways (such as signing a petition), that voter is deemed "inactive," which initiates Ohio's purging process. The next step is that that voter is sent a "confirmation notice" in the form of a postcard. If that "inactive" voter fails to respond to the postcard, and then fails to vote in the ensuing four years, Ohio purges her from the voting rolls altogether.[424] As the federal Sixth Circuit opinion striking down the process concluded: "In sum, under the Supplemental Process, a voter is purged from the rolls after six years of inactivity—even if he or she did not move and otherwise remains eligible to vote."[425] (A long legal battle ended in a 5-4 United States Supreme Court decision reversing the Sixth Circuit and allowing the process to continue.)

Over the decade, the "supplemental process" became a wrecking ball smashing directly into large swaths of the Ohio electorate. Deep problems inevitably result from what is a fundamentally flawed approach—and, as Justice Breyer explained, from simple math. While only about four percent of people move out of their county on an annual basis, and fewer than one percent of Americans pass away every year, in some years more than 50% of voters choose not to vote.[426] So by using a short window of failing to vote as the proxy for when voters have moved, which then triggers the purging process, the approach is absurdly overbroad—sweeping into its net countless voters who have neither moved nor passed away.

Breyer scrutinized one year as an example. In its 2012

purge, Ohio sent confirmation notices to 1.5 million(!) voters, 20% of the state's entire electorate at the time. While 235,000 voters returned cards confirming they had not moved, another one million (!) simply didn't respond (about 13% of Ohio's voting population). To suggest a large percentage of this non-responsive group had moved to a different county or state doesn't come close to approximating data on the number of people who actually move. Nor does it square with localized census figures. As Breyer suggests, this far more likely reflects "the human tendency not to send back cards received in the mail."[427] Especially when, for most of the decade, that postcard failed to explain the consequences of not returning it, and also required voters to send it back, fully filled out, even if they had never moved.[428]

As you'd expect, the numbers emerging from this grotesquely overbroad approach exploded. Over the decade, more than two million voters were purged from Ohio's rolls, most via the "supplemental process" as opposed to the lists flagging when someone actually moved or passed away.[429] And as with other voting procedures and obstacles, the purging disproportionally impacted voters of color and young voters. Studies found that voters in Ohio's large, urban and diverse counties bore a disproportionate share of the purging.[430] And even within those counties, voters of color in poor communities (i.e., those who voted for Obama in large numbers) were far more likely to be purged (twice as much or more[431]) than white, more affluent communities nearby.[432] Other analyses have found that young voters and Democratic-leaning voters are also more likely to be purged.[433]

As if the sheer number and disproportionate impact weren't bad enough, things only got worse in 2019. That's when we learned that the process purges a huge chunk of registered voters in error. Not errors by voters, mind you, but *errors made by government officials and staff* in compiling, managing and sharing the lists of purged voters.

Here's how the disastrous incompetence came to light. In 2019, Frank LaRose entered the secretary of state's office under the (since broken) promise of reform and continued the purge process. One issue frustrating voting rights advocates was that they'd never before seen a list of actual purged voters. Frank changed that in 2019 when he publicly shared a list of the 235,000 voters slated to be removed in a few months. His aim was to give voting rights activists a chance to call voters on the list and urge them to return the confirmation notices.

These groups pored over the list before the purge took place, and volunteers did contact numerous voters. But in the process of scanning the list and making those calls, they, along with journalists and Democratic legislators, found that *tens of thousands of voters were on that list in error.* Thousands of them *had* voted since 2015, many as recently as 2018, meaning they weren't "inactive" at all yet were still scheduled to be purged.[434] Others had recently signed petitions, which also should've kept them off the "inactive" list.[435] And others were simply on the list due to vendor or staff error, or miscoding. Even the executive director of Ohio's League of Women Voters, one of the organizations leading the effort to scrutinize the list of voters to be purged, found *herself* on the list even though she had voted three times in the prior year.[436] In all, a stunning 20% (half from the Democratic stronghold of Franklin County) of the voters on the list of 235,000 were there in error. Remember, this was the *first and only* "to be purged" list that had ever been made public.[437] As far as we know, LaRose has not gone back in time to see how many errors were made in prior purges. But simple math—a 20% error rate projected across more than two million Ohioans purged—shows a catastrophic number of purged Ohioans from government error alone. These are outcome-changing numbers, and not just in close races.

Given that alarming error rate, voting rights advocates immediately demanded that the upcoming purge be halted; a lawsuit (yours truly) tried but failed to get a court to halt it from moving forward.[438] But the legislative majority said nothing, and LaRose, having removed the 40,000 names that were on the list in error, stubbornly moved forward on the planned purge even while confessing that the process was rife with flaws.[439] He was immediately proven right . . . on the flaws, that is. After the purge moved forward, it only took a few weeks to find names of *more* voters that had been purged in error.[440]

While common sense dictated halting the process amid these scandalous errors, Ohio's legislative majority remained silent. But that was par for the course over the decade. In 2015, Democratic legislators proposed eliminating the deeply flawed "use it or lose it" process, using only the traditional lists other states use to clean the rolls.[441] The bill didn't even get a hearing. The same bill was introduced again in the next legislative term. Still no hearing. The legislature also showed no interest in modernizing the process as other states had—if you're doing automatic voter registration, much of the purging process is no longer necessary.

But the legislature didn't just do nothing, it pushed for *more* purging. In 2014, the legislature passed a bill that increased the frequency of purges, while providing the secretary of state even more opportunity to cancel voters' registrations by authorizing him to use additional databases to identify voters to purge.[442] The primary database they had in mind was a national "program" called Cross-Check. Led by a close Trump ally and Kansas secretary of state, Cross-Check claimed that its goal was to detect voters who illegally voted in more than one state at the same time. But its error rate was so high it made Ohio's purging process look like a stickler for accuracy. One *Washington Post* study found that the Cross-Check system is "overrun with false positives, creating a high risk of disenfranchising legal voters"— the *Post* estimating that its system flagged for elimination, incorrectly, 200 legal voters for every voter it identified as voting more than once.[443]

By decade's end, Ohio's aggressive purging had its intended effect. From 2008 to 2020, despite robust registration drives in each presidential election (which re-registered many purged voters), total registrations were down in Ohio's six largest counties by more than 225,000 votes,[444] even though, according to the Census, those counties' populations had together *grown* by more than 100,000 people. Cuyahoga, the most important county in Obama's 2008 and 2012 wins, fell 20%, tumbling from over 1.1 million registered voters to 888,000, even as its population declined by less than five percent. Those "lost" voters totaled 90% of Obama's margin of victory in the county in 2012, and that was the county that had made the difference between him winning and losing Ohio.[445]

Even more important, these large counties saw an especially steep decline in core urban areas. For example, Cleveland's registered voter count fell by almost 33% between 2008 and 2020; East Cleveland fell by almost 50%, from more than 20,000 voters to under 11,000.[446] And amid Hamilton County's slight decline in registered voters, Cincinnati's registrations were down 8.7% (even as its population grew); this was driven by far greater declines in predominantly Black neighborhoods like Avondale, which saw its registrations fall by more than 26%.[447] Same stories in other cities: Toledo— down 12.5%.[448] Dayton—down 16.7%.[449] Many of these urban areas did see population declines. But just as Justice Breyer predicted, the declines in registration came at a far greater clip than any decline in actual population. For example, while Cleveland's registered voter count fell by almost 33%, its actual population fell by under 13% in the same years. And Dayton's population fell by 9.2% versus its 16.7% registration drop.

Bottom line: when Ohio's secretary of state and legislature aimed their fire at the heart of Obama's Ohio coalition through purging, they scored a direct hit, If some others were also tossed off the rolls as a consequence, that was collateral damage they could live with.

Wave 3. Young Voters

Amid these attacks, the legislature still found time to target those pesky college voters who'd cost Romney Ohio and the presidency in 2012.

The first attempt came in 2013, and was as cynical as it gets: pitting the financial interests of Ohio's universities and colleges against their own students. They did this through a budget amendment penalizing universities and colleges for providing out-of-state students with the requisite identification information (usually a school-issued letter or utility bill indicating an on-campus address) that allowed them to register as Ohio voters. Per the amendment, any student who registered using such university-issued documents would pay in-state tuition instead of higher out-of-state tuition. Since this would cost the schools more than $100 million in lost tuition,[450] the goal was clearly to discourage schools from facilitating their students voting in-state. Downright devilish.

But the scheme proved too cute by half. To their credit, college and university leaders called the legislators' bluff.

Refusing to be party to blatant suppression of their own students, they publicly insisted that despite the threatened penalty, they would continue to provide the needed information to students. Fearing the unintended consequence of providing students with a huge financial *incentive* to register in-state, the legislature dropped the idea.

But they weren't done trying.

In 2015, they added a different amendment into a bill funding transportation projects around the state, and it was just as brash. The measure required that college students who registered to vote in Ohio also needed to get an Ohio driver's license, and register their vehicles in Ohio, within 30 days. Obtaining a license and an Ohio registration would've cost each student $75 at the time. And failure to do so would constitute a minor-misdemeanor, punishable with up to a $150 fine; *and* that student would no longer be allowed to drive in Ohio with their prior license.[451] So here we have a time-consuming bureaucratic hoop, poll tax, and criminal penalty, all wrapped into one. 1950s Alabama wants its toolkit back!

This bill actually passed the house and senate. But after a firestorm among college students across the state (I confess to having encouraged a fair number of phone calls), including some college Republicans, Governor Kasich vetoed it.[452]

One last attack on young Ohioans came in 2016. Since 1981, Ohio law had permitted seventeen-year-olds to vote in the presidential primary so long as they turned eighteen by the November election. But in 2016, Secretary of State Husted issued an out-of-the-blue directive barring all seventeen-year-olds from participating in the March presidential primary. A court made mincemeat of that directive, and Husted didn't appeal.[453]

Attacking Unions

Chapters Six and Seven addressed the aggressive attacks against public union collective bargaining in 2011. Make no mistake, that was a political attack as much as it was an economic one. Averaging between 600,000 and 700,000 union members over the past decade,[454] Ohio enjoys one of the largest unionized workforces in the country. Those workers not only made up another big chunk of the electorate that turned Ohio blue in 2008 and 2012, but their unions provide large financial support to the operations—candidate, party and otherwise—that turn out Democratic voters.[455] Together, these unions provide the financial counterweight to the big corporate dollars supporting the ALEC/Koch agenda. More broadly, by promoting a strong middle class and involving a cross-section of Americans in civic and political life, unions also play an important democracy-supporting role at a time when many traditional civic institutions have disappeared. Although it ultimately failed, Senate Bill 5 was clearly an attempt to neutralize and defund a core pillar of the coalition that had turned Ohio blue.

Lessons from the Ohio Voter Suppression Lab

Other bills attacking voting came forward; some became law, some died like those attacks on young voters. No need to review them all here. The central point is that Ohio legislators understood the direct threat posed by the coalition that had turned the state blue in 2008 and devoted the entire decade to dismantling it. And just like they had on other issues, Ohio's legislators learned valuable lessons along the way.

Lesson 1: It Worked

First, their attacks worked, in too many ways. Black participation and Black turnout in the 2016 Ohio election decreased from its 2008 and 2012 levels, eroding the Obama base and making Ohio far tougher for Democrats to win.[456]

As one example, a drop in registered voters in the communities that anchored Obama's win makes it far more difficult for Democrats to win the state. By 2016 and still more in 2020, most of Ohio's largest cities were well below the number of registered voters from 2008: Cleveland, down 120,000 voters;[457] Cincinnati, down 20,000 voters;[458] Dayton, down 17,000;[459] Akron, down 10,000.[460] If a candidate starts out from a smaller base of her own voters, she has to perform that much better to succeed—and thanks to cutbacks in early voting, now she has less time to do so. For example, Hillary Clinton actually received a higher percentage of the registered voters in Cuyahoga County than Obama did in 2008—44.7% to 41.3%.[461] But because the number registered was so much lower, her margin of victory from the county was only 214,000 votes. Recall that Obama's margin in 2008 was 258,000. Clinton needed to make up ground in other counties as well.[462]

The attack on voting rolls also forces campaigns to devote enormous resources and time in a never-ending effort to re-register purged communities, taxing work that takes away from the vital get out the vote and persuasion efforts (with swing voters) that are also essential. In scanning Ohio in August of 2015, the Clinton campaign would've seen that Cleveland registrations were down from their 2008 level of 374,000 to 246,000,[463] a colossal drop that threatened the campaign from the outset. Registrations were also down elsewhere. After the primary ended, until early vote started, the campaign dedicated almost its entire field effort to registering voters in Democratic areas across the state. In Cleveland, they lifted registrations to 264,000 by the campaign's end, not nearly enough to reach Obama margins of victory. In the meantime, they'd hardly campaigned on the ground outside of those core areas, and that was one reason they lost those areas by far greater numbers than Obama had. Traditional get out the vote organizing with *registered voters* also started far later than necessary.

Now fast forward to October 2019. Thanks to more purging, Cleveland registrations were right back down to 245,000,[464] so the Biden campaign would've faced the same Catch-22 of balancing registration and persuasion. By the end, Biden carried Cuyahoga County by *an even greater percentage* of total registered voters than either Clinton or Obama—46.8%[465] versus 44.7% and 41.2%. But again, because of fewer registered voters than 2008 and 2016, Biden's 213,477 vote margin was lower than both.

Bottom line: around the state, the GOP's endless attacks on the Obama coalition were brutally effective. From purging to narrowing early voting to other obstacles, they used official government actions to directly undermine the emerging political coalition that most threatened them. Not only were the Democratic campaigns unable to claw back those losses, but like a game of "whack a mole," successive campaigns were forced to divert precious resources to combat the obstacles as best they could, hampering other critical campaign work.

If the goal was to crush the involvement of voters who had been so energized in 2008, the state's efforts might have worked even better than they imagined. In the modern era of campaigning, purging has a far bigger effect than what happens on election day. To a fault, today's campaign tactics utilize that list of registered voters for everything they do. In the world of 21st century campaigns, if you're purged from the voter list, you're essentially banished to a political netherworld. No phone calls. No mail. No door knocks. While that may make life a little quieter around election time, it also means communities with high levels of purging are far less engaged politically than those with less purging. And overall participation drops from there. It's a downward spiral.

And the effect goes way beyond the presidential elections. In 2005, a young me ran for mayor of Cincinnati. I lost in a tight race, 37,206 to 34,268.[466] The 2009 race was a low-profile re-election, but the next two elections were not. Still, total turnout was way down in 2013—less than 58,000 total votes. And in 2017, it was still under 61,000. The Black portion of turnout was precipitously lower than in 2005.

In Dayton, the winning mayor candidate in 2005 won 18,258 out of more than 33,000 votes. Eight years later, only half that number of voters showed up to vote for mayor. In a city of more than 140,000 people, the winner of the mayor's race secured victory by winning just over 9,000 votes.[467] Toledo saw 79,000 residents vote for mayor in 2001; in a fiercely contested race in 2015, only 51,500 did. [468]

Bottom line: the past ten years confirmed for the legislature that altering the rules of elections through official actions can kneecap their political competition come election time, with consequences at all levels.

Lesson 2: Never Stop Fighting

The decade of attacks on voting rights also reconfirmed the lesson of Chapter Seven—throw as much forward as possible, and never stop fighting.

Some proposals will advance, some won't. Some earn unwelcome attention, others fall under the radar. Some get stopped in court, some don't. But the harder you push, the more become law.

And the more you put forward, and the more you keep fighting, the more you can adjust strategies and correct errors along the way.

In 2011, a petition drive stopped the legislature's biggest voting bill in its tracks. So, they pulled the law back, cancelled the election, and repackaged it into other mini-bills in the coming years. According to former representative Clyde:

> they were incensed. [So] they took that bill and shoved it down our throats by splitting it up into ten or fifteen bills so we couldn't possibly hit them again with a referendum. And the first one out of the gate was a bill reducing the number of days you have to collect signatures for a referendum.

Many became law, and multiple lessons were learned.

Court fights all the way to the United States Supreme Court stopped key provisions of some bills, but also illuminated legal errors that could be corrected. So they repackaged the laws, brought them back, and some still got enacted. "Golden Week" was finally eliminated on the third try.

Even the 2011 Senate Bill 5 labor fight forced Ohio's unions to spend millions just to maintain the status quo only a year prior to a presidential election.

Bottom line: the decade proved that the more the legislature kept pressing forward, the more it succeeded.

Lesson 3: No accountability:
You'll get re-elected—even promoted

The third lesson from the decade also mirrors that of Chapter Seven: there's no reason to stop pressing forward because there's no accountability for even the most egregious attempts to suppress the vote. Walled off in rigged districts and protected by monied interests and anonymity, statehouses turn out to be the perfect launch point of attacks on voting. They can keep firing away without ever worrying about consequences.

Think about how far they went, beyond just the basic offense of attacking voting rights:

They publicly admitted that their goal was to target Black and young voters . . . no problem, even in court.

They denied the citizens their constitutionally-granted right to repeal a law they didn't like, after they'd gathered 100,000s of signatures . . . no problem.

Federal judge after federal judge ruled that they violated the constitutional rights of their own voters. They wasted millions of tax dollars defending against all those suits, and the bill was paid for by the very people whose rights they violated. Yet still, no problem. They've never been held accountable for any of it.

Volunteers discovered that hundreds of thousands of voters have been kicked off the rolls by *government error and incompetence.* The legislature doesn't even bother to correct the problem, or even look into it. They move forward, and even more errors result. No matter.

You get the point. Gerrymandering and the overall frenzy of activity means individual legislators can do all these things, and more, and still coast to reelection. While they've secured huge gains politically by attacking voting rights, they've paid zero political price for doing so.

Worse, some have even been promoted.

Frank LaRose was a state senator who, by his own admission,[469] voted for every anti-voter bill described above. He led the charge on the attack on "Golden Week" that finally took hold, with its clearly disproportionate impact on Ohio's Black voters.[470] He voted to enhance Ohio's purging with the disastrous Cross-Check system. He voted to keep counties from prepaying postage on absentee ballots. He voted for each wave of attacks on the final three days of voting which were found unconstitutional, and he voted to preemptively repeal the 2011 bill that citizens had successfully gathered signatures for. With that shameful record of attacking voting rights, it took some chutzpah for LaRose to run for secretary of state, *claiming to be a moderate*. But it worked! In endorsing him, the *Columbus Dispatch* wrote that LaRose had shown "bipartisanship and civility," a "record of support for easier voting," and was the "go-to lawmaker for bills aimed at improving voting and elections."[471]

State Rep. Kathleen Clyde was LaRose's opponent, having spent the prior eight years fighting to end purging, add automatic voter registration, and reject all the other anti-voter bills. She served as an expert witness in court. And was proven right again and again in her predictions. According to the *Dispatch*, her tireless efforts to stop the legislature's rampant suppression made *her the one* who was "more partisan in a time when the need for nonpartisan leadership in Ohio has never been greater."[472] Even papers who endorsed Clyde framed it as a decision between "two good choices," as Clyde puts it, not mentioning the leading role LaRose had played suppressing votes all decade.

LaRose won narrowly, and—surprise—immediately continued the same anti-voter measures he had voted for in the legislature.

Why not aggressively suppress the vote year after year if even the newspapers paying attention give you a pass, enabling you to do it again?

Lesson 4: The Legislature Remains in the Driver's Seat

A final lesson, drawing on the reality from Chapter Two that state legislators control the terms of elections, is that in the end, they're the boss. And that shapes so much of their behavior, as well as the behavior of the secretary of state.

The legislature sets the rules, passing law after law which the secretary of state is then responsible for implementing. He chooses whether to endorse these proposals, but is stuck with them either way. Most of the time, Jon Husted simply defended what they did, in public and in court. LaRose was so deferential, he'd claim the legislature was in charge even when they weren't. He spent two years refusing to allow voters to request absentee ballots on-line or by email, saying only the legislature could allow that—a lawsuit (yes, we filed that one too) proved him wrong again.[473]

Of course, if legislators support what the secretary of state is doing, they can sit back and let it happen while protecting his actions if others try to stop it. Or they can take steps to urge it on. That was the purging story in Ohio, where the legislative majority refused to let colleagues fix or even slow the process even when its problems became painfully clear. Eliminating the same-day registration opportunity of "Golden Week" while never taking up automatic voter registration were other backdoor ways of ensuring that the pain of purging stuck.

At the same time, when the secretary of state wants to pursue something the legislators don't like, they can step in to stop it. LaRose, for example, requested funding to pay for postage for absentee ballots in the 2020 election. The legislature said no, and that was that.

The legislature can even get ahead of issues proactively, as they did when they banned county officials from sending out absentee ballot applications or pre-paying postage. And would later do so by limiting drop boxes.

In fact, so much of what they did served as a preview for 2021. But before we get there, let's widen our lens on the attacks on voters. Once again, as aggressive as Ohio was, it was just a bellwether.

2011-2020: Attacks on Voters Everywhere

As the lawsuit challenging Ohio's purging process made its way through the courts, states from across the country watched closely. So, too, did voting rights advocates. At the time, at least nine states pursued a similar "use it or lose it" purging approach.[474] Most others stayed away, for good reason. On paper, at least, federal law forbids states from using a person's "failure to vote" as a reason to purge the rolls. But Ohio's system actually considers a person's failure to vote *twice*—for two years on the front end, and for four more years after the confirmation notice is sent. On its face, that would appear to violate federal law, and it's why Ohio gained the reputation as the most aggressive state in the country when it came to purging voters (again, #1 in all the wrong things). And it's the likely reason that more states didn't use a process as aggressive as Ohio's.

So, when Justice Alito (writing for a 5-4 majority) reached the head-scratching conclusion that sending a postcard to voters cleansed the process of any violation of federal law,[475] it meant all nine states were in the clear. Georgia, which purged 1.4 million voters over the decade,[476] could keep doing what it was doing, just as its secretary of state was running for governor; and Georgia's next secretary of state would continue to purge right up until the 2020 presidential election. Other states would do the same. But it also meant that any other states holding back before the decision now had a new, Court-approved model of purging to pursue in coming years. In celebrating the decision, Husted proudly declared that the Ohio process "can serve as a model for other states to use."[477] Other conservative voices echoed him.[478] Advocates of voting rights understandably feared that other states would do exactly that.[479] By pursuing the most aggressive model of purging in the country, and winning in court, Ohio had just opened a path every other state could pursue.

Sound familiar?

As in Chapter Seven, this purging example captures the broader dynamic that played out across the country on voting rights. Motivated by the 2008 election loss and empowered to take action by the 2010 GOP election wins, states aggressively attacked voting rights in a wide variety of ways. As they rushed forward in pursuit of similar goals, they created models of voter suppression others could adopt. And as with purging, these attacks received a series of boosts from the Supreme Court along the way—clearing the way for new and more aggressive laws all over the country, with new court precedents leading to the next round of laws.

Stricter voter identification laws were among the first to appear, emerging even before 2010. In 2008, the Supreme Court upheld Indiana's new photo ID law even when more than 40,000 Hoosiers lacked the required ID.[480] The Court ruled that states didn't need to prove fraud to justify these voter ID laws (fraud almost never actually occurs, so the proof would be next to impossible), but only assert that preventing fraud was the generalized reason behind the law. With that flashing green light, other states moved quickly. Now, nineteen states have photo identification requirements, and another four have "strict"[481] non-photo identification requirements. Another thirteen have "non-strict" identification requirements which don't require photo identification.[482] Along the way, the Supreme Court gave these efforts a second thumbs up, letting stand a sweeping new voter ID law in Texas in 2014 after a lower court had struck it down for being discriminatory.[483]

Then came attacks on the early vote process. As in Ohio, the success of the Obama campaign with early vote invited a fierce backlash in other states. In 2012, Georgia slashed its early vote window from 45 to 21 days. Florida, Wisconsin, West Virginia, Tennessee, Nebraska and other states also cut back. North Carolina reduced its early vote window in 2013.[484] Texas saw a surge in early voting over the decade, then cracked down on the use of early voting locations in 2019.[485] North Carolina also cut back on the number of those locations.[486] Laws were also passed around absentee/mail-in voting, usually taking the form of strict signature match requirements that led to ballots being thrown out.[487]

The motivation behind these laws was as clear as in Ohio. A Pennsylvania legislator bragged that their voter ID law "is gonna allow Governor Romney to win the state of Pennsylvania."[488] And in North Carolina, one state senator used virtually the same words as the Ohio officials to justify reducing early voting. Since the state had loosened early voting, it's "been altered over the years, maybe *tainted* in one direction," (my emphasis) the state senator explained. "It got abused. It was never designed to give one group an advantage over another."[489] As Ari Berman pointed out, it's hard to imagine he wasn't referring to the fact that 70% of Black North Carolinians voted early in 2012, as opposed to 50% of White voters.[490]

Between 2010 and 2020, a dozen states threw obstacles into the process of registering to vote, both as individual voters and groups. Some states required proof of citizenship (Alabama, Kansas, Georgia, Tennessee), others enacted "strict match" requirements which make the registration process more difficult (Georgia), particularly for people of color, and others added limitations on how groups can mount registration drives (Georgia, Florida, Iowa, Tennessee, Texas, Virginia). Still others, such as North Carolina and Iowa, followed Ohio in eliminating opportunities for same-day registration.[491] Again, their intent was plain, as Georgia's then-secretary of state made clear when defending an effort to hinder voter registration drives: "Democrats are working hard . . . , you know, registering all these minority voters out there . . . ., if they can do that, they can win these elections in November."[492]

The effect of individual laws alone was enormous. For example, voter ID requirements keep millions of voters from voting. According to the Brennan Center: "As many as 11 percent of eligible voters do not have the kind of ID that is required by states with strict ID requirements, and that percentage is even higher among seniors, minorities, people with disabilities, low-income voters, and students."[493] And as one 2017 study summarized: "strict identification laws have a differentially negative impact on the turnout of racial and ethnic minorities in primaries and general elections."[494] In reviewing the impact on the 2014 election, the Center for American Progress and other groups estimated that one million voters were negatively impacted by the Texas strict voter ID law alone, and found sizeable impacts elsewhere:

- the Alabama strict voter ID law negatively impacted between 250,000 and 500,000 voters;

- the North Carolina early vote reduction, 200,000 people;

- the Virginia strict photo ID law, almost 200,000 people; and

- registration delays in Georgia, 40,000 people.[495]

These impacts were larger than the margin of victory in some state-wide elections in those years.[496] In Wisconsin, for example, best estimates were that 300,000 voters lacked the types of identification required by a voter ID law that passed in 2011 (the legal fight over which ended in 2015).[497] In 2016, Wisconsin saw its lowest voter turnout since 2000, and after-election analysis found many voters—and disproportionally minority and low-income voters—didn't show up because they didn't have the proper ID or were confused about what the law required.[498] Trump won the state by only 22,000 votes.[499]

Importantly, the Supreme Court's 2013 decision in *Shelby County v. Holder* allowed new restrictions to explode in places where they wouldn't have been permitted before. By gutting Section 5 of the Voting Rights Act, the Court empowered states that would've previously needed to receive pre-approval by the Department of Justice for any proposed voting changes. Faced with no pre-clearance requirement and the less onerous standards of Section 2 of the VRA, these states were liberated to rush forward with new laws. In North Carolina, for example, only three weeks after *Shelby* came down, that state's legislature introduced legislation that: added strict voter ID rules; shortened early vote by a week (900,000 had voted in that week in 2012); eliminated same-day registration (100,000 had registered and voted on the same day); eliminated state supported voter registration drives; and increased the frequency of purging.[500] Stopping such an aggressive law would likely have been a "slam dunk" under Section 5.[501] But without that tool, challenges to the North Carolina changes proved mostly unsuccessful. Other Southern states noted this clear lesson and charged forward with equal vigor in the years that followed.

Finally, not only did attacks on unions undermine states' economies and delivery of public services,[502] they had their desired effect of undermining a core part of the political coalition resisting ALEC/Koch interests. The unionized segment of the American workforce declined over the decade by almost two million workers, eroding on the public side while falling especially fast on the private side.[503] The results varied dramatically by region, but some of the targeted states suffered the steepest decline. In Wisconsin, for example, the attacks were "wildly successful."[504] Union membership plummeted after Governor Walker's victory—dropping from 14.2% of the state's workforce in 2010 (above the national average), to 8.7% in 2020 (below).[505] It was 24% in 1979.[506] Public sector union membership fell from 60% in 2010 to under 20% only seven years later.[507] Wisconsin, long viewed as a labor stronghold, now sits in the bottom third of the nation.[508]

Not surprisingly, national groups like ALEC played a key role in fomenting many of these battles. ALEC itself was a prime behind-the-scenes driver of strict voter ID laws and proof of citizenship registration laws.[509] The laws passed in Wisconsin, Texas, Pennsylvania and many other states were all based on ALEC's model ID law.[510] When a number of corporations fled ALEC following the Trayvon Martin killing, ALEC publicly claimed to shut down its voter suppression work along with its criminal justice work (they had been housed in the same Public Safety and Elections task force). But just as with "Stand Your Ground" laws, the consequences of their work continued. The model laws were still out there,

ALEC members kept plugging away on other laws, and by 2019, ALEC was back at it directly, convening a new working group on elections to tackle voting issues such as vote by mail and purging.[511] They had an "exclusive" call in June 2020 to discuss mail-in voting with members across the country.[512] And in a preview of things to come, they did this work in partnership with other dark-money groups dedicated to attacking voting rights.[513]

No surprise, after attending a national ALEC meeting where voting issues were discussed, Ohio's Cindy Abrams, a first-term legislator and ALEC member, put forward the 2020 legislation forbidding pre-paid postage from absentee ballots. Advocates who scrutinized the bill and observed her describe it said it was clear she hadn't written it: "[I]t became evident that she didn't realize the bill included changes to election administration beyond emergencies and the upcoming general election."[514]

After 2016: Undermining Election Outcomes

Finally, late in the decade, another form of legislative attack emerged. A new wrinkle, and a sneak preview of a far bigger trend that would explode in 2021.

In Chapter Five, we reviewed the twisted consequences of an entire generation of political majorities never experiencing a real election. Well, most in that generation also never faced a statewide official from the other party. For most of the decade, in most states, these legislatures shared power with governors of the same party. But that changed beginning in 2016. And as they did after 2008 and 2012 nationally, some of these legislatures took losing . . . sorely.

Their responses weren't attacks on voting rights per se— those continued regardless. What followed in some states were attacks on the *very outcome* that voters had forged in the recent election. They attacked democracy not on the front end, but after the fact.

It started in North Carolina after a Democrat won the governor's race there in 2016. Within weeks, the legislature and losing governor came together to rush through a series of restrictions binding the new governor. For the first time, the state's governor would need legislative approval for his cabinet selections. The legislature also slashed the size of his administration (by two-thirds), and the size and makeup of the state- and county-level boards of elections. And they rigged it so that Republicans could control those boards in election years—and keep control out of the hands of the governor.[515] They next stripped the governor of his power to name trustees to the University of North Carolina board. And having just lost the majority on the North Carolina Supreme Court, the legislature also mandated that party identification appear on the ballot next to judicial candidates, while boosting the jurisdiction of the appeals court, which remained in the hands of Republican-endorsed judges.[516]

No surprise, these maneuvers exploded in controversy, leading to vetoes, veto overrides, and litigation that played out for years. The new governor spent much of his term fighting them, and a precedent was set. Unhappy with an election's outcome (both for governor and the state supreme court), a legislature had taken the audacious step to overturn as much of the impact of that election as it could. One branch of government attacking another; or in North Carolina's case, attacking both other branches.

In 2018, Democrats swept into governorships and other statewide offices in a number of states where the GOP, thanks to gerrymandering, still remained in firm control of legislatures. Would other states follow the North Carolina model?

Wisconsin did so eagerly. In a lame duck session, the Wisconsin legislature rushed through laws eroding the new governor's and attorney general's powers on everything from intervening in (or withdrawing from) law suits on behalf of the state, taking executive action on voter ID and anti-labor laws, and appointing members to Wisconsin's economic development agency. These all negated specific pledges the new governor had made as a candidate on each of these issues—such as promising to pull out of a suit opposing the Affordable Care Act.[517] Legislative leaders admitted this was their way of stopping outcomes they didn't agree with. Robin Vos, Wisconsin's Speaker and former travel companion of Cliff Rosenberger, was blunt: "[W]e are going to have a very liberal governor who is going to enact policies that are in direct contrast to what many of us believe in."[518] The Wisconsin Supreme Court ultimately upheld the changes in a 4-3 decision.[519]

With Democrats (and women) taking every state-wide office in Michigan, Michigan legislators also made a run at undermining the outcome. As in Wisconsin, they tried to block the new governor's and attorney general's ability to dictate the state's positions on legal cases, and they tried to strip the new secretary of state's oversight of campaign finance issues.[520] To his credit, outgoing Governor Rick Snyder vetoed the bill on legal cases, and other power-stripping bills died in the legislature.[521]

Overall, the current Democratic chair of Wisconsin described the precedent in appropriately bleak terms: "Republican legislatures, even in defeat, reaching out from the political grave to pull the democratically elected victors down with them."[522] But the "victors" they pulled down weren't only elected officials. They often were the people themselves, because the precedent also carried over into another type of elections— direct initiatives and referenda.

Partly in response to the extreme direction of these legislatures, citizens and groups waged statewide ballot fights around the country, succeeding on a wide range of issues. In 2016, the voters of Maine directly raised the minimum wage while hiking taxes on the most well-off to support education. In South Dakota, citizens voted in campaign finance reform and curbs on lobbying. In Nevada, they enacted background checks for gun sales.[523] In 2018, Missouri voters overwhelmingly amended the districting process while also reforming campaign finance and lobbying practices.[524] And in Florida, voters ended a years-long practice of disenfranchising Floridians with felony records.

All of these successful elections rejected the ALEC-style direction set by these states' gerrymandered legislatures. So, what did the politicians do? They defied every one of these initiatives. They repealed the measures outright in Maine and South Dakota. In Nevada, it took two years and a new legislature to finally fulfil the will of the voters on background checks. In Florida, the legislature required that all felons pay off all fees, fines and restitution before being allowed to vote, which disqualified nearly 800,000 from voting directly contrary to the will of Florida's voters.[525] And in Missouri, the legislature ignored the citizen-led reform for two years before placing its own districting "reform" measure on the ballot, which essentially reversed the real reform from 2018. Carried by Trump's fifteen-point victory, the measure barely passed with 51% of the vote.[526]

At the same time that they defied their own voters' will in state after state, these same legislators got to work on a new priority project: how to make these citizen-led ballot initiatives as difficult as possible. After 2016, in classic 80/20 fashion, legislators across the country began working feverishly to "reform" the initiative process, usually to make it more difficult.[527] Twenty-five such bills passed, adding hurdles and hoops to the citizen-led process in Arizona, Maine, South Dakota and other states.[528] Of course, this overall effort to strip citizens of their direct democratic power vis-a-vis gerrymandered legislatures dovetailed perfectly with a model policy that ALEC had long ago passed: a resolution to "Preserve the Legislative Process" and discourage ballot initiatives.[529]

*   *   *

Whew. That's a lot. All in one decade.

Before we move on, take a step back. Think about what this last section in particular tells us.

For a decade, legislators in numerous states, who were largely in office thanks to rigged districts and the other dynamics described in Chapters Two through Six, fiercely pursued measures to strip voters of their rights. And they did it with the (sometimes express) purpose of changing the outcome of national and statewide elections by targeting the coalition that had bested them in 2008 and 2012. That's called cheating. That alone is anti-democratic.

Despite that, in 2016 and 2018, in multiple ways and in multiple states, some of the cheaters lost. Sure, they won in some places, but lost in others.

And they didn't simply lose in that Democrats won governorships and other offices. Or that voters approved ballot measures that ran counter to their policies. In many of these states, these legislators "lost" in another way. Remember Chapter Four. In Michigan, across the state, voters voted for Democratic statehouse candidates by a combined 52%-47% over Republican candidates. Only the egregious gerrymander kept the losing side in power. Same story in Wisconsin, where voters opted for Democrats by 54%-45% but the state's rigged map kept Republicans in power.

Let that sink in:

The winning governors had won on an unrigged map, having powered over and through steep voter suppression obstacles the legislators had tossed their way. Still, they prevailed.

Even with all that suppression, the legislative leaders *lost* across the same states, remaining in power only due to a wholly rigged and undemocratic system that assures they can never lose.

Despite *all* of that, it was these undemocratic legislatures that asserted power. Imagine Wisconsin's Vos, entirely comfortable stripping the newly elected governor of power because that governor would advocate policies "in direct contrast to what many of us believe in."[530] *Many* of you, yes. But not the majority. Not even close. Just those locked into power due to a rigged system propped up by monied interests and egged on by groups like ALEC.

State voters had spoken as clearly as possible. A clear majority.

But state representatives across the country—who most voters in their own district couldn't name, who've never faced a true election beyond their first primary, whose ecosystem rewards them for doing the polar opposite of what's needed in their struggling hometowns—didn't care.

Same story in states where voters overwhelmingly passed initiatives. Again, a generation of undemocratic legislators faced the reality that their own voters wholly reject their approach on a given issue. What did they do? They defied their own voters, overturned the new laws however they could, and then set out to make it harder for those voters to ever again undertake such efforts going forward.

And through all this defiance of democracy and its traditional outcomes, the laboratory just kept chugging away, always learning how to do its work more effectively. As in Ohio, many of their attacks on voting and democracy succeeded. And when they failed, they picked up the pieces, learned from other states' successes, and tried again. And despite the audacity of this egregiously anti-democratic behavior, they still learned the other key lesson: there is *never* accountability.

Keep fighting. Make progress. Never retreat from short-term failure. And no worries, you'll never be held accountable.

Scary stuff.

And the clearest preview possible.

CHAPTER 9

2021: The Culmination

EMEMBER HOW VOTING rights groups found all those purging mistakes in Ohio in 2019?

Their work represented the best of American democracy. Volunteers heroically poring over the list of voters to be purged, calling thousands of their fellow Ohioans to alert them that they were on the list and needed to take action. Along the way, uncovering the truth . . . that 40,000 were listed in error. If it weren't for these groups' actions, so many more voters would've been purged going into the 2020 election, many due to no fault of their own. And Ohio would never have known about how broken its purging process is.

And recall how the legislature refused to do anything about this?

Well, in 2021, that changed.

They finally acted.

They passed a law forbidding the secretary of state from collaborating with or expending any resources working with groups like these to register voters or undertake other election-related activities.[531] So as Ohio keeps purging voters through an error-strewn process, never again, the legislature commanded, should groups be able to play their 2019 role of working with the secretary of state's office to uncover those errors or re-register purged voters.

That law came at the same time as the bill to ban more drop boxes was moving forward. That same bill would also eliminate the final Monday of early vote (which 60,000 voters used in 2020). And would add ID requirements for vote by mail. And reduce the time to request a vote-by-mail ballot. Months later, a new bill was introduced to eliminate *all* drop boxes, while also eliminating the entire early vote process that came after the disastrous 2004 election. And all of these laws are coming on the heels of an election that Ohio Republicans like Frank LaRose have touted as having been clean and fraud-free. So clearly, combating fraud is not the motivation behind these new changes.

Meanwhile, on the same day the legislature voted to hamstring those groups, a different kind of elections bill sailed through. More so than the others, it represented a fundamental breach of another core principle of American governance. Yet amid the flurry, it got far less attention.

Here's the background:

The greatest Democratic overperformance in the 2020 election occurred in Ohio, when appellate Judge Jennifer Brunner toppled a sitting Ohio Supreme Court Justice by ten points. In Ohio, judicial races don't have a party ID listed on the ballot. But the parties do endorse candidates. Brunner was the Democratic-endorsed candidate; the opponent she toppled, the Republican-endorsed candidate. An eighteen-point swing (Donald Trump won Ohio by eight points) is a decisive win, especially in an election when only five Democratic candidates in the entire nation picked up statewide seats in states Trump won.

But the win wasn't a fluke. It was the third win in four races for the Democratic-endorsed candidate for the Ohio Supreme

Court, taking the Court from 7-0 to 4-3 in only two years. Along the way, Democratic-endorsed judicial candidates also unseated numerous incumbents at the appellate level across the state, securing a majority of Ohio's appellate judicial seats for the first time in memory. Democratic-endorsed candidates also made big gains in large counties such as Hamilton, Franklin (Columbus) and Summit (Akron). Together these changes provided much-needed balance in state government, where an independent bench can review laws that emerge from the legislature (including the new legislative districts), with the power to strike them down if they violate the Ohio Constitution.

Checks and balances. Y'know, how it's supposed to work in America.

There are a number of reasons why these judicial candidates did so well in recent years. Most important, many of the winning candidates, like Justice Brunner, previously Ohio's secretary of state, were long-time public servants with strong reputations. And they campaigned well. But due to a lot of hard work by folks at all levels, they also were boosted by another phenomenon called "drop-off." In a change from prior decades, Democratic voters showed a far higher propensity to vote all the way through their ballot (including in the judicial elections, where no party affiliation appeared on the ballot). Voters who showed up largely to vote for Donald Trump were less informed on judicial races, and far fewer voted in them as a result (not voting in those lower races is what we call "drop-off"). The difference in the two levels of "drop-off" provided a boost to Democratic-endorsed candidates all around the state, and that's one reason the court has reached a close balance for the first time in a generation.

Now we worked hard to reduce drop-off on our end. And in the spring of 2021, Republicans unveiled their "drop-off" plan.

Recruit better candidates? Nah. Better inform their voters with slate cards and digital ads (like we had done)? Nope.

Simpler than that. They went to the statehouse and did something they and so many other statehouses have grown accustomed to doing over the past decade. They changed the rules. They passed a bill that, for the first time in Ohio history, makes judicial elections fully partisan. Forever more, judicial candidates will have their party ID listed on the ballot. The proposal met with pushback from every level of the judicial bench and bar—in fact, the last two Ohio Chief Justices (both Republican-endorsed) had advocated steps to make the courts *less* partisan. But the law making the Court *fully partisan* passed with little overall fanfare or attention. The legislators clearly hope this change will solve their "drop-off" problem without the GOP having to spend a dime to better inform their voters who's who.

While the proponents of the change claimed it was somehow principled, those watching understood why they took this action now. Most telling was that while their new law requires party ID on the ballot for appellate and supreme court races, it continues to *leave out* party ID at the county level. Why? Because if party ID were on the ballot at the county level, every remaining Republican-endorsed judge in Ohio's larger counties (which have all turned blue) would be swept from office. So, they changed the rule to benefit their candidates at the appellate and supreme court levels, but adopted the *opposite* approach to protect valued judgeships at the county level. All power, no principle. Truly rigging the rules to maximize election outcomes.

While breathtakingly simple, like North Carolina after 2016, what the legislature did here represents a fundamental breach of democratic norms. Ohio's Supreme Court has jurisdiction over everything the legislature does, including gerrymandering. It plays a crucial role in the checks and balances of Ohio government. Ohio's new, independent judiciary has arisen as the greatest threat to the legislature's rigged grip on power, so the statehouse immediately went to war on its co-equal branch to undermine its ability to play that role.

And the legislature won.

My guess is almost no Ohioans know this change happened. There were a few headlines, but that was it. Why did a law this breathtaking get so little attention? Because again, it was lost amid the far-right budget, and the other new voting rules, and a torrent of other laws in Ohio and across the nation. Laws which not only attacked voting rights, and there were plenty of those. But laws that built on what happened in North Carolina in 2016, and Wisconsin in 2018. Laws attacking other core tenets of democratic government. So many, no one could keep up with them all.

*   *   *

2021: The Gun Goes Off

November 3, 2020 will go down as one of the most consequential days in our nation's long history. The day that Donald Trump was defeated.

But beneath the surface, November 3 was consequential for an entirely different reason. It was the day that the gerrymandered statehouse maps of 2011 held. If the "blue wave" of 2018 wasn't enough to topple the rigged statehouse districts that were drawn back in 2011, 2020 wasn't even close. In fact, in many states, Republicans saw a rebound from 2018, picking up seats all over. Despite more focus and investment than in 2010—including an effort by former president Obama and his attorney general, Eric Holder—Democrats failed to pick up a single statehouse from the ones they had lost in 2010, which were then gerrymandered in 2011. (Virginia and Nevada flipped earlier in the decade).

Amid the drama in the days after the election—as Biden victories were confirmed in Georgia, Pennsylvania, Michigan and Arizona, and Trump began to claim that the election had been stolen—the statehouse story hardly made news.

But the awareness exploded a few months later, as hundreds of bills moved forward attacking democracy more aggressively than even the prior decade.

These attacks were met with shock and surprise by many observers. They were usually framed as an outgrowth of Trump's "Big Lie" that the election was stolen. As some kind of effort to save Trump. But that narrative was overly simplistic. The "Big Lie" might've provided a cover for these actions; fealty to Trump an added bonus. But these laws weren't new at all. They were a natural extension of prior years—a culmination of a decade of dry runs, perfected over time by all that these laboratories of autocracy had learned. Like 2011, many of the new laws targeted the modes and mechanisms of voting that Democratic voters had most utilized in the 2020 election, such as drop boxes and other vote by mail opportunities. Others drew from the most effective suppression tactics from around the country in recent years—sadly, Ohio's tactics proved to be quite popular. Still others followed the model of Wisconsin and North Carolina legislators after 2018 and 2016 losses—directly attacking other branches of government. Not only as a way to undo recent results and weaken emerging threats to power, but as a way to rig *future* outcomes.

Doubling Down on Voting Rights Attacks

Like a decade before, statehouses kicked off their 2021 terms by immediately targeting voting rights. And as in 2011, when their goal was to dismantle the Obama coalition, they again focused on the modes of voting that had most boosted their opponents in the preceding election.

Amid the pandemic and an overall surge in turnout, *early voting by mail (including by drop boxes)* played a huge role in the 2020 election, its usage more than twice what it was in 2016.[532] So that was first up on the legislative hit list, with half of the nation's statehouses pushing bills to limit early vote in a variety of ways.[533] They shortened the windows for voting by mail (and requesting ballots), limited the proactive mailing of absentee ballots by elections boards, threw new wrenches in the process of receiving a vote-by-mail ballot, and added voter ID and signature requirements for mail voting.[534]

As in Ohio, *drop boxes* became an especially popular target even though they hadn't previously been a source of either controversy or problems. Or even partisan strife. Georgia elections boards had provided drop boxes widely in the 2020 election. Most were at local libraries, conveniently located outside and accessible 24/7. These drop boxes were used far more by minority and urban voters than rural voters. Overall, Biden won almost two of every three of Georgia's 1.3 million absentee votes,[535] and in the four Georgia counties where Biden performed best, 56% of those early voters dropped their ballot in a drop box.[536]

Georgia legislators changed that right quick. First, they dramatically reduced the number of drop boxes overall (from 94 to 23 in metropolitan Atlanta). They also mandated that drop boxes only be located within in-person early vote locations, and only be operated at the same time those sites are open. Going forward, drop boxes will also now close down the Friday before election day. As in Ohio, these changes largely defeat the purpose of drop boxes while adding to congestion at already busy early vote centers.[537] While they were at it, Georgia also reduced early voting hours in numerous counties, and eliminated "mobile" voting centers, which more than 11,000 Fulton County voters had used to cast their ballots.[538]

Other states followed suit. A Florida bill would entirely ban drop boxes, where 1.5 million Floridians cast their ballots in the 2020 election.[539] Iowa reduced the overall period of early voting and limited local discretion on both the use of drop boxes and early, in-person vote centers.[540] Texans had flocked to 24-hour early voting sites, including drive-through voting, so a Texas law cut those hours while banning drop boxes and prohibiting the drive-through option.[541] A Wisconsin bill would require that drop boxes be attached to clerk of elections buildings, both reducing the total number of drop boxes and adding to congestion.[542]

Jon Husted's dream that other states would adopt Ohio's "use it or lose it" *purging policies* also came true. Iowa enacted a law deeming voters "inactive" for missing a single federal election.[543] Arizona used the same approach for voters on lists to receive absentee ballots, potentially knocking off hundreds of thousands of voters and, disproportionately, Latinos.[544] A new Texas law levies financial penalties on elections officials for not adequately purging voters from the rolls,[545] and other states pushed for new, suspect lists to be used to ramp up purging.[546]

Other states built on practices refined over the prior decade: ratcheting up voter ID requirements (85 bills in 32 states),[547] eliminating same-day registration, banning automatic voter registration, reducing the amount of time voters have to correct errors (Arizona), and forbidding funding support from third-party groups that had helped pay for pro-voter activities or infrastructure in 2020.[548] Ohio's approach of tossing ballots for small mistakes emerged elsewhere.[549] Georgia and Florida prohibited anyone but poll workers from handing out food and water to any voters stuck waiting in lines thanks to all these other restrictions.[550] Not coincidentally, wait times averaged more than 45 minutes in each of the counties of metro Atlanta, the diverse region that delivered victory for Biden and other Democratic candidates.[551]

As occurred after 2011, many of these new laws will face court fights. The Department of Justice filed suit in June against the new Georgia law, alleging intentional racial discrimination. We can only hope some of these suits are successful, although a 2021 Supreme Court decision "gutted most of what remains of the landmark Voting Rights Act," making the battle to overturn these laws more difficult.[552] As a result, many of these new rules will inevitably remain intact, with other states sure to adopt those that survive scrutiny. That's how 80/20 works.

But these more standard voter suppression tactics were only the beginning of the 2021 legislative onslaught against democracy.

Knee-Capping Emerging Threats

Just as the Ohio legislature took aim at an emerging independent Supreme Court, legislatures around the country targeted other officials they saw as threats—both when it came to elections, and the overall balance of power in their states. As opposed to attacks on voters, which rig the rules *before* the votes are counted, these changes risk altering outcomes both *as and after* votes are counted.

Most troubling, they stripped power from secretaries of state in two states where the 2020 election was closest.

After the 2020 election, Georgia Secretary of State Brad Raffensperger became a household name after rebuffing Trump's attempts to reverse the outcome there. Even though he'd been an active participant in suppression efforts heading into the election, good for him for defending the Georgia election outcome. He did exactly what we should hope (and once assumed) every secretary of state would do.

Apparently, the Georgia legislature had different expectations. So within their broader bill attacking voting rights, they stripped away some of the secretary's core powers. Specifically, they removed the secretary from chairing the State Elections Board, and in his place, the legislature anointed itself as the appointee of the board chair. Combined with its two other legislative appointments to the five-person board, the gerrymandered legislature essentially grabbed control of Georgia elections. The law also gave the newly constituted state board the power to replace local elections officials and boards outright with individual administrators of their choosing—and shortly thereafter began targeting officials in Fulton County, the state's largest county, where Biden won 73% of the vote.[553] One of the most important roles these local boards play is determining voter eligibility, and what ballots should be disqualified. Rather than insulating that process from politics, now those decisions and others ultimately fall under the state legislature via the State Elections Board.[554]

Arizona was another key state that swung the election Biden's way. In fact, the networks' (including Fox News) calling Arizona on election night proved to be the back breaker of the Trump campaign; Trump had counted on having the electoral college majority undecided as he discredited outcomes in close states like Michigan and Pennsylvania that would be counting mail-in votes for days. The Arizona call foiled that plan, so there was hell to pay in the Grand Canyon State. One of many steps the legislature took was targeting the secretary of state by shifting her power to manage election-related lawsuits over to the state's attorney general, a Republican. To be clear, the power to direct the state's legal position in an election lawsuit is the power to change the outcome. And like the Ohio judicial change, any principle behind this law was negated by the fact that the change only lasts for the remainder of the term of the current secretary of state, a Democrat.[555]

While these were the most high-profile changes, other states took similar steps, curbing both executive and local elections officials' powers and discretion over elections, or lawsuits that arise from them. From Arkansas to Texas, Missouri to Tennessee, state officials are pushing bills to restrain local elections officials over a wide variety of decisions, such as sending out absentee ballots.[556] And just as Georgia added a mechanism for the new state board to terminate elections officials, numerous states added similar measures, including replacement mechanisms, fines and even criminal sanctions.[557]

Like secretaries of state, state supreme courts had frustrated legislatures both before and after the 2020 election with various rulings. As a result, numerous legislatures—including Arizona, Georgia, Kansas, Kentucky and others—passed or are considering laws limiting state courts' ability to rule in election-related cases.[558] More broadly, the Brennan Center identified at least 93 proposed laws in at least 26 states which "politicize[d] or undermine[d] the independence of state courts."[559] From restricting judicial powers, to ramping up discipline against state judges, to the "gerrymandering" of judicial districts to rig the makeup of state courts, the full-out assault on independent courts in these states is breathtaking.[560]

And as in Ohio, numerous legislatures took up legislation making the election or appointment of judges and justices more partisan. Seven other states considered laws to add partisan labels to some or all judicial races. And in a number of states where judges are appointed as opposed to elected, legislators pushed bills to make the process more political and less subject to non-partisan checks currently in place (such as diluting the role played by non-partisan judicial selection commissions).[561]

Beyond legislation itself, state legislators played a leading role in the unprecedented effort to independently (translation: illegitimately) "audit" the results of the 2020 election long after President Biden was sworn in. Back in Arizona, after four standard audits confirmed that the results were valid, the state senate subpoenaed more than two million ballots and voting machines from Maricopa County. It then selected a cybersecurity firm called Cyber Ninjas—which had no experience conducting post-election audits—to review those ballots and overall results again.[562] This audit didn't follow any of the standard election audit procedures, including that officials from both parties observe the work; at one point, Cyber Ninjas proposed going door to door as part of the audit, but the DOJ stepped in to stop it. The secretary of state has announced that all the machines the firm handled must now be replaced for security reasons, costing millions, and even local Republican officials decried it as illegitimate.[563] And the widespread distribution of voting machinery and software as part of these "audits" has heightened the risk of future election meddling.[564] Still, even before the audit results were in, the vice chair of the Arizona Senate's judiciary committee tweeted that she was ready to decertify the election.[565]

Legislators elsewhere adopted the Arizona approach,

with a number making personal pilgrimages to Arizona to observe Cyber Ninjas' work up close. State legislators in Michigan,[566] Pennsylvania,[567] and Wisconsin[568] have all called for similar audits in their states. Wisconsin's Speaker Robin Vos announced his intention to hire a police official and an attorney to look into the election outcome.[569] And even though the Georgia secretary of state of his own party verified the election there through multiple audits, the Georgia Republican chair is calling for an Arizona-style audit in the Peach State.[570] Audit fever has even spread into states that Trump *won*, with legislators in Utah, North Carolina, Florida, Texas and others pushing to audit their 2020 results.[571]

If they're willing to overturn a presidential outcome, state legislators certainly don't shy from overturning the results of referenda, as they proved after 2016 and 2018. Missouri voters learned that for a second time in early 2021. Back in August of 2020, voters amended the state's constitution to allow expansion of Medicaid,[572] something neither the state's governors nor legislators had been willing to do. Learning from the experience in other states,[573] the measure even included a provision that prohibited the state legislature from limiting state Medicaid eligibility beyond the limitations in Medicaid itself.[574] Still basking in their victory of having overturned the 2018 gerrymandering amendment, the legislature instantly neutered this one as well. They simply allocated zero funds in the budget for the approved expansion, leaving close to 200,000 Missourians who would've been eligible without coverage.[575] While the governor had initially promised to follow the will of the voters, he ultimately went along with the legislature's decision. The senate minority leader accused him of "caving to the new Authoritarian Republican Regime that doesn't respect the outcome of elections."[576] It took the Missouri Supreme Court to step in and reverse the legislature.[577] No surprise, Missouri is one of the states where the legislature is trying to undermine the Supreme Court's power.[578]

Behind the Scenes Scheming

Of course, building on the model of the prior decade, this flurry of laws is not occurring by happenstance. A conservative think tank called Heritage Foundation, along with ALEC and other groups, has been working behind the scenes to draw up, disseminate and advocate for many of these bills.

The executive director of the Heritage Foundation was recorded touting its work secretly drafting some of the most controversial legislation in 2021, taking credit for provisions in the Georgia and Texas laws (including the limit on drop boxes);[579] the Arizona law forbidding the acceptance of outside dollars to support pro-voting efforts; and the law adding Iowa voters to "inactive status" for missing one election. "In some cases, we actually draft them for them . . . Or we have a sentinel on our behalf give them the model legislation, so it has that grassroots, from-the-bottom-up type of vibe."[580] As ALEC has done for years, Heritage also offers expert witnesses and analysis to legislators who bring forward its bills.[581] Perhaps the preeminent expert at Heritage is a suppression expert named Hans von Spakovsky. Public records revealed that a staff member for Ohio's LaRose consulted with von Spakovsky prior to announcing Ohio's drop box ban.[582] So with Heritage and von Spakovsky working with numerous states, it's not a surprise that Ohio's logjam approach to drop boxes is spreading so quickly.

In her briefing, Heritage's executive director told supporters she was surprised by the simplicity of it all: "Honestly, nobody even noticed. My team looked at each other, and we're like, 'it can't be that easy.'"[583] (ALEC folks no doubt chuckled—"it really is"). Many of the recommendations that became law are listed right on their website and were included in a newsletter sent earlier in the year.[584]

While ALEC tries to maintain a low profile around voting laws, its fingerprints remain all over the flood of bills. Heritage documents referred to a two-year partnership with ALEC and the State Policy Network to churn out model voting legislation.[585] The new Honest Elections Project, which ALEC had partnered with in 2020, also is playing an advocacy role in the 2021 push. And ALEC organized a call in March 2021 with Ted Cruz to urge on state legislators in their suppression efforts.[586] The watchdog Center for Media and Democracy identified 100 ALEC legislators who sponsored voter suppression laws in at least six states—including members of the ALEC elections working group that started meeting in 2019.[587] In June, Common Cause, Fair Fight Action, the League of Women Voters and other groups launched a new effort to convince ALEC corporate members to leave the organization, pointing out that many corporate supporters of ALEC had also made statements decrying the attacks on voting rights.[588]

Beyond the bill-writing and dissemination, Heritage is partnering with other national organizations to lobby and advocate for passage of these laws once they're presented in states. Partners include Susan B. Anthony List, Tea Party Patriots, and FreedomWorks, with tens of millions of dollars budgeted on key swing states—Arizona, Michigan, Florida, Georgia, Iowa, Nevada, Texas, and Wisconsin.[589] The Republican National Committee has also formed its own committee to coordinate voter attacks, chock full of officials who were part of the "stop the steal" conspiracy theory of early 2021.[590] Finally, this same network of ALEC, the Honest Elections Project, the

Heritage Foundation and the big money bankrolling them are also playing a behind-the-scenes role in the frenzied effort to undermine the 2020 election results—from backing the audits in Arizona to pursuing court cases.[591]

Broader Moves Against Democracy

To a degree not seen in the prior decade, as they have pursued these blunt-force attacks on voting, elections and officeholders, legislators spent early 2021 taking Putin-style whacks at other aspects of functioning, healthy democracies.

Protests

In the summer of 2020, following the murder of George Floyd by a Minneapolis police officer, widespread protests dominated both city streets and the public airwaves. Despite right-wing hyperventilating, 96% of the 2020 protests were peaceful.[592] They also became an important site of political organizing and empowerment. In June, when the protests were at their peak, Democrats saw voter registration skyrocket in state after state, far above the same period in 2016. In Iowa, for example, party registrations jumped 49% for Democrats in June 2020 over June 2016, and up only 3.5% for Republicans; in Michigan, Democratic registrations were up 25%, while GOP registrations fell 20%.[593] Across the board, newly registered voters were disproportionately young and people of color.[594]

Back in session in 2021, legislators in Ohio and more than 30 other states took swift action to crack down on future protests, introducing more than 100 bills.[595] These new laws punished people for engaging in a variety of activities associated with protests, lowering the bar on what is considered a criminal offense while also increasing penalties.[596] Others added secondary consequences for being convicted of protest-related crimes, such as being cut off from state employment, forms of public assistance such as student loans, or public office. On the flip side, other states—including Iowa, Florida and Oklahoma—passed measures granting immunity to those whose vehicles injure protesters on public streets,[597] while justifying the use of force by those who feel threatened by demonstrators.[598]

Stoking Vigilantism and Evading Court Review

That final aspect of protest legislation—stoking and protecting vigilantism—also is part of a broader trend of statehouses empowering individual citizens to take the law into their own hands. In the voting context, numerous states are taking up legislation giving poll watchers more powers to observe both the voting and vote-counting process—at a time that election workers are already receiving threats of violence and worse.[599] And as this book went to print, a Texas law went into effect empowering individual citizens to operate as litigation "bounty hunters" enforcing a six-week abortion ban against their fellow Texans. In quintessential laboratory of autocracy form, within days of the United States Supreme Court allowing the Texas law to go into effect, legislators in other states—Florida, Arkansas and South Dakota—announced they were considering the same approach.[600]

Not only do these laws enlist one group of citizens to directly challenge the rights of other citizens, but they complicate the traditional path used by the targets of these laws to assert their legal rights in court. States have thus found yet another way to attack their own constituents' constitutional rights, while undermining independent review of that attack.

Censoring History

Few maneuvers augur a descent away from a healthy democracy more than government trying to reshape the teaching of its own history, especially censoring out critical viewpoints and approaches. And in state after state in 2021— 27 in total—legislatures took up this task as well.[601] While the formal term many railed against publicly was "critical race theory,"[602] the legislative book-burning spanned far wider into limitations that, if taken seriously, would fundamentally alter the teaching of basic American history. As the Brookings Institute summarized, many states barred "any discussions about conscious and unconscious bias, privilege, discrimination, and oppression."[603] In Arizona, the legislature banned teaching history in a way that "presents any form of blame or judgment on the basis of race, ethnicity or sex."[604] And in Michigan, a proposed law banned an entire list of "anti-American and racist theories" from being taught,[605] including any suggestion that the Constitution—and its notorious 3/5s clause—was a racist document.

Yale historian and autocracy expert Timothy Snyder (from Wilmington, Ohio) points out that beyond particular topics, many of these new "memory laws" forbid curricula that might engender "discomfort, guilt, anguish or any other form of psychological distress on account of the individual's race or sex." This forces teachers to "self-censor, on the basis of what students might feel," a far wider ambit than even other countries that have censored their history.[606] As he explains: "Since the aim of the law is to protect feelings over facts, teachers will feel pressure to discuss the event in a way that would not give rise to controversy."[607] And as he points out, these laws also circle back to the simultaneous attack on voting rights:

In most cases, the new American memory laws have been passed by state legislatures that, in the same session, have passed laws designed to make voting more difficult. The memory management enables the voter suppression. The history of denying Black people the vote is shameful. This means that it is less likely to be taught where teachers are mandated to protect young people from feeling shame.[608]

Legislating "The Big Lie"

Another disturbing shift away from democracy has come through many legislators' ever intensifying embrace of the "Big Lie" in their rhetoric and political work.

"Big Lie" politics—where politicians and their supporters propagate bold, audacious and easily disprovable lies—have become commonplace in recent American discourse. Early examples were Birtherism and the false claim of widespread voter fraud that led to the prior decade's attacks on voting rights. Yes, voter fraud is practically non-existent; the entire public justification for all this suppression was an absolute fabrication.[609] Then came widespread climate change denial, followed more recently by the frenzied denial of science around the pandemic. Trump, of course, advanced whopping lies both as a candidate and throughout his time as president, beginning on day one with his infamous inauguration crowd-size inflation. But the most prominent example of the "Big Lie" turned out to be his final act at the White House—the false claim that he actually won the 2020 election, but was stopped by a multi-pronged conspiracy of fraudulent actions.

Together, these lies have dominated the national political conversation over the past decade, amplified by right wing media and social media, and buoyed by the silence of so many Republicans who knew them to be false. And in statehouses across the country, many legislators have proactively embraced them—recall that Ohio committee hearing where legislators invited a revolving door of anti-vaccination crackpots to testify. As intended, one general consequence of the Big Lie is that large portions of the electorate come to live in a world unconnected to truth, bouncing between one lie and the next spewed by the leader or leaders they follow. Hannah Arendt explained "Big Lie" politics at its most extreme:

> In an ever-changing, incomprehensible world the masses had reached the point where they would, at the same time, believe everything and nothing, think that everything was possible and nothing was true ... The totalitarian mass leaders based their propaganda on the correct psychological assumption that, under such conditions, one could make people believe the most fantastic statements one day, and trust that if the next day they were given irrefutable proof of their falsehood, they would take refuge in cynicism; instead of deserting the leaders who had lied to them, they would protest that they had known all along that the statement was a lie and would admire the leaders for their superior tactical cleverness. [610]

To a striking degree, we are seeing this impact now in the United States, where on issue after issue, outlandish lies are swaying large swaths of American citizens. Anti-COVID vaccination rates peaked in the summer of 2021, with few additional Americans getting vaccinated despite wide availability. Why? Polls in the summer of 2021 revealed that 90% of the unvaccinated believed that the consequences of the vaccine were worse than COVID itself. More than half thought the vaccine was a plot to place microchips in the US population, and 49% believed it would lead to autism in kids.[611] Or in politics, even as the Arizona "audit" ran into one snafu after the next, with only a few hundred improper votes uncovered, Arizona Republicans surveyed were confident (by a 62%-21% figure) that the audit would show that Trump had won that state's election.[612]

But beyond creating a critical mass of misinformed citizens, these lies have also begun to motivate lawmaking in state legislatures. Dissident Alexander Solzhenitsyn famously said of the Soviet Union: "the lie has become not just a moral category but a pillar of the State." Well, statehouses have begun to make these lies a central "pillar" of their legislative work, on everything from energy to vaccines, and even spanning into "auditing" of election results. And whether measured in public outcomes, untold lives lost, or a dysfunctional political system, these lie-driven policies have rendered wide and deep damage.

More fundamentally, legislating lies marks yet another dangerous step away from a healthy democracy and toward authoritarianism. The "Big Lie" has long been a powerful tool in the toolbelt of autocrats for a multitude of reasons beyond a misinformed public or private profiteering. First, bold, audacious lies engender and signal loyalty, and breed subordination: "When a subordinate repeats an obviously ridiculous claim he or she is degraded, and bound more closely to the leader."[613] As Jacob Levy writes: "Saying something obviously untrue, and making your subordinates repeat it with a straight face in their own voice, is a particularly startling display of power over them. It's something that was endemic to totalitarianism."[614] Embracing the Big Lie also makes a person "complicit" in the lie—"[y]our ability to stand on your own moral two feet and resist or denounce is lost.

Part of this is a general tool for making people part of immoral groups."[615]

In this way, beyond individual subordination, the Big Lie also "creates tribes . . . If you believe [the Big Lie], it separates you from the rest of the world. It makes you feel like you have to carry out some kind of desperate or violent action."[616] By repeatedly embracing the Big Lie, and legislating on the foundation of that lie, state legislatures themselves become *the tribes,* charging headlong in dystopian directions that advance the Big Lie *through laws themselves.*

Now *that* is dangerous.

CHAPTER 10

What's Next?
And to What End?

A S BAD AS the last decade has been, things are getting worse.

The frenzy of anti-democratic activity and action is intensifying. Its span widening. The downward spiral is only accelerating. All driven by statehouses, populated by largely anonymous officials, who are locked into power no matter what their states' voters do.

And as bad as 2021 already is, the risks going forward are even more foreboding. Here's why:

2022 Is the Next Decade

In addition to the raft of anti-voter laws and attacks on co-equal branches of government, the 2022 election looms large because legislators can once again lock up election results for another decade.

Most state legislatures have an unobstructed path to repeat their 2011 gerrymandering handiwork all over again before the 2022 election. They can adjust to population shifts that eroded their majorities in some areas, and they will have perfected the science of rigging districts after another ten years of learning. And as always, they'll get help. In advance of the districting process, ALEC, the SPN, and Heritage have already hosted sessions instructing these statehouses on how best to rig elections for the next decade.[617] Private bunkers are no doubt operational around the country, where this work is being done.

In recent years, some states, including Ohio and Michigan, passed Constitutional amendments reforming the process by which districts are drawn. Still, the legislative majorities comfortably in control in those states will do all they can to keep it that way. As this book goes to print, led by GOP statehouse leaders, Ohio officials have just jammed through a new, rigged statehouse map which blatantly violates the new constitutional requirements, and will no doubt end up in court. (Yet another reason legislatures are so eager to rig results in state court elections).

Beyond locking in another decade of guaranteed majorities, a number of statehouses have the opportunity to enhance their power vis-a-vis other statewide officials. Both North Carolina and South Carolina are only several votes shy of having GOP supermajority control, meaning they can override any vetoes of a Governor—either of the other party, or their own.[618]

Overall, the broader risk is of a second and third generation of legislative majorities and leaders at the seat of power who've still never experienced real elections or any semblance of robust democracy in their own rise. In most of these states, an election in 2010 will have dictated almost every result not just for the initial ten years that followed, but for the ensuing 20 years, at least. From John Adams to Nino Vitale to his successor, and thousands of similar districts across the nation, rarely a real election. We therefore will see a doubling down of the pernicious consequences that arise when statehouses lack real democracy. On the flip side, a generation of American voters will have been locked out of their statehouses for all that time. On both sides, a deeply broken system will have become the norm of state politics.

The 2021 gerrymandering will also allow statehouses to re-gerrymander the U.S. House of Representatives. The math is clear: GOP statehouses exert direct control over the shape of many more U.S. House seats (187) than Democratic statehouses do (75).[619] And they will control the process in states with large Congressional delegations—such as Florida, Texas, North Carolina and Georgia.[620] This makes it possible for the GOP to rig their way back to most of the seats they need to retake the U.S. House majority before a single vote is cast. And it means they can win the House majority back in 2022 even if they fall well short of earning the majority of U.S. House votes across the country. In this way, anonymous, unaccountable statehouse politicians can not only lock themselves into power permanently, they have the ability to hand the reins of federal power over to the likes of Kevin McCarthy, Jim Jordan and Marjorie Taylor Greene. Given that a majority of Republican House members voted against certifying the 2020 election despite its clear outcome, that alone is a dangerous prospect.

That's '22, and the decade it shapes. But the damage grows even worse with time.

2024 and Beyond

When Donald Trump and his backers dreamed of overturning the 2020 election, one source of their hope lay in state legislatures. After all, as explained in Chapter Two, the

Constitution grants state legislatures the sole and awesome responsibility of determining how a state's electors are divvied up in a presidential election. And countless state legislators were devoted Trumpers, even flying into Washington D.C. to meet with the president after his loss.

Give Trump credit—he knew where the power lay. His problem was that he was too late. Even though the Constitution is clear about the legislatures' sole power to allocate electors, federal law establishes that a state can not change the way it allots electors *after* the election has taken place. Once states set the rules on how to allocate electors, and the voters vote, those rules are locked in and must be followed. (Almost all states allocate all their electors to the popular winner of their state). In the end, even Trump's supporters in close states shied away from changing those rules after the fact.[621]

But what about 2024, now that there's time to change the rules beforehand? Or 2028? We've seen that these legislatures are always learning from past mistakes and setbacks. They assess the precise reasons why they lost and change the rules so it doesn't happen again. Could they somehow rig the electoral college formula to favor their preferred outcome just like they have in almost every other election?

Some—including Ohio's secretary of state during the notorious 2004 election—already advanced a plan to do just that after Mitt Romney's 2012 loss. Their idea? Don't allocate all the state's electors to the overall popular winner of a state, with the loser getting nothing. Instead, allocate an elector for each Congressional district a campaign wins within a state.[622]

It's misleadingly simple. And sounds technical. But in raw political terms, the idea superimposes the election rigging of gerrymandering onto the presidential election, rigging that outcome as well. No matter the vote in Ohio, for example, the Republican presidential candidate would've won twelve out of sixteen electors based on Ohio's rigged 2011-2020 map; thus, Obama's sixteen electoral vote haul by winning Ohio in 2012 would have instead resulted in an eight-elector vote deficit (twelve for Romney, four for Obama). Not because Obama lost, but because the gerrymandered map would've guaranteed that outcome.

Far-fetched? Well, Maine and Nebraska partially do this already. Ohio's Jon Husted mentioned the concept in a speech in 2013, but later said he was only speaking hypothetically.[623] And legislators in multiple states crafted legislation to get it done after 2012.[624] No surprise, this included Michigan, Wisconsin, and Pennsylvania—states where using gerrymandered districts to allocate presidential electors would convert decisive electoral college losses into gains.

Another option laid out by scholar Rick Hasen is that legislators could learn from what happened in the 2020 election and step in sooner in a tight 2024 presidential election. Specifically, the legislature itself could claim that a court order or election rule issued amid the election violated the rules they had established for determining the electoral college winner, negate the outcome, then themselves vote to choose the winner. As Hasen points out, a number of Supreme Court Justices have expressed support for an argument along these lines—that the legislature is ultimately "supreme" in making this determination.[625] In Arizona, a state representative and candidate for secretary of state put forward a bill formalizing exactly this theory.[626] Sad to say, it's easy to see a gerrymandered House GOP majority—as part of its duty to accept the electoral college total from each state—happily accepting such an argument.[627]

C'mon, some are saying. Would they really go this far?

After reading the first nine chapters of this book, after looking at the debacle of 2021, you tell me: have they ever shied away before? Has there been a line they wouldn't cross when the moment to seize power arrived? And it would only take a few states to change the outcome of a presidential election.

Rewriting the Constitution

A final step statehouses could take to lock in their non-democratic hold on power is to amend the Constitution.

Since our Founding, when Americans have amended the Constitution, they've always used the same process. Per Article V, two-thirds of Congress passed the Amendment, and then three-quarters of the states ratified it.

But Article V provides an alternative, if never-before-used, path. If two-thirds of the states call for a convention, and three-quarters of the states approve a specific change at that convention, that change is also written into the U.S. Constitution.

Let me say that again.

Thirty-eight states, without any vote of the people or any say by those in Congress, can rewrite our Constitution. That's right, thirty eight states, most with legislatures that were rigged in 2011 and haven't had true legislative elections since, can rewrite the foundational law of our land.

Surely, again, this sounds nuts. Who would even try such a thing?

Well, ALEC, for one.

For years, one of ALEC's task forces has been circulating model legislation guiding state legislatures on how to pass a resolution calling for a convention of states on a variety of issues, from term limits to a national balanced budget amendment.[628] Other organizations have emerged *solely* to serve this goal. An organization called Convention of States Action is hard at work advocating a convention. It's led by the likes of former

South Carolina Senator Jim DeMint, and enjoys support from Jeb Bush, Marco Rubio, Mike Huckabee, Ron DeSantis, Rand Paul and others. According to its tabulation, fifteen states have fully passed resolutions to join a states convention; nine others have passed a resolution in one chamber; and seventeen others have legislation before them calling for their participation.[629]

. . . And to What End?

This book has largely focused on the practical mechanisms, concrete actions and real-world ramifications of statehouses emerging as laboratories of autocracy. I've focused on the institutional weaknesses that have invited so much trouble, the perverse incentives, the national effort to weaponize them, and the acceleration downward in recent years. And I've outlined the risks going forward.

But to what end is all this work. Power for power's sake? One-off corrupt deals like William Lager's? Or something deeper?

Others have explained the most deep-seated motivations behind anti-democratic agglomeration of power in America and elsewhere. I won't repeat that work here, or claim to share their expertise.

But let me summarize a few directions.

Large, Private Interests Seeking Economic Liberty . . . For Themselves

The agenda of ALEC and its backers in hard-wiring statehouses to serve their interests isn't subtle. They describe the goal as "economic liberty," but at its heart, they mean cordoning off capital and property from the control of everyday Americans.

As Nancy MacLean writes: the goal is "the insulation of private property rights from the reach of government."[630]

Let's return to the ALEC/Laffer ranking of states. It perfectly summarizes this definition of "economic liberty": reduce taxes as much as possible (ideally, to zero), weaken workers as much as possible, minimize regulation as much as possible. Not because these goals generate strong public outcomes for the states being ranked, or because a high ranking correlates with a higher quality of life for a state's constituents. But because those results forge the greatest economic "liberty" for the big money interests who are funding ALEC and all those legislators to do the work. Tiny government, huge accumulation of wealth at the top.

Their big problem is that a robust political system is a direct threat to this top-down vision of economic liberty. A system where an empowered popular majority exerts its control through fair elections wouldn't stand for that Koch vision of economic liberty. The agenda is too deeply unpopular, and too clearly counter to the broader public good on issue after issue, to survive for long. And they know it: the Koch Brothers' own research found that what the average American "wanted from politics . . . was quite different from their business-dominated free-market orthodoxy."[631]

Maximizing economic liberty as they desire it thus requires systematically obstructing American majorities from imposing their will through a healthy democratic process. It means identifying the institutions that are most sealed off from public accountability, and then further walling them off so they can carry out their assigned tasks with as little interference as possible. It also means harnessing those institutions to lock the broader electorate out of imposing their will at other levels of politics—national, federal, or local.

Statehouses turn out to be the perfect places to accomplish

all aspects of this vision, locking up both economic and political power simultaneously. They've done it for more than a decade now, and a new round of gerrymandering and voter suppression positions them to keep right on doing it.

Protecting White Dominance in an Increasingly Diverse Country

It's also a sobering constant of American history that a strand of white supremacy permanently haunts us, often below the surface, other times bursting above it in plain, ugly sight for years or generations at a time. As the iconic Southern historian C. Vann Woodward explained: "All the elements of fear, jealousy, proscription, hatred and fanaticism ha[ve] long been present, as they are present in various degrees of intensity in any society."[632] More recently, Isabel Wilkerson captures the ever-present reality in the compelling frame of caste systems.

And however it's framed, American history has followed an ugly but predictable course: those in the dominant caste—the forces of white dominance—lash out most fiercely when their grip on power is threatened by the traditionally subordinate caste.

The pattern repeats itself like clockwork.

When reconstruction lifted Blacks into an elevated status after the Civil War, including elected office, the backlash was fast, furious, and violent, leading to a century of Jim Crow.

After the passage of civil rights laws in the 1960s, the entire political world turned upside down, with Southern states flipping from Democratic to Republican in a relentless effort to block further Black progress. The "Southern Strategy" dominated politics for decades.

And we're seeing it again now.

Barack Obama's ascendance to the presidency, powered

by the rise of the energized and diverse Obama coalition as a potent political force, marked "the greatest departure from the script of the American caste system" and white dominance in American history.[633] And the backlash again was predictably fierce. It included: demeaning and explicitly racist attacks against Obama himself; fierce resistance to every item on his agenda (even a health care plan that was based on a Republican model), both by other public officials and large grassroots movements across the country; political and legal attacks on multiple policy fronts; and a spike in racist hate groups and white supremacist violence and terrorism throughout the country.[634] The backlash peaked with the ascendancy of Donald Trump to the White House, through racial overtones and appeals that began on the first day of his campaign and persisted to the end of his presidency, and voting divided more starkly along racial lines than in any election in 36 years.[635]

State legislative activity since Obama's win has paralleled this backlash, and mirrors in disturbing ways the activity that ushered in the Jim Crow era in the late 1800s. Voting laws directly targeted African American voters. Public justification of those laws through open appeals to race, and as a way to maximize the "quality" of votes[636]—almost the precise words used at the dawn of Jim Crow. The passage of laws that whitewash the most racist elements of our history, and battles over the very symbols of white supremacy. Courts weakening laws put in place to protect civil rights. Laws criminalizing protest, after demonstrations dominated by Black Americans protesting violence against Black Americans; and laws granting immunity to those who commit violence against those protesting. New gun laws that dovetail precisely with historic white supremacist notions of vigilante violence against "dangerous" Black Americans—the very narrative that allowed George Zimmerman to track and kill Trayvon Martin with impunity. Large numbers of White working class Americans expressing in surveys a fear that they are losing "their" country.[637] And the open and unabashed discussion of "replacement theory" on the public airwaves, a racist conspiracy that has sparked violence from New Zealand to Charlottesville.[638]

As Stacey Abrams describes, "[t]hose who see their relative influence shrinking are using every tool possible to limit access to political power."[639] And today's legislatures have become the central institutional bulwark holding the emerging and diverse "New American Majority" at bay as much and for as long as possible. But of course the bigger threat still looms in raw demographics—census figures project White Americans will become a numeric minority by 2042.[640]

Will ongoing suppression, gerrymandering and other laws keep the reins of government out of reach of the non-White population even as it emerges as the new majority? Or will legislatures intensify their effort even further?

If 2021 is any indicator, they're going for broke on the latter.

A Veneer of Legitimacy

These are dramatic parallels to a horrific past. Surely, some will react, we're not returning to the violent apartheid conditions of Jim Crow. And we're not about to become a police state or a Russian-style oligarchy.

Perhaps not, but that's also not necessary to achieve the agendas discussed above.

There's another path. Political scientists call it "competitive" autocracy or authoritarianism, and it's a system that locks a minority into power without the brute force of police states or apartheid regimes. It's alive and well in numerous countries today.

And in one way, it's even more dangerous. Because on the

surface it looks legitimate. The formal process of elections takes place. Millions vote. Results are generally covered as legitimate, and celebrated or bemoaned accordingly. The losers concede. The winner takes or stays in power, thanking the voters for their support.

But it fails to reflect the will of the people, because the rules are so rigged in one side's favor that the other side had no chance at victory from the start.

Two scholars, Lucan Way and Steven Levitsky, described the phenomenon back in 2002, citing numerous examples at the time: Russia, Ukraine, Serbia and others. In those countries:

> formal democratic institutions are widely viewed as the principal means of obtaining and exercising political authority. Incumbents violate those rules so often and to such an extent, however, that the regime fails to meet conventional minimum standards for democracy.[641]

And as Zack Beauchamp explains, despite the undemocratic reality, a key to these systems' survival is to "[convinc[e] citizens that they are living in a democracy. That's how they maintain their legitimacy and prevent popular uprisings."[642] Maintaining a formal election process remains critical, even if in many states, the "political systems [] no longer meet the minimum conditions for free and fair elections. "[643] To talk brass tacks, you don't de-register everyone like they did in the South by 1904. You don't run an election that's a sham on its face. But you change enough rules, eliminate enough voters through voter ID and purging, rig enough districts, and systematically target your opponent's favored mode of voting (e.g., early in-person, dropboxes, etc.) that the outcome is still guaranteed, and you never lose control, in election after election. At the state level in places like Ohio, at least, where decades of elections were pre-determined in rooms in 2011, politics already feels eerily close to this description.

One of the most prominent examples of an emerging autocracy founded on competitive authoritarianism in 2021 is Hungary, led by prime minister Viktor Orbán. Over a decade, Orbán and his party have locked out the opposition with a variety of tools: gerrymandering—his party enjoyed a two-thirds supermajority in parliament even after winning less than half of the vote; [644] attacks on the courts; attacks on an independent media; and takeover of other institutions such as the country's electoral commission.[645] Still, since Orbán has not used the tactics seen in more aggressive autocracies, Hungary is treated as a peer by Western nations even though it no longer functions as a viable democracy.[646] So, the fact that Tucker Carlson, the most watched right-wing commentator on cable TV, spent early August 2021 fawning over Hungary and Orbán's leadership is no fluke. As Beauchamp writes: "Many conservative intellectuals in America have come to see the Orbán regime as a model for America."[647]

An Autocrat in Waiting

There's one other potential end to this statehouse agglomeration of power, and that is the transition to outright autocracy itself.

Now I don't think that was the goal those who rigged maps in 2011 had in mind. And it wasn't the endgame of those engaged in the initial round of voter suppression. But it risks being the ultimate consequence of all their anti-democratic work nonetheless. And it would be entirely consistent with another bleak pattern in history. That when enough pillars protecting democratic governance erode, and when enough figures in positions of power are willing to defy both the law and bedrock democratic norms, autocracy arises.

We are close enough to those conditions now that it would be naive to declare this couldn't happen in America. Rigged election outcomes. Attacks on independent courts. Big Lie politics. Unchecked abuses of power at the highest level. Statehouses perfectly positioned to impact elections at all levels, both before and after they happen. And the same White working class Americans (60%, at least) who fear the rise of a diverse majority expressing strong support for "a strong leader who is willing to break the rules."[648]

Some argue that the Trump presidency—where countless abuses happened yet were largely normalized—already marked the first stage of the process.[649] While Trump's activity was interrupted by Biden's win, the 2021 statehouse frenzy makes clear that broader conditions remain ripe for further stages in coming election cycles. Scholars of democracy from across the country warned that these conditions "could enable some state legislatures or partisan election officials to do what they failed to do in 2020: reverse the outcome of a free and fair election."[650] Hundreds of state legislators from across the country took part in the "stop the steal" rally on January 6, signed off on letters or legal briefs to overturn the 2020 election results, or actively spread the lie that the 2020 elections were rigged for Biden.[651] That alone indicates that there's a base of politicians ready to overturn outcomes *who actually wield significant power to do exactly that.*

And once they go there, there's no turning back.

PART III

I N 1888, THERE were 127,993 registered Black voters in Louisiana, compared to 126,884 registered White voters. This reflected the approximate 50/50 split in the state's population.[652]

By 1906, only 1,342 Black voters remained on the rolls.

Four years after that, only 730—under .5% of the actual Black population. Close to half of the state's 60 parishes didn't have a single registered Black voter.[653]

Almost overnight, a brutal round of poll taxes, literacy tests, character tests, and racially exclusive primaries worked to devastating effect, there and elsewhere.

Other states saw similar declines. Alabama's registration fell from a peak of 140,000 to 3,742 by 1883. After 1900, only 3,000 of 181,471 of Alabama's Black males remained registered.[654]

Between 1876 and 1898, South Carolina plummeted from 92,081 to 2,832. Mississippi: from 52,705 (1876) to 3,573 (1898).[655]

The disintegration in registration carried immediate consequences: as historian John Hope Franklin summarized, "[o]nce Blacks were disenfranchised, everything else necessary for white supremacy could be done."[656]

It started with representation. For a generation after the Civil War, Blacks in the south served as jury members, judges, sheriffs, mayors and other local positions.[657] Many served in the conventions that wrote and approved the new constitutions of formerly Confederate states.[658] Then between the 1860s and early 1900s, Blacks served in elected office in Southern states in impressive numbers.[659] In that time, 52 Black legislators served in the North Carolina state legislature,[660] while 87 served in South Carolina's (at one point, they comprised the majority).[661] In 1890, Louisiana's legislature included ten Black representatives. Mississippi's first Reconstruction legislature had 40 Black members.[662] And Virginia had at least one Black state representative in every legislative session from 1869 to 1891. In every Congressional term but one, between 1869 and 1901, the South sent at least one Black House member to Washington, 20 in total.[663] Mississippi elected two Blacks Senators in that time.[664] Blacks occupied other statewide leadership posts, including three lieutenant governors (one temporarily served as governor), state supreme court justices, secretaries of state, and statehouse Speakerships.[665]

But after those waves of attacks on voting rights and democracy, pernicious court rulings, revisions to the new state constitutions, along with white supremacist violence and terrorism and far too many political compromises among Whites of all political persuasions,[666] not one Black legislator remained in the South after 1901. Black voter turnout fell to almost zero—in presidential elections in the former Confederate states, for example, Black turnout cratered from 61% in 1880 to 2% in 1912.[667]

This was accompanied by a ruthless era of racial segregation and apartheid in almost every other aspect of Southern life. "All private and human activities were segregated from birth to death, from hospital wards to railroad platforms to ambulances, hearses, and cemeteries."[668] But the effect was national. James Loewen describes the period that followed as "the Nadir," where "America took a wrong turn, North as well as South. In fact, we took perhaps the wrongest turn we have ever taken as a nation, a turn so wrong that we have not yet been able to comprehend all that it has done to us."[669]

One of the most important books covering this shameful period of American history is called *The Strange Career of Jim Crow,* by the revered Yale historian C. Vann Woodward. It is a haunting read.

But Woodward's short book didn't earn outsized attention because it described the descent into Jim Crow. That painful story has been told by many, often in more detail. What stuck out was its central assertion: that for most of the 20th century, historians were wrong about the *inevitability* of Reconstruction's collapse. To the contrary, Woodward argued that the slide into Jim Crow was avoidable.[670] That different strategies and different decisions at key moments might've changed the outcome and spared our country, and generations of Black Americans, the living hell and ongoing terrorism that was the Jim Crow era, and the consequences that are still suffered today.

So if we could go back to the 1870s, what would Woodward and others have us tell those fighting for democracy and equality?

First, we'd have to sound the alarm: "If you don't act fast, all those gains will be gone in a few years. For a century."

Many then would've dismissed this as hyperbole. Of course life was difficult, and the future uncertain. But they had won the Civil War, changed the Constitution three times, passed civil rights laws, opened up the franchise to Blacks throughout the south, so much so that Black legislators walked the halls of statehouses and the U.S. House. The nation's leading party appeared committed to protecting these gains. It would've taken forceful persuasion to convince people that it all might go away, so quickly, for so long.

But if you woke people up to that impending danger, what next? What would you tell them to do about it?

If you trust Woodward, John Hope Franklin and other historians, you'd urge them: Resist! Newly-freed slaves and their Southern and Northern White allies, take none of the gains for granted . . . it can all end almost overnight. Don't reduce one iota of federal support for newly freed Black Southerners. Pass even more robust laws, and don't let the courts weaken your newly-won rights. To vindicate those rights and protect Blacks as they exercise them, keep the troops in the states far longer than you think you need to or racist terrorism and bloody violence will follow. Don't let them rewrite history, cleansing it of our worst moments. Don't fall for the scare tactics about Black crime and corruption, and the need to cleanse the vote. Northern and Southern politicians alike, don't cut short-term political deals that compromise any of this. Don't let economic or political crises, or foreign affairs, goad you into playing racial politics, "moving on," or watering down in *any way* your commitment to full democracy and equal rights. Because if you do let up, or divide, the united and dedicated forces of Jim Crow will move in immediately. They will take over.

Do all of this, and you *may* stop what's coming. Do nothing, and you'll lose your democracy for almost a century.

*   *   *

My goal in this book's first ten chapters has been to sound the same alarm now. To make the case that we too face grave risk to the essence of our democracy—not simply because of one man's antics, but because powerful institutions have become impregnable laboratories of autocracy. That 2021 bears too many similarities to the late 1800s to ignore. In fact, some of the monied forces controlling statehouses now are more entrenched, and more sophisticated, than what existed back then. There was a lot of flux in the 1870s and 1880s; there's far less in most of the laboratories of autocracy today.

So we must act as if we face a threat to democracy equal to the one faced back then.

And just as I asked what we would advise folks in the 1870s, we must ask ourselves now: What do *we* do? What do *I* do?

Knowing what we know now, learning from that tragic history, this Part will outline *30 steps* I propose:

CHAPTER 11

Reclaiming Democracy

Step 1. Reframe the Battle: Fulfilling a Constitutional Guarantee

"[I]n grave matters it is best to call things by their right names. . . . "—Edward Everett, Gettysburg

THIS IS A fight for democracy, and in 2021, democracy is losing.

The Founders understood this fight; they had endured it, and they knew fights would occur again. They did not take democracy for granted. Knowing how fragile their new creation was, they erected numerous protections to sustain it at the federal level. But they didn't stop there. Even as they created a federalist system, paying great deference to states on most matters, they did so on one essential condition. State governments, too, needed to reflect and represent the will of the people.

This was such an important element in their Constitutional framework that they placed a remarkable responsibility on the new federal government. They felt so strongly about it, they described it with language found nowhere else in the Constitution.

They *guaranteed* it.

It's an often overlooked sentence in the U.S. Constitution.

The Guarantee Clause.

"The United States shall guarantee to every State in this Union a Republican Form of government . . . ."[671] As explicitly and bluntly as can be—"shall" is the strongest verb in law there is—the Founders *required* that the federal government fulfill this role.

And what did they mean by "Republican Form of government"?

Scholars and political figures have examined and debated the phrase for generations—its history, its many appearances in the founding documents, its frequent usage by the Founders. The term "Republicanism" lay at the heart of the founding conversation—a revolutionary concept the first Americans believed separated the new country from all others before it. And while there's some disagreement on its precise contours, there's a consensus on what they meant generally. As scholar Akhil Amar emphasizes, its roots tell the story: *publica; poplicus.*[672] Government must be derived from the *people. The people are sovereign.*

James Madison dedicated Federalist 39 to defining "republican form" of government; at its essence, he wrote, it is "a government which derives all its powers directly or indirectly from the great body of the people." When describing Republicanism, Madison twice refers to "self-government."[673] In Federalist 37, he emphasized that in a republic, "all power should be derived from the people." Power is "derived from the great body of the society, not from an inconsiderable portion or a favored class of it."[674] These definitions reflected similar notions of the day.[675]

Looking at these and other references, Amar concluded that "[t]he central meaning of Republican Government revolved tightly around popular sovereignty, majority rule and the people's right to alter or abolish."[676] Amar and scholar Edwin Chemerinsky note that much of Republicanism was framed in contrast to monarchy: "What was so objectionable about a monarchy? In a monarchy, citizens do not get to choose their rulers, power is fixed and inherited; in a republican form of government, the people ultimately retain sovereignty and choose their officeholders."[677]

And why did the Founders place the onus of enforcing that guarantee on the federal government? First, as Madison wrote in Federalist 10, they feared that individual states—being smaller in size—risked the formation of anti-democratic factions: "Men of factious tempers, of local prejudices, or of sinister designs, may, by intrigue, by corruption, or by other means, first obtain the suffrages, and then betray the interests, of the people." This reflected their recent lived experience. In fact, a prime motivator of the new Constitution was the behavior of "vile" state legislatures—their "corruption and mutability," as Madison put it[678]—in the years immediately prior.

But the risk went beyond concerns about individual states. Corruption in one state could spill over into others. As Amar explains, one reason for the Constitution's residency requirement for elected office was a concern that "Rich men of neighboring States, may employ with success the means of corruption in some particular district and thereby get into the Public Councils after having failed in their own State."[679] Hmmm—you don't say!

But the risk went even further than that. As Madison wrote in Federalist 43, it stemmed from the fact that they were granting states a wide range of roles and powers within the new nation's overall governing structure, including over elections themselves. "The more intimate the nature of such a union may be, the greater interest have the members in the political institutions of each other; and the greater right to insist that the forms of government under which the compact was entered into should be SUBSTANTIALLY maintained."[680] Intertwined as they were, if states were sufficiently tainted in their own governance, they could upend the entire national project (sound familiar?). As Amar writes:

[A]n unrepublican state government might tend to undermine the republican character of the *federal* government, whose own institutions would rest largely on state-law pillars. For example, a warped state government might corrupt the integrity of that state's elections to the federal House, Senate, and electoral college.[681]

Madison even foresaw the risk of gerrymandering: "the inequality of the Representation in the Legislatures of particular states, would produce a like inequality in their representation in the National Legislature."[682] So in the end, "the superintending government ought clearly to possess authority to defend the system against aristocratic or monarchial innovations."[683] Or as Amar writes, think of it as "a kind of democratic insurance policy."[684] A guaranteed one.

Strong language creating a critical safeguard.

And that is the broad lens through which we should examine what's happening in states across our country today.

But we don't.

Today, the debate about statehouse actions usually takes place within the narrower construct of individual rights. Most of the offending statehouse laws and practices are examined or challenged as an attack on equal rights, or voting rights, or first amendment rights. And no doubt, those rights are under attack, and must be protected.

But in framing and responding to what's happening in our statehouses, pro-democracy leaders need to think more broadly, in the same way the Founders framed the issue—as part of a broader guarantee about governance at the state and national level. That all 50 states must be run by governments where the people are sovereign. That anti-democratic takeovers of states run afoul of that Constitutional promise. And that they must be stopped before they spill over into poisoning the entire nation's governance.

Ironically, America knows how to do this because it's how we've approached international work for years. Our nation has engaged in the business of democracy building across the world. We provide technical assistance on everything from election administration to all the other aspects necessary to build a viable democracy. We guide pro-democracy parties, candidates and regimes.

And as we do this work in other countries, we treat descents into autocracy for what they are. What would we say if leaders of a country, in a short time, did all of the following? Rigged rules so they could never lose elections; engaged in rampant corruption; changed public laws to make it harder for voters and parties who opposed them to win elections; undermined other elected offices which are designed to play independent roles in elections; undermined the independence of their courts; directly defied the outcomes of referenda; took steps to question the results of recent elections; cracked down on protests; and censored the teaching of history to whitewash some of its worst elements, while relentlessly attacking independent media. How would we react if groups of oligarchs drafted legislation in private and then handed it to politicians (who couldn't lose elections) to enact, and they did so again and again? We wouldn't simply describe these steps narrowly, as attacks on various individual rights. We would say, far more loudly and with greater concern, that the country in question was abandoning democracy. That they were becoming an autocracy. And we would respond accordingly.

But that's not how we approach the equivalent problem at home. Understandably, we've taken for granted that the essence of democracy is understood and valued here. Sure, nations may slip elsewhere, but not on our shores. But the Guarantee Clause makes clear that our Founders weren't as confident.

So, we have to re-apply our pro-democracy mission, mindset and work back into our own country. Into state after state. We must call it what it is: a fight for democracy. A fight against spreading authoritarianism and a path to autocracy. And we start by recognizing that countless statehouses no longer meet even the most generous definition of a "Republican Form" of government; that, to use Madison's words, "aristocratic . . . innovations" have walled them off from accountability to "the great body of the society," placing them at odds with the will of their own citizens on issue after issue, and raising the multiple risks the Founders described. Not just to the states and their own citizens, but to the entire national endeavor. We must take steps to buttress the firewall Madison and the Founders constructed for us, such that "[t]he influence of factious leaders may kindle a flame within their particular States, but will be unable to spread a general conflagration through the other States."[685]

Once framed this way, the stakes change. Even the teams change. Those who care about democracy must unite to wage that fight more broadly than just along party lines. Sure, disagree over various ideas and policies. But for those concerned about the broader direction described above, protecting and supporting democracy itself must now lay at the heart of our politics. Or we will make the mistake of the late 1800s, where divisions over economics and foreign affairs ushered in the Jim Crow era.

And once we call it what it is, the tools change as well. Yes, whenever possible, we still must battle every attack on grounds of equal protection, and due process, and freedom of association, and the right to vote. Fight as relentlessly *for* those rights as they are against them. The Department of Justice and lawyers across the country are doing all they can to protect these rights.

But we also must fight to uphold the broader commitment to "guarantee to every State in this Union a Republican Form of government." And even though it's been sitting in the toolbox, unused for more than a century, the Guarantee Clause turns out to be an incredibly powerful tool. Senator Charles Sumner of Massachusetts once called it the "sleeping giant" of the Constitution.[686]

Why is it so robust? For one, the directness of the command speaks for itself. But second, the Supreme Court has long held it to be in the exclusive possession of the US Congress—the "political department"[687]—and over which courts have no jurisdiction to second guess.[688] Yes, on the one hand that means you can't sue a state for violating the Guarantee Clause. But on the other hand, if the question is whether a state is upholding a Republican Form of government, *that* is for Congress alone to decide. And if a state no longer meets that standard, it is for Congress to take action. More than a century ago, for example, the United States Senate refused to seat a Senator from Louisiana because it concluded that the election had been so tainted—officials had "manipulated the 'machinery of the election' with a 'systematic purpose' to decrease black voter turnout"—it did not comport with the Guarantee Clause.[689] A century of precedent holds that that is beyond courts' purview.

It's long past time that the United States government lived up to that guarantee in every state in the country. Remember, the Constitution instructs that it "shall" do so. That's an order.

CHAPTER 12

Resistance at the National Level

National-Level Response—Federal Action

Step 2. Resist through Federal Legislation and Enforcement

> *"Reconstruction did not end abruptly as the result of congressional or presidential action. Rather it came to a gradual end as restraints were relaxed and stringent legislation repealed."*[690]—John Hope Franklin

> *"The South's adoption of extreme racism was due not so much to a conversion as it was to a relaxation of the opposition . . . an almost simultaneous decline in the effectiveness of restraint by"* forces opposed to racist policies.[691]—C. Vann Woodward

THE MOST IMPORTANT lesson history teaches us about attacks on democracy is to resist as fiercely and as long as it takes. Indeed, to never stop resisting, or even let resistance weaken. Diminishing resistance at multiple levels is what allowed the forces of Jim Crow to prevail. A similar history can be told in countries that plunged into authoritarianism and autocracy.

As the Founders signaled by their very writing of the Guarantee Clause, the most powerful entity that can mount that resistance is the federal government. And if history is any indication, lackluster federal resistance amid aggressive state-level attacks on democracy will assure the fight is ultimately lost.

So, what should the federal government do in response to what's happening across our states? Resist with all its might.

And what does resistance look like? It starts with laws providing the strongest protection of democratic governance possible, including fair elections and the equal opportunity to exercise voting rights. And it's followed by relentless enforcement of those laws.

In 2021, several bills have passed the House that do this work. The John Lewis Voting Rights Act revives and updates key parts of the Voting Rights Act that were disemboweled by the *Shelby* decision. Most important, it revives the pre-clearance process, requiring states with a history of discrimination to seek and receive Department of Justice approval before they can move forward with election laws and process changes. The bill not only expands the scope of practices that must be approved in advance—including voter ID changes, purging practices and voting locations—but expands the jurisdictions required to abide by the preclearance process. Others have proposed that pre-clearance be required of *all states*. Voters in states like Ohio would certainly benefit from the widest scope of pre-clearance possible.

A second act, called the For the People Act, goes even further, adding more protections to assure fair elections and end forms of suppression. Under the Act, states must offer a baseline of voter protections, including same-day registration, automatic voter registration, and a window of early voting. And states are barred from attacking modes of voting that have proven popular in recent years. Among other provisions, the bill also takes aim at extreme partisan gerrymandering by requiring that states utilize independent commissions to draw district lines, and that no state can draw a map that "unduly favors or disfavors" one party or another.

If passed, these acts would dismantle many of the tools statehouses have used to seal themselves off from the voters for the past generation and for the foreseeable future. As the Brennan Center concluded, the For the People Act alone "would thwart virtually every vote suppression bill currently pending in the states."[692] And the districting provision would re-empower the people to be part of the selection of their legislators, and avoid the state-by-state race to the bottom that inevitably occurs without a national standard for fair districts. Together, this is the type of *robust federal resistance* needed to halt the intensifying attacks on democracy; it's similar to types of protections eschewed more than a century ago, the failure of which brought on Jim Crow.

History tells us that when democracy is under attack, a failure of federal resistance guarantees the attack succeeds.

So, resist.

Pass the John Lewis Act.

Pass the For the People Act.

And as it does so, Congress should anchor this democracy work in the Guarantee Clause itself. First, that grounding offers a far stronger legal defense of some provisions—such as the reforms to stop extreme gerrymandering—than is currently available under standard voting rights precedent, which the Roberts Court has steadily eroded. Mounting a Guarantee Clause defense of democracy also opens the door to other steps if necessary.

Step 3. Don't Let the Filibuster Stop You

In 2021, both these acts are stuck in the Senate, doomed by a filibuster that requires them to earn 60 votes—which today means ten votes from Republican Senators. That's right, under this sometimes used procedural rule, those resisting attacks against democracy must somehow persuade *ten allies of those attacking democracy* to vote to *stop* those attacks. Now I'm just a guy from Ohio, but that seems to be stacking the deck against democracy.

Many advocate for filibuster reform of various types,[693] including an exception in cases involving voting rights. No less than Vice President Kamala Harris and Representative James Clyburn have raised this exception.

I couldn't agree more.

Think about it. There've been more than 161 exceptions to the filibuster carved out between 1969 and 2014.[694] The McConnell majority in 2017 even created an exception for Supreme Court Justice nominations, allowing them to appoint three Justices in the years that followed. If there are sound reasons for all these exceptions, it's hard to argue with Stacey Abrams that "protection of democracy is so fundamental that it should be exempt from the filibuster rules."[695]

But the on-the-ground reality described in this book, with statehouses operating as laboratories of autocracy wholly unmoored from any semblance of a democratic process, makes use of the filibuster even less defensible here.

Defenders of the filibuster insist that minority voices in the senate must be respected. That the filibuster assures that those voices are considered, while also forcing two sides to work together. That's what Democratic Senator Joe Manchin argued in April 2021.[696] And in some contexts, the filibuster can certainly work that way.

But that argument collapses on itself once you widen the lens to witness the full, multi-layered war taking place over democracy. The side attacking democracy nationally has chosen statehouses as the impregnable high ground from which to wage their frontal assault with no accountability. As they launch wave after wave of attacks, those gerrymandered state-level majorities aren't seeking an iota of minority approval—or popular input of any sort. Many of the bills are being drafted out-of-state and simply rammed through without a thought of in-state views whatsoever. Meanwhile, the same forces attacking democracy rammed through a new generation of federal justices and judges, without use of the filibuster, who are hacking away at the federal laws designed to protect against their attacks.

It's asymmetric warfare at its worst.

When on *offense* at the state level, those attacking democracy happily trample over minorities. When on *offense* at the federal level, their allies have seated judges without the filibuster, with no mind to minority voices. But when on *defense* at the federal level, their allies block all laws by insisting that minority voices must not only be heard, but included. Applying different rules at different levels guarantees that exactly what folks like Manchin say they want—minority voices to be heard and respected—doesn't happen in state after state. In fact, those voices are locked out forever, even when they grow to be a majority in multiple states. So, in this case, the filibuster safeguards the very behavior its defenders say they want to prevent.

In the area of voting laws, another defense mounted for the filibuster is that it's needed to defend states' rights. Manchin, for one, says without the filibuster, small states will be overrun.[697] But this argument runs up against the promise and logic of the Guarantee Clause. States' autonomy on many issues is worthy of deference, but on the pre-supposition that those state governments are legitimately representative of the people in the first place. But if a state no longer satisfies the basic definition of a Republican form of government—if its operation no longer has any connection back to the people of that state—states' rights offers a hollow objection to federal corrective action. And if the actions in question are steps to further wall off those in power from their own people, the objection makes even less sense. The Guarantee Clause states that in such moments, the federal government *"shall"* correct the problem. Of all occasions where the filibuster might be used, using it to block Congress from fulfilling a guarantee by citing the concerns of states who are the object of that guarantee—and falling woefully short of it—makes no sense.

Finally, some argue on practical grounds that if the filibuster is used to support democracy, then "nothing else will get done" in Congress because Senate Republicans will block everything else. This argument has three related flaws. First, it's giving in to bullying—and we should've learned from Trump, never do that! Second, it's prioritizing getting "something done" on other matters by essentially agreeing to getting nothing done to protect democracy; that itself is a choice. Third, a look back at the history referenced above will show that the willingness to countenance attacks on democracy to get "other things done" is exactly the mindset that ushered in the Jim Crow era. It's a losing trade-off, and always has been.

The filibuster is not a legitimate obstacle to either the For the People Act or the John Lewis Act.

Pass them both. Then enforce them relentlessly.

Step 4: Robust Federal Corruption Enforcement

In rigged Ohio, unless the federal government cracks down on the corruption that is endemic to today's laboratories of autocracy, nothing will be done about it. *Every* major scandal in Ohio of the past decade was rooted out by the FBI and DOJ. In most of those cases, Ohio's attorney general or auditor had at least an indirect relationship with the scandals or their perpetrators, which posed obvious conflicts of interest and kept the office from fighting corruption. In some cases, the AG or auditor didn't just look the other way, but took steps that *aided* the perpetrators.[698]

Other factors now almost guarantee that in-state enforcement will be anemic at best. Generally, as explained in Chapter Three, attorneys general here and elsewhere engage in the same pay to play politics as those in the statehouses.[699] And Republican attorneys general have only gotten more absorbed in the far-right world that has consumed legislatures, waging legal battles that undermined the 2020 election outcome while actively participating in the planning of January 6.[700] It's safe to say, most have abandoned any claim to be independent arbiters of the rule of law.

And as we're seeing in Ohio, whether it's altering jurisdiction over corruption or changing the rules of judicial elections, corrupt legislatures happily rig the rules of courts and the criminal justice system to evade accountability for misdeeds. And they can get away with it knowing that gerrymandering protects them at the ballot box.

In states awash in the corruption that accompanies these laboratories of democracy, robust federal enforcement against corruption is the only path to cleaning it up.

Step 5: Legislation To Buttress Democracy on Other Fronts

To the extent the laboratories of autocracy, urged on by ALEC and other allies, have attacked other pillars of democracy, federal legislation shoring up those pillars is essential. The relentless attacks on labor unions and the right to organize, the fulsome teaching of history, and the right to protest, should all be seen as part of the broader state-by-state attack on democracy. So too, the new laws stoking vigilantism against fellow citizens in exercising their rights. It's the Orbán model right here in America, gaining speed. So beyond voting laws themselves, the federal government has an obligation to step in and do what it can to protect *all* pillars of a healthy, democratic society—including affirmatively protecting federal rights that are under attack in states.

National-Level Response—Advocates of Democracy

Beyond resistance from the federal government, most of the resistance to the statehouse attacks on democracy will take place at the source—the state level. But in order for those to be successful, those who support democracy must also make some strategic decisions at the national level.

Big ones.

Step 6: Define the Teams Differently

In 2020, Republicans overall did far better than Donald Trump did. They picked up U.S. House seats and statehouse seats even in states that Trump himself lost. As in 2018, gerrymandering played the decisive role in that mixed outcome. But in some areas at least, many Republican candidates got votes that Trump himself didn't get. Enough voters to matter showed up and voted for Joe Biden because they couldn't stand Trump, but then voted Republican for the rest of the ticket.

Why?

In some cases, because too many others—commentators and even Democratic candidates—told them to. Not intentionally. Maybe not even out loud. But too many who care about democracy were blinded by their antipathy of Trump so that *he* became the dividing line. So politicians on the right who didn't act like Trump or feel like Trump (and even many who did) went on to get thousands of votes Trump himself didn't get. And now what are those politicians doing? Working as hard as they can to undermine democracy. Maybe more politely than Trump would have, but doing it all the same.

We can't make that mistake again.

We have to change our lexicon away from Never-Trump. That's too narrow a view—too short-term—of what's happening in states. That would've been like having a Never-Johnson test after the civil war, as opposed to Never Jim Crow. It lets too many off the hook who have voted against democracy for years, and will keep doing so.

Let's redefine it as <u>Always-democracy</u>. *That's* what's at stake in the coming elections. A commitment to democracy must be the dividing line. Are you for it or not? Do you want to stop attacks on voters, or don't you? Do you want to win by rigging elections, or not? Do you stand up against moves toward autocracy—such as by supporting the January 6 Commission or opposing outrageous audits—or not? For those that do, embrace them as part of the pro-democracy effort even if major disagreements exist on other issues. But that genteel politician who posts nice photos marching across the Edmund Pettus Bridge while voting against democracy at every opportunity (ahem, Ohio Senator Rob Portman and Frank LaRose)? Or writing op-eds bemoaning partisanship while rigging elections in backrooms (Husted). He or she is on the wrong team. Make that as clear as day.

In case this seems like some unfair partisan test, be clear that only a few years ago, George W. Bush signed the reauthorization of the Voting Rights Act in 2006, after a 98-0 vote in the Senate and a 390-33 vote in the House. Ronald Reagan signed the prior VRA extension in 1982, after 85-8 approval in the Senate and a 389-24 vote in the House. Amid countless and bitter disagreements in both years, extending the protection of voting rights was something that both parties agreed to. We must make that the case again.

Never Trump? Better than pro-Trump, but doesn't tell me enough.

Never Democracy? Vote 'em out.

Always Democracy? Welcome aboard!

And that also means infighting between so-called progressives and so-called moderates on all sorts of issues needs to take a back seat to the fierce unity on democracy that's so essential. Disagree, by all means. But not so rancorously that deep divisions open up opportunities for the other side.

Step 7. Fight for Democracy Everywhere

Go to the map of the United States on the State Policy Network website—the think tank that works with ALEC to push their corporate-written policies all over the country: it's at https://spn.org/directory/ [701]

What's interesting about this map is it's not divided into red states and blue states. It doesn't simply highlight the states that Republicans already control, or that the Republicans need to win to secure the presidency or the Senate majority.

No, every state is the same color. And when you click on each state, you'll see every single one has at least one state affiliate identified. The most are in red states, of course. But they also exist in the bluest of states.

In Stowe, Vermont, they've got the Ethan Allen Institute. In Chicago, they've got the Illinois Policy Institute. In Honolulu, they've got the Grassroot Institute of Hawaii.

The point is, the fight *against* democracy is being waged everywhere, even in states that are as blue as it gets.

In contrast, those who *support* democracy too often let the presidential map—the electoral college map—dictate where they wage *their* fight. Whether it's legal battles or registration efforts or targeted races or where we invest large amounts of political money, we focus on the handful of swing states in the nation that will determine the presidential election. And with a few exceptions, these states overlap with where U.S. Senate seats and other state-wide offices are contested. Ken Martin, chair of the Minnesota Democratic-Farmer-Labor (DFL) Party and President of the Association of State Democratic Committees, sums its up bluntly: "the Democratic party has been myopically focused on federal races to our own peril for too long."

What happens if the side attacking democracy is waging the battle in 50 states, but those resisting only fight in half those states or fewer? The anti-democracy side is always making gains. And to the extent that the pro-democracy side gives up on states once they're on the wrong side of the presidential map, the anti-democracy side's gain in that state becomes permanent.

The damage is especially great when states are pursuing the "laboratories of autocracy" model described above: always pushing new approaches, always testing, always learning, always sharing, never relenting. The more petri dishes, the better. Before you know it, a number of states have adopted new measures with scant resistance, which builds momentum to push those measures elsewhere.

The defense for democracy must take place in all 50 states. On a permanent basis.

My friend Stacey Abrams writes: "Those of us who believe in the promise of democracy must become outraged about even a single act of suppression . . . . the loss of a single voter's right to participate is a wrong that cannot be tolerated."[702]

I'll add this corollary: *Not a single American* should live in a state that doesn't come anywhere close to meeting the definition of a functioning democracy. And we must organize accordingly—as opposed to forcing people to move out-of-state to return to democratic governance.

Step 8. Invest Every Year, Everywhere

Fighting back in all 50 states sounds expensive. And it will be.

But just like we cannot let the presidential map determine *where* we fight our battles, we can't let our presidential calendar determine *when* we fight our battles. And *when we* invest. And that's another mistake forces of democracy made for too long.

Presidential years have seen explosions of spending, both at the top and in targeted federal races across the board. The Center for Responsive Politics estimates that at least $14 billion was spent in 2020 from all sides—almost $7 billion spent by Democratic candidates, campaigns, and groups, and another $2.6 billion by so-called "Super PACs," political parties and dark money groups.[703] Most of this money flowed into the pockets of television stations in the form of 30-second ads.

I'm not suggesting winning the presidency or those targeted seats are not critical causes. They're essential (but not enough). And television ads *do* matter.

But at the risk of oversimplifying things, I will make a bold suggestion:

Take a small percentage of that presidential year spending, invest it to fight for democracy all over the country *every year*, and not only might you save democracy, but you'll *enhance* your prospects in the presidential year as well.

Three percent of the rough total spent by the side fighting for democracy? That's around $240 million. (As a comparison, Rove's effort in 2010 cost $24 million.)

Five percent of the total? $400 million.

Really want to save democracy? Take it to ten percent. $800 million.

Sound crazy?

Well, it's exactly what the forces attacking democracy decided to do years ago. Invest nationally, every year, in all states. And it's worked out pretty well for them.

I think it's worth fighting *for* democracy just as hard, don't you? Plus, it's not a zero-sum game. Remember, if you firm up democracy everywhere, you'll do *better* in the presidential year.

More on how to invest those dollars below. But the bottom line is we shouldn't let the most high-profile races dictate where and when all the investment to save democracy occurs. *Most* of it, sure. But not *all*. We need to fight for democracy in all 50 states, all the time, or democracy erodes.

Investing a seed amount in defending democracy every year, everywhere is an investment that will pay off time and again. The money's there—we just need to make saving democracy a higher priority.

One piece of good news is that the Democratic National Committee has been moving in this direction since 2016. When I first arrived as a DNC member (membership comes with being chair of a state party), the big debate was whether the

DNC should allocate $5,000 or $10,000 to state parties (where most of the on-the-ground work is done) on a monthly basis. That was *it*. And for many parties in red states, that was a big chunk of their overall budget. Even at the time, I thought ALEC and Rove and the Koch Brothers must've loved seeing that that was the big debate.

Under Chairs Tom Perez and now Jaime Harrison, that number has been increased, not just in the monthly allocations, but in larger one-time grants awarded to state parties for certain programs and approaches. As Harrison told me, "[w]e must protect democracy everywhere and therefore must be able to compete everywhere." Still, to catch up with what's happening on the other side—to replicate some of the success stories I describe in the next chapter—the overall amount invested in state-based efforts to protect democracy needs to go way higher, from a wide range of pro-democracy funders.

Step 9: Challenge Laws Everywhere

When Frank LaRose announced his ban on all but one drop box per county, he justified it on legal grounds even though he'd never received a legal opinion on the matter. Still, he proclaimed he had no authority to add any more drop boxes.

I'm a lawyer, and I knew he was lying. My team of lawyers knew it too. And we're stubborn, so we sued . . . and won in every court at every level. Each court found that LaRose had ample authority to add multiple drop boxes in multiple locations. He didn't need legislative approval as he was falsely claiming.

LaRose never thought we'd sue. He had strung out the decision for weeks and assumed we wouldn't take on the high expense of disproving this lie, especially when funds were desperately needed in the election's closing months. But like I said, we're stubborn. Still, the case was damn expensive—we scrambled to raise some funds, the Democratic National Committee helped, but it will still take the party a long time to pay off that legal bill.

In many states, his bet would've paid off. Many state parties or other pro-democracy organizations simply don't have the funds to wage the legal fights necessary to win, especially in cases where the entire Republican Party and national campaign (as happened in our drop box suit) enter the case to make it even more time-consuming and costly. So, too often the legal challenges only take place in swing states. But that gives up the fight in too many places. It allows egregious lies like LaRose's to settle in, unchallenged, and become that state's truth. And it risks setting dangerous precedents for elsewhere.

The legal fight must be fought *everywhere* the attacks happen. Or anti-democratic precedents will take hold in state after state and spread from there.

Just as forces for democracy must invest everywhere, they need to provide support to fight court battles for democracy everywhere. Not only during presidential years. Not only in swing states.

But to be truly effective, this support must go beyond simply litigation support *after* suits are filed. Each state requires an infrastructure for ongoing voter protection and election observation with enough capacity to ensure votes aren't being suppressed through administrative decisions on the ground.

CHAPTER 13

Resistance at the State Level

State Response—Policy and Government

Step 10. ALWAYS Resist—Never Cut Deals Against Democracy

RECALL CHAPTER EIGHT. All that voter suppression in Ohio and across the country, aimed right at the Obama coalition.

Remember that horrible bill that required college students who registered to vote in Ohio to also change their driver's license and registration within 30 days or be sanctioned? The one college kids from across Ohio convinced Kasich to veto?

Some Democrats in the Ohio Statehouse voted *for* it.

Why? Because they wanted to be on record in support of the road projects at the heart of the bill. While they made clear that they didn't back the voting provision, many still voted yes on the overall bill.

Other times, county-level Democratic elections officials in Ohio supported anti-voter election changes, such as eliminating early vote opportunities like Golden Week. Representative

Clyde describes "feeling like you're running on a hamster wheel trying to get Democratic elections officials from supporting some of these anti-voter policies."[704] And occasionally, eyeing a handful of districts favorable to themselves, Democrats across the country will join Republicans in support of badly gerrymandered maps.

Lesson for the future: in a fight for democracy, don't *ever* go along. With any aspect of it. For whatever tradeoff is offered.

Those attacking democracy love to tout *any* bipartisan support for their tactics. Heck, they'll take *any* trace of non-extreme support—so when a Democrat joins up, it's like Christmas. Or as Charles P. Pierce colorfully stated, it's become a "cheap alibi . . . a lock-pick."[705] It's the first rebuttal they'll offer publicly in defense of a bad bill, and they'll throw it in the face of all those fighting for democracy—casting them as the partisan ones. And it's one of the first things they'll include in their legal defense when they're sued.

Beyond boosting the wrong side, when those who support democracy go along, the average voters will understandably assume the change must not be that bad. "Well, if it was less important than a road . . . " It normalizes it all; it makes it seem like a legitimate trade-off, when it's not.

Nothing is worth trading democracy for, especially at a time when one side is trying to crush it.

Never compromise on that.

Step 11. Resist Fiercely and Unconventionally

In the summer of 2021, looking at a bill that would shred voting rights across Texas, Texas Democrats faced a choice. Show up, vote against it, and watch it pass—gutting voting rights for a generation. Or leave.

They left. The Statehouse, and the state. And the effort stopped for some time.

Good.

Those Texas resisters spent the next few weeks in the media spotlight, explaining to the country how undemocratic the Texas legislation was.

Even better.

The attacks on voting rights at the state level are so illegitimate, being led by gerrymandered bodies that themselves are illegitimate, that resisting in unconventional ways is precisely what is called for.

As former Ohio State Senator Nina Turner likes to say, "when your hair is on fire, act like your hair is on fire."

Call the illegitimacy out for what it is. These measures are *way* out of bounds. Don't leave any impression that any of this is normal politics.

And remember, competitive autocracies rely on the public impression that everything is fine. That tainted elections are fair and attempts to rig them are perfectly okay. The perpetrators of all this need to "convince citizens that they are living in a democracy." Don't let them.

Days after the end of her historic run for governor of Georgia, Stacey Abrams acknowledged that her opponent was the legal victor in a tight race, and that she had no legal course to change that. But she also emphasized that hers was "not a speech of concession. Concession means to acknowledge an action is right, true or proper. As a woman of conscience and faith, I cannot concede."[706] She next called out all the offenses against democracy that had occurred in Georgia in the prior eight years: the purging of millions of voters, the disqualification of thousands of ballots and registrations, the lack of training and sufficient equipment, the long lines: "I know that eight years of systemic disenfranchisement, disinvestment and incompetence had its desired effect on the electoral process in Georgia."[707]

Stacey knew this unconventional speech would bring criticism:

> Pundits and hyper-partisans will hear my words as a rejection of the normal order. I'm supposed to say nice things and accept my fate. They will complain that I should not use this moment to recap what was done wrong or to demand a remedy. As a leader, I should be stoic in my outrage and silent in my rebuke. But stoicism is a luxury and silence is a weapon for those who would quiet the voices of the people, and I will not concede because the erosion of our democracy is not right.[708]

Concession, she later wrote, "would validate the system that slashed voters from the rolls, ensured thousands could not cast ballots, and blocked thousands more from being counted."[709]

Shortly thereafter, she filed a suit challenging the state's entire election system.[710] It took on multiple aspects of Georgia's election infrastructure and voting laws, including: the purging of millions of voters from their Ohio-style "use it or lose it" approach; the "exact match" voter registration requirement that eliminated 53,000 registrations, which disproportionately impacted (80%) people of color;[711] the closure of hundreds of precinct locations; inaccurate and error-strewn voting rolls which disenfranchise voters; underfunded elections sites, creating long lines, ballot shortages and inoperable machines; inadequate training; and other issues. In sum, the suit concludes: "Georgia citizens try to exercise their constitutional rights but are denied the ability to elect their leaders because of an unconstitutional elections process."[712] Her aim wasn't to reverse her numeric loss, but to repel the attacks on Georgia's democracy.

Edward Everett, the man who preceded Lincoln at Gettysburg, said: *"In grave matters it is best to call things by their right names. . . . "* At the risk of being criticized, that's exactly what Stacey did. A standard concession speech would've normalized outrageous, anti-democratic behavior that she had challenged for years. It would've left the impression that even she could overlook the thousands who'd had their votes suppressed. Instead, she called it all out, then challenged it after the fact. Like those Texas resisters, she ensured the entire state and nation focused on all the continuing wrongs in Georgia.

Good!

Never stop resisting. Don't *ever* let what's happening appear normal.

Step 12. When in Power, *Create* Laboratories of Democracy

A few years ago, Washington and Oregon added voter drop boxes, extended early voting, and began mailing ballots to every voter. These simple steps have led to some of the highest voter turnout numbers in the country year in and year out. Thank you, Washington and Oregon, for showing the way. Many other states have since added these features. And it was a conversation with the chair of the Washington Democratic Party that inspired me to push so fiercely for more drop boxes in Ohio.

When those who support democracy have the power to *strengthen* democracy, they *must* do so.

And do it as soon as the opportunity presents itself.

In short, be like Virginia.

After grabbing the majority in 2019, Virginia lawmakers passed a slew of pro-voter reforms, including repealing the state's strict voter ID law, opening up a 45-day window of no-excuse early voting, and enacting automatic voter registration. Like the Voting Rights Act it was once subject to, Virginia also created an in-state pre-clearance process for local election changes that impact voters.[713] Other states are doing the same in 2021, passing a flood of expansive laws, including expanding drop boxes, broadening early voting more generally, restoring voting rights, easing voter ID requirements, and others.[714]

Pushing these reforms is crucial, for reasons even beyond lifting the voters within individual states.

First, going back to Brandeis' vision, forces of democracy must create models of success the whole nation can learn from. Learn lessons from what works and figure out what needs improvement. Let the forces that *support* democracy pursue the 80/20 approach, whether it's drop boxes, same-day registration, automatic voter registration or novel pre-clearance processes. Do the same work around election security, and truly robust post-election audits. Virginia Governor Ralph Northam got it right when he said his state's goal was to create a "model for how states can provide comprehensive voter protections that strengthen democracy and the integrity of our elections."[715]

These models also allow champions of democracy to disprove the myths and lies spread about pro-voter innovations. For example, widespread use of drop boxes has *not* resulted in fraudulently cast votes, while automatic voter registration turns out to be a far more cost-effective and less error-prone way of updating your voter rolls than the pony express of purging infrequent voters. Similarly, same-day registration has worked incredibly well in the states that use it, disproving the myths of fraud those attacking democracy try to spread.

Yet another benefit is that it eliminates one of the prime defensive tactics used in "laboratory of autocracy" states. Those pushing to restrict voting laws know exactly which states in Democratic hands have *not* modernized or adopted robust voting practices. Just as they will tout any Democrat who joins their attacks on voters, they happily cite those states to distract from their anti-voter policies: "Well, Ohio has better laws than . . . X" was a refrain I heard again and again. Their intent *in Ohio* has been to curtail days or means of voting that were disproportionally used by voters of color. Because they can't defend that, pointing to other states allows them to change the subject. Too often, it works.

Champions of democracy *must* take that argument away from them, and some are. New York was the most commonly cited state for poor voting laws. So, it's great to see in 2021, numerous reforms moving forward in the Empire State to change that, including on-line requests of absentee ballots and that absentee ballots postmarked by election day will count.[716] Keep going! Your work there helps your own voters, builds momentum for reforms everywhere, and helps those fighting back against the "laboratories of autocracy."

If you believe in a robust democracy, make it happen whenever you have the power to do so. Go on offense. Create "laboratories of democracy" wherever we can. Spread the successes, and share the lessons. Take away their counterarguments.

State Response—Political Effort

"That's all well and good," some are no doubt saying. "But what if you don't have that power? What if you're behind the lines, and you face a rigged system? What can you do?" This is no doubt the most difficult hurdle, especially if Congress doesn't step up. But there are success models here as well.

Step 13: Run a Candidate in Every Legislative District

Ohio Speaker Larry Householder was indicted for the largest bribery scandal in the history of Ohio right in the middle of the 2020 election.

And then was re-elected with more than 70% of the vote.

One major reason for his win? He faced four candidates—all write-ins.

Write-ins almost never win. Four write-ins will *never* win.

Even indicted, Householder was a shoe-in.

Bottom line: run someone in *every* district, every year. For a lot of reasons:

First, in the current statehouse cultures where corruption is a central feature, incumbents are out of touch, and public outcomes are paltry, you never know who the next Larry Householder or Cliff Rosenberger will be. They should *never* get a pass, and some might lose. Unless, of course, they don't have an opponent.

Second, incumbents with no challengers become increasingly sealed off from the people. From democracy itself. Remember that judge who was so relieved when no one filed against her? Allowing incumbents to feel that relief— walled off from the voters for another term, feeling entitled to keep doing what they're doing, or go even further—is a gift we should never give. Democracy and voters without choices are the ones who pay the price. And once sealed off from the people for some time, that relief evolves into fear of the people, and of the democratic process.

Third, *every* district is an opportunity to carry the message to communities that need to hear it. On corruption. On democracy. And most importantly, on the shameful public outcomes that local communities are experiencing. The citizens of Manchester shouldn't *only* hear from a politician telling them to leave because failure is inevitable; they should also hear an alternative vision by someone challenging those officials. If the incumbent isn't challenged, voters hear nothing. That's *their* loss.

Finally, think 80/20 like they do. You're far more likely to unseat incumbents *somewhere* if you challenge them *everywhere*. In Ohio, the 2011 gerrymandering was so bad, Democrats didn't flip a single seat in 2012, 2014 or 2016. Not one. But in 2018, for the first time, that changed when we flipped six seats. Not coincidentally, that was the only year of the decade where the Democratic House Caucus ran a candidate in all 99 Ohio districts. Every incumbent Republican was challenged. Not one member felt that "relief" of filing day. That's not the only reason we gained seats, but it mattered.

And after you run everywhere once, keep doing it. Keep building.

Again, look at Virginia. Entering 2017, Republicans controlled 66 of 100 seats. In 2017, Democrats ran a candidate in more districts than any cycle in recent history[717]— including in numerous districts where they had little chance of winning. Overall, Democrats left twelve seats uncontested while the GOP left 27 uncontested. Democrats went on to pick up fifteen seats. Only a lost coin toss kept their total to 49-51. Two years later, they wouldn't need that coin. They contested even more seats (leaving only seven uncontested, versus 28 by Republicans!), and flipped six more to take a 55-45 majority.[718]

Two cycles, incumbents challenged everywhere, and the whole state flips. And then they got right to work enhancing democracy with one law after the next.

Run in every district if at all possible.

Step 14: Run on Corrosion as much as Corruption: In Kansas, "There's No Place Like . . . Public Schools"

As early chapters of the book make clear, a broken democracy, combined with corruption and/or the ALEC model of governing, inevitably leads to failing public outcomes. Why inevitably? Because the *goal* of the corruption and private takeover of the public process is to rip away public resources for private gain, on issue after issue. The policies to do that are deeply unpopular, and the results predictably horrific for communities. Ironically, those woeful outcomes also open up political opportunity for those challenging the corrupt status quo. And those failures can ultimately be *the* way out.

Just look at Kansas. It's a deep red state that twice voted for Trump, by 20% and 14%. Its two Republican Senators also win handily, by 11% and 30% in their most recent elections.

But in 2018, Kansas elected a Democratic governor in Laura Kelly.[719] How? Because among other things, she campaigned relentlessly on the disastrous public outcomes Kansans had suffered through eight years of her predecessor. And what had her predecessor done? He'd worked with the legislature to unleash the full-on, failed ALEC model on Kansas and its communities.

As background, Kansas' Governor Sam Brownback came to power in 2010 and, guided by Arthur Laffer—the namesake of the ALEC index—worked with the state legislature on what they called the "March to Zero." Slash income taxes to nothing. Along the way, Kansas' legislature advanced countless other ALEC model laws.[720] No surprise, the ALEC/Laffer ranking rewarded Laffer's own handiwork, lifting Kansas from 26th to 11th in 2013.[721]

ALEC might've been the only place that praised the work.

In the non-ALEC real world, what followed was one disaster after the next. A massive revenue shortfall led to exploding deficits and downgrades of Kansas bonds, adding to the cost of infrastructure projects.[722] Education funding was slashed to the point where the state's supreme court ruled it unconstitutional; some schools ended the year early because they ran out of money,[723] while others went to four days a week.[724] To make up for shortfalls, taxes were hiked for the less well-off via higher sales taxes to pay for the income tax cuts.[725] And despite big promises and their higher ALEC ranking for "competitiveness," Kansas' job growth was half the national average and lower than its neighboring states.[726] The state became a case study of how tax cut obsession can crater public outcomes.[727] The disastrous results were so clear that some statehouse Republicans joined Democrats to repeal some of the tax cuts in the later years of Brownback's tenure. (As you'd expect, even amid the wreckage, ALEC concluded that "the case can certainly be made that the reforms are having a positive effect."[728] And as Kansas saw some recovery after abandoning the worst of the ALEC policies, the Laffer/ALEC ranking *punished* Kansas by dropping its ranking back down to 27th by 2016.[729])

Enter Laura Kelly, a long-time state senator who entered the governor's race in 2018. What did she run on from the moment she started? Basic delivery of public goods—education, Medicaid expansion, and highway construction.[730] And the egregious failures of the ALEC-inspired extremism.

Her opponent, Kris Kobach, was infamous for his attacks on voting rights, but her strategy was to be "relentless in trying to tie Mr. Kobach to former Gov. Sam Brownback" and his failed policies.[731]

Relentless is right. One TV ad reminded voters what Brownback had done to Kansas' public schools: "[t]o me, Sam Brownback's attacks and massive education cuts weren't numbers on a spreadsheet. They were an attack on who we are as Kansans."[732] Another: "Sam Brownback sacrificed our schools to pay for his big tax experiment. Now, we're seeing bigger classes, fewer programs, and shorter school years. I'm running for governor to undo that harm."[733] And after Governor Kelly won, her victory speech stuck to the same theme: "[W]e have faced challenges here over the last eight years like in no other state. We've seen our schools devastated and the opportunities for our children put at risk. Partisanship was put above all else and it tore our state apart."[734]

Kansas was not the only state where this strategy worked. In Michigan, the winning message was "fixing the damn roads."[735] And while Scott Walker was toxic for many reasons in Wisconsin, his opponent, an educator, focused on school cuts and roads, and also won.[736]

Bottom line: the extreme and insider/ALEC-driven agenda that dominates current statehouses is deeply unpopular and leads to terrible results for everyday people. Corruption and pay-to-play inevitably lead to public decay. So, no doubt, call out corruption whenever it occurs. Highlight extremists, in some crowds. Perhaps mention where some of the worst ideas originate from. But most important, focus relentlessly on the failed results that everyday people and communities feel directly, and care about the most. Always connect back to that.

Step 15: Focus on Any Seat with Leverage over Power

In recent years, largely because of the Trump margins of victory here and those gerrymandered districts, the nation has declared Ohio to be a red state. (That's an over-simplistic misreading, but this book is not the place to debate that). National forces on the Democratic side of things have invested accordingly (i.e., not as much as they used to). It also doesn't help that campaigning across Ohio and its multiple media markets is very expensive.

At the same time, in 2018 and 2020, Democratic-endorsed candidates for the Ohio Supreme Court won three out of four statewide elections (ousting two incumbents), taking the court from 7-0 to 4-3. This represents a huge shift in one of the most important levers of power in the state.

How did this happen when Ohio has been deemed a predictably red state, with less national Democratic support than before?

Because we prioritized those seats. We knew how strategically important they were. We did a deep dive into why we'd been losing them in prior years and how we could win them back. We concluded that even without national support, they were attainable if we recruited good candidates and increased our voters' awareness on those races—if we reduced "drop-off." And then we created a strategic plan and stuck to it through three cycles. And we learned and adjusted as we went.

This is how Karl Rove operated in 2010. Head down. Ignore the national chatter. Focus on seats that matter, even if they're below the radar. And *especially* because they're below the radar, the amount of resources involved may be far less.

Give Rove credit—he made a return appearance in Ohio in 2020, trying to beat back our effort to take the third Supreme

Court seat. But it was too late. Justice Brunner won going away, the biggest overperformance in the nation. We crushed Rove. And now an independent court provides an important balance against the extremism of the statehouse.

We earned a similar strategic win in the 2020 Franklin County prosecutor race. As explained in Chapter Seven, that office has jurisdiction over all the corruption in the capital city, and was occupied by an incumbent who'd won handily for a generation, yet never did a thing about the corruption in his party. We invested a good amount into that race as well, and won.

Bottom line: Many positions in politics play a role in protecting democracy. Legislatures, of course—so run in every district. Statewide offices such as governors, secretaries of state, and attorneys general are critical. Even auditors, as those miners in Utah learned from their bosses. And state court seats are playing a critical role on so many issues.

And even in a badly gerrymandered world, whether they be in Kansas or Arizona or Ohio, some of these seats are winnable.

Focus on them, put together a plan, and execute.

Step 16: Go Right to the People to Protect Democracy

Almost everyone said it couldn't be done. At least, it couldn't be done without millions of dollars which we didn't have, and had no way of raising.

Almost everyone. A small group of good government reformers and I saw it differently.

The post-2016 marches in Washington spilled over into an incredible grassroots movement all across Ohio, usually in the form of marches and regular protests outside the offices of gerrymandered GOP Congressmen. It was a level of energy we hadn't seen since Senate Bill 5 in 2011. And these were mostly new people coming forward, a diverse coalition of progressives from cities and suburbs (more women than men) appalled by the early Trump attacks on health care and immigrants. But these protesters learned quickly that no matter the size of their rallies, not one GOP Congressman in Ohio cared what they thought. They voted in lock-step for all the worst stuff.

The protests and marches were so large and spirited, our small group convinced ourselves—there's got to be a way to channel all that frustration and energy into positive change here in Ohio. To go on *offense*. Perhaps if we could turn these protesters into petition-gatherers, we could get something big done. So, despite the naysaying from political professionals, we asked a coalition of these new groups if they wanted to channel their unbounded energy into a drive to end the worst gerrymandering in Ohio history. To make the House members ignoring them more accountable.

And boy did they!

The first meeting where we all agreed to take on gerrymandering was March 2017. Within months, we'd finalized the constitutional language, gotten it approved by the state's ballot board, and on Memorial Day, all the grassroots and good government groups kicked off the signature gathering effort. By late fall, with only volunteers doing the work (most big petition drives involve paid circulators, costing those millions we didn't have), they'd gathered hundreds of thousands of signatures from all over the state. And late in the year, scared of the momentum they saw, the legislature itself took up a modified version of the measure and placed it on the ballot.[737] The overall reform remained significant enough that the groups endorsed it. And in May 2018, Ohio voters showed that they despised the rigging of elections as much as we did. The measure passed with more than 70% of the vote.

Now no one who worked hard on that effort was naive enough to assume that was the end of it. Legislators who've only known rigged districts will still try to get away with a rigged map if they can. Some Republican officials still can't hide their intent to ignore the people's will—and law—and rig elections for another decade.[738] So after adding the new language to the Ohio Constitution in May 2018, many of those grassroots activists threw their energy into ensuring the new rules would be enforced by electing an independent Supreme Court. Want fair districts? Elect yourself a fair court. And that's what they did. That broad grassroots understanding provided a critical base of support behind the three winning Supreme Court campaigns in 2018 and 2020 that ushered in an independent court. (Compare that to 2009-2010, when no one knew a thing about the districting process).

Ohio wasn't unique in this success. Michigan did the same thing Ohio did in 2018, passing a measure to end gerrymandering while adding other voter protections. Florida voters ended felony disenfranchisement. Nevadans voted for same-day registration.[739] I've told the Missouri story above.

The lesson is: many state constitutions allow citizens to forge the change they want directly.[740] Changes to shore up democracy, or changes to improve policy. If you're in a state that allows you to go straight to the voters, these measures can succeed—even when hardened political professionals are convinced they can't. One reason they succeed: as Ohio experienced with Senate Bill 5, and as with gerrymandering, the corrupt, extreme and anti-public approach of most of these statehouses is deeply unpopular when understood. Going right to the people and exposing these problems—calling an up-or-down vote on corruption or broken politics or common good issues such as health care—can work even when the odds appear long. (Which is another reason why ALEC and some statehouses are trying to make these efforts more difficult).

Want to go on *offense* for democracy? Use these tools whenever you can. And don't let the naysayers convince you otherwise. And yes, after you win, the statehouse will likely still try defy the change. But keep fighting.

One other thing, where possible, do all you can to repeal terrible laws when they're passed. Do what Ohio did with Senate Bill 5. And here, the political professionals are right: because the timeframe for gathering signatures is short, these efforts will usually take money. And this is where, as with legal issues, national funding to wage repeal efforts on an ongoing basis is critical.

Step 17: Treat *Every* Candidate as a Champion of Democracy

It's tough as hell to run for office in a gerrymandered world. It's tough to be told that in the best-case scenario, you're part of an 80/20 strategy—and you're more likely with the 80 who don't make it than the 20. It's painful to know that you can put most of your life on hold, ask everyone you know to help, out-hustle and outwork and outshine your opponent in every way, and still get fewer votes because it was all rigged from the outset. That's what happened to "Toro," Ken Harbaugh, Betsy Rader, and Desiree Tims. That's what happened to the young candidate who lost to the worst candidate I've ever seen. It happens to thousands of candidates every cycle. It drives most of them out of politics. It keeps most from running in the first place.

But **Step 13** requires that we need to run in every district.

So how do we solve this dilemma?

Let me return to a common theme: *do what Stacey Abrams did.*

Redefine the run. Redefine the purpose of running in the first place. And redefine what victory looks like.

The battle for democracy has always been an uphill one. Look at the multiple generations of women who fought for suffrage. Look at John Lewis and all those who put their lives on the line (and the many who lost them) to end the (last) Jim Crow era. And in our new battle, we face an organized, deep-pocketed force relentlessly working to make that uphill battle ever steeper—in state after state, they're trying to beat democracy into submission.

Fighting back against the Koch Brothers and ALEC and all those gerrymandered politicians involves both a *long game* and an enormous *team effort*. Even if most won't change outcomes of a particular district in a single election, *every single run* is part of that years-long, team effort.

The individual candidates who step up to run in a gerrymandered district are the heart of that effort. Simply by running, they are performing as honorable an act of public service as there is. They are giving voters the choice that the gerrymandered majority didn't want them to have. "Laboratories of autocracy" thrive when there is no attention on most districts or candidates, or the statehouse, or the corruption, or the failed public outcomes. When there are no debates or forums. Their dream scenario is to have no conversation at all—a victory party on filing day—in as many places as possible. So, each run itself is something to celebrate. The odds may be long on election day, but the challenger disrupts the other side's ideal outcome the moment they file to run. In that alone, they are already a *champion of democracy.* We should be the ones celebrating on filing day!

And if they run hard, celebrate the hell out of that as well—even when most don't get more votes than their opponents. As Stacey said in her non-concession speech: "We won".[741] How? "[W]inning doesn't always mean you get the prize. Sometimes you get progress, and that counts."

"Progress."

Like what?

Again, in a gerrymandered district, progress starts with giving voters that choice in the first place. *Every* conversation is progress. Every door knock, every forum, every parade—all are offering a different view than what the gerrymandered incumbent would have them believe. Many are challenging voters to think about the statehouse for the first time in a long time, if ever.

And without that run? Not one of these things would've happened. Silence. Inactivity. And silence and inactivity crush democracy. *Their* ideal state.

But progress comes in so many other tangible ways too. Newly registered voters—voters who now won't be purged. Newly engaged voters. Higher turnout. Inspired volunteers, who then become activists or even candidates down the road.

These are not simply moral victories, by the way. All those tangible steps inure beyond a single campaign. Done right, each concrete step of a campaign—each door knock, each phone call, each vote—is *additive*. Over time, and across districts, all those steps build on one another to forge bigger change. And even, ultimately, victories at the ballot box.

How?

First, the battle for democracy is a team sport, so even in loss, one candidate's spirited run may lift other candidates on the same ballot to victory. I've seen it happen again and again.

Remember Betsy Rader's run for Congress? Betsy ran a robust turnout operation in her race, with wide and spirited grassroots support. It wasn't enough to overcome the rigged district, but *two* of the statehouse districts where we flipped a seat that year were in Betsy's House district. One race was decided by 707 votes (1.2%);[742] the other by under 3,000 votes (under 3%).[743] Betsy's turnout operation helped turn out many more voters than those narrow margins. She played a key role in those breakthrough wins. 80/20 at work!

Like Betsy, in 2018, a candidate named Aftab Pureval took on a gerrymandered district in Cincinnati. Aftab inspired many, and his campaign anchored a robust get-out-the-vote operation that year. The rigged district got the best of him, but the turnout from his effort built a blue wave in Hamilton County. Where did we win another one of those house seats? Northern Hamilton County (by 56 votes—.1%).[744] And that year, we didn't give incumbent judges the gift of a free pass, and almost every one of our judicial candidates unseated them. It's a whole new courthouse now, which far better reflects the people of the community. Thank you, Aftab.

A candidate named Shannon Freshour took on Jim Jordan in 2020. She knew it was an uphill battle in a hopelessly gerrymandered district that criss-crossed 14 counties (in the shape of a duck). But active on social media and facing a nationally notorious opponent, Shannon built a large on-line following and raised more than $1.4 million dollars (!) in small dollar donations. With her opponent's notoriety and her resources, Shannon spent the campaign lifting others in their runs as much as she did her own. She supported field offices in five rural counties, lifted statehouse and Supreme Court candidates everywhere she went, and essentially became the team captain in the 14 counties of that district. I don't recall seeing a more team-oriented campaign *ever*. Why'd Shannon do this? Because, as she told me: "I knew [running that way] had a much better chance of doing more good long-term for our state." Now *that* is a true champion of democracy, running hard until the last day even knowing the odds were long. I'm so glad Shannon ran.

Similarly, others who ran in tougher statehouse districts in 2018 owned a part of the six statehouse flips we gained that year. Ninety-nine candidates running forced their opponents and party bigshots to devote time and resources in all of those districts. No one got a pass—no one celebrated filing day. We flipped six districts because we contested all 99. *Make sure those who don't win understand that those pick-ups were their victories too.*

"Progress" in the long game of democracy can also come *later*. Remember, done right, it's all additive. Play the long game.

Look at Georgia. Stacey's run, and the fact that she never stopped fighting for the cause of voters and democracy, set the table for the enormous Georgia wins in 2020 that allowed Democrats to take back both the White House and the Senate. If a voter registered to vote and showed up for Stacey in 2018, that voter very likely did the same for Biden and the Senate candidates in 2020. Maybe that voter told others to join them. As Stacey did, you just keep adding. Keep building.

Or look again at Ohio, at those flipped six statehouse seats in 2018, all in districts that had been gerrymandered in 2011. All six who won those races were great candidates. But three of those six winners had run hard in 2016 and *lost*. After coming up short in the prior cycle, they went right back at it for the next election. Everything they'd built for 2016 became their jumping off point for 2018. Then they added from there; new volunteers, new registered voters, new donors, new doors knocked on. And ultimately, new voters—enough to win. In

2020, they each built more, and won by more. Again, if done right, it's all additive.

Too often, after a single loss, we let these champions of democracy walk away, thinking they failed. We celebrate the breakthrough wins, but fail to give credit to too many who were in the fight. It's a huge mistake. These candidates did exactly the opposite of what those attacking democracy want to happen. And if they ran hard, they built something— for their district, for their state, and for the future. Thank them. Celebrate them. Keep everything they built intact for the next time. Keep them in the fold in any way you can, including in other forms of service. I'm thrilled that Desiree, who ran that great race in Dayton, now runs Innovation Ohio, a progressive think tank here; and that Aftab Pureval will likely be Cincinnati's next mayor. Shannon and Toro are still fighting the good fight on social media with their 100,000s of followers, and Ken runs several popular podcasts.

Theodore Roosevelt summed it up in one of his most memorable speeches:

> It is not the critic who counts; not the man who points out how the strong man stumbles, or where the doer of deeds could have done them better. The credit belongs to the man who is actually in the arena, whose face is marred by dust and sweat and blood; who strives valiantly; who errs, and comes short again and again, because there is no effort without error and shortcoming; but who does actually strive to do the deeds; who knows the great enthusiasms, the great devotions; who spends himself in a worthy cause; who at the best knows in the end the triumph of high achievement, and who at the worst, if he fails, at least fails while daring greatly, so that his place

shall never be with those cold and timid souls who know neither victory nor defeat.

Politicians in office often assume that Roosevelt is referring to them. That the "arena" means those *in* elected office. But especially now, let's broaden it—those who *run* for office are smack dab in the middle of the arena. If they're doing it in an uphill, rigged district amid a wave of attacks on democracy, they're "daring greatly" for as "worthy [a] cause" as there is. And that's how we should treat them from start to finish, and after.

Step 18: No "Off-Year" Elections

As important as running in every legislative or Congressional district is, it still isn't enough. Go further, go deeper. If politics is truly about democracy, the people, and public service—and not just power—*every* election matters.

So, you run hard at every level, every year.

You reject the term "off-year" election.

An odd-numbered year isn't an "off year" at all. In most places, it's a chance to lift community in countless ways through municipal elections, or schools and students and teachers through school board elections, or improve the justice system through judicial elections. In crises like a pandemic, it's where you save lives (or cost them if you're reckless). All that is pretty "on" if you ask me, or most voters. Communities everywhere are in desperate need of good, capable, service-minded leaders. And each of these elected offices offers an opportunity for someone to perform public service and make a difference in the world. *Nothing* matters more than that.

Campaigns for all of these offices enhance democracy.

Again, each is additive. Every door knock, every phone call, every vote, every petition signed—all build on one another. Each registered voter, each new voter. If a person votes in a local school board race in a so-called "off year," they're far more likely to turn around and vote in a statehouse or congressional or presidential race the next year. And that voter just took herself off the "to be purged" list if she lives in Ohio, Georgia, Arizona, or another "use it or lose it" state.

Most of these local races aren't gerrymandered, so they're more winnable. And when champions of democracy win, their public service also changes the conversation. Their leadership provides an important contrast to the gerrymandered leaders who do little more than what ALEC demands at the statehouse. In 2019, for example, four Democratic candidates took on incumbent mayors in four small, rural Ohio towns Trump won handily in 2016: Archbold, Ironton, Norwalk and Coshocton. Like Governor Kelly in Kansas, each ran on the fact that their towns were failing in too many ways. And each candidate won by 60%-40% or better. Now they're pushing for change in a way that dramatically contrasts with the work those communities' legislators are doing at the statehouse. Or in 2021, look at all the local officials—school leaders in particular—who stood up to governors and legislators who refused to be responsible during the pandemic. These leaders not only saved the lives of kids, but they provided a stark contrast from gerrymandered leaders and partisan governors too removed from the people they're supposed to represent. These local officials showed the country the best democracy and public service offer.

Needless to say, these local officeholders also happen to be some of the people best suited to run for legislative districts down the road. They're your "pro-democracy bench." That's important too. But don't jump to that too quickly. Even if many never seek higher office, their run for local office and the service they perform at that level are both huge wins for democracy and their communities.

Step 19: Reflect America, Represent the New Majority

It's a painful reality that one of the core motivations behind the attacks on democracy is fighting back against an ever more diverse America. Abject fear of a non-white majority, and of empowered women.

What's the best response to that? *Embrace that new majority*, and the fact that women *are* already the majority. Reflect it as best you can in who runs for all these offices, at all levels, and who gets the support it takes to win. The country is changing, states are changing, and communities are changing—so you'll get better election results and better public service results if you represent that new majority.

We've seen this even in a tough state like Ohio. Take our Supreme Court wins. Two victors in two years were women, including Melody Stewart, who broke an ignoble glass ceiling when she became the first Black woman to win a statewide election on the Democratic ticket. Of those 2018 and 2020 statehouse wins, five out of seven were women, and one of the men was the first African American to ever win his suburban district. Tina Maharath flipped a state senate district in 2018, making her the first Laotian-American and first Asian-American woman ever to serve in the Ohio senate. Local victories were driven by our diversity as well. Reynoldsburg is a suburb of Columbus, long dominated by Republicans. We ran a strong slate of candidates in 2015 and 2019, unseating some incumbents in '15, then winning every race on the ballot in 2019, including the mayor's office and council majority.

Never before had Reynoldsburg had a Black woman on its council—after 2019, there are three, including the council president. And Reynoldsburg also elected the first Nepali-Bhutanese official in the country.[745] Suburbs in particular are growing more diverse; run candidates who reflect that diversity, and who will represent it in office.

Or look more closely at Virginia's historic success. Same story. Virginia Democrats ran a record number of women in 2017, and eleven out of their fifteen flips that year were by women.[746] Among those winners were the first two Latinas to ever serve in the Virginia General assembly, the first Asian-American woman to serve, and the first open transgender and lesbian legislators in Virginia history.[747]

And federally, America is seeing not only more diversity in the halls of Congress, but a growing trend of candidates of color succeeding in majority-White districts. Eight of the nine new Black members of Congress in 2018 won in districts that had 21 percent Black voters or fewer—six of them having succeeded Republicans in those districts.[748]

In the long run, the racism anchoring so much of the attack on democracy isn't just wrong to its core and another stain on our history. In an ever more diverse America, it also turns out to be a losing political strategy—as long as the side fighting *for* democracy is committed to true representation in who runs for office and *how* they run.

Step 20: Register, Register, Register

In an age where poor and disproportionately minority voters move all the time, and laboratories of autocracy purge all the time, nothing matters more than registering voters. And then continually engaging those voters so they become consistent voters.

But if you leave it to campaigns themselves to do all that work, you've likely already lost. That's way too late in the process, and most campaigns will only get to a certain subsection of voters. In a world of finite resources, campaigns spend most of their time and dollars on a more narrow set of registered voters who are most likely to vote.

So, everyone else: start earlier. In fact, never stop. And get to everyone you can.

Needless to say, the more organizations dedicated to registering voters, the better—including those whose sole purpose it is to do that hard work. That's what Stacey Abrams did for years in Georgia, which ultimately helped flip the state blue. By 2021, 95% of eligible Georgia voters were registered to vote, a truly impressive number forged by years of hard work long before anyone thought Georgia could be blue.[749] There are similar efforts in other states. And part of the 50-state, every-year investment I referenced in **Step 8** must include investing in this type of grassroots registration and engagement work in *every state, all the time*—with special focus on communities of color that are purged the most. Whether it be state parties or other grassroots groups that do this work (need both, ideally), they need to be funded robustly every year so they can go deep into communities and empower voters. Not just at election time. But *way before*—indeed, always. Just as the State Policy Network has its 50-state map of institutions fighting its battles from the right, we must have a 50-state map of robust pro-democracy organizations registering voters non-stop.

Minnesota DFL Chair Ken Martin explains that since the goal is to "re-engage voters with their democracy . . . your investment is going to go much further if you invest locally. In organizations that are closest to voters. We need people to be engaged in intimate, face-to-face conversations with voters."

But we must go way beyond just those organizations. We must adopt a different mindset altogether. Automatic voter registration has shown the way. In the states that have it, AVR makes the process far easier because registration is incorporated into all sorts of other everyday activities people are already doing. So in states *without* AVR, let's replicate that logic and benefit in every way we can.

How do you do that if it's not the state process? To use the military term, let's force multiply. Every organization interacting with the public should broaden its mission to include enhancing democracy, which starts with registering voters. Each organization should think of itself as a *voter registration hub*. And those that interact with those most likely to be purged should lean in the most.

Go to a public health clinic or a children's hospital. Register. (On paper, or online).

Go to the local rec center. Register. (same).

Go to Kroger, or Publix. Register.

Get your union card. Register.

Rent a new apartment. Register.

Register for college courses. Register to vote.

Any City Hall service. Any courthouse service. Any public-facing non-profit that receives public support. Any social service organization or food bank. Register. Register. Register. Register.

If state-level laboratories of autocracy are going to dedicate so much of their time and energy purging voters—often punishing them for being poor and moving a lot, or due to the color of their skin—local governments and organizations whose constituents are disproportionately purged should fight back just as hard to re-register those same folks. *Their* folks. It's both in their constituents' interest, as well the local institutions' interest, that their members and residents fully participate in the political process. (Just as many of these institutions dedicate a lot of time and resources to be sure people are counted in the Census—they know it's in their interest).

So, every mayor, every councilmember, county official, school board member, etc. who believes in democracy—who believes her community benefits from maximum representation—should add voter registration to her core mission. Leaders should then think through every function in their footprint that interfaces with the public and incorporate registration into those services—and especially do so with those services that touch the folks most swept up in the purging net. Then they should train front-line staff accordingly and create an intake system (paper or online) to get the job done in a way that complies with state law. (As a city councilman, I once put together an effort to ensure Cincinnati residents properly claimed the Earned Income Tax Credit. Our free clinics helped thousands of people and brought millions of dollars back to the city. *Registration work* is far easier than helping people do their taxes).

And for all the companies supporting ALEC (more on them below), let's find hundreds more who actually want to register and empower their customers.

Barbershops and beauty salons.

Coffee shops and restaurants and diners.

Grocery stores and ice cream shops.

Apartment complexes and churches.

Big business and small businesses.

All can serve as *voter registration hubs*. All can empower their customers and clients and employees. All can have their front-line staff trained to ask one simple question—"hey, are you registered to vote?" And maybe one more—"hey, did you move?"

Then let's scale it up from there. Picture a recognizable sticker in every business window where businesses, non-profits and government offices tout that they are "voter registration hubs." Like the Better Business Bureau, but for democracy. Imagine a box near each of their entrances with registration and other materials. And a list of all these businesses on a website, so the rest of us can reward them by getting our haircuts or coffee at these establishments *because* they're a voter hub, and telling our friends to do the same. Let's reward all those organizations who are fighting for democracy.

This is all the right thing to do. But it also makes a huge practical difference. It means that campaigns don't spend most of their time and money simply playing a never-ending game of "whack a mole" with those who are purging voters. Let's go to where people are and re-register them all the time—before the campaigns ever start. And if these folks *are* re-registered, they're back in the databases and far more likely to hear from the campaigns.

Last thing, these voting hubs can go beyond simply registration work once elections are under way. They can engage voters in other ways as well, such as providing early vote application materials for their customers.

Step 21: Boosting Journalism

Above, I wrote that challenging incumbents everywhere is one of the best ways to disrupt the conditions that allow laboratories of autocracy to thrive. That silence is a huge boost to their work, so disrupt it.

Well, that silence is also created by the hollowing out of in-state and local journalism. Given everything described above about the power and problems with statehouses, it should scare anyone who cares about democracy that states average only three full-time journalists covering statehouses. That is a dream come true for a strategy anchored in 80/20— throw so much forward, ferociously, and abandon the things that get too much negative attention while ramming the rest through. Three journalists per state capital, along with the demise of local papers, guarantees that approach will succeed. It only gets worse when you throw in state-based faux-news bureaus supported by the SPN/ALEC/Koch network described in Chapter Six.

How do we solve this? It's another tough one, but there are ways to fight back.

First, if you're reading this, and care about democracy, subscribe to good in-state and local papers, especially those that *do* cover the statehouse. Don't try to avoid paywalls— subscribe. Then read and share their articles widely, especially those that address statehouse issues. In Ohio, we are blessed with an incredibly talented and professional corps of statehouse reporters. You'll see how often I've cited their work above. I know them well enough to know that 1) they're exhausted; and 2) after they've written a good story, it's all about clicks and opens. It's how success is measured. If they work on a long piece probing deeply into a statehouse scandal, and no one opens it, that's likely the last time the paper will devote the resources to dive into that issue. If it goes viral, the odds are better they'll keep going. Reward good journalism by subscribing, clicking and sharing.

Second, there's a new trend happening that's encouraging. Non-profit journalism is emerging to fill in some of the gaps left by the struggles in for-profit papers, both through entirely new media outlets, as well as former for-profit papers converting to non-profit status.[750] And some national foundations and organizations, such as the American

Journalism Project, are doing their best to invest in this new model.[751] It's not a silver bullet, but it allows these outlets to broaden their streams of revenue while also pursuing targeted priorities.

Perhaps the best example of this is the *Texas Tribune*, whose self-proclaimed mission is to intensely cover politics in the Lone Star State: "We are trying to make the biggest audience possible in Texas care deeply about politics and policy here."[752] Ironically, the *Tribune* too emerged from drawings on napkins around 2009, after the Texas statehouse press corps had shrunk from 95 reporters in 1989 to 30 in 2008.[753] With some early venture capital support and strong leadership by experienced journalists, by 2018, the Tribune had grown to 80 staff members and a $9 million budget. Around two million unique visitors check into the Tribune's website each month, and it disseminates its news through events, podcasts, a digital newsletter, along with its highly trafficked social media feeds.[754] In 2019 alone, more than 250 other outlets shared its content.[755]

I can attest that in Ohio, a new non-profit called the *Ohio Capital Journal* has had immediate impact. Opening in 2019, its team of scrappy young reporters has churned up story after story, built a strong social media presence, caught more than one politician engaged in misleading tactics,[756] and much of its work was picked up by other news outlets.

Do what you can to help these new and innovative approaches succeed. They're desperately needed. Subscribe, click and share.

Step 22: Expose Statehouses; Disrupt the Silence

The model I'm advocating for above is *real journalism* anchored by the work of real reporters.

But advocacy also has a key role to play. Activists need to go *on offense* at the state level. Remember, these statehouses are used to doing most of their work without much attention. So are their supporters. Silence and anonymity create the perfect environment for them to get away with it all.

Change that. Disrupt that.

One of the most active groups in Ohio since 2016 has been Indivisible, playing a spirited role on issue after issue. If it weren't for their many chapters gathering petition signatures, we would never have changed the Ohio Constitution to reform districting. And they've understood here and elsewhere that too few of their members, or the broader electorate, understand what goes on in statehouses. On their website, they first explain much of what I've talked about here. The basics of how statehouses work, what powers they have, and how they operate.[757] They then walk through tactics to advocate change at the statehouse level, such as: "Mass calls to offices doesn't take as much time as in-person action, but it can have a huge impact at the state level, where staffers are not used to getting a large volume of calls."[758] They encourage folks to submit pieces into local newspapers so legislators actually see that the people they represent (in theory) are aware of what they're doing. They direct folks to go to committee hearings, where much of the work is done.

This is good stuff. *Every* activist group in *every* community in *every* state should add this type of statehouse agenda to their work. Use the Indivisible guide, or find another, or write your own.

To be clear, statehouse politicians will often ignore this advocacy, as loud as it may get. Other times, they may actually cave. The most effective such advocacy I've witnessed was amid a budget crisis, when a large cut was proposed for libraries across Ohio. Supporters of libraries pushed back fiercely from every corner, and the calls flew to Columbus at an unprecedented volume. The legislators actually backed off. It won't happen most times, but this shows you that it can.

But even if you don't win every time, or even most times, the only thing worse than that is silence. Inactivity.

That's what laboratories of autocracy want. That's when they thrive. And that is what we can't afford to give them.

CHAPTER 14

Resistance at the Individual Level

"Freedom is not a state; it is an act. It is not some enchanted garden perched high on a distant plateau where we can finally sit down and rest. Freedom is the continuous action we all must take, and each generation must do its part to create an even more fair, more just society."

—John Lewis

"Unless someone like you cares a whole awful lot, Nothing is going to get better. It's not."

—Dr. Seuss, The Lorax

IF YOU WEREN'T alarmed when you picked up this book, I hope you are now.

And if you were alarmed when you picked up this book, I hope you are *more* alarmed now.

I'm more alarmed after writing it.

But my hope is that you're also inspired to resist what's happening in states across this country. And that I've given enough examples of successful resistance and action that you see that it can make a difference.

Be alarmed, but don't give up hope.

Resist.

So, what you can do, personally?

To the extent you can be part of *any* of the steps I've listed above, please take them. And encourage others to do the same. Organize to do the same.

If you are in a position to do more—you hold public office, you run a business or a non-profit, you run or are part of a political or advocacy group, you are a major donor—take even more of these steps. Convince others who are similarly situated to do the same. Call them all together to do something jointly. You can *lead*.

But whatever your station in life, I want to break it down further than that.

Every person has a toolkit of resources at her or his disposal: your time, your voice, your network, your passion, your dollars.

Your plan to resist what's happening should include how you can use each of these personal resources in various ways.

Step 23: Once Aware, Spread the Word

Remember that *the* core problem of all this is not nearly enough people are aware of what's happening in states. State-level government isn't understood, lost amid the higher profile stuff. And that's *exactly why* it's where the real action is. Some may know some of the basics, but very few know what's *really* happening, or how bad it *really is*. Until they do know, with enough understanding to be alarmed by it, we will never inspire enough people to get involved to make a difference. That's why I wrote this book.

Well, you can help change that. Help spread the word. Again, we need as many people as possible not simply to be aware that there *is* a problem, but to be so alarmed about it that they take action. Help spread the word to get that started. Then tell others to spread the word too.

The easiest way is to get others to **read this book**, and/or other materials within that especially helped clarify what's happening. Five people. Ten people. Family. Friends. Your Facebook friends and Twitter followers. Your book club. The grassroots group you're an active member of. The college political club you're a part of. Your county party. Spread the word and talk about it.

By the way, I'm happy to join any group, anytime, to discuss it as well. We have to spread the word. And fast.

Also, don't stop at this book. Become aware of what's happening in your own state, since that's where you can make the biggest difference. Right away. And spread the word about those details as well.

Step 24: Connect!

I read a lot of good books. I take notes. And then they end. And that's usually that.

I don't want this book to be static. I want it to start a larger conversation. So along with the book, I've created a website called www.laboratoriesofautocracy.com. If you're interested in connecting directly and helping organize, connecting with others, learning more, please go to the website and sign up. My goal is to begin the biggest conversation and movement possible. If a lot of people go to the site, we'll build it up as big as we can to help.

If there's interest, we'll use the site to start building our own models of laboratories of democracy that are working. On the best ways to resist. We'll use it to connect like-minded groups, and to connect *you* to those groups.

You should also follow me on twitter at @davidpepper—I promise you'll get your fill.

Step 25: Know Your Legislator, or His/Her Opponent

The other core problem of all this is that not nearly enough people are aware of who their legislators are or what they're doing—or, if it's election season, who their opponents are.

Well, you can change that too. Get to know who your state rep and state senator are. Size up if they're champions of democracy. It's not hard to figure out. If they are, great. Help them, and ask them *who else* you should help. If they're *not* a champion of democracy, find out if they have an opponent yet. If they do, get to know *them*. See how you can help. Keep helping. And . . . .

Step 26: Run for Office, or Make Sure Someone Else Does

. . . if they don't have an opponent, do whatever you can to change that. Contact your local or state party and see if a candidate is thinking about it. If not, consider running yourself. Be a champion of democracy—like I said, I *loved* running for office. If running isn't for you, get a friend to run. Or a family member. Or a work colleague. Someone who's really impressed you.

But whatever you do, don't let an officeholder who's not a champion of democracy celebrate filing day without an opponent. That's how voters lose, and that's how communities in your district lose. And it's how the laboratories of autocracy win.

Whoever runs, do what you can to help them. Volunteer.

Donate. Introduce them to your network. Keep helping. A few really active people can make a *huge* difference in any campaign.

If they're stepping up to run in a rigged district, they are a champion of democracy. They're in the arena! Celebrate them and support them.

Step 27: Register Voters

Whatever you can do to help register voters, please do. Volunteer with a group that does it. Do it as part of your work on a campaign. Convince a group that you're in to take it up as part of its mission. Provide financial support to local organizations that register people (be sure to check them out first). Ask your local elected officials to create local voter hubs. Convince your employer, whether it be private or public, to become a permanent voter hub. Convince your favorite restaurant or barbershop or gym to become a voter hub. Help them figure out how to set it up. Better yet, make a checklist of all the places that could do it, and convince every one.

Stacey Abrams got registration up to 95% in Georgia! It took years, but it worked. Then Georgia turned blue. Every community and state should be aiming for that goal.

When big numbers of people vote, democracy wins.

Step 28: Put Your Money Where Democracy Is

If a business is part of ALEC, cut them off. Immediately. They don't support democracy, which means they don't respect you. Check out Common Cause, Color of Change and other groups to get the most current list of companies who are attacking democracy.

But don't stop there. I listed above all the mainstream

business groups that supported the likes of John Becker and other state representatives who are on the far fringes and attacking democracy relentlessly. Accountants. The Board of Realtors. NFIB. And others. Let them know they have *no business* endorsing someone with views that extreme—someone happy to tear our democracy asunder. If you run a business, are part of a business, are part of groups like these, etc., make clear that *nothing* is worth putting your good names or dollars behind candidates that are openly tearing down democracy. Tell them that *nothing* is worth trading democracy for.

But go even further than that. Reward *good* behavior. If you run a local or national business, support democracy in any way you can—starting with voter registration and other steps (i.e., election day off) to make it easier for your constituents, clients, customers and employees to vote. Pair up with other businesses in your community to do it all together. Then go public and challenge others to join you.

And if you see local or national businesses supporting voters and democracy, spend your dollars *there*. And tell other people about it. Tweet or tell your friends about the restaurants and beauty salons and city halls that are registering voters. Frequent those places and thank them for what they're doing. Tell others to do the same.

When democracy is being permanently attacked, we need permanent champions of democracy. And the best way to enlist many is to show that we support them *because* they are helping the cause. Again, like the Better Business Bureau, but for voting and democracy. From the biggest national businesses to the smallest mom and shop businesses.

And don't forget, subscribe and support local papers. Share articles and spread the word.

If you have more to spend, help candidates. Not just U.S.

Senate candidates in far-away states, but state representative and state senate candidates in your community, or nearby, or somewhere in your state. And the earlier you help them, the better. The more diverse the candidates, the better too. It's better for representation, and a broad coalition is far more likely to win.

One tip: if you get a call from a candidate you don't know, don't jump off the phone right away. Thank them for running and check them out. It may feel like an annoying telemarketing call, but this caller could very well be a champion of democracy running in a tough district, playing a critical role in our democracy that the election riggers hoped they wouldn't play. And if they're calling you, it's a sign that they're actually sophisticated enough to do what *they need to do* to have a chance at winning. (Many won't make calls, which almost guarantees they will lose). If they win you over, help them out. Offer to do even more than send support.

If you want to dig deeper than that, find organizations that are helping those candidates and help them too. Your party's legislative caucus. Organizations like Run for Something, EveryDistrict, and The Collective PAC, which recruit and support diverse slates of candidates all over the country, and likely in your state. They are doing critical work to add focus and resources at this critical level of politics. Help them if you can. Remember, as Ken Martin says, "invest in people closest to the ground."

Second tip: there's a lot of spam out there, and even a lot of politicians who send emails claiming that your dollars will be spent on all sorts of things—voter protection, grassroots work, local candidates, etc. Read the fine print and ask questions. Lots of these emails are using words and algorithms to get your money even though the money won't go to the cause promised. *We don't have enough money as it is, so we can't afford to waste it on that stuff.* My best advice is to give to the candidates directly if your goal is to help *their* campaigns; to local and state parties that appear to be well run; and to organizations you've looked into and find credible that are doing strong voter outreach/registration work or candidate recruitment and support work.

Step 29: Put Your Time and Voice Where Democracy Is

Laboratories of autocracy thrive in silence. Inattention. Don't let them.

If there's an issue, call legislative offices about it. Write local letters to the editor. Post on social media. Organize for others to do the same.

Show up and testify, and give 'em hell. Show up and march, or protest a statehouse office or a God-awful bill. This is not *normal* politics so don't leave the impression from your tone that you think it is.

Know when you take these actions, just like that crowd that chanted "do something," a majority of voters in your state likely agree with you. It's the gerrymandered legislators that are usually in the deep minority on whatever position they're taking.

And be active on social media. We know how much bad information and propaganda are being shared every day on Twitter, Facebook, and other outlets—both by people and anti-democratic organizations, and by bots and other countries that want to upend American democracy. What's the best way to fight back? Share *the truth* as much as you can. Make sure your networks know what's really happening, and how they can help. And as you do this, I'd recommend reading books like George Lakoff's *Don't Think Like an Elephant* and *The Political Mind*, or Drew Westen's *The Political Brain*, so that every time you communicate you are doing so as effectively as possible.

And don't forget to keep sending letters to the editor to local papers along the same lines.

No silence allowed.

Step 30: Election Time

Vote as early as you can.

Then spend the rest of the election helping make sure other voters vote too. You can do that by helping a candidate, a party, or other organizations who get the vote out. Remember, even in a local election year, every call or text or door knocked is additive. It's always building.

Take election day off and do whatever you can to help make sure people vote.

Minnesota's Ken Martin summed it up well: "the antidote to our current assault on democracy is engaging the electorate in a way that they understand their power, their agency and are inspired to take action." Up to and during election time, do all you can to help voters find their power and take that action.

* * *

There's so much more to do, but these 30 steps are a start. Sign on at www.laboratoriesofautocracy.com and I'll work to add far more to this conversation than I can put in one book.

I'll close on a somber note.

I'm haunted by the thought of the 20- or 30-something Black Alabaman or Georgian or South Carolinian in the 1870s and 80s.

Much was wrong in the world in which he lived. But by that

point, he had the opportunity to vote (unfortunately, women still didn't). And with the franchise, he now saw Black elected officials at every level of government, advocating for a better future. He could even aspire to be one of them some day, leading the way to a better American future as the 20th century dawned.

In just a few years, all of that hope would be gone. The new representation, vanished. And that young Black American would spend the *rest of his life* trapped in a world of no democracy for him or almost anyone he knew—and suffer all the horrific consequences that came without it.

Haunting. A preventable American tragedy.

Thanks to laboratories of autocracy across the country, plugging away as you read this, too many conditions are present that an event or two could quickly lead to some twisted 21st century model of no democracy.

And there's a risk that today's 20-somethings, or teenagers, or my two sons, seven and four, will be saddled with such a warped system, forced to dedicate much or most of their lives clawing back from our failure to stop it.

But that dark fate too is preventable. As long as millions of us who believe in democracy get to work. And, of course, another benefit of that work, if successful, is that a robust democracy is essential if states like Ohio are going to break free from their current, steady decline, and instead lift themselves up in this challenging 21st century economy.

However you can get involved to help, please do.

Robert Kennedy famously said: "Each time a man stands up for an ideal, or acts to improve the lot of others, or strikes out against injustice, he sends forth a tiny ripple of hope, and crossing each other from a million different centers of energy and daring, those ripples build a current that can sweep down the mightiest walls of oppression and resistance."

Send your first ripple for democracy today.

If you've already sent some, stir up some more. Then more tomorrow. Then keep going.

Get others to do the same. Build the current. Then the flood. Resist.

Endnotes

Introduction

[1] Thomas, Bradley W. "Affidavit of Bradley W. Thomas." (20CV005634, Franklin County, Ohio., 2020.), Exhibit 2.

[2] Livingston, Doug. "Traffic congestion drives away early some voters." Akron Beacon Journal. October 15, 2020. https://www.beacon journal.com/story/news/politics/2020/10/15/traffic-congestion-keeps-some-voting-early-summit-county/3666369001/

[3] Thomas, Bradley W. "Affidavit of Bradley W. Thomas." (20CV005634, Franklin County, Ohio., 2020.), Exhibit 2.

[4] Povich, Elaine S. "Rise in Use of Ballot Drop Boxes Sparks Partisan Battles." Pew Charitable Trusts. October 16, 2020. https://www.pewtrusts.org/en/research-and-analysis/blogs/stateline/2020/10/16/rise-in-use-of-ballot-drop-boxes-sparks-partisan-battles

[5] Tobias, Andrew J. "Ohio Secretary of State Frank LaRose: no extra ballot drop boxes for November election." Cleveland.com. August 12, 2020. https://www.cleveland.com/open/2020/08/ohio-secretary-of-state-frank-larose-no-extra-ballot-drop-boxes-for-november-election.html

[6] Tobias, Andrew J. "Ohio judge says Secretary of State Frank LaRose's one ballot drop box per county rule is 'arbitrary and unreasonable." Cleveland.com. September 15, 2020. https://www.cleveland.com/open/2020/09/ohio-judge-rules-against-secretary-of-state-frank-laroses-arbitrary-and-unreasonable-one-ballot-drop-box-per-county-rule.html

[7] Balmert, Jessie. "Ohio's elections chief Frank LaRose: No off-site ballot drop boxes." Cincinnati Enquirer. October 5, 2020. https://www.cincinnati.com/story/news/politics/elections/2020/10/05/ohio-secretary-of-state-frank-larose-multiple-drop-boxes-ballot-decision/3622081001/

[8] "Where To Vote-- 2020 General Election." Denver.org. https://www.denvergov.org/maps/map/electionservices

[9] "Boxes-- King County." Kingcounty.gov.

[10] Livingston, Doug. "Traffic congestion drives away early some voters." Akron Beacon Journal. October 15, 2020. https://www.beaconjournal.com/story/news/politics/2020/10/15/traffic-congestion-keeps-some-voting-early-summit-county/3666369001/

[11] Castele, Nick. "Ohio Supreme Court Reverses LaRose on Blocked Summit County BOE Member." Ideastream Public Media. April 28, 2021. https://www.ideastream.org/news/ohio-supreme-court-reverses-larose-on-blocked-summit-county-boe-member

[12] "Secure Democracy Ohio Track." The Tyson Group. Poll. April 21, 2021-April 23, 2021.

[13] Hancock, Laura. "Ohio bill to overhaul voting laws would only allow ballot drop boxes at county board of elections." Cleveland.com. May 6, 2021. https://www.cleveland.com/open/2021/05/ohio-bill-to-overhaul-voting-laws-would-only-allow-ballot-drop-boxes-at-county-boards-of-elections.html

[14] Cassidy, Christina A. "GOP Targets ballot drop boxes in Georgia, Florida, elsewhere." Associated Press. April 19 2021. https://apnews.com/article/donald-trump-georgia-elections-coronavirus-pandemic-gubernatorial-elections-c083f5e0af7855c9dbb5a1659840c4a9

[15] "Voting Laws Roundup: May 2021." Brennan Center for Justice. May 28, 2021. https://www.brennancenter.org/our-work/research-reports/voting-laws-roundup-may-2021

[16] Millhiser, Ian. "There are 2 kinds of GOP bills-- and one is much worse." Vox Media. June 3, 2021. https://www.vox.com/22463490/

voting-rights-democracy-texas-georgia-suppression-jim-crow-supreme-court-sb7

[17] David Wright and Eric Bradner. "Arizona house passes legislation that weakens secretary of state." CNN. June 25, 2021. https://www.cnn.com/2021/06/25/politics/arizona-bills-secretary-of-state/index.html

[18] Nick Corasaniti and Reid J. Epstein. "What Georgia's Voting Law Really Does." The New York Times. April 2, 2021. https://www.nytimes.com/2021/04/02/us/politics/georgia-voting-law-annotated.html

[19] Patricia Mazzei and Reid J. Epstein "G.O.P Bills Target Protesters (and absolve Motorists Who Hit Them)." June 16, 2021. https://www.nytimes.com/2021/04/21/us/politics/republican-anti-protest-laws.html

[20] Alice Bannon, Douglas Keith, Patrick Berry. "Legislative Assaults on State Courts-- 2021." Brennan Center for Justice. May 19, 2021. https://www.brennancenter.org/our-work/research-reports/legislative-assaults-state-courts-2021

[21] *New State Ice Co. v. Liebmann*, 285 U.S. 262, 311 (1932) (Brandeis, dissenting)

[22] Baker, Keeling. "A Progressive Call to Arms: Laboratories of Democracy." Harvard Political Review. December 3, 2020. https://harvardpolitics.com/laboratories-of-democracy/https://harvardpolitics.com/laboratories-of-democracy/

Chapter 1: Ohio, Ohio, Ohio: A Bellwether for Good and Bad

[23] Feran, Tom. "Gov. John Kasich says 60 percent of U.S. population is within 600 miles of Ohio." Politifact.com. May 13, 2011. https://www.politifact.com/factchecks/2011/may/13/john-kasich/gov-john-kasich-says-60-percent-us-population-with/

[24] Desjardins, Jeff. "Animation: The 20 Largest State Economies by GDP in the Last 50 Years." VisualCapitlist.com. August 22, 2019. https://www.visualcapitalist.com/animation-the-20-largest-state-economies-by-gdp-in-the-last-50-years/

[25] Jobsohio.com   https://www.jobsohio.com/why-ohio/business-climate/

[26] Joe Hallet and Michael F. Curtin. *Ohio Politics Almanac*. Michael F. Curtain, 3rd Edition. (Kent, Ohio. Kent State University Press, 2015), 5-6. "For most of the twentieth century, Ohio indeed mirrored the nation as closely as any state. On most demographic counts, Ohio did not differ from national averages by more than a percentage or two."

[27] Ohio voted for the national winner of the presidential election in 23 of the 25 elections of the 20th century.

[28] Joe Hallet and Michael F. Curtin. *Ohio Politics Almanac*. Michael F. Curtain, 3rd Edition. (Kent, Ohio. Kent State University Press, 2015), 6.

[29] Read Brian Alexander's *Glass House* and Sam Quinones' *Dreamland* to learn the sad details of those two towns.

[30] Fran Stewart and William Shkurti. "Toward a New Ohio: Questions Every Candidate Should Answer." The John Glenn College of Public Affairs at The Ohio State University. Academic Paper. March 29, 2018.

[31] Ohio Department of Development. "Ohio Major Employers Historic Data." 2018. https://www.development.ohio.gov/files/research/B2021.pdf

[32] Brynn Epstein and Daphne Lofquist. "U.S. Census Bureau Today Delivers State Population Totals for Congressional Apportionment." United States Census Bureau. April 26, 2021. https://www.census.gov/library/stories/2021/04/2020-census-data-release.html

[33] "Annual 2020 United Van Lines National Movers Study." United Van Lines. January 4, 2021. https://www.unitedvanlines.com/newsroom/movers-study-2020?utm_source=prnewswire.com&utm_medium=press&utm_campaign=National-Movers-Study&utm_content=2020-movers-study

[34] Meibers, Bonnie. "2020 Census: Why Ohio's population growth seems to be lagging." Dayton Daily News. April 30, 2021. https://www.

daytondailynews.com/local/2020-census-why-ohios-population-growth-seems-to-be-lagging/JVKUX6AP7JHNHON3HTM4T
67VK4/

[35] "Overview of Ohio." U.S. News and World Report. 2020. https://www.usnews.com/news/best-states/ohio

[36] "Map: A-F Grades, Rankings for States on School Quality." Education Week. September 1, 2020. https://www.edweek.org/policy-politics/map-a-f-grades-rankings-for-states-on-school-quality/2020/09#top-to-bottom-rankings; Candisky, Catherine. "Ohio schools slide in national rankings." The Columbus Dispatch. January 7, 2016. https://www.dispatch.com/article/20160107/NEWS/301079757.

[37] Maciag, Mike. "High School Graduation Rates by State." Governing.com. December 3, 2012. https://nces.ed.gov/programs/coe/pdf/coe_coi.pdf. https://www.governing.com/archive/high-school-graduation-rates-by-state.html

[38] Cieslewicz, Bill. "Ohio ranks as top state for residents with student loans." Sept. 6, 2021. Cincinnati Business Courier. Boomer, Harry. "The cost of college: Ohio leads the nation in college debt." Cleveland19.com. August 4, 2017. https://www.cleveland19.com/story/36060259/ohio-leads-the-nation-in-college-debt/www.cleveland19.com

[39] "2021 Health Value Dashboard." Health Policy Ohio. 2021. https://www.healthpolicyohio.org/2021-health-value-dashboard/.

[40] "2019 Health Value Dashboard." Health Policy Ohio. 2019. https://www.healthpolicyohio.org/wp-content/uploads/2019/04/2019__HealthValueDashboard.pdf

[41] "2019 Health Value Dashboard." Health Policy Ohio. 2019. https://www.healthpolicyohio.org/wp-content/uploads/2019/04/2019__HealthValueDashboard.pdf

[42] Campbell, Emily. "Cleveland is now the poorest big city in the country." The Center for Community Solutions. September 21, 2020.

https://www.communitysolutions.com/cleveland-now-poorest-big-city-country/

[43] Exner, Rich. "Every Ohio city and county ranked for poverty, child poverty: census estimates." Cleveland.com. January 3, 2020. https://www.cleveland.com/datacentral/2020/01/every-ohio-city-and-county-ranked-for-poverty-child-poverty-census-estimates.html

[44] Exner, Rich. "Every Ohio city and county ranked for poverty, child poverty: census estimates." Cleveland.com. January 3, 2020. https://www.cleveland.com/datacentral/2020/01/every-ohio-city-and-county-ranked-for-poverty-child-poverty-census-estimates.html

[45] Fran Stewart and William Shkurti. "Toward a New Ohio: Questions Every Candidate Should Answer." The John Glenn College of Public Affairs at The Ohio State University. Academic Paper. March 29, 2018.

[46] "Working for Less: Too Many Jobs Still Pay Too Little, 2019," *Policy Matters Ohio*, May 1, 2019, https://www.policymattersohio.org/research-policy/fair-economy/work-wages/minimum-wage/working-for-less-too-many-jobs-still-pay-too-little-2019

[47] Walliser-Wejebe, Maria. "Communities Across the State Declare Racism as a Public Health Crisis, The State Considers It." Greater Ohio Policy Center. July 21, 2020. https://www.greaterohio.org/blog/2020/7/16/communities-across-the-state-declare-racism-as-a-public-health-crisis-the-state-considers-it

[48] Rick Rouan, "Despite years of efforts to combat infant mortality in Ohio, racial disparity increases." The Columbus Dispatch. Dec. 17, 2020.   https://www.dispatch.com/story/news/politics/government/2020/12/17/ohio-infant-mortality-drops-but-black-babies-still-more-likely-die-gov-mike-dewine-forms-task-force/3945254001/

[49] Bischoff, Laura A."In a league of its own': Ohio is number 1 state when it comes to corruption, experts say." The Columbus Dispatch. May 10, 2021. https://www.dispatch.com/story/news/2021/05/10/ohio-householder-prosecution-top-state-political-corruption-hb-6/4922865001/

[50] King, Lori. "State of turmoil: The Coingate Scandal." The Toledo Blade. March 16, 2005. https://www.toledoblade.com/coingate

[51] Meckler, Laura. "How the demise of an online charter school is roiling Ohio Politics." October 20, 2018. https://www.washingtonpost.com/local/education/how-the-demise-of-an-online-charter-school-is-roiling-ohio-politics/2018/10/20/1e9f55d2-c1d7-11e8-b338-a3289f6cb742_story.html

[52] Siegel, Jim. "Cliff Rosenberger under investigation for possible bribery, extortion." August 27, 2018. https://www.dispatch.com/news/20180827/cliff-rosenberger-under-investigation-for-possible-bribery-extortion

[53] Bischoff, Laura A. "'In a league of its own': Ohio is number 1 state when it comes to corruption, experts say." The Columbus Dispatch. May 10, 2021. https://www.dispatch.com/story/news/2021/05/10/ohio-householder-prosecution-top-state-political-corruption-hb-6/4922865001/

[54] Balmert, Jessie. "Columbus lobbyist Neil Clark, accused in HB 6 scandal, died by suicide, autopsy confirms." The Cincinnati Enquirer. June 8, 2021.

[55] Exner, Rich "Ohio Democrats nearly match Republicans in Statehouse votes, but will remain in the deep minority; what's ahead for gerrymandering." Cleveland.com. November 15, 2018. https://www.cleveland.com/news/erry-2018/11/0f32e762411182/ohio-democrats-outpolled-repub.html

[56] Rosenberg, Gabe. "Ohio Governor Signs 'Stand Your Ground' Law After Suggesting He'd Veto It." NationalPublicRadio.org. January 4, 2021. https://www.npr.org/2021/01/04/953405793/ohio-governor-signs-stand-your-ground-law-after-suggesting-hed-veto-it

[57] Tebben, Susan. "A complete abortion ban isn't law in Ohio, but some Ohioans still think abortion is illegal." Ohio Capital Journal. February 22, 2021. https://ohiocapitaljournal.com/2021/02/22/a-complete-abortion-ban-isnt-law-in-ohio-but-some-ohioans-still-think-abortion-is-illegal/

[58] Pollit, Katha. "Half of the Abortion Clinics in Ohio Have Closed. And Kasich Is a 'Moderate'?" The Nation. March 31, 2016. https://www.thenation.com/article/archive/half-of-the-abortion-clinics-in-ohio-have-closed-and-kasich-is-a-moderate/

[59] Wilkinson, Joseph. "SEE IT: Ohio nurse hilariously fails to prove COVID vaccine makes people magnetic, key falls from her neck." The Washington Post. June 9, 2021. https://www.washingtonpost.com/nation/2021/06/09/sherri-tenpenny-magnetized-vaccine-ohio/.

[60] Balmert, Jessie. "Where did this Ohio lawmaker get his ideas about implanting ectopic pregnancies?" The Columbus Dispatch. December 11, 2019. https://www.dispatch.com/news/20191211/where-did-this-ohio-lawmaker-get-his-ideas-about--implanting-ectopic-pregnancies

[61] Fieldstadt, Elisha. "Ohio lawmaker refuses to wear mask because he says it dishonors God." NBCNews.com. May 6, 2020. https://www.nbcnews.com/news/us-news/ohio-lawmaker-refuses-wear-mask-because-he-says-it-dishonors-n1201106

[62] Pelzer, Jeremy. "Ohio legislator says America's public education system is 'socialism,' should be privatized." Cleveland.com. March 19, 2014. https://www.cleveland.com/open/2014/03/ohio_lawmaker_americas_public.html

[63] Bischoff, Laura A. "Lawmaker asks if 'colored population' not washing their hands as well as others behind COVID rates." Dayton Daily News. June 11, 2020. https://www.daytondailynews.com/news/local/lawmaker-asks-colored-population-not-washing-their-hands-often-behind-covid-rates/mnI4I0D4DHS5uscmbpqcQL/

Chapter 2: With Great Power Comes Great Anonymity

[64] Joe Hallet and Michael F. Curtin. Ohio Politics Almanac. Michael F. Curtin, 3rd Edition. (Kent, Ohio. Kent State University Press, 2015), 2.

[65] Knepper, George W. Ohio and its People. (Kent, Ohio: The Kent State University Press, 2003), 93.

[66] Joe Hallet and Michael F. Curtin. *Ohio Politics Almanac*. Michael F. Curtin, 3rd Edition. (Kent, Ohio. Kent State University Press, 2015), 82.

[67] Ohio Const. Art. II, § 22.

[68] "Investing in Ohio's Future: The Budget of the State of Ohio | Fiscal Years 2022-2023." Ohio.gov. February 9, 2021. https:// archives.obm.ohio.gov/Files/Budget_and_Planning/Operating_ Budget/Fiscal_Years_2022-2023/FY22-23%20Highlights%20 Book-Final-02-09-2021.pdf; "State and Local Expenditures." The Urban Institute. 2011. https://www.urban.org/policy-centers/cross-center-initiatives/state-and-local-finance-initiative/state-and-local-backgrounders/state-and-local-expenditures

[69] Iris J. Lav and Michael Leachman. "At Risk: Federal Grants to State and Local Governments." Center on Budget and Policy Priorities. March 13, 2017. https://wwgkw.cbpp.org/research/state-budget-and-tax/at-risk-federal-grants-to-state-and-local-governments

[70] Ohio Const. Art. XVIII, § 3.

[71] U.S. Const. Art. I, § 4, Clause 1.

[72] US Const. Art. II, § 1, Clause 2.

[73] Young people—there was no cable yet. No internet or Facebook or twitter. Those Sunday shows were where you got your political fill. It was all so calm.

[74] Rosen, Jill. "Americans don't know much about state government, survey finds." Hub at Johns Hopkins University. December 14, 2018. https://hub.jhu.edu/2018/12/14/americans-dont-understand-state-government/

[75] Rosen, Jill. "Americans don't know much about state government, survey finds." Hub at Johns Hopkins University. December 14, 2018. https://hub.jhu.edu/2018/12/14/americans-dont-understand-state-government/

[76] "Stumped: Just 2 In 5 Americans Could Name One of Their Local Congress Members." StudyFinds.org. September 16, 2019. https://

www.studyfinds.org/stumped-just-2-in-5-americans-could-name-local-congress-members/

[77] Famer, Liz. "Who's Your Governor? 1 in 3 Americans Don't Know." Governing.org. December 19, 2018. https://www.governing.com/archive/gov-americans-knowledge-state-government.html

[78] Baker, John R., Linda L. Bennett, Stephen E. Bennett, Richard S. Flickinger. 1996. "Citizens' Knowledge and Perceptions of Legislatures in Canada, Britain and the United States." The Journal of Legislative Studies, 2, 2 (Summer): 44-62.

[79] Yes, all things said to me walking down the street.

[80] "Legislative Session Length." National Conference of State Legislatures. July 7, 2021. https://www.ncsl.org/research/about-state-legislatures/legislative-session-length.aspx "Session Schedules." State Scape.com. 2021. http://www.statescape.com/resources/legislative/session-schedules

[81] Jan Lauren Boyles and Katerina Eva Matsa. "Who Covers the Statehouses?" Pew Research Center. July 10, 2014. https://www.journalism.org/2014/07/10/who-covers-the-statehouse/

[82] Smith, Edward. "A declining statehouse press corps leaves readers less informed about lawmakers' efforts." National Conference of State Legislatures. https://www.ncsl.org/press-room/sl-magazine-disappearing-act.aspx; Wilson, Reid. "The precipitous decline of state political coverage." The Washington Post. July 10, 2014. https://www.washingtonpost.com/blogs/govbeat/wp/2014/07/10/the-precipitous-decline-of-state-political-coverage/

[83] Barber, Gregory. "Study: Statehouse Press Corps In Decline" NationalPublicRadio.org. July 10, 2014. https://www.npr.org/sections/itsallpolitics/2014/07/10/330456166/study-statehouse-press-corps-in-decline

[84] Grieco, Elizabeth. "Fast facts about the newspaper industry's financial struggles as McClatchy files for bankruptcy." Pew Research Center. February 14, 2020. https://www.pewresearch.org/fact-tank/2020/02/14/fast-facts-about-the-newspaper-industrys-

financial-struggles/; Hendrickson, Clara. "Local journalism in crisis: Why America must revive its local newsrooms." The Brookings Institute. November 12, 2019. https://www.brookings.edu/research/local-journalism-in-crisis-why-america-must-revive-its-local-newsrooms/; David Bauder and David A. Lieb. "Decline in readers, ads leads hundreds of newspapers to fold." Associated Press. March 11, 2019. https://apnews.com/article/north-america-waynesville-mo-state-wire-us-news-newspapers-0c59cf4a09114238af55fe18e3 2bc454; Abernathy, Penelope Muse. "The Expanding News Desert." University of North Carolina School of Media and Journalism. 2018. https://www.cislm.org/wp-content/uploads/2018/10/The-Expanding-News-Desert-10_14-Web.pdf.

[85] "Legislative Broadcasts and Webcasts." National Conference of State Legislatures. July 16, 2021. https://www.ncsl.org/research/about-state-legislatures/legislative-webcasts-and-broadcasts.aspx

[86] Pelzer, Jeremy. "Ohio House moves toward long-sought goal to publicly broadcast all committee hearings." Cleveland.com March 19, 2021. https://www.cleveland.com/politics/2019/03/ohio-house-moves-toward-long-sought-goal-to-publicly-broadcast-all-committee-hearings.html

[87] Kurtz, Karl. "As Term-Limit Laws Turn 30, Are States Better Off?" National Conference of State Legislatures. February 8, 2021. https://www.ncsl.org/bookstore/state-legislatures-magazine/state-legislative-term-limit-laws-turn-30-magazine2021.aspx

Chapter 3: The Insiders Know: Ordering at the Statehouse Grille

[88] Pogue, James. "The GOP's Biggest Charter School Experiment Just Imploded." Mother Jones. March/April 2018 Issue. https://www.motherjones.com/politics/2018/01/the-gops-biggest-charter-school-experiment-just-imploded/; Catherine Candisky and Jim Siegel. "How ECOT founder William Lager cooked up a lucrative charter school." The Columbus Dispatch. June 30, 2017. https://www.dispatch.com/news/20170730/how-ecot-founder-william-lager-cooked-up-lucrative-charter-school

[89] Pogue, James. "The GOP's Biggest Charter School Experiment Just Imploded." Mother Jones. March/April 2018 Issue. https://www. motherjones.com/politics/2018/01/the-gops-biggest-charter-school-experiment-just-imploded/

[90] Pogue, James. "The GOP's Biggest Charter School Experiment Just Imploded." Mother Jones. March/April 2018 Issue. https://www. motherjones.com/politics/2018/01/the-gops-biggest-charter-school-experiment-just-imploded/

[91] Rich, Motoko. "Online School Enriches Affiliated Companies if Not Its Students." The New York Times. May 18, 2016. https://www. nytimes.com/2016/05/19/us/online-charter-schools-electronic-classroom-of-tomorrow.html

[92] O'Donnel, Patrick. "ECOT attendance inflated by 9,000 students, audit finds; $60 million in state funding in jeopardy." Cleveland.com. September 21, 2016. https://www.cleveland.com/metro/2016/09/ ecot_attendance_inflated_by_9000_students_audit_finds_60_million_in_state_funding_in_jeopardy.html

[93] Harold, Benjamin. "ECOT Fallout: Missing Students, Returned Donations, Criminal Accusations." Education Week. July 10, 2018. https://www.edweek.org/policy-politics/ecot-fallout-missing-students-returned-donations-criminal-accusations/2018/07

[94] Liming, Katherine. "Nearly $600 Million Dollars Went from Local School Districts to ECOT." InnovationOhio.org. June 6, 2018. http:// innovationohio.org/2018/06/06/nearly-600-million-dollars-went-from-local-school-districts-to-ecot/

[95] Lager is estimated to have made more than $2.5 million in political donations. Siegel, Jim. "Which side is right in political battle over ECOT blame?" The Columbus Dispatch. September 2, 2018. https://www.dispatch.com/news/20180902/which-side-is-right-in-political-battle-over-ecot-blame; Dyer, Stephen. "ECOT Campaign Contributions." InnovationOhio.org. May 15, 2018. https://innovationohio.org/featured/ecot-contributions/https:// innovationohio.org/featured/ecot-contributions/

[96] Pogue, James. "The GOP's Biggest Charter School Experiment Just Imploded." Mother Jones. March/April 2018 Issue. https://www. motherjones.com/politics/2018/01/the-gops-biggest-charter-school-experiment-just-imploded/

[97] Bischoff, Laura. "Two Decades of ECOT political giving detailed in info sent to federal investigators." Sept. 7, 2021. The Columbus Dispatch. https://www.dispatch.com/story/news/2021/09/07/two-decades-of-electronic-classroom-of-tomorrow-political-giving-detailed/5702493001/

[98] Ben Wieder, Chris Zubak-Skees, and Yue Qiu. "Here Are The Interests Lobbying In Every Statehouse." PublicIntegity.org. February 11, 2016. https://publicintegrity.org/politics/state-politics/here-are-the-interests-lobbying-in-every-statehouse/

[99] Ben Wieder and Lizzy Essley Whyte. "Amid Federal Gridlock, Lobbying Rises In The States." PublicIntegity.org. February 12, 2016. https://publicintegrity.org/politics/state-politics/amid-federal-gridlock-lobbying-rises-in-the-states/

[100] Bischoff, Laura. "Ohio House speaker Rosenberger rents luxury condo from top GOP donor." The Columbus Dispatch. February 1, 2017. https://www.dispatch.com/news/20170201/ohio-house-speaker-rosenberger-rents-luxury-condo-from-top-gop-donor?rssfeed=true

[101] Bischoff, Laura. "House speaker owes back rent on luxury Columbus condo." Springfield News-Sun. May 16, 2017. https://www.springfieldnewssun.com/news/house-speaker-owes-back-rent-columbus-condo/daQeiRvajasEpxX5jj8ftO/

[102] Balmert, Jessie. "Former Ohio Speaker Cliff Rosenberger's travel log: France, England, D.C., Key West." Cincinnati.com. August 28, 2018. https://www.cincinnati.com/story/news/politics/2018/08/28/former-ohio-speaker-cliff-rosenbergers-travel-france-england-key-west/1119656002/

[103] Siegel, Jim. "Cliff Rosenberger under investigation for possible bribery, extortion." The Columbus Dispatch. August 27, 2018.

https://www.dispatch.com/news/20180827/cliff-rosenberger-under-investigation-for-possible-bribery-extortion

[104] Pelzer, Jermey. "Thirteen things we found in ex-Ohio House Speaker Cliff Rosenberger's travel records." Cleveland.com. September 12, 2018. https://www.cleveland.com/news/erry-2018/09/e2acc0c8108434/thirteen-things-we-found-in-ex.html

[105] Chrissie Thompson and Jessie Balmert. "Ohio speaker, under FBI investigation, thought Disney might move to Cincinnati. He was wrong." WKYC.com. May 2, 2018. https://www.wkyc.com/article/news/local/ohio/ohio-speaker-under-fbi-investigation-thought-disney-might-move-to-cincinnati-he-was-wrong/95-548229041

[106] Chrissie Thompson and Jessie Balmert. "Ohio speaker, under FBI investigation, thought Disney might move to Cincinnati. He was wrong." WKYC.com. May 2, 2018. https://www.wkyc.com/article/news/local/ohio/ohio-speaker-under-fbi-investigation-thought-disney-might-move-to-cincinnati-he-was-wrong/95-548229041

[107] Borchardt, Jackie. "Ex-Speaker Cliff Rosenberger dashed off to California to discuss Disney Ohio project that turned out to not exist." Cleveland.com. May 2, 2018. https://www.cleveland.com/metro/2018/05/ex-speaker_cliff_rosenberger_d.html

[108] We'll cover the second in Chapter Four.

[109] Let me be clear: there are all sorts of folks lobbying on issues in Columbus and other state capitals that are perfectly appropriate. Or are good for people. Or which serve the common good. People dedicating their lives to support schools or kids or senior citizens or fight poverty or climate change or for Ohioans with disabilities. People have every right to advocate for their interests, and many of those interests are as noble or common sense as can be. But it's fair to say that they are outmatched and outgunned by those aiming for other, less noble goals. And too often in statehouses across this country, these deep-pocketed interests are the ones who dominate.

[110] Bischoff, Laura A. "Vendors gave big to DeWine, GOP." Dayton Daily News. July 19, 2014. https://www.daytondailynews.com/

news/state--regional-govt--politics/vendors-gave-big-dewine-gop/
ZMEcHuU1e1xFhYKACN7pJP/

[111] Pelzer, Jeremy. "Ex-FirstEnergy CEO denies wrongdoing in House Bill 6 bribery scandal." Cleveland.com. July 23, 2021. https://www.cleveland.com/open/2021/07/ex-firstenergy-ceo-denies-wrongdoing-in-house-bill-6-bribery-scandal.html

[112] Larkin, Brent. "The obscene conniving in Hunting Valley to get residents out of paying public school taxes." Cleveland.com. October 24, 2019. https://www.cleveland.com/opinion/2019/10/the-obscene-conniving-in-hunting-valley-to-get-residents-out-of-paying-public-school-taxes.html

[113] Tobias, Andrew J. "Gov. Mike DeWine blocks stealthy budget change that would have helped Hunting Valley, cost Orange schools." Cleveland.com. July 19, 2019. https://www.cleveland.com/open/2019/07/gov-mike-dewine-blocks-stealthy-budget-change-that-would-helped-hunting-valley-hurt-orange-schools.html

[114] Beyerlein, Tom. "Ohio legislation favors White Hat charter schools." Springfield News-Sun. May 28, 2011. https://www.springfieldnewssun.com/news/local/ohio-legislation-favors-white-hat-charter-schools/nT5UKhii9ToTksc2yR0o9H/

[115] Beyerlein, Tom. "Ohio legislation favors White Hat charter schools." Springfield News-Sun. May 28, 2011. https://www.springfieldnewssun.com/news/local/ohio-legislation-favors-white-hat-charter-schools/nT5UKhii9ToTksc2yR0o9H/

[116] O'Donnell, Patrick. "Ohio is the "Wild, Wild West" of charter schools, says national group promoting charter standards." Cleveland.com. January 12, 2019. https://www.cleveland.com/metro/2014/07/ohio_is_the_wild_wild_west_of.html

[117] Siegel, Jim. "Which side is right in political battle over ECOT blame?" The Columbus Dispatch. September 2, 2018. https://www.dispatch.com/news/20180902/which-side-is-right-in-political-battle-over-ecot-blame

[118] Livingston, Doug. "School's out for White Hat: David Brennan's pioneering for-profit company exits Ohio charter scene." Akron Beacon Journal. August 7, 2018. https://www.beaconjournal.com/news/20180807/schools-out-for-white-hat-david-brennans-pioneering-for-profit-company-exits-ohio-charter-scene

[119] Siegel, Jim. "Which side is right in political battle over ECOT blame?" The Columbus Dispatch. September 2, 2018. https://www.dispatch.com/news/20180902/which-side-is-right-in-political-battle-over-ecot-blame

[120] Lager used his graduation ceremonies to honor the Columbus politicians who had been most helpful to his cause. https://www.youtube.com/watch?v=VC9WH53MuRs In hindsight, it's a helpful list of those who enabled the scam at critical moments.

[121] Siegel, Jim. "Which side is right in political battle over ECOT blame?" The Columbus Dispatch. September 2, 2018. https://www.dispatch.com/news/20180902/which-side-is-right-in-political-battle-over-ecot-blame. Brennan also gave generously to Husted. http://www.jointhefuture.org/join-the-future/tag/ann https://vindyarchives.com/news/2001/nov/18/foxes-closing-in-on-ohios-charter-school-henhouse/

[122] Siegel, Jim. "Which side is right in political battle over ECOT blame?" The Columbus Dispatch. September 2, 2018. https://www.dispatch.com/news/20180902/which-side-is-right-in-political-battle-over-ecot-blame

[123] Siegel, Jim. "Which side is right in political battle over ECOT blame?" The Columbus Dispatch. September 2, 2018. https://www.dispatch.com/news/20180902/which-side-is-right-in-political-battle-over-ecot-blame

[124] "How State Rate Limits Affect Payday Loan Prices." Pew Charitable Trusts. April 2014. https://www.pewtrusts.org/~/media/legacy/uploadedfiles/pcs/content-level_pages/fact_sheets/stateratelimitsfactsheetpdf.pdf?la=e

[125] Borchardt, Jackie. "Payday loan reform bill stalls (again) amid Rosenberger FBI inquiry." Cleveland.com. April 11, 2018. https://

www.cleveland.com/metro/2018/04/payday_loan_reform_bill_
stalls.html

126 Borchardt, Jackie. "Payday lenders say ex-Ohio House Speaker Cliff Rosenberger threatened them, delayed bill." Cleveland.com. May 24, 2018. https://www.cleveland.com/metro/2018/05/payday_lenders_say_ex-ohio_hou.html

127 Borchardt, Jackie. "Payday loan reform bill stalls (again) amid Rosenberger FBI inquiry." Cleveland.com. April 11, 2018. https://www.cleveland.com/metro/2018/04/payday_loan_reform_bill_stalls.html

128 Siegel, Jim. "Cliff Rosenberger under investigation for possible bribery, extortion." The Columbus Dispatch. August 27, 2018. https://www.dispatch.com/news/20180827/cliff-rosenberger-under-investigation-for-possible-bribery-extortion

129 Borchardt, Jackie. "Payday lenders say ex-Ohio House Speaker Cliff Rosenberger threatened them, delayed bill." Cleveland.com. May 24, 2018. https://www.cleveland.com/metro/2018/05/payday_lenders_say_ex-ohio_hou.html

130 Kowalski, Kathiann M. "Ohio researchers show how solar could help turn around Appalachian economy." Energy News Network. September 21, 2020. https://energynews.us/2020/09/21/ohio-researchers-show-how-solar-could-help-turn-around-appalachian-economy/

131 Anderson, Dave. "Murray Energy's War on Clean Energy in Ohio." Energy and Policy Institute. March 9, 2018. https://www.energyandpolicy.org/murray-energy-vs-renewable-energy/

132 Anderson, Dave. "Attacks on wind and solar power by the coal and gas industries." Energy and Policy Institute. February 19, 2019. https://www.energyandpolicy.org/attacks-renewable-energy/

133 Roberts, Dave. "Ohio just passed the worst energy bill of the 21st century." Vox Media. July 27, 2019. https://www.vox.com/energy-and-environment/2019/7/27/8910804/ohio-gop-nuclear-coal-plants-renewables-efficiency-hb6

[134] Zhang, Sharon. "Fossil fuel knocks the wind out of renewable energy movement in Ohio." Salon Magazine. January 5, 2020. https://www.salon.com/2020/01/05/fossil-fuel-knocks-the-wind-out-of-renewable-energy-movement-in-ohio_partner/

[135] Tsao, Stephanie. "Ohio wind development lags nearby states as strict siting rules worry developers." S&P Global. February 7, 2020. https://www.spglobal.com/marketintelligence/en/news-insights/latest-news-headlines/ohio-wind-development-lags-nearby-states-as-strict-siting-rules-worry-developers-56699280

[136] Zhang, Sharon. "Fossil fuel knocks the wind out of renewable energy movement in Ohio." Salon Magazine. January 5, 2020. https://www.salon.com/2020/01/05/fossil-fuel-knocks-the-wind-out-of-renewable-energy-movement-in-ohio_partner/

[137] Pelzer, Jeremy. "Ohio cities can't ban plastic bags for at least one year, under legislation signed by Gov. Mike DeWine." Cleveland.com. October 13, 2020. https://www.cleveland.com/open/2020/10/ohio-cities-cant-ban-plastic-bags-for-at-least-one-year-under-legislation-signed-by-gov-mike-dewine.html

[138] Pelzer, Jeremy. "Ohio cities can't ban plastic bags for at least one year, under legislation signed by Gov. Mike DeWine." Cleveland.com. October 13, 2020. https://www.cleveland.com/open/2020/10/ohio-cities-cant-ban-plastic-bags-for-at-least-one-year-under-legislation-signed-by-gov-mike-dewine.html

[139] Siegel, Jim. "Lawmakers use Petland bill to ban Ohio cities from upping minimum wage." The Columbus Dispatch. December 6, 2016. https://www.dispatch.com/content/stories/local/2016/12/06/lawmakers-set-to-ban-ohio-cities-from-increasing-minimum-wage.html

[140] Zuckerman, Jake. "How a powerful state law blocks Ohio cities from gun regulation." WTOL.com. April 6, 2021. https://www.wtol.com/article/news/state/powerful-state-law-blocks-ohio-cities-from-gun-regulation/512-4fd0010e-c1c9-487e-bf40-181f26af27ef

[141] Cleveland v. State, 128 Ohio St.3d 135, 2010-Ohio-6318. https://www.supremecourt.ohio.gov/rod/docs/pdf/0/2010/2010-ohio-6318.pdf

[142] Harrison, Rachel. "States Laws Limit Local Control Over Guns, Favor Gun Rights." NYU.edu. May 20, 2021. https://www.nyu.edu/about/news-publications/news/2021/may/states-laws-limit-local-control-over-guns.html

[143] Slagle, Jim. "Ohio Transparency Report—The Elephant in the Room." League of Women Voters and Ohio Citizen Action. December 12, 2011. https://my.lwv.org/sites/default/files/leagues/wysiwyg/%5Bcurrent-user%3Aog-user-node%3A1%3Atitle%5D/the_elephant_in_the_room_-_transparency_report.pdf

Chapter 4: Rigged in the Bunker: A Decade of Predetermined Elections

[144] Slagle, Jim. "Ohio Transparency Report—The Elephant in the Room." League of Women Voters and Ohio Citizen Action. December 12, 2011. https://my.lwv.org/sites/default/files/leagues/wysiwyg/%5Bcurrent-user%3Aog-user-node%3A1%3Atitle%5D/the_elephant_in_the_room_-_transparency_report.pdf

[145] "Endangered Species." Time Magazine. May 18, 2009. http://content.time.com/time/covers/0,16641,20090518,00.html

[146] Grunwald, Michael. "One Year Ago: The Republicans in Distress." Time Magazine. May 7, 2009. http://content.time.com/time/subscriber/article/0,33009,1896736,00.html

[147] Grunwald, Michael. "One Year Ago: The Republicans in Distress." Time Magazine. May 7, 2009. http://content.time.com/time/subscriber/article/0,33009,1896736,00.html

[148] Naymik, Mark. "Gov. Ted Strickland's approval rating drops with economy, poll shows." Cleveland.com. April 30, 2009. https://www.cleveland.com/naymik/2009/04/gov_ted_stricklands_approval_r.html

[149] Grunwald, Michael. "One Year Ago: The Republicans in Distress." Time Magazine. May 7, 2009. http://content.time.com/time/subscriber/article/0,33009,1896736,00.html

[150] Guillen, Joe. "ProgressOhio near the mark on spending increases by Ohio auditor candidate Dave Yost." Politifact.com. July 29, 2010.

https://www.politifact.com/factchecks/2010/jul/29/progressohio/liberal-group-progressohio-near-mark-attack-ohio-a/

[151] Dave Yost for Ohio, Contribution Results. Office of the Ohio Secretary of State. 2010. https://www6.ohiosos.gov/ords/f?p=CFDIS CLOSURE:45:4170365261306::NO::P45_ENTITY_ID:12822

[152] Williams, Carter. "Looking back at the Crandall Canyon Mine collapse 10 years later." KSL.com. August 6, 2017. https://www.ksl.com/article/45302392/looking-back-at-the-crandall-canyon-mine-collapse-10-years-later; "Crandall Canyon Mine operator to pay nearly $1M in fines." Deseret News. September 27, 2012. https://www.deseret.com/2012/9/27/20438362/crandall-canyon-mine-operator-to-pay-nearly-1m-in-fines#this-file-photo-shows-an-aerial-view-of-the-crandall-canyon-mine-in-huntington-utah-monday-aug-6-2007

[153] Brittany Patterson and Dave Mistich. "Bob Murray, Who Fought Against Black Lung Regulations As A Coal Operator, Has Filed For Black Lung Benefits." WestVirginiaPublicBroadcasting.org. September 30, 2020. https://www.wvpublic.org/energy-environment/2020-09-30/bob-murray-who-fought-against-black-lung-regulations-as-a-coal-operator-has-filed-for-black-lung-benefits

[154] Lucas Iberico and Michelle Conlin. "The new U.S. office politics: funding your boss's political causes." Reuters. May 11, 2015. https://www.reuters.com/article/us-usa-election-workers-insight/the-new-u-s-office-politics-funding-your-bosss-political-causes-idUSKBN0NW0AC20150511; MacGillis, Alec. "Coal Tycoon Bob Murray Is Still Urging His Employees to Give to Republicans." The New Republic. October 2, 2014. https://newrepublic.com/article/119689/murray-energy-ceo-bob-murray-still-urging-employees-give-gop

[155] Eaton, Sabrina. "Despite recommendations, FEC won't pursue charges that Murray Energy coerced campaign donations from employees." Cleveland.com. May 23, 2016. https://www.cleveland.com/open/2016/05/deadlocked_federal_election_co.html; Lacey, Stephen. "Coal Workers Say Murray Energy 'Coerces' Them To Make GOP Donations: 'If You Don't Contribute, Your Job's At Stake'."

ThinkProgress.org. October 5, 2012. https://archive.thinkprogress. org/coal-workers-say-murray-energy-coerces-them-to-make-gop-donations-if-you-don-t-contribute-your-job-s-f5af46d17b0b/

[156] "Dave Yost Award Presentation." Youtube.com. ECOT School. March 23, 2015. https://www.youtube.com/watch?v=mXrEgr5FR1Y

[157] Pogue, James. "The GOP's Biggest Charter School Experiment Just Imploded." Mother Jones. March/April 2018 Issue. https://www. motherjones.com/politics/2018/01/the-gops-biggest-charter-school-experiment-just-imploded/; "ECOT says no records kept of students' offline work." The Columbus Dispatch. August 4, 2016. https://www. dispatch.com/content/stories/local/2016/08/04/ecot-log-books-dont-exist.html

[158] "ECOT says no records kept of students' offline work." The Columbus Dispatch. August 4, 2016. https://www.dispatch.com/ content/stories/local/2016/08/04/ecot-log-books-dont-exist.html

[159] "White Hat Management Political Contributions." JoinTheFuture. org. May 2, 2011. http://www.jointhefuture.org/join-the-future/tag/ ann

[160] If you watch the movie Larry Flynt, he's the guy played by James Carville.

[161] Rove, Karl. "The GOP Targets State Legislatures." The Wall Street Journal. March 4, 2010. https://www.wsj.com/articles/SB1000142405 2748703862704575099670689398044

[162] Daley, David. *Ratf**d: Why Your Vote Doesn't Count.* Daley, David. (New York, New York. Liveright Publishing Corporation, 2017), xvi-xx.

[163] Daley, David. *Ratf**d: Why Your Vote Doesn't Count.* Daley, David. (New York, New York. Liveright Publishing Corporation, 2017), xxi.

[164] Daley, David. *Ratf**d: Why Your Vote Doesn't Count.* Daley, David. (New York, New York. Liveright Publishing Corporation, 2017), xx.

[165] Daley, David. *Ratf**d: Why Your Vote Doesn't Count.* Daley, David. (New York, New York. Liveright Publishing Corporation, 2017), xx.

[166] Daley, David. *Ratf**d: Why Your Vote Doesn't Count.* Daley, David. (New York, New York. Liveright Publishing Corporation, 2017), xx-xxi.

[167] Slagle, Jim. "Ohio Transparency Report—The Elephant in the Room." League of Women Voters and Ohio Citizen Action. December 12, 2011. https://my.lwv.org/sites/default/files/leagues/wysiwyg/%5Bcurrent-user%3Aog-user-node%3A1%3Atitle%5D/the_elephant_in_the_room_-_transparency_report.pdf

[168] Slagle, Jim. "Ohio Transparency Report—The Elephant in the Room." League of Women Voters and Ohio Citizen Action. December 12, 2011. https://my.lwv.org/sites/default/files/leagues/wysiwyg/%5Bcurrent-user%3Aog-user-node%3A1%3Atitle%5D/the_elephant_in_the_room_-_transparency_report.pdf

[169] Slagle, Jim. "Ohio Transparency Report—The Elephant in the Room." League of Women Voters and Ohio Citizen Action. December 12, 2011. https://my.lwv.org/sites/default/files/leagues/wysiwyg/%5Bcurrent-user%3Aog-user-node%3A1%3Atitle%5D/the_elephant_in_the_room_-_transparency_report.pdf

[170] Slagle, Jim. "Ohio Transparency Report—The Elephant in the Room." League of Women Voters and Ohio Citizen Action. December 12, 2011. https://my.lwv.org/sites/default/files/leagues/wysiwyg/%5Bcurrent-user%3Aog-user-node%3A1%3Atitle%5D/the_elephant_in_the_room_-_transparency_report.pdf

[171] Slagle, Jim. "Ohio Transparency Report—The Elephant in the Room." Appendix, Volume 1. League of Women Voters and Ohio Citizen Action. December 12, 2011. https://my.lwv.org/sites/default/files/leagues/wysiwyg/%5Bcurrent-user%3Aog-user-node%3A1%3Atitle%5D/appendix_i-_page_1-401.pdf

[172] Slagle, Jim. "Ohio Transparency Report—The Elephant in the Room." League of Women Voters and Ohio Citizen Action. December 12, 2011. https://my.lwv.org/sites/default/files/leagues/

wysiwyg/%5Bcurrent-user%3Aog-user-node%3A1%3Atitle%5D/
the_elephant_in_the_room_-_transparency_report.pdf

173 "Ohio's Gerrymandering Problem: Why Haven't We Fixed This Yet?" League of Women Voters of Ohio and Ohio Common Cause. https://my.lwv.org/sites/default/files/leagues/wysiwyg/%5Bcurrent-user%3Aog-user-node%3A1%3Atitle%5D/ohios_gerrymanding_problem.pdf; Slagle, Jim. "Ohio Transparency Report—The Elephant in the Room." Appendix, Volume 1. League of Women Voters and Ohio Citizen Action. December 12, 2011. https://my.lwv.org/sites/default/files/leagues/wysiwyg/%5Bcurrent-user%3Aog-user-node%3A1%3Atitle%5D/appendix_i-_page_1-401.pdf

174 Slagle, Jim. "Ohio Transparency Report—The Elephant in the Room." League of Women Voters and Ohio Citizen Action. December 12, 2011. https://my.lwv.org/sites/default/files/leagues/wysiwyg/%5Bcurrent-user%3Aog-user-node%3A1%3Atitle%5D/the_elephant_in_the_room_-_transparency_report.pdf

175 "Ohio's Gerrymandering Problem: Why Haven't We Fixed This Yet?" League of Women Voters of Ohio and Ohio Common Cause. https://my.lwv.org/sites/default/files/leagues/wysiwyg/%5Bcurrent-user%3Aog-user-node%3A1%3Atitle%5D/ohios_gerrymanding_problem.pdf

176 Slagle, Jim. "Ohio Transparency Report—The Elephant in the Room." League of Women Voters and Ohio Citizen Action. December 12, 2011. https://my.lwv.org/sites/default/files/leagues/wysiwyg/%5Bcurrent-user%3Aog-user-node%3A1%3Atitle%5D/the_elephant_in_the_room_-_transparency_report.pdf

177 Slagle, Jim. "Ohio Transparency Report—The Elephant in the Room." League of Women Voters and Ohio Citizen Action. December 12, 2011. https://my.lwv.org/sites/default/files/leagues/wysiwyg/%5Bcurrent-user%3Aog-user-node%3A1%3Atitle%5D/the_elephant_in_the_room_-_transparency_report.pdf

178 Slagle, Jim. "Ohio Transparency Report—The Elephant in the Room." League of Women Voters and Ohio Citizen Action. December 12, 2011. https://my.lwv.org/sites/default/files/leagues/

wysiwyg/%5Bcurrent-user%3Aog-user-node%3A1%3Atitle%5D/
the_elephant_in_the_room_-_transparency_report.pdf

[179] Slagle, Jim. "Ohio Transparency Report—The Elephant in the Room." League of Women Voters and Ohio Citizen Action. December 12, 2011. https://my.lwv.org/sites/default/files/leagues/ wysiwyg/%5Bcurrent-user%3Aog-user-node%3A1%3Atitle%5D/ the_elephant_in_the_room_-_transparency_report.pdf

[180] Husted, Jon. "From Ohio, lessons in redistricting reform." The Washington Post. February 6, 2014. https://www.washingtonpost. com/opinions/from-ohio-lessons-in-redistricting-reform/ 2014/02/06/626b5b32-76f3-11e3-af7f-13bf0e9965f6_story.html

[181] Husted once tweeted that he and Chuck Todd had lunch, and both agreed on the need to reform gerrymandering. Husted, Jon. "Enjoyed having lunch today with NBCs @chucktodd - he and I agree Redistricting reform needs to happen in OH and across the US." Jan. 26, 2013. https://twitter.com/JonHusted/ status/295243263345057792

[182] Slagle, Jim. "Ohio Transparency Report—The Elephant in the Room." League of Women Voters and Ohio Citizen Action. December 12, 2011. https://my.lwv.org/sites/default/files/leagues/ wysiwyg/%5Bcurrent-user%3Aog-user-node%3A1%3Atitle%5D/ the_elephant_in_the_room_-_transparency_report.pdf

[183] Slagle, Jim. "Ohio Transparency Report—The Elephant in the Room." League of Women Voters and Ohio Citizen Action. December 12, 2011. https://my.lwv.org/sites/default/files/leagues/ wysiwyg/%5Bcurrent-user%3Aog-user-node%3A1%3Atitle%5D/ the_elephant_in_the_room_-_transparency_report.pdf

[184] Slagle, Jim. "Ohio Transparency Report—The Elephant in the Room." Appendix, Volume 1. League of Women Voters and Ohio Citizen Action. December 12, 2011. https://my.lwv.org/ sites/default/files/leagues/wysiwyg/%5Bcurrent-user%3Aog-user- node%3A1%3Atitle%5D/appendix_i-_page_1-401.pdf

[185] Slagle, Jim. "Ohio Transparency Report—The Elephant in the Room." League of Women Voters and Ohio Citizen Action.

December 12, 2011. https://my.lwv.org/sites/default/files/leagues/
wysiwyg/%5Bcurrent-user%3Aog-user-node%3A1%3Atitle%5D/
the_elephant_in_the_room_-_transparency_report.pdf

[186] Hoefeller, Thomas B. "What I've Learned About Redistricting—
The Hard Way." National Conference of State Legislatures. January 24,
2011. https://www.ncsl.org/documents/legismgt/The_Hard_Way.pdf

[187] Hoefeller, Thomas B. "What I've Learned About Redistricting—
The Hard Way." National Conference of State Legislatures. January
24, 2011. https://www.ncsl.org/documents/legismgt/The_Hard_Way.
pdf

[188] Hoefeller, Thomas B. "What I've Learned About Redistricting—
The Hard Way." National Conference of State Legislatures. January 24,
2011. https://www.ncsl.org/documents/legismgt/The_Hard_Way.pdf

[189] Chang, Alvin. "The man who rigged America's election map."
Vox Media. October 17, 2019. https://www.vox.com/videos/2019/
10/17/20917852/gerrymander-hofeller-election-map

[190] Chang, Alvin. "The man who rigged America's election map."
Vox Media. October 17, 2019. https://www.vox.com/videos/2019/
10/17/20917852/gerrymander-hofeller-election-map

[191] Daley, David. *Ratf**d: Why Your Vote Doesn't Count.* Daley,
David. (New York, New York. Liveright Publishing Corporation,
2017), 141-142.

[192] Daley, David. *Ratf**d: Why Your Vote Doesn't Count.* Daley,
David. (New York, New York. Liveright Publishing Corporation,
2017), 122-135.

[193] Daley, David. *Ratf**d: Why Your Vote Doesn't Count.* Daley,
David. (New York, New York. Liveright Publishing Corporation,
2017), 44.

[194] Laura Roydon and Michael Li. "Extreme Maps." The Brennan
Center for Justice at New York University School of Law. 2017. https://
www.brennancenter.org/sites/default/files/2019-08/Report_
Extreme%20Maps%205.16_0.pdf

[195] Quigley, Rob. "The worst U.S. State Legislative Partisan Gerrymanders." USC Schwarzenegger Institute for Global Policy. September 5, 2019. https://issuu.com/robquigley/docs/the_worst_gerrymanders_of_2018_us_state_legislatur

[196] Quigley, Rob. "The Worst U.S. State Legislative Partisan Gerrymanders." USC Schwarzenegger Institute for Global Policy. September 5, 2019. https://issuu.com/robquigley/docs/the_worst_gerrymanders_of_2018_us_state_legislatur

Chapter 5: "Just Move": A Terrible Incentive Package

[197] MacGillis, Alec. "Forced to Choose Between a Job—and a Community." Propublica. May 23, 2018. https://www.propublica.org/article/adams-county-ohio-coal-forced-to-choose-between-a-job-and-a-community

[198] MacGillis, Alec. "Forced to Choose Between a Job—and a Community." Propublica. May 23, 2018. https://www.propublica.org/article/adams-county-ohio-coal-forced-to-choose-between-a-job-and-a-community

[199] Alley, Megan. "Uecker resigns from State Senate to go to work for ODOT." The Clermont Sun. August 14, 2019. https://www.clermontsun.com/2019/08/14/uecker-resigns-from-state-senate-to-go-to-work-for-odot

[200] Filby, Max. "Ohio spends less per capita on public health than nearly every other state." The Columbus Dispatch. April 2, 2020. https://www.dispatch.com/news/20200402/ohio-spends-less-per-capita-on-public-health-than-nearly-every-other-state/1

[201] Patton, Wendy. "Ohio local governments lost $1 billion since 2010." Policy Matters Ohio. January 3, 2017. https://www.policymattersohio.org/press-room/2017/01/03/ohio-local-governments-lost-1-billion-since-2010

[202] Karl, Jonathan. "State of the Union: The Hottest Seats in Town." ABCNews.com. January 24, 2012. https://abcnews.go.com/blogs/politics/2012/01/state-of-the-union-the-hottest-seats-in-town

[203] Powell, William. "A PODIATRIST AND A TRUCK DRIVER WALK INTO A GENERAL ELECTION." Cincinnati Magazine. October 1, 2012. https://www.cincinnatimagazine.com/features/a-podiatrist-and-a-truck-driver-walk-into-a-g1/

[204] Powell, William. "A PODIATRIST AND A TRUCK DRIVER WALK INTO A GENERAL ELECTION." Cincinnati Magazine. October 1, 2012. https://www.cincinnatimagazine.com/features/a-podiatrist-and-a-truck-driver-walk-into-a-g1/

[205] Zapanta, Victor. "Rep. Jean Schmidt tells birther 'I agree with you'." ThinkProgress.org. September 8, 2009. https://web.archive.org/web/20090910073952/http://thinkprogress.org/2009/09/08/jean-schmidt-birther/

[206] Powell, William. "A PODIATRIST AND A TRUCK DRIVER WALK INTO A GENERAL ELECTION." Cincinnati Magazine. October 1, 2012. https://www.cincinnatimagazine.com/features/a-podiatrist-and-a-truck-driver-walk-into-a-g1/

[207] Cillizza, Chris. "Who had the worst week in Washington? Rep. Jean Schmidt (R-Ohio)." The Washington Post. March 9, 2012. https://www.washingtonpost.com/opinions/who-had-the-worst-week-in-washington-rep-jean-schmidt-r-ohio/2012/03/08/gIQAcA6J1R_story.html

[208] Terris, Ben. "The Curse of the State of the Union Aisle Seat. The Atlantic. February 11, 2013. https://www.theatlantic.com/politics/archive/2013/02/curse-state-union-aisle-seat/318501/

[209] Cillizza, Chris. "Who had the worst week in Washington? Rep. Jean Schmidt (R-Ohio)." The Washington Post. March 9, 2012. https://www.washingtonpost.com/opinions/who-had-the-worst-week-in-washington-rep-jean-schmidt-r-ohio/2012/03/08/gIQAcA6J1R_story.html

[210] "After Upset, Wenstrup Ready To Get Back To Work." WLWT.com. March 7, 2012. https://www.wlwt.com/article/after-upset-wenstrup-ready-to-get-back-to-work/3520733

[211] Powell, William. "A PODIATRIST AND A TRUCK DRIVER WALK INTO A GENERAL ELECTION." Cincinnati Magazine. October 1, 2012. https://www.cincinnatimagazine.com/features/a-podiatrist-and-a-truck-driver-walk-into-a-g1/

[212] Greenwood, Max. "Poll: 82 percent support a ban on bump stocks." The Hill. October 13, 2017. https://thehill.com/blogs/blog-briefing-room/news/355376-poll-82-support-a-ban-on-bump-stocks; Margot Sanger-Katz and Quoctrung Bui. "A Bump Stock Ban Is Popular With the Public. But Experts Have Their Doubts." The New York Times. October 12, 2017. https://www.nytimes.com/interactive/2017/10/12/upshot/a-bump-stock-ban-is-popular-but-experts-have-their-doubts.html

[213] Alec Tyson and Brian Kennedy. "Two-Thirds of Americans Think Government Should Do More on Climate." Pew Charitable Trusts. June 23, 2020. https://www.pewresearch.org/science/2020/06/23/two-thirds-of-americans-think-government-should-do-more-on-climate/

[214] Kinder, Molly. "Even a divided America agrees on raising the minimum wage." The Brookings Institute. November 13, 2020. https://www.brookings.edu/blog/the-avenue/2020/11/13/even-a-divided-america-agrees-on-raising-the-minimum-wage/

[215] Hannah Hartig and Leslie Davis. "Two-thirds of Americans favor raising federal minimum wage to $15 an hour." Pew Charitable Trusts. July 30, 2019. https://www.pewresearch.org/fact-tank/2019/07/30/two-thirds-of-americans-favor-raising-federal-minimum-wage-to-15-an-hour/

[216] Talev, Margaret. "Axios-Ipsos poll: Most Americans favor mandates." Axios. August 17, 2021. https://www.axios.com/axios-ipsos-poll-mandates-masks-vaccinations-f0f105a7-3c2e-4953-aac9-f25516128b11.html

[217] Rosenberg, Gabe. "Ohio House Elects Bob Cupp As Speaker After Householder's Removal." WOSU.org. July 30, 2020. https://news.wosu.org/news/2020-07-30/ohio-house-elects-bob-cupp-as-speaker-after-householders-removal

[218] Staff. "We now know Dave Greenspan was one of the heroes of the FBI probe of the corrupted HB6: The Wake Up podcast." Cleveland. com. September 25, 2020. https://www.msn.com/en-us/news/ politics/we-now-know-dave-greenspan-was-one-of-the-heroes-of-the-fbi-probe-of-the-corrupted-hb6-the-wake-up-podcast/ ar-BB19pGjo

[219] Journals of the senate and house of representatives. Ohio House of Representatives Journal. July 30, 2020. https://search-prod.lis.state. oh.us/solarapi/v1/general_assembly_133/journals/House/2020-07-30?format=pdf

[220] Siegel, Jim. "Which side is right in political battle over ECOT blame?" The Columbus Dispatch. September 2, 2018. https://www. dispatch.com/news/20180902/which-side-is-right-in-political-battle-over-ecot-blame

[221] "GOP House bill would change public corruption jurisdiction." Associated Press. June 24, 2021. https://apnews.com/article/oh-state-wire-bills-6ab1e9482b370d87450e8d912813a7b4

[222] Rader, Betsy. "I was born in poverty in Appalachia. 'Hillbilly Elegy' doesn't speak for me." The Washington Post. September 1, 2017. https://www.washingtonpost.com/opinions/i-grew-up-in-poverty-in-appalachia-jd-vances-hillbilly-elegy-doesnt-speak-for-me/2017/08/30/734abb38-891d-11e7-961d-2f373b3977ee_story. html

[223] All data obtained at "Election Results and Data." Office of the Ohio Secretary of State. https://www.sos.state.oh.us/elections/election-results-and-data/

[224] Yes, if you raise a lot of money into a campaign account, but actually don't need money to spend on campaigns because they're rigged, there are temptations to spend it on things you shouldn't.

[225] He even posted a video pushing anti-mask conspiracy theories.

[226] Carey, Tyler. "State Rep. Nino Vitale, DeWine administration critic, urges Ohioans to 'STOP GETTING TESTED' for coronavirus." WKYC.com. July 7, 2020. https://www.wkyc.com/article/news/

politics/state-rep-nino-vitale-dewine-administration-critic-urges-ohioans-to-stop-getting-tested-for-coronavirus/95-1ac4c167-e7cc-4b0c-a342-df1472448f43

[227] Naymik, Mark. "State Rep. Nino Vitale offers ignorant assessment of the poor and media in bizarre email about energy bill." Cleveland. com May 6, 2019. https://www.cleveland.com/news/2019/05/state-rep-nino-vitale-offers-ignorant-assessment-of-the-poor-and-media-in-bizarre-email-about-energy-bill-mark-naymik.html

[228] Bischoff, Laura A. "Urbana lawmaker says he's 'darker' than members of black caucus." The Springfield News-Sun. June 11, 2020. https://www.springfieldnewssun.com/news/state--regional-govt--politics/urbana-lawmaker-says-darker-than-members-black-caucus/35fKLe5o40q84H1yQvCmcL/

[229] Naymik, Mark. "State Rep. Nino Vitale offers ignorant assessment of the poor and media in bizarre email about energy bill." Cleveland. com May 6, 2019. https://www.cleveland.com/news/2019/05/state-rep-nino-vitale-offers-ignorant-assessment-of-the-poor-and-media-in-bizarre-email-about-energy-bill-mark-naymik.html

[230] "Legislator Nino Vitale." BillTrack.com. https://www.billtrack50. com/LegislatorDetail/20812

[231] Siegal, Jim. "Bill making cockfighting a felony passes House." The Columbus Dispatch. February 24, 2016. https://www.dispatch.com/article/20160224/news/302249813

[232] Larkin, Brent. "A red county, Clermont County, Ohio, and its far-right state rep." Cleveland.com. July 7, 2013. https://www.cleveland.com/opinion/2013/07/a_red_county_clermont_county_o.html

[233] Larkin, Brent. "A red county, Clermont County, Ohio, and its far-right state rep." Cleveland.com. July 7, 2013. https://www.cleveland.com/opinion/2013/07/a_red_county_clermont_county_o.html

[234] I'll use his words. "The following is not a proposal but rather an academic exercise for the purposes of discussion, debate, and consideration. (Maybe it should be a proposal…)" Becker, John. "Musings of a Free Ohio – "The Becker Doctrine"." John Becker

for Ohio. 2019. https://www.beckergop.com/the-issues/the-becker-doctrine/

[235] He explicitly defends the use of the phrase "so-called civil war": "History is written by the victors to be whatever they say it is. The Confederate States had no interest in conquering the United States. They were simply asserting and defending their independence." Becker, John. "Musings of a Free Ohio – "The Becker Doctrine." John Becker for Ohio. 2019. https://www.beckergop.com/the-issues/the-becker-doctrine/

[236] Horne, Sarah. "Greater Cincinnati Republican deletes controversial Facebook post involving daughter and shotgun." Cincinnati Enquirer. May 30, 2019. https://www.google.com/amp/s/amp.cincinnati.com/amp/1290079001

[237] Siegel, Jim. "Powell legislator stirs controversy over views on public schools." The Columbus Dispatch. March 19, 2014. https://www.dispatch.com/article/20140319/NEWS/303199763; Klein, Rebecca. "GOP Lawmaker: 'Public Education In America Is Socialism'." The Huffington Post. March 14, 2014. https://www.huffpost.com/entry/andrew-brenner-education-socialism_n_4961201

[238] "Rep. Brenner compares Planned Parenthood to Nazis." The Columbus Dispatch. July 23, 2015. https://www.dispatch.com/article/20150723/blogs/307239865

[239] Siegel, Jim. "Rep. Brenner claim about ECOT donations draws fire." The Akron Beacon-Journal. May 21, 2018. https://www.beaconjournal.com/news/20180521/rep-brenner-claim-about-ecot-donations-draws-fire

[240] Buchanan, Tyler. "GOP lawmaker says he won't let Jewish health director turn Ohio into Nazi Germany." The Ohio Capital Journal. April 22, 2020. https://ohiocapitaljournal.com/2020/04/22/gop-lawmaker-says-he-wont-let-jewish-health-director-turn-ohio-into-nazi-germany/

Part II

[241] Campbell, Jon. "New York corruption scandals: Here's who has been convicted in 2018." The Democrat and Chronicle. July 20, 2018. https://www.democratandchronicle.com/story/news/politics/albany/2018/07/20/new-york-corruption-scandals-heres-who-has-been-convicted-2018/795849002/

[242] Cournoyer, Caroline. "Rhode Island House Speaker Resigns After Home, Office Raids." Governing.com. March 24, 2014. https://www.governing.com/news/headlines/rhode-island-house-speaker-resigns-after-home-office-raids.html

[243] Richey, Eric. "MISSOURI GETS D- GRADE IN 2015 STATE INTEGRITY INVESTIGATION." PublicIntegrity.org. November 9, 2015. https://publicintegrity.org/politics/state-politics/state-integrity-investigation/missouri-gets-d-grade-in-2015-state-integrity-investigation/

[244] Dick Simpson, Marco Rosaire Rossi, and Thomas J. Gradel. "Corruption Spikes in Illinois." University of Illinois at Chicago Department of Political Science. February 22, 2021. https://pols.uic.edu/wp-content/uploads/sites/273/2021/02/Corruption-Spikes-in-IL-Anti-Corruption-Rpt-13-final2.-1.pdf

[245] Hicks, Justin P. "Speaker of the House testifies in Michigan politician's bribery, extortion case." MLive.com. December 5, 2019. https://www.mlive.com/news/2019/12/speaker-of-the-house-testifies-in-michigan-politicians-bribery-extortion-case.html

[246] Flowers, Steve. "Alabama corruption giving Louisiana a run for its money." St. Clair Times. April 18, 2017. https://www.annistonstar.com/the_st_clair_times/steve-flowers-alabama-corruption-giving-louisiana-a-run-for-its-money-opinion/article_f375dc52-23a1-11e7-8a0b-9bedb4becc5e.html

[247] Harper, Mark. "Ghost candidates, dark money and a 'winning formula': Florida corruption case linked to Republican insiders." The Palm Beach Post. July 30, 2021. https://www.palmbeachpost.com/story/news/state/2021/07/30/florida-ghost-candidate-election-corruption-frank-artiles-republican-lawmakers-third-party/5391308001/

[248] Shaw, William. "Column: Corruption in the General Assembly Must Be Rooted Out at the Ballot Box." The Pilot. September 26, 2020. https://www.thepilot.com/opinion/column-corruption-in-the-general-assembly-must-be-rooted-out-at-the-ballot-box/article_d5e84cd4-ff75-11ea-96ed-1b278fd9f418.html

[249] Glenn Smith and Tony Bartelme. "Targets of influence: Investigation zeroes in on how money and power are peddled in South Carolina politics." The Post and Courier. March 19, 2017. https://www.postandcourier.com/politics/targets-of-influence-investigation-zeroes-in-on-how-money-and/article_0049f2be-0b43-11e7-9c24-5feb8d6a203b.html

[250] Hooks, Christopher. "In a System that Encourages Corruption, Prison-Bound Senator Carlos Uresti was Inevitable." The Texas Observer. June 28, 2018. https://www.texasobserver.org/in-a-system-that-encourages-corruption-prison-bound-senator-carlos-uresti-was-inevitable/ ("The state of Texas has built a political system that is effectively designed to produce petty grifters, which it succeeds in doing with great regularity.")

[251] Hogan, Shanna. "Arizona's Top 10 Disgraced Politicians." The Phoenix New Times. Aug 1, 2016. https://www.phoenixnewtimes.com/news/arizonas-top-10-disgraced-politicians-8486446

[252] McGreevy, Patrick. "Corruption scandals haven't curbed lavish gift-giving to California lawmakers." The Los Angeles Times. March 3, 2018. https://www.latimes.com/politics/la-pol-ca-gift-limits-2018 0303-story.html

[253] Greenblat, Alan. "5 Reasons State House Speakers May Be Prone to Corruption." Governing.com. January 26, 2015. https://www.governing.com/archive/gov-speakers-indicted-new-york-rhode-island-south-carolina-alabama.html

[254] Michael Johnston and Oguzhan Dincer. "Measuring Illegal and Legal Corruption in American States: Some Results from the Corruption in America Survey." Harvard University Edmund J. Safra Center for Ethics. December 1, 2014. https://ethics.harvard.edu/blog/measuring-illegal-and-legal-corruption-american-states-some-results-safra

[255] "How the Right Trounced Liberals in the States." Democracy Journal. Winter 2016. Issue #39. https://democracyjournal.org/magazine/39/how-the-right-trounced-liberals-in-the-states/ ("Radical policy changes, often undoing decades of progress on liberal issues, have not been limited to traditionally very conservative areas in the Deep South and inner West. "Purple" states in the upper South and once "blue" states in the Midwest have also been the sites of sharp rightward policy turns.")

[256] Drutman, Lee. "Why There Are So Few Moderate Republicans Left." FiveThirtyEight.org. August 24, 2020. https://fivethirtyeight.com/features/why-there-are-so-few-moderate-republicans-left/

[257] Cohen, Matt. "The Most Radical Republicans Aren't in Congress. They're in the Statehouses." Mother Jones Magazine. March 17, 2021. https://www.motherjones.com/politics/2021/03/radical-republicans-statehouses/

[258] Cournoyer, Caroline. "Abortion Restrictions Vetoed by Pennsylvania Governor." Governing.com. December 17, 2019. https://www.governing.com/archive/tns-wolf-veto-abortion.html

[259] Shannon, Bill. "Gov. Wolf vetoes bills on firearms during emergency, gas drilling." WTAJ News. November 26, 2020. https://www.wearecentralpa.com/news/regional-news/gov-wolf-vetoes-bills-on-firearms-during-emergency-gas-drilling/

[260] "Gov. Wolf Vetoes Republican Bill Rolling Back Environmental Protection Standards For Conventional Oil & Gas Drilling." PA Environment Daily. November 25, 2020. http://paenvironmentdaily.blogspot.com/2020/11/gov-wolf-vetoes-republican-bill-rolling.html

[261] Esack, Steve. "Is 2015 the worst year in Pennsylvania political history?" The Morning Call. December 12, 2015. https://www.mcall.com/news/pennsylvania/mc-pa-worst-year-in-state-politics-20151212-story.html

[262] Kiesel, Megan. "From the State House to Big House: Bipartisan Cellmates." ABCNews.com. June 5, 2012. https://abcnews.go.com/blogs/politics/2012/06/political-rivals-now-bunk-mates-in-jail

263 Cillizza, Chris. "How the ugly, racist White 'replacement theory' came to Congress." CNN. April 15, 2021. https://www. cnn.com/2021/04/15/politics/scott-perry-white-replacement-theory-tucker-carlson-fox-news/index.html; Taylor, Jessica. "Pennsylvania GOP Rep. Patrick Meehan Resigns After Sexual Harassment Scandal." NPR.org. April 27, 2018. https://www. npr.org/2018/04/27/606545237/pennsylvania-gop-rep-patrick-meehan-resigns-after-sexual-harassment-scandal; Lopez, German. "The fall of Tom Marino, Trump's pick for drug czar, explained." Vox Media. October 17, 2017. https://www.vox.com/policy-and-politics/2017/10/17/16482620/tom-marino-drug-czar-dea-opioid.

264 After all, the LWV were the ones who brought the successful suit. "PENNSYLVANIA REDISTRICTING LAWSUIT." The Public Interest Law Center. 2018. https://www.pubintlaw.org/cases-and-projects/pennsylvania-redistricting-lawsuit/.

Chapter 6: Weaponizing Statehouses into a National Force

265 Pelzer, Jeremy. "Ohio Senate GOP budget proposal would ban municipal broadband programs." Cleveland.com. June 15, 2021. https://www.cleveland.com/open/2021/06/ohio-senate-gop-budget-proposal-would-ban-municipal-broadband-programs.html; "Worst Connected Cities 2019." National Digital Inclusion Alliance. 2019. https://www.digitalinclusion.org/worst-connected-cities-2019/

266 Buchanan, Tyler. "Ohio Senate leadership wants no additional $ for broadband expansion." Ohio Capital Journal. June 2, 2021. https://ohiocapitaljournal.com/2021/06/02/ohio-senate-leadership-wants-no-additional-for-broadband-expansion/

267 Wendy Patton and Zach Schiller. "Senate tax cuts would go mostly to the affluent." Policy Matters Ohio. June 3, 2021. https:// www.policymattersohio.org/research-policy/quality-ohio/revenue-budget/tax-policy/senate-tax-cuts-would-go-mostly-to-the-affluent

268 Brodkin, Jon. "Ohio Republicans close to imposing near-total ban on municipal broadband." Ars Technica. June 17, 2021. https:// arstechnica.com/tech-policy/2021/06/ohio-republicans-close-to-imposing-near-total-ban-on-municipal-broadband/

[269] Schladen, Marty. "Experts overwhelmingly agree rural broadband will grow Ohio's economy, reduce inequality. Senate leaders don't." Ohio Capital Journal. June 23, 2021. https://ohiocapitaljournal. com/2021/06/23/experts-overwhelmingly-agree-rural-broadband-will-grow-ohios-economy-reduce-inequality-senate-leaders-dont/

[270] Emily Mills and Jim Mackinnon. "State could kill municipal broadband services such as FairlawnGig, critics fear." The Akron Beacon Journal. June 13, 2021. https://www.beaconjournal.com/ story/news/2021/06/13/municipal-broadband-fairlawngig-ohio-budget-summit-medina-county/7654789002/

[271] Pelzer, Jeremy. "Ohio Senate GOP budget proposal would ban municipal broadband programs." Cleveland.com. June 15, 2021. https://www.cleveland.com/open/2021/06/ohio-senate-gop-budget-proposal-would-ban-municipal-broadband-programs.html

[272] Cooper, Tyler. "Municipal Broadband Is Restricted In 18 States Across the U.S. in 2021." BroadbandNow. April 6, 2021. https:// broadbandnow.com/report/municipal-broadband-roadblocks/

[273] Cooper, Tyler. "Municipal Broadband Is Restricted In 18 States Across the U.S. in 2021." BroadbandNow. April 6, 2021. https:// broadbandnow.com/report/municipal-broadband-roadblocks/

[274] "Municipal Telecommunications Private Industry Safeguards Act Exposed." ALECExposed.org. Date Accessed: March 15, 2016. Edited: October 12, 2017. https://www.alecexposed.org/wiki/Municipal_ Telecommunications_Private_Industry_Safeguards_Act_Exposed

[275] Hertel-Fernandez, Alexander. *State Capture: How conservative activists, big businesses, and wealthy donors reshaped the American states—and the nation.* (New York, New York: Oxford University Press. 2019).

[276] Greenblatt, Alan. "ALEC Enjoys A New Wave of Influence and Criticism." Governing.com. November 29, 2011. https://www. governing.com/archive/alec-enjoys-new-wave-influence-criticism. html

[277] Greenblatt, Alan. "ALEC Enjoys A New Wave of Influence and Criticism." Governing.com. November 29, 2011. https://www.

governing.com/archive/alec-enjoys-new-wave-influence-criticism. html; Olsson, Karen. "Ghostwriting the Law." Mother Jones Magazine. September/October Issue 2002. https://www.motherjones. com/politics/2002/09/ghostwriting-law/

[278] In 2009, ALEC membership included "speakers, presidents, and majority and minority leaders in 22 senates and 30 houses." Olsson, Karen. "Ghostwriting the Law." Mother Jones Magazine. September/ October Issue 2002. https://www.motherjones.com/politics/2002/09/ ghostwriting-law/

[279] "About ALEC." Alec.org. 2021. https://www.alec.org/about/

[280] "About ALEC." Alec.org. 2021. https://www.alec.org/about/

[281] "Federalism." Alec.org. 2021. https://www.alec.org/issue/ federalism/

[282] "Rich States, Poor States." richstatespoorstates.org. 2021. https:// www.richstatespoorstates.org

[283] Gale, William G. "The Kansas tax cut experiment." The Brookings Institute. July 11, 2017. https://www.brookings.edu/blog/ unpacked/2017/07/11/the-kansas-tax-cut-experiment/

[284] "Policy Basics: Taxpayer Bill of Rights (TABOR)." The Center of Budget and Policy Priorities. November 5, 2019. https://www.cbpp. org/research/state-budget-and-tax/taxpayer-bill-of-rights-tabor

[285] "Washington." richstatespoorstates.org. 2021. https://www.rich statespoorstates.org/states/WA/

[286] "Wyoming." richstatespoorstates.org. 2021. https://www.rich statespoorstates.org/states/WY/

[287] How do we know when an item in a state comes from the ALEC menu? For years, that too was a secret, but after the 2011 surge in exposure, people figured it out. First, the legislators don't put in much effort to change the wording, so journalists and others can track similarities between ALEC's model bills and real bills that become law. A Brookings Institute scholar, for example, used string searches to match language from model ALEC bills and actual legislation in states to find when ALEC was behind a bill. For 2011-2012 alone,

he identified 169 of ALEC's "model bills" that generated 132 actual bills back in statehouses. https://www.brookings.edu/articles/alecs-influence-over-lawmaking-in-state-legislatures/ ProPublica created a database of these laws, and wrote a "how-to" guide on how to track the connection between ALEC laws in states. Beckett, Lois. "Our Step-By-Step Guide to Understanding ALEC's Influence on Your State Laws." Propublica. August 1, 2011. https://www.propublica.org/article/our-step-by-step-guide-to-understanding-alecs-influence-on-your-state-laws Other times, legislators haven't even deleted words on model legislation that make it clear that ALEC did the work. For example, in Florida, a legislator forgot to remove the boilerplate language at the top of the bill she introduced at the legislature—so a Sunshine State bill urging a limit on federal corporate taxation also made clear that ALEC is dedicated to "Jeffersonian principles of free markets, limited government, federalism, and individual liberty...." Muzenrieder, Kyle. "Dumb Florida Legislator Accidentally Tried to Make Lobbyist Group's Mission Statement a Law." The Miami New Times. February 2, 2012. https://www.miaminewtimes.com/news/dumb-florida-legislator-accidentally-tried-to-make-lobbyist-groups-mission-statement-a-law-6555315 Florida residents must've been thrilled by the news.

[288] Greenblatt, Alan. "ALEC Enjoys A New Wave of Influence and Criticism." Governing.com. November 29, 2011. https://www.governing.com/archive/alec-enjoys-new-wave-influence-criticism.html

[289] Harney, Sarah. "What Makes Alec Smart?" Governing.com. November 5, 2010. https://www.governing.com/archive/what-makes-alec-smart.html

[290] Graves, Lisa. "About ALEC Exposed." PRWatch.org. July 13, 2011. https://www.prwatch.org/news/2011/07/10883/about-alec-exposed

[291] Nichols, John. "ALEC Exposed." The Nation Magazine. August 1/8, 2011 Issue. https://www.alecexposed.org/w/images/7/73/Nation20110801.pdf

[292] Greely, Brendan. "ALEC's Secrets Revealed: Corporations Flee." Bloomberg. May 3, 2012. https://www.bloomberg.com/news/articles/2012-05-03/alecs-secrets-revealed-corporations-flee

[293] Rob O'Dell and Yvonne Wingett Sanchez. "What is ALEC? 'The most effective organization' for conservatives, says Newt Gingrich." USA Today. April 3, 2019. https://www.usatoday.com/story/news/investigations/2019/04/03/alec-american-legislative-exchange-council-model-bills-republican-conservative-devos-gingrich/3162357002/

[294] Millbank, Dana. "ALEC stands its ground." The Washington Post. December 4, 2013. https://www.washingtonpost.com/opinions/dana-milbank-alec-stands-its-ground/2013/12/04/ad593320-5d2c-11e3-bc56-c6ca94801fac_story.html

[295] Rob O'Dell and Yvonne Wingett Sanchez. "What is ALEC? 'The most effective organization' for conservatives, says Newt Gingrich." USA Today. April 3, 2019. https://www.usatoday.com/story/news/investigations/2019/04/03/alec-american-legislative-exchange-council-model-bills-republican-conservative-devos-gingrich/3162357002/

[296] Olsson, Karen. "Ghostwriting the Law." Mother Jones Magazine. September/October Issue 2002. https://www.motherjones.com/politics/2002/09/ghostwriting-law/

[297] Pelzer, Jeremy. "Ohio Senate GOP Budget Proposal Would Ban Municipal Broadband Programs." cleveland.com June 14, 2021. https://www.cleveland.com/open/2021/06/ohio-senate-gop-budget-proposal-would-ban-municipal-broadband-programs.html

[298] Laura Macomber and Tom Casciato. "The End of the (Wire) Line." The Benton Institute. July 24, 2013. https://www.benton.org/headlines/end-wireline; Bruce Kushnick and Dave Rosen. "ALEC, Tech and the Telecom Wars: Killing America's Telecom Utilities." The Huffington Post. July 24, 2012. https://www.huffpost.com/entry/alec-tech-and-the-telecom_b_1696830

[299] Greenblatt, Alan. "ALEC Enjoys A New Wave of Influence and Criticism." Governing.com. November 29, 2011. https://www.governing.com/archive/alec-enjoys-new-wave-influence-criticism.html

[300] "Buying Influence." Alec Exposed, D.B.A Press, and Common Cause. 2012. https://www.alecexposed.org/w/images/f/fa/BUYING_INFLUENCE_Main_Report.pdf

[301] "Buying Influence." Alec Exposed, D.B.A Press, and Common Cause. 2012. 14-15. https://www.alecexposed.org/w/images/f/fa/BUYING_INFLUENCE_Main_Report.pdf

[302] Greenblatt, Alan. "ALEC Enjoys A New Wave of Influence and Criticism." Governing.com. November 29, 2011. https://www.governing.com/archive/alec-enjoys-new-wave-influence-criticism.html

[303] Hertel-Fernandez, Alexander. *State Capture: How conservative activists, big businesses, and wealthy donors reshaped the American states—and the nation.* (New York, New York. Oxford University Press. 2019), 82.

[304] Nick Penzenstadler and Rob O'Dell. "Copy, Paste, Legislate: You elected them to write new laws. They're letting corporations do it instead." USA Today. December 16, 2019. https://www.usatoday.com/in-depth/news/investigations/2019/04/03/abortion-gun-laws-stand-your-ground-model-bills-conservatives-liberal-corporate-influence-lobbyists/3162173002/

[305] Rob O'Dell and Yvonne Wingett Sanchez. "What is ALEC? 'The most effective organization' for conservatives, says Newt Gingrich." USA Today. April 3, 2019. https://www.usatoday.com/story/news/investigations/2019/04/03/alec-american-legislative-exchange-council-model-bills-republican-conservative-devos-gingrich/3162357002/

[306] Rob O'Dell and Yvonne Wingett Sanchez. "What is ALEC? 'The most effective organization' for conservatives, says Newt Gingrich." USA Today. April 3, 2019. https://www.usatoday.com/story/news/investigations/2019/04/03/alec-american-legislative-exchange-council-model-bills-republican-conservative-devos-gingrich/3162357002/

[307] Rob O'Dell and Yvonne Wingett Sanchez. "What is ALEC? 'The most effective organization' for conservatives, says Newt

Gingrich." USA Today. April 3, 2019. https://www.usatoday.com/ story/news/investigations/2019/04/03/alec-american-legislative- exchange-council-model-bills-republican-conservative-devos- gingrich/3162357002/

[308] "Buying Influence." Alec Exposed, D.B.A Press, and Common Cause. 2012. https://www.alecexposed.org/w/images/f/fa/BUYING_ INFLUENCE_Main_Report.pdf

[309] Millbank, Dana. "ALEC stands its ground." The Washington Post. December 4, 2013. https://www.washingtonpost.com/opinions/ dana-milbank-alec-stands-its-ground/2013/12/04/ad593320-5d2c- 11e3-bc56-c6ca94801fac_story.html

[310] "ALEC in Ohio." People for the American Way, Progress Ohio, Common Cause, and ALEC Exposed. 2012. https://www. commoncause.org/wp-content/uploads/2019/08/ALEC-in-Ohio.pdf

[311] "ALEC in Ohio." People for the American Way, Progress Ohio, Common Cause, and ALEC Exposed. 2012. 11. https://www. commoncause.org/wp-content/uploads/2019/08/ALEC-in-Ohio.pdf

[312] "ALEC in Ohio." People for the American Way, Progress Ohio, Common Cause, and ALEC Exposed. 2012. https://www. commoncause.org/wp-content/uploads/2019/08/ALEC-in-Ohio.pdf

[313] "ALEC in Ohio." People for the American Way, Progress Ohio, Common Cause, and ALEC Exposed. 2012. https://www. commoncause.org/wp-content/uploads/2019/08/ALEC-in-Ohio.pdf

[314] "ALEC in Ohio." People for the American Way, Progress Ohio, Common Cause, and ALEC Exposed. 2012. 12. https://www. commoncause.org/wp-content/uploads/2019/08/ALEC-in-Ohio.pdf

[315] "ALEC in Ohio." People for the American Way, Progress Ohio, Common Cause, and ALEC Exposed. 2012. https://www. commoncause.org/wp-content/uploads/2019/08/ALEC-in-Ohio.pdf

[316] "Ohio." ALECExposed.org. Last Edited: September 26, 2017. https://www.alecexposed.org/wiki/Ohio "ALEC in Ohio." People for the American Way, Progress Ohio, Common Cause, and

ALEC Exposed. 2012. https://www.commoncause.org/wp-content/uploads/2019/08/ALEC-in-Ohio.pdf

[317] Marshall, Aaron. "Ohio House approves legislation requiring state photo ID to vote." Cleveland.com. March 24, 2011. https://www.cleveland.com/open/2011/03/ohio_house_approves_legislatio.html

[318] "ALEC Exposed in Wisconsin." The Center for Media and Democracy. 2012. https://www.alecexposed.org/w/images/c/cd/ALEC_Exposed_in_Wisconsin.pdf

[319] Marley, Patrick. "Assembly Speaker Robin Vos received $57,000 in travel and other perks since 2014." Milwaukee Journal Sentinel. May 3, 2018. https://www.jsonline.com/story/news/politics/2018/05/03/robin-vos-last-year-received-13-000-travel-and-other-perks/577176002/

[320] "ALEC Exposed in Wisconsin." The Center for Media and Democracy. 2012. https://www.alecexposed.org/w/images/c/cd/ALEC_Exposed_in_Wisconsin.pdf

[321] "ALEC Exposed in Wisconsin." The Center for Media and Democracy. 2012. https://www.alecexposed.org/w/images/c/cd/ALEC_Exposed_in_Wisconsin.pdf

[322] "ALEC Exposed in Iowa." Progress Iowa, Center for Media and Democracy, Common Cause, People for the American Way, and Progress Now. https://www.commoncause.org/wp-content/uploads/2019/08/Iowa.ALEC_.report.pdf

[323] "ALEC in Arizona." Arizona Working Families, Center for media and Democracy, Common Cause, People for the American Way, Progress Now Education. 2013. https://www.commoncause.org/wp-content/uploads/2019/08/ALEC_In_Arizona_2013.pdf

[324] "Stand Up To ALEC—Exposed: ALEC's influence on Kansas and Missouri." Progress Missouri, ALEC Exposed, Common Cause, Missouri Jobs With Justice, Voter Action. https://www.commoncause.org/wp-content/uploads/2018/03/exposed-alecs-influence-in.pdf

[325] "ALEC Exposed in Michigan—Who is writing Michigan's laws?" Progress Michigan, Common Cause, ALEC Exposed, People for

the American Way. July 19, 2012. https://www.commoncause.org/
wp-content/uploads/2019/08/Who-is-Writing-Our-Laws-ALEC-
Exposed-in-Michigan.pdf

[326] "ALEC in Florida." Progress Florida, Florida Watch, Common
Cause, People for the American Way, ALEC Exposed. 2012. https://
www.commoncause.org/wp-content/uploads/2019/08/alecinflorida.
pdf

[327] "ALEC in Texas." Common Cause, Exposed by The Center for
Media and Democracy. August 2019. https://www.commoncause.
org/wp-content/uploads/2019/08/ALEC-Report-Texas_FINAL_
WEB.pdf

[328] "ALEC in Louisiana." Common Cause. August 2018. https://www.
commoncause.org/wp-content/uploads/2019/08/ALEC-Report-
Texas_FINAL_WEB.pdf

[329] "Exposed: The State Policy Network." Center for Media and
Democracy. November 2013. https://www.prwatch.org/files/spn_
national_report_final.pdf

[330] Mayer, Jane. *Dark Money*, First Edition. (New York, New York:
Doubleday, 347.

[331] Davis, Walker. "Americans for Prosperity tripled state lobbyists
in past four years." Citizens for Ethics and Responsibility in
Washington. August 16, 2016. https://www.citizensforethics.org/
reports-investigations/crew-investigations/americans-prosperity-
tripled-state-lobbyists-past-four-years/

[332] Davis, Walker. "Americans for Prosperity tripled state lobbyists
in past four years." Citizens for Ethics and Responsibility in
Washington. August 16, 2016. https://www.citizensforethics.org/
reports-investigations/crew-investigations/americans-prosperity-
tripled-state-lobbyists-past-four-years/

[333] Davis, Walker. "Americans for Prosperity tripled state lobbyists
in past four years." Citizens for Ethics and Responsibility in
Washington. August 16, 2016. https://www.citizensforethics.org/

reports-investigations/crew-investigations/americans-prosperity-tripled-state-lobbyists-past-four-years/

[334] Alex Roatry and National Journal "A Conservative Juggernaut's Long Game." The Atlantic. June 16, 2014. https://www.theatlantic.com/politics/archive/2014/06/the-koch-brothers-pac-is-just-warming-up/372851/

[335] Davis, Walker. "Americans for Prosperity tripled state lobbyists in past four years." Citizens for Ethics and Responsibility in Washington. August 16, 2016. https://www.citizensforethics.org/reports-investigations/crew-investigations/americans-prosperity-tripled-state-lobbyists-past-four-years/

[336] Ben Wieder and Lizzy Essley Whyte. "Amid Federal Gridlock, Lobbying Rises In The States." PublicIntegity.org. February 12, 2016. https://publicintegrity.org/politics/state-politics/amid-federal-gridlock-lobbying-rises-in-the-states/

[337] Ben Wieder and Lizzy Essley Whyte. "Amid Federal Gridlock, Lobbying Rises In The States." PublicIntegity.org. February 12, 2016. https://publicintegrity.org/politics/state-politics/amid-federal-gridlock-lobbying-rises-in-the-states/

[338] *Democracy Unchained*, Andrew Gumbel, Bakari Kitwana, David W. Orr, and William S. Becker. (New York, New York: The New Press, 2020), 305.

Chapter 7: Laboratories at Work: A Decade of Dry Runs

[339] Suddes, Thomas. "GOP lost the handle on Senate Bill 5 early." Cleveland.com. October 15, 2011. https://www.cleveland.com/opinion/2011/10/gop_lost_the_handle_on_senate.html

[340] Staver, Anna. "After a gunman killed 9, Gov. DeWine heard chants of 'Do something!' and rolled out a plan. A year later, Ohio laws haven't changed a bit." USA Today. August 4, 2020. https://www.usatoday.com/story/news/nation/2020/08/04/dayton-shooting-one-year-anniversary-ohio-gun-laws/5574324002/

[341] Wong, Wilson. "Ohio Gov. DeWine reverses course on veto, signs 'stand your ground' bill eliminating duty to retreat." NBCNews.

com. January 5, 2021. https://www.nbcnews.com/news/us-news/ohio-gov-dewine-reverses-course-veto-warning-signs-stand-your-n1252823

[342] Strauss, Daniel. "Poll: Ohio voters favor universal background checks." The Hill. March 1, 2013. https://thehill.com/blogs/blog-briefing-room/news/285677-poll-ohio-voters-favor-universal-background-checks

[343] WKYC Staff. "Poll says 90% of Ohioans support gun background checks." WKYC.com. July 26, 2019. https://www.wkyc.com/article/news/poll-says-90-of-ohioans-support-gun-background-checks/95-ea935860-d94f-4682-90a5-89bf9fb80b88

[344] "Ohio Poll Results Show Overwhelming Support for Lifesaving Gun Violence Prevention Policies." Giffords.org. November 19, 2020. https://giffords.org/press-release/2020/11/ohio-poll-overwhelming-support-for-gun-violence-prevention/

[345] "Ohio Poll Results Show Overwhelming Support for Lifesaving Gun Violence Prevention Policies." Giffords.org. November 19, 2020. https://giffords.org/press-release/2020/11/ohio-poll-overwhelming-support-for-gun-violence-prevention/

[346] Welsh-Huggins, Andrew. "Bill Would Eliminate Required Ohio Conceal Carry License." WOSU 89.7 NPR News. August 16, 2021. https://news.wosu.org/politics/2021-08-16/bill-would-eliminate-required-ohio-conceal-carry-license

[347] Julia A Wolfson et al., "US Public Opinion on Carrying Firearms in Public Places." American Journal of Public Health. (American Public Health Association, June 2017), https://www.ncbi.nlm.nih.gov/pmc/articles/PMC5425856/

[348] Kaffer, Nancy. "The Legislature wants more guns. Michiganders don't." The Detroit Free Press. November 12, 2017. https://www.freep.com/story/opinion/columnists/nancy-kaffer/2017/11/12/gun-control-policy-lansing/850377001/

[349] Hertel-Fernandez, Alexander. *State Capture: How conservative activists, big businesses, and wealthy donors reshaped the American*

states—and the nation. (New York, New York: Oxford University Press. 2019), 254.

[350] Bellin, Jeffrey. "How 'duty to retreat' became 'stand your ground'." CNN. March 3, 2021. https://www.cnn.com/2012/03/21/opinion/bellin-stand-your-ground-law/index.html

[351] "Florida Standard Jury Instructions—Criminal." TheLawOfSelf Defense.com. https://lawofselfdefense.com/jury-instruction/fl-3-6f-justifiable-use-of-deadly-force/

[352] Caputo, Mark A. "Jury talked Stand Your Ground before not-guilty Zimmerman verdict, juror says." Miami Herald. Jul. 18, 2013, http://www.miamiherald.com/2013/07/16/3502481/juror-we-talked-stand-your-ground.html.

[353] Caputo, Mark A. "Jury talked Stand Your Ground before not-guilty Zimmerman verdict, juror says." Miami Herald. Jul. 18, 2013, http://www.miamiherald.com/2013/07/16/3502481/juror-we-talked-stand-your-ground.html.

[354] Sloan, Calvin. "ALEC: The Hidden Player Behind 'Stand Your Ground' Laws." People For The American Way. March 21, 2012. https://www.pfaw.org/blog-posts/alec-the-hidden-player-behind-stand-your-ground-laws/

[355] Sloan, Calvin. "ALEC: The Hidden Player Behind 'Stand Your Ground' Laws." People For The American Way. March 21, 2012. https://www.pfaw.org/blog-posts/alec-the-hidden-player-behind-stand-your-ground-laws/

[356] "NRA Presents ALEC Model Legislation In Grapevine, Texas." August 12, 2005. https://www.prwatch.org/files/NRA_2005.png

[357] "ALEC Castle Doctrine." ALECExposed.org. March 23, 2012. https://www.alecexposed.org/wiki/ALEC_Castle_Doctrine

[358] Krugman, Paul. "Lobbyists, Guns and Money." The New York Times. March 25, 2012. https://www.nytimes.com/2012/03/26/opinion/krugman-lobbyists-guns-and-money.html

[359] "Stand Your Ground." Giffords Law Center. 2021.https://giffords. org/lawcenter/gun-laws/policy-areas/guns-in-public/stand-your-ground-laws/#footnote_11_5647

[360] Kovac, Marc. "Dayton mayor unhappy as Gov. Mike DeWine signs 'stand your ground' legislation into law." January 4, 2021. https://www.dispatch.com/story/news/politics/state/2021/01/ 04/ohio-gov-mike-dewine-acts-on-stand-your-ground-bill/ 4008228001/

[361] Scola, Nancy. "Exposing ALEC: How Conservative-Backed State Laws Are All Connected." The Atlantic. April 14, 2012. https:// www.theatlantic.com/politics/archive/2012/04/exposing-alec-how-conservative-backed-state-laws-are-all-connected/255869/

[362] Hertel-Fernandez, Alexander. *State Capture: How conservative activists, big businesses, and wealthy donors reshaped the American states—and the nation.* (New York, New York: Oxford University Press. 2019), 58-59; Hamburger, Tom." Trayvon Martin shooting spurs protests against companies with ties to legislative group." The Washington Post. April 12, 2012. https://www.washingtonpost. com/politics/trayvon-martin-shooting-spurs-protests-against-com panies-with-ties-to-legislative-group/2012/04/12/gIQAs8HuDT_ story.html.

[363] Hertel-Fernandez, Alexander. *"State Capture: How conservative activists, big businesses, and wealthy donors reshaped the American states—and the nation."* (New York, New York: Oxford University Press. 2019), 133.

[364] Graves, Lisa. "Let's end Stand Your Ground." Politico. July 17, 2013. https://www.politico.com/story/2013/07/after-zimmerman-lets-end-stand-your-ground-094357; Gertz, Matt. "ALEC Eliminates Task Force That Did NRA's Bidding." Media Matters for America. April 17, 2012. https://www.mediamatters.org/national-rifle-association/alec-eliminates-task-force-did-nras-bidding

[365] "ALEC Castle Doctrine," ALECExposed.org. March 23, 2012. https://www.alecexposed.org/wiki/ALEC_Castle_Doctrine

[366] Hertel-Fernandez, Alexander. *State Capture: How conservative activists, big businesses, and wealthy donors reshaped the American states—and the nation.* (New York, New York: Oxford University Press. 2019), 134-135. One study found that 41% of primarily "consumer-facing" companies in ALEC left, versus 13% of "non-consumer-facing" companies. 43% of public employee held companies similarly left ALEC. Hertel-Fernandez, Alexander. *State Capture: How conservative activists, big businesses, and wealthy donors reshaped the American states—and the nation.* (New York, New York: Oxford University Press. 2019), 135.

[367] Weinstein, Casey. Twitter Post. June 29, 2021. https://twitter.com/repweinstein/status/1409862011782111235?s=21

[368] Zuckerman, Jake. "Senate passes bill creating new hurdles for wind, solar development." Ohio Capital Journal. June 3, 2021. https://ohiocapitaljournal.com/2021/06/03/senate-passes-bill-creating-new-hurdles-for-wind-solar-development/. Jesse Balmert and Gere Goble. "DeWine signs bill adding local input, additional hurdle for wind and solar projects in Ohio." *USA Today.* June 12, 2021. https://www.usatoday.com/story/news/2021/07/12/dewine-signs-bill-adding-hurdle-wind-solar-projects-ohio/7943554002/

[369] Zuckerman, Jake. "State budget blocks Ohio cities from taxing grocery bags." 10TV.com. June18, 2021. https://www.10tv.com/article/news/politics/state-budget-blocks-ohio-cities-from-taxing-grocery-bags/530-71c3a1db-270a-4148-ade1-61f0bc2a337f

[370] Hertel-Fernandez, Alexander. *State Capture: How conservative activists, big businesses, and wealthy donors reshaped the American states—and the nation.* (New York, New York: Oxford University Press. 2019), 246-247.

[371] "Ohio Collective Bargaining Fight Takes New Turn; Recut Television Ad Makes SB5 Opponent Look Like A Supporter." LRIS.com. October 13, 2011. https://lris.com/2011/10/13/ohio-collective-bargaining-fight-takes-new-turn-recut-television-ad-makes-sb5-opponent-look-like-a-supporter/

[372] The Associated Press. "Ohio police, firefighters decry collective bargaining limits." MassLive.com. March 25, 2019. https://www.masslive.com/news/2011/03/ohio_police_firefighters_decry.html

[373] Suddes, Thomas. "GOP lost the handle on Senate Bill 5 early." Cleveland.com. October 15, 2011. https://www.cleveland.com/opinion/2011/10/gop_lost_the_handle_on_senate.html

[374] Suddes, Thomas. "GOP lost the handle on Senate Bill 5 early." Cleveland.com. October 15, 2011. https://www.cleveland.com/opinion/2011/10/gop_lost_the_handle_on_senate.html

[375] Fields, Reginald. "Television stations pulling SB5 commercial over concerns it is misleading." Cleveland.com. January 12, 2019. https://www.cleveland.com/open/2011/10/television_stations_pulling_sb.html

[376] "Wisconsin Gov. Scott Walker says National Guard ready for any unrest over anti-union bill." WisconsinSituation.com from Green Bay Press Gazette. May 22, 2011. https://wisconsinsituation.wordpress.com/2011/05/22/wisconsin-gov-scott-walker-says-national-guard-ready-for-any-unrest-over-anti-union-bill/

[377] "Despite Exemption from Anti-Union Bill, Wisconsin Firefighters Stand with Public Sector Workers." Democracy Now. February 25, 2011. https://www.democracynow.org/2011/2/25/despite_exemption_from_anti_union_bill

[378] Suddes, Thomas. "GOP lost the handle on Senate Bill 5 early." Cleveland.com. October 15, 2011. https://www.cleveland.com/opinion/2011/10/gop_lost_the_handle_on_senate.html

[379] Haglund, Rick. "Why Michigan police, firefighters were exempted from new right-to-work legislation." MLive.com. December 20, 2012. https://www.mlive.com/politics/2012/12/policy_reasons_for_exempting_p.html

[380] Scheiber, Noam. "Public Pension Cuts Exempt Police and Firefighters." The New York Times. March 19, 2015. https://www.nytimes.com/2015/03/20/business/economy/police-officers-and-firefighters-are-exceptions-to-new-public-sector-rules.html

381 Grant Rodgers and William Petroski. "Union sues over Iowa's new collective bargaining law." Des Moine Register. February 20, 2017. https://www.desmoinesregister.com/story/news/crime-and-courts/2017/02/20/iowa-collective-bargaining-law-terry-branstad-legislature/98155452/

382 "Policy Working Groups." State Policy Network. 2021. https://spn.org/core_program/policy-working-groups/

383 Bragdon, Trevor. "State Workplace Freedom Toolkit." State Policy Network. https://s3.documentcloud.org/documents/6563106/SPN-State-Workplace-Freedom-Toolkit.pdf

384 Bragdon, Trevor. "State Workplace Freedom Toolkit." State Policy Network. https://s3.documentcloud.org/documents/6563106/SPN-State-Workplace-Freedom-Toolkit.pdf

385 Bragdon, Trevor. "State Workplace Freedom Toolkit." State Policy Network. https://s3.documentcloud.org/documents/6563106/SPN-State-Workplace-Freedom-Toolkit.pdf

386 Bragdon, Trevor. "State Workplace Freedom Toolkit." State Policy Network. https://s3.documentcloud.org/documents/6563106/SPN-State-Workplace-Freedom-Toolkit.pdf

387 Hertel-Fernandez, Alexander. *State Capture: How conservative activists, big businesses, and wealthy donors reshaped the American states—and the nation.* (New York, New York: Oxford University Press. 2019), 245-46.

Chapter 8: Laboratories of Autocracy: Warming Up

388 Andy Sullivan and John Whiteside. "In Ohio, a spelling error could cost you your vote." Reuters. November 1, 2016. https://www.reuters.com/article/us-usa-election-ohio-insight/in-ohio-a-spelling-error-could-cost-you-your-vote-idUSKBN12W3LQ

389 The Northeast Ohio Coalition for the Homeless vs. Jon Husted in his official capacity as Secretary of the State of Ohio, Case No. 2:06-CV-896, (S.D. OH. 2016) at 29. https://moritzlaw.osu.edu/electionlaw/litigation/documents/NEOCH-opinion060716.pdf.

[390] The Northeast Ohio Coalition for the Homeless vs. Jon Husted in his official capacity as Secretary of the State of Ohio, Case No. 2:06-CV-896, (S.D. OH. 2016) at 28. https://moritzlaw.osu.edu/electionlaw/litigation/documents/NEOCH-opinion060716.pdf

[391] The Northeast Ohio Coalition for the Homeless vs. Jon Husted in his official capacity as Secretary of the State of Ohio, Case No. 2:06-CV-896, (S.D. OH. 2016) at 28. https://moritzlaw.osu.edu/electionlaw/litigation/documents/NEOCH-opinion060716.pdf

[392] Wendel, Emily E. "Ohio Legislative Service Commission Analysis of S.B. 205." Ohio Legislative Service Commission. June 1, 2014. https://www.lsc.ohio.gov/documents/gaDocuments/analyses130/14-sb205-130.pdf; Wendel, Emily E. "Ohio Legislative Service Commission Analysis of S.B. 216." Ohio Legislative Service Commission. June 1, 2014. https://www.lsc.ohio.gov/documents/gaDocuments/analyses130/s0216-rh-130.pdf

[393] Borchardt, Jackie. "Ohio ballot laws challenged in federal court as unconstitutional." Cleveland.com. October 31, 2014. https://www.cleveland.com/open/2014/10/ohio_ballot_laws_challenged_in.html; Wendel, Emily E. "Ohio Legislative Service Commission Analysis of S.B. 216." Ohio Legislative Service Commission. June 1, 2014. https://www.lsc.ohio.gov/documents/gaDocuments/analyses130/s0216-rh-130.pdf; Wendel, Emily E. "Ohio Legislative Service Commission Analysis of S.B. 205." Ohio Legislative Service Commission. June 1, 2014. https://www.lsc.ohio.gov/documents/gaDocuments/analyses130/14-sb205-130.pdf ; Siegel, Jim. "GOP bill alters Ohio rules for provisional ballots." The Columbus Dispatch. February 19, 2014. https://www.dispatch.com/article/20140219/NEWS/302199748

[394] Andy Sullivan and John Whiteside. "In Ohio, a spelling error could cost you your vote." Reuters. November 1, 2016. https://www.reuters.com/article/us-usa-election-ohio-insight/in-ohio-a-spelling-error-could-cost-you-your-vote-idUSKBN12W3LQ Those counties were: "Lucas, home to the city of Toledo; Cuyahoga, which includes Cleveland; Franklin, home to the state capital, Columbus; Summit, which includes Akron, the fifth-largest city in the state; and Hamilton County, home of Cincinnati."

[395] "The 14 Ohio counties with the most restrictive enforcement accounted for 53 percent of Ohio's total vote in 2012 and gave Democratic President Barack Obama 60 percent of the votes he won in Ohio." Andy Sullivan and John Whiteside. "In Ohio, a spelling error could cost you your vote." Reuters. November 1, 2016. https://www.reuters.com/article/us-usa-election-ohio-insight/in-ohio-a-spelling-error-could-cost-you-your-vote-idUSKBN12W3LQ

[396] The Northeast Ohio Coalition for the Homeless vs. Jon Husted in his official capacity as Secretary of the State of Ohio, Case No. 2:06-CV-896, (S.D. OH. 2016) at 30-32. https://moritzlaw.osu.edu/electionlaw/litigation/documents/NEOCH-opinion060716.pdf

[397] The Northeast Ohio Coalition for the Homeless vs. Jon Husted in his official capacity as Secretary of the State of Ohio, Case No. 2:06-CV-896, (S.D. OH. 2016) at 47. https://moritzlaw.osu.edu/electionlaw/litigation/documents/NEOCH-opinion060716.pdf

[398] The Northeast Ohio Coalition for the Homeless vs. Jon Husted in his official capacity as Secretary of the State of Ohio, Case No. 2:06-CV-896, (S.D. OH. 2016) at 23. https://moritzlaw.osu.edu/electionlaw/litigation/documents/NEOCH-opinion060716.pdf ("[T]he district court was not presented with a shred of evidence of mail-in absentee- voter fraud.")

[399] The Northeast Ohio Coalition for the Homeless vs. Jon Husted in his official capacity as Secretary of the State of Ohio, Case No. 2:06-CV-896, (S.D. OH. 2016) at 73. https://moritzlaw.osu.edu/electionlaw/litigation/documents/NEOCH-opinion060716.pdf

[400] The Northeast Ohio Coalition for the Homeless vs. Jon Husted in his official capacity as Secretary of the State of Ohio, Case No. 16-3603; 16-3691 (S.D. OH. 2016). https://www.scotusblog.com/wp-content/uploads/2017/10/16-980-bsac-NAACP.pdf

[401] The Northeast Ohio Coalition for the Homeless vs. Jon Husted in his official capacity as Secretary of the State of Ohio, Case No. 2:06-CV-896, (S.D. OH. 2016). https://moritzlaw.osu.edu/electionlaw/litigation/documents/NEOCH-opinion060716.pdf

[402] The Northeast Ohio Coalition for the Homeless vs. Jon Husted in his official capacity as Secretary of the State of Ohio, Case No. 2:06-CV-896, (S.D. OH. 2016) at 28. https://moritzlaw.osu.edu/ electionlaw/litigation/documents/NEOCH-opinion060716.pdf

[403] "Young Voters Supported Obama Less, But May Have Mattered More." Pew Research Center. November 26, 2012. https://www. pewresearch.org/politics/2012/11/26/young-voters-supported-obama-less-but-may-have-mattered-more/. These were the largest margins among under 30 voters since the Goldwater/Nixon election.

[404] "Young Voters Supported Obama Less, But May Have Mattered More." Pew Research Center. November 26, 2012. https://www. pewresearch.org/politics/2012/11/26/young-voters-supported-obama-less-but-may-have-mattered-more/.

[405] "Young Voters Supported Obama Less, But May Have Mattered More." Pew Research Center. November 26, 2012. https://www. pewresearch.org/politics/2012/11/26/young-voters-supported-obama-less-but-may-have-mattered-more/. "In Florida, Ohio, Virginia and Pennsylvania, Obama [] failed to win a majority of voters 30 and older. Yet he swept all four battleground states, in part because he won majorities of 60% or more among young voters."

[406] Conaway, Laura. "Student voting rights seem 'peculiar' to Ohio GOP." NBCNews.com. May 17, 2013. https://www.nbcnews. com/news/world/student-voting-rights-seem-peculiar-ohio-gop-flna1c9978664

[407] Conaway, Laura. "Student voting rights seem 'peculiar' to Ohio GOP." NBCNews.com. May 17, 2013. https://www.nbcnews. com/news/world/student-voting-rights-seem-peculiar-ohio-gop-flna1c9978664

[408] Carrington vs. Rash, 380 U.S. 89, (United States Supreme Court, 1965), at 94. ("'fencing out' from the franchise a sector of the population because of the way they may vote is constitutionally impermissible"). Cipriano v. City of Houma, Case No. 395 US 701, (United States Supreme Court, 1969).

[409] Dunn v. Blumstein, 405 U.S. 330, 355 (United States Supreme Court, 1972).

[410] The Northeast Ohio Coalition for the Homeless vs. Jon Husted in his official capacity as Secretary of the State of Ohio, Case No. 2:06-CV-896, (S.D. OH. 2016) at 4. https://moritzlaw.osu.edu/electionlaw/litigation/documents/NEOCH-opinion060716.pdf; The Ohio Organizing Collaborative vs. Jon Husted, Case No. 215-cv-1802, (United States District Court, Southern District of Ohio, Eastern Division, 2016), at 39. https://drive.google.com/file/d/0BxDmhRN9Ij2ccnBrc0pwTzVWQlk/view?resourcekey=0-kG_OQJ8tK60TQPI6jQ_0xQ

[411] The Northeast Ohio Coalition for the Homeless vs. Jon Husted in his official capacity as Secretary of the State of Ohio, Case No. 2:06-CV-896, (S.D. OH. 2016), at 55. https://moritzlaw.osu.edu/electionlaw/litigation/documents/NEOCH-opinion060716.pdf.

[412] Obama for America, Democratic National Committee, Ohio Democratic Party vs. Jon Husted, Ohio Secretary of State, Mike DeWine, Ohio Attorney General, Case No. 2:12-cv-00636, (United States Court of Appeals, Sixth Circuit, 2012), at 5. https://moritzlaw.osu.edu/electionlaw/litigation/documents/Opinion_006.pdf

[413] Obama for America, Democratic National Committee, Ohio Democratic Party vs. Jon Husted, Ohio Secretary of State, Mike DeWine, Ohio Attorney General, Case No. 2:12-cv-00636, (United States Court of Appeals, Sixth Circuit, 2012), at 4. https://moritzlaw.osu.edu/electionlaw/litigation/documents/Opinion_006.pdf

[414] The Northeast Ohio Coalition for the Homeless vs. Jon Husted in his official capacity as Secretary of the State of Ohio, Case No. 2:06-CV-896, (S.D. OH. 2016), at 55. https://moritzlaw.osu.edu/electionlaw/litigation/documents/NEOCH-opinion060716.pdf.

[415] Ohio State Conference of the NAACP vs. Jon Husted, Case No. 2:14-cv-404, (United States District Court, Southern District of Ohio, Eastern Division, 2014), at 38. https://s3.amazonaws.com/s3.documentcloud.org/documents/1283696/economus-golden-week.pdf.

[416] A number of counties had sent out absentee ballot applications in 2008 and 2010. The Ohio Organizing Collaborative vs. Jon Husted, Case No. 215-cv-1802, (United States District Court, Southern District of Ohio, Eastern Division, 2016), at 68. https://drive.google.com/file/d/0BxDmhRN9Ij2ccnBrc0pwTzVWQlk/view?resourcekey=0-kG_OQJ8tK60TQPI6jQ_0xQ .

[417] Ohio State Conference of the NAACP vs. Jon Husted, Case No. 2:14-cv-404, (United States District Court, Southern District of Ohio, Eastern Division, 2014), at 7. https://s3.amazonaws.com/s3.documentcloud.org/documents/1283696/economus-golden-week.pdf

[418] The Ohio Organizing Collaborative vs. Jon Husted, Case No. 215-cv-1802, (United States District Court, Southern District of Ohio, Eastern Division, 2016), at 36. https://drive.google.com/file/d/0BxDmhRN9Ij2ccnBrc0pwTzVWQlk/view?resourcekey=0-kG_OQJ8tK60TQPI6jQ_0xQ Looking at "homogenous" geographic blocks of voters, homogenous Black blocks were 3.5 times more likely to vote in person during "Golden Week" than homogenous white blocks.

[419] Jon Husted vs. Philip A. Randolph Institute, Case No. 16-980, 584 (United States Supreme Court, 2018), at 9. https://www.scotusblog.com/wp-content/uploads/2017/10/16-980-bsac-NAACP.pdf

[420] Guillen, Joe. "Ohio House votes to repeal controversial election law." Cleveland.com. May 8, 2012. https://www.cleveland.com/open/2012/05/ohio_house_votes_to_repeal_con.html

[421] Obama for America, Democratic National Committee, Ohio Democratic Party vs. Jon Husted, Ohio Secretary of State, Mike DeWine, Ohio Attorney General, Case No. 2:12-cv-00636, (United States Court of Appeals, Sixth Circuit, 2012). https://moritzlaw.osu.edu/electionlaw/litigation/documents/Opinion_006.pdf

[422] Almost half of Franklin County's early-person votes cast in 2008 came during weekday evening hours. Rowland, Darrel. "Voting in Ohio | Fight over poll hours isn't just political." The

Columbus Dispatch. August 19, 2012. https://www.dispatch.com/article/20120819/NEWS/308199804

[423] "Automatic Voter Registration, a Summary." The Brennan Center for Justice. July 10, 2019. https://www.brennancenter.org/our-work/research-reports/automatic-voter-registration-summary

[424] Jon Husted vs. Philip A. Randolph Institute, Case No. 2:16-cv-00303 (United States Court of Appeals, Sixth Circuit, 2016), at 4. https://www.brennancenter.org/sites/default/files/legal-work/2016_09_23_Opinion_Reversing_District_Court.pdf

[425] Jon Husted vs. Philip A. Randolph Institute, Case No. 2:16-cv-00303 (United States Court of Appeals, Sixth Circuit, 2016), at 4. https://www.brennancenter.org/sites/default/files/legal-work/2016_09_23_Opinion_Reversing_District_Court.pdf.

[426] Jon Husted vs. Philip A. Randolph Institute, Case No. 16-980, 584 (United States Supreme Court, Slip Opinion, 2018) (J. Breyer, dissenting), at 12. https://www.supremecourt.gov/opinions/17pdf/16-980_f2q3.pdf

[427] Jon Husted vs. Philip A. Randolph Institute, Case No. 16-980, 584 (United States Supreme Court, Slip Opinion, 2018), at 13. https://www.supremecourt.gov/opinions/17pdf/16-980_f2q3.pdf

[428] Jon Husted vs. Philip A. Randolph Institute, Case No. 2:16-cv-00303 (United States Court of Appeals, Sixth Circuit, 2016), at 4. https://www.brennancenter.org/sites/default/files/legal-work/2016_09_23_Opinion_Reversing_District_Court.pdf.

[429] Andy Sullivan and Grant Smith. "Use it or lose it: Occasional Ohio voters may be shut out in November." Reuters. June 6, 2016. https://www.reuters.com/article/us-usa-votingrights-%20ohio-insight/use-it-or-lose-it-occasional-ohio-voters-may-be-shut-out-%20in-november-idUSKcN0yO19D

[430] Jon Husted vs. Philip A. Randolph Institute, Case No. 16-980, 584 (United States Supreme Court, 2018), at 18. https://www.scotusblog.com/wp-content/uploads/2017/10/16-980-bsac-NAACP.pdf

[431] "In the state's three largest counties that include Cleveland, Cincinnati and Columbus, voters have been struck from the rolls in Democratic-leaning neighborhoods at roughly twice the rate as in Republican neighborhoods." https://www.reuters.com/article/us-usa-votingrights-%20ohio-insight/use-it-or-lose-it-occasional-ohio-voters-may-be-shut-out-%20in-november-idUSKcN0yO19D

[432] Jon Husted vs. Philip A. Randolph Institute, Case No. 16-980, 584 (United States Supreme Court, 2018), at 18. https://www.scotusblog.com/wp-content/uploads/2017/10/16-980-bsac-NAACP.pdf

[433] "The young were disproportionately purged: Nearly 1 out of 3 purged voters was age 25 to 34. And where a party preference could be determined based on the last partisan primary in which the voter cast a ballot, Democrats outnumbered Republicans almost 2 to 1." Doug Caruso and Rick Rouan, "Ohio's voter registration purge targeted thousands in error. Now, a call for change." USA Today. January 22, 2020. https://www.usatoday.com/in-depth/news/investigations/2020/01/22/errors-ohio-voter-registration-purge-prompt-call-change/4490821002/

[434] Doug Caruso and Rick Rouan. "Vendor's errors lead to hundreds of voters targeted for purge in Ohio." The Columbus Dispatch. August 25, 2019. https://www.dispatch.com/news/20190825/vendors-errors-lead-to-hundreds-of-voters-targeted-for-purge-in-ohio/1

[435] Rouan, Rick. "Dozens of Ohio voters improperly on purge list in Franklin County." The Columbus Dispatch. August 5, 2019. https://www.dispatch.com/news/20190805/dozens-of-ohio-voters-improperly-on-purge-list-in-franklin-county

[436] Casey, Nicholas. "Ohio Was Set to Purge 235,000 Voters. It Was Wrong About 20%." The New York Times. October 14, 2019. https://www.nytimes.com/2019/10/14/us/politics/ohio-voter-purge.html

[437] Casey, Nicholas. "Ohio Was Set to Purge 235,000 Voters. It Was Wrong About 20%." The New York Times. October 14, 2019. https://www.nytimes.com/2019/10/14/us/politics/ohio-voter-purge.html

[438] Tobias, Andrew J. "Ohio to continue with voter purge Friday after federal judge declines to block it." Cleveland.com. September 3, 2019.

https://www.cleveland.com/open/2019/09/ohio-to-continue-with-voter-purge-friday-after-federal-judge-declines-to-block-it.html

[439] Tobias, Andrew J. "Ohio Secretary of State Frank LaRose says Ohio's system of maintaining voter registrations rife with problems." Cleveland.com. September 24, 2019. https://www.cleveland.com/open/2019/09/ohio-secretary-of-state-frank-larose-says-ohios-system-of-maintaining-voter-registrations-rife-with-problems.html

[440] Tobias, Andrew J. "Another possible error springs up in Ohio voter-purge process." Cleveland.com. September 18, 2019. https://www.cleveland.com/open/2019/09/another-possible-error-springs-up-in-ohio-voter-purge-process.html; Rose, Bride. "Rep. Sweeney Finds Hundreds Purged in Error over the Past Week." Sweeney News Release. September 12, 2019. https://ohiohouse.gov/members/bride-rose-sweeney/news/rep-sweeney-finds-hundreds-purged-in-error-over-the-past-week-101141

[441] Siegel, Jim. "Democrats call Ohio's purgings of voter rolls too aggressive." The Columbus Dispatch. December 3, 2015. https://www.dispatch.com/article/20151203/NEWS/312039811

[442] Roth, Zachary. "Ohio voting bill could lead to long lines, voter purges." MSNBC.com. December 12, 2013. https://www.msnbc.com/msnbc/ohio-republican-voting-bill-msna229536; "Status Report of Legislation, Senate Bill 0200." Legislative Service Commission of Ohio. October 30, 2013. http://lsc.state.oh.us/pages/reference/archives/notes/srl/default.aspx?G=130&T=SB&N=0200

[443] Ingraham, Christopher. "This anti-voter-fraud program gets it wrong over 99 percent of the time. The GOP wants to take it nationwide." The Washington Post. July 20, 2017. https://www.washingtonpost.com/news/wonk/wp/2017/07/20/this-anti-voter-fraud-program-gets-it-wrong-over-99-of-the-time-the-gop-wants-to-take-it-nationwide/

[444] "Election Results and Data." The Office of the Ohio Secretary of State. 2021. https://www.ohiosos.gov/elections/election-results-and-data/

[445] Montgomery County (18,000 fewer registers voters less) and Lucas County (17,000) saw their registrations fall at a rate higher than their population declines. Hamilton County saw its registered population drop slightly, even as its population grew. And while Franklin County saw strong population growth (15%), registrations were up less than a third of that rate (4.4%).

[446] "Voter Registration Statistics." Cuyahoga County Board of Elections. 2021. https://boe.cuyahogacounty.gov/en-US/VoterRegis trationStatistics.aspx

[447] "Election Results." Hamilton County Board of Elections. 2021. https://votehamiltoncountyohio.gov/results/

[448] "Historic Election Results." Lucas County Board of Elections. 2021. https://www.lucascountyohiovotes.gov/historic-election-results

[449] "Election Results." Montgomery County Board of Elections. 2021. https://www.montgomery.boe.ohio.gov/election-results/

[450] Siegel, Jim. "Tuition saver or vote suppressor? GOP plan for college-student residency stirs controversy." The Columbus Dispatch. April 23, 2013. https://www.dispatch.com/article/20130423/NEWS/ 304239687

[451] Ludlow, Randy. "How will Ohio enforce new voting rules for out-of-state students?" The Columbus Dispatch. April 1, 2015. https:// www.dispatch.com/content/stories/local/2015/04/01/enforcing-new-rules-looms-as-gray-area.html

[452] Ludlow, Randy. "Kasich's veto removes voting target for out-of-state college students." The Columbus Dispatch. April 1, 2015. https://www.dispatch.com/article/20150401/NEWS/304019721

[453] "Judge rules 17-year-olds can vote in presidential primary." The Columbus Dispatch. March 11, 2016. https://www.dispatch.com/ article/20160311/NEWS/303119693

[454] "Union Members in Ohio—2020." Bureau of Labor Statistics. February 21, 2021. https://www.bls.gov/regions/midwest/news-release/unionmembership_ohio.htm

[455] Carl Dean and Tia Lessin. "The Next Phase of the Koch Brothers' war on Unions." The Daily Beast. April 14, 2017. https://www. thedailybeast.com/the-next-phase-of-the-koch-brothers-war-on-unions

[456] John Halpin and Ruy Teixeira. "Voter Trends in 2016." Center for American Progress. November 1, 2017. https://www.americanprogress. org/issues/democracy/reports/2017/11/01/441926/voter-trends-in-2016/

[457] "Voter Registration Statistics." Cuyahoga County Board of Elections. 2021. https://boe.cuyahogacounty.gov/en-US/VoterRegis trationStatistics.aspx

[458] "Election Results." Hamilton County Board of Elections. 2021. https://votehamiltoncountyohio.gov/results/

[459] "Election Results." Montgomery County Board of Elections. 2021. https://www.montgomery.boe.ohio.gov/election-results/

[460] "Election Results." Summit County Board of Elections. August 2, 2021. https://www.summitcountyboe.gov/boe-reports/election-results/

[461] "2016 Official Election Results." The Office of the Ohio Secretary of State. 2021. ://www.ohiosos.gov/elections/election-results-and-data/2016-official-elections-results/

[462] "Of the five counties with the highest overall removal rates, four went for Hillary Clinton in the 2016 presidential election...[M]ore than a million [voters] were removed [from those counties' rolls] between November 2014 and February of 2018, [accounting] for 43 percent of all removals statewide despite making up just 30 percent of the state's registered voters in 2016." Angela Caputo, Geoff Hing, and Johnny Kauffman. "They Didn't Vote ... Now They Can't." APM Reports. October 19, 2018. https://www.apmreports.org/story/2018/10/19/georgia-voter-purge

[463] "Voter Registration Statistics." Cuyahoga County Board of Elections. 2021. https://boe.cuyahogacounty.gov/en-US/VoterRegis trationStatistics.aspx

[464] "Voter Registration Statistics." Cuyahoga County Board of Elections. 2021. https://boe.cuyahogacounty.gov/en-US/VoterRegis trationStatistics.aspx

[465] "2020 Official Election Results." The Office of the Ohio Secretary of State. 2021. https://www.ohiosos.gov/elections/election-results-and-data/2020/

[466] "Election Results." Hamilton County Board of Elections. 2021. https://votehamiltoncountyohio.gov/results/

[467] "Election Results." Montgomery County Board of Elections. 2021. https://www.montgomery.boe.ohio.gov/election-results/

[468] "Historic Election Results." Lucas County Board of Elections. 2021. https://www.lucascountyohiovotes.gov/historic-election-results

[469] Kovac, Marc. "Clyde, LaRose announce bids for Ohio's secretary of state." My Town Neo. May 21, 2017. https://www.mytownneo.com/news/20170521/clyde-larose-announce-bids-for-ohios-secretary-of-state?template=ampart ("Almost all of the legislation that pertains to elections issues over the last seven years has either been something I've written or worked very personally on.")

[470] One columnist wrote: "There's no reason -- none -- to think Frank LaRose, fellow Republicans who voted for his bill, or Kasich are racially prejudiced. But in terms of what a given piece of legislation does, facts are facts…" Suddes, Thomas. "Nothing fair, or right, about Golden Week ban." The Columbus Dispatch. September 4, 2016. https://www.dispatch.com/content/stories/editorials/2016/09/04/1-nothing-fair-or-right-about-golden-week-ban.html

[471] "Editorial endorsement: For Ohio secretary of state: Frank LaRose." The Columbus Dispatch. September 16, 2018. https://www.dispatch.com/opinion/20180916/editorial-endorsement-for-ohio-secretary-of-state-frank-larose

[472] "Editorial endorsement: For Ohio secretary of state: Frank LaRose." The Columbus Dispatch. September 16, 2018. https://www.dispatch.com/opinion/20180916/editorial-endorsement-for-ohio-secretary-of-state-frank-larose

[473] Ingles, Jo. "Franklin County Court Rules All Ohioans Should Be Able To Request Absentee Ballots Online." WKSU.org. September 11, 2020. https://www.wksu.org/government-politics/2020-09-11/franklin-county-court-rules-all-ohioans-should-be-able-to-request-absentee-ballots-online

[474] The nine were: Alaska, Georgia, Montana, Ohio, Pennsylvania, South Dakota, Oklahoma, Oregon and West Virginia. Johnny Kauffman. "They Didn't Vote ... Now They Can't." APM Reports. October 19, 2018. https://www.apmreports.org/story/2018/10/19/georgia-voter-purge

[475] Congress had explicitly said that voters should not be removed from the rolls "due to their failure to respond to a mailing." Bains, Chiraag. "Opinion: You have the right to vote. Use it or lose it, the Supreme Court says." The Washington Post. June 13, 2018. https://www.washingtonpost.com/opinions/vote-or-be-purged-thats-wrong/2018/06/13/5e9730d6-6f27-11e8-afd5-778aca903bbe_story.html

[476] Abrams, Stacey. *Our Time is Now*, First Edition. (New York, New York: Henry Holt and Company, 2021), 66.

[477] Chung, Andrew. "U.S. top court backs Ohio voter purge; Democrats blast ruling." Reuters. June 11, 2018. https://www.reuters.com/article/us-usa-court-purge/u-s-top-court-backs-ohio-voter-purge-democrats-blast-ruling-idUSKBN1J71QQ

[478] Totenberg, Nina. "Supreme Court Upholds Controversial Ohio Voter-Purge Law." NPR.org. June 11, 2018. https://www.npr.org/2018/06/11/618870982/supreme-court-upholds-controversial-ohio-voter-purge-law

[479] Abdel-Baqui, Omar. "9 states where the rules for voting have been changed or challenged ahead of 2020." NBCNews.com. July 13, 2019. https://www.nbcnews.com/politics/2020-election/9-states-where-rules-voting-have-been-changed-or-challenged-n1026886; Totenberg, Nina. "Supreme Court Upholds Controversial Ohio Voter-Purge Law." NPR.org. June 11, 2018. https://www.npr.org/2018/06/11/618870982/supreme-court-upholds-controversial-

ohio-voter-purge-law ("This provides another tool for those states... to remove eligible voters from the voting rolls, and that will have a disproportionate effect likely on voters who tend to vote for Democrats.")

480 Crawford v. Marion County Election Board, 553 U.S. 181 (United States Supreme Court, 2008).

481 "Strict" identification requirements generally mean that without the required identification, voters must vote a provisional ballot and then take an additional step (return to show their ID) to have their vote count. "Non-strict" means that when they don't have the identification with them when they vote, elections officials will take steps to ensure that they are a legally registered voter. "Voter Identification Requirements | Voter ID Laws." National Conference of State Legislatures. September 8, 2021. https://www.ncsl.org/research/elections-and-campaigns/voter-id.aspx

482 "Voter Identification Requirements | Voter ID Laws." National Conference of State Legislatures. September 8, 2021. https://www.ncsl.org/research/elections-and-campaigns/voter-id.aspx

483 Liptak, Adam. "Supreme Court Allows Texas to Use Strict Voter ID Law in Coming Election." The New York Times. Oct. 18, 2014. https://www.nytimes.com/2014/10/19/us/supreme-court-upholds-texas-voter-id-law.html

484 "New Voting Restrictions in America." The Brennan Center for Justice. September 2019. https://www.brennancenter.org/sites/default/files/2019-11/New%20Voting%20Restrictions.pdf; Brait, Ellen. "Voting restrictions in the US since the 2010 election: state by state." The Guardian. https://www.theguardian.com/us-news/2015/jul/13/voting-restrictions-2010-election

485 "New Voting Restrictions in America." The Brennan Center for Justice. September 2019. https://www.brennancenter.org/sites/default/files/2019-11/New%20Voting%20Restrictions.pdf

486 "New Voting Restrictions in America." The Brennan Center for Justice. September 2019. https://www.brennancenter.org/sites/default/files/2019-11/New%20Voting%20Restrictions.pdf

487 Abrams, Stacey. *Our Time is Now*, First Edition. (New York, New York: Henry Holt and Company, 2021), 101.

488 Berman, Ari. "Ohio GOP Admits Early Voting Cutbacks Are Racially Motivated." The Nation. August 20, 2012. https://www.thenation.com/article/archive/ohio-gop-admits-early-voting-cutbacks-are-racially-motivated/

489 Berman, Ari. *Give Us the Ballot*, (New York, New York: Picador Farrar, Straus and Giroux, 2015), 296.

490 Berman, Ari. *Give Us the Ballot*, (New York, New York: Picador Farrar, Straus and Giroux, 2015), 296.

491 "New Voting Restrictions in America." The Brennan Center for Justice. September 2019. https://www.brennancenter.org/sites/default/files/2019-11/New%20Voting%20Restrictions.pdf

492 Abrams, Stacey. *Our Time is Now*, First Edition. (New York, New York: Henry Holt and Company, 2021), 54.

493 "Voter ID." Brennan Center for Justice. 2021. https://www.brennancenter.org/issues/ensure-every-american-can-vote/vote-suppression/voter-id

494 Zoltan Hajnal, Nazita Lajevardi, and Lindsay Nielson. "Voter Identification Laws and the Suppression of Minority Votes." The Journal of Politics. (2): 363-379 https://www.journals.uchicago.edu/doi/full/10.1086/688343

495 Ben Jealous and Ryan P. Haygood. "The Battle to Protect the Vote." Center for American Progress, Legal Defense Fund, and Southern Elections Foundation. November 2014. https://tminstituteldf.org/wp-content/uploads/2017/08/The-Battle-to-Protect-the-Vote.pdf

496 Kennedy, Liz. "Voter Suppression Laws Cost Americans Their Voices at the Polls." Center for American Progress. November 11, 2016. https://www.americanprogress.org/issues/democracy/reports/2016/11/11/292322/voter-suppression-laws-cost-americans-their-voices-at-the-polls/

[497] Van Egeren, Jessica. "Voter ID would disenfranchise 300,000 Latinos, African-Americans in Wisconsin." The Capital Times. May 1, 2014. https://madison.com/ct/news/local/writers/jessica_vanegeren/voter-id-would-disenfranchise-300-000-latinos-african-americans-in-wisconsin/article_09763594-d0a1-11e3-8aaf-0019bb2963f4.html

[498] Wines, Michael. "Wisconsin Strict ID Law Discouraged Voters, Study Finds." The New York Times. Sept. 25, 2017 https://www.nytimes.com/2017/09/25/us/wisconsin-voters.html

[499] "Wisconsin voter ID law proved insurmountable for many voters." CBSNews.com. May 9, 2017. https://www.cbsnews.com/news/wisconsin-voter-id-law-turned-voters-estimate/

[500] Berman, Ari. Give Us the Ballot, (New York, New York: Picador Farrar, Straus and Giroux, 2015), 294-95.

[501] Berman, Ari. Give Us the Ballot, (New York, New York: Picador Farrar, Straus and Giroux, 2015), 305.

[502] Alex Rowell and David Madland. "Attacks on Public-Sector Unions Harm States: How Act 10 Has Affected Education in Wisconsin." American Progress Action. November 15, 2017. https://www.americanprogressaction.org/issues/economy/reports/2017/11/15/169146/attacks-public-sector-unions-harm-states-act-10-affected-education-wisconsin/

[503] Maisano, Chris. "Labor Union Membership Has Just Hit an All-Time Low. We Need to Reverse This Trend." Jacobian. January 23, 2020. https://jacobinmag.com/2020/01/labor-union-membership-density-bls-2019

[504] Elbow, Steven. "Labor report chronicle severe decline of unions in Wisconsin." The Capital Times. August 31, 2019. https://madison.com/ct/news/local/govt-and-politics/labor-report-chronicles-severe-decline-of-unions-in-wisconsin/article_431d8c33-c0c0-5237-bac3-7e4c1caf3b40.html

[505] Johnson, Shawn "A Decade After Act 10, It's A Different World For Wisconsin Unions." WPR.org. February 11, 2021 https://www.wpr.org/decade-after-act-10-its-different-world-wisconsin-unions

[506] Murphy, Bruce. "The Incredible Decline of Wisconsin Unions." UrbanMilwaukee.com. May 4, 2020. http://urbanmilwaukee. com/2020/05/04/murphys-law-states-unions-continue-to-decline/

[507] Elbow, Steven. "Labor report chronicle severe decline of unions in Wisconsin." The Capital Times. August 31, 2019. https://madison. com/ct/news/local/govt-and-politics/labor-report-chronicles-severe-decline-of-unions-in-wisconsin/article_431d8c33-c0c0-5237-bac3-7e4c1caf3b40.html

[508] Umhoefer, Dave. "For unions in Wisconsin, a fast and hard fall since Act 10." Milwaukee Journal Sentinel. November 27, 2016. https://projects.jsonline.com/news/2016/11/27/for-unions-in-wisconsin-fast-and-hard-fall-since-act-10.html

[509] Nichols, John. "ALEC Exposed: Rigging Elections." The Nation. July1,2011.https://www.thenation.com/article/archive/alec-exposed-rigging-elections/; "ALEC's Legislative Agenda on Voting Rights." ALECexposed.org. https://www.alecexposed.org/w/images/c/ca/ALEC_on_Voting.pdf

[510] Nichols, John. "ALEC Exposed: Rigging Elections." The Nation. July1,2011.https://www.thenation.com/article/archive/alec-exposed-rigging-elections/

[511] Nichols, John. "ALEC's Corporate Funders Are Complicit in State-Based Assaults on Voting Rights and Democracy." The Nation. June 17, 2021. https://www.thenation.com/article/politics/alec-corporations-democracy/; Corey, Jamie. "Creates Secret Internal Project to Work Redistrictiing and Election Issues." Document.net. June 5, 2020. https://documented.net/2020/06/corporate-backed-alec-creates-secret-internal-project-to-work-on-redistricting-and-election-issues/; Kotch, Alex. "ALEC Legislator Introduces Bill to Suppress the Vote in Ohio." PRWatch.org. June 4, 2020.https://www.prwatch.org/comment/47047.

[512] Armiak, David. "ALEC Invite to "Mail-In Voting: Exclusive Call with Former FEC Official & Honest Elections." Exposed by CMD. June 3, 2020. https://www.exposedbycmd.org/featured-documents/

alec-invite-to-mail-in-voting-exclusive-call-with-former-fec-
official-honest-elections/

513 Armiak, David. "ALEC Invite to "Mail-In Voting: Exclusive Call
with Former FEC Official & Honest Elections." Exposed by CMD.
June 3, 2020. https://www.exposedbycmd.org/featured-documents/
alec-invite-to-mail-in-voting-exclusive-call-with-former-fec-
official-honest-elections/

514 Kotch, Alex. "ALEC Legislator Introduces Bill to Suppress the
Vote in Ohio." PRWatch.org. June 4, 2020.https://www.prwatch.org/
comment/47047

515 Golson, Tara. "North Carolina wrote the playbook Wisconsin
and Michigan are using to undermine Democracy." Vox Media.
December 5, 2018. https://www.vox.com/policy-and-politics/2018/
12/5/18125544/north-carolina-power-grab-wisconsin-michigan-
lame-duck

516 Hersher, Rebecca. "North Carolina Governor Signs Law Limiting
Power Of His Successor." NPR.org. December 16, 2016. https://
www.npr.org/sections/thetwo-way/2016/12/16/505872501/north-
carolina-governor-signs-law-limiting-power-of-his-successor

517 White, Laurel. "Wisconsin Supreme Court Sides With GOP
Lawmakers To Limit Democratic Governor's Power." NPR.org. June
21, 2019. https://www.npr.org/2019/06/21/734722467/wisconsin-
supreme-court-sides-with-gop-lawmakers-to-limit-democratic-
governors-p; Berman, Russell. "The Republicans" Midwest 'Power
Grab'." The Atlantic. December 4, 2018. https://www.theatlantic.
com/politics/archive/2018/12/gop-power-grab-wisconsin-and-
michigan/577246/ ("The core promise of the winning candidates
for governor and attorney general would be blocked by this power
grab.")

518 Golson, Tara. "North Carolina wrote the playbook Wisconsin
and Michigan are using to undermine Democracy." Vox Media.
December 5, 2018. https://www.vox.com/policy-and-politics/2018/
12/5/18125544/north-carolina-power-grab-wisconsin-michigan-
lame-duck

[519] Smith, Mitch. "Last-Minute Laws Took Democrats' Power. Court Says That's Fine." The New York Times. June 21, 2019. https://www.nytimes.com/2019/06/21/us/wisconsin-lame-duck-laws-upheld.html

[520] Herndon, Astead W. "Michigan G.O.P. Starts Limiting Power of Incoming Democratic Leaders." The New York Times. Dec. 6, 2018. https://www.nytimes.com/2018/12/06/us/politics/michigan-republicans-power.html

[521] Smitch, Mitch. "Fears of Republican Power Grab in Michigan Fade as Governor Vetoes Bill." The New York Times. Dec. 28, 2018. https://www.nytimes.com/2018/12/28/us/michigan-snyder-power-veto.html

[522] Berman, Russell. "The Republicans" Midwest 'Power Grab'." The Atlantic. December 4, 2018. https://www.theatlantic.com/politics/archive/2018/12/gop-power-grab-wisconsin-and-michigan/577246/

[523] Chang, Clio. "How GOP Lawmakers Ignore the Will of the People." The New Republic. October 16, 2017. https://newrepublic.com/article/145006/gop-lawmakers-ignore-will-people-voters-passed-liberal-ballot-initiatives-republicans-throwing-them-out

[524] Skala, Karl. "The legislature should not ignore the will of the people." Columbia Daily Tribune. Apr 9, 2019. https://www.columbiatribune.com/news/20190409/legislature-should-not-ignore-will-of-people

[525] Langston Taylor and Lawrence Mower. "In Florida, the Gutting of a Landmark Law Leaves Few Felons Likely to Vote." Propublica. Oct. 7, 2020. https://www.propublica.org/article/in-florida-the-gutting-of-a-landmark-law-leaves-few-felons-likely-to-vote

[526] Lieb, David A. "Missouri voters reverse redistricting reforms before they could be used." PBS.org. Nov 5, 2020. https://www.pbs.org/newshour/politics/missouri-voters-reverse-redistricting-reforms-before-they-could-be-used

[527] Chang, Clio. "How GOP Lawmakers Ignore the Will of the People." The New Republic. October 16, 2017. https://newrepublic.

com/article/145006/gop-lawmakers-ignore-will-people-voters-passed-liberal-ballot-initiatives-republicans-throwing-them-out

[528] "Changes in 2017 to laws governing ballot measures." Ballotpedia. org. 2017. https://ballotpedia.org/Changes_in_2017_to_laws_govern ing_ballot_measures

[529] "ALEC Exposed." ALECexposed.org. https://www.alecexposed. org/w/images/f/f9/7G12-Resolution_to_Preserve_the_Legislative_ Process_Exposed.pdf

[530] Golson, Tara. "North Carolina wrote the playbook Wisconsin and Michigan are using to undermine Democracy." Vox Media. December 5, 2018. https://www.vox.com/policy-and-politics/2018/12/5/18125544/north-carolina-power-grab-wisconsin-michigan-lame-duck

Chapter 9: 2021: The Culmination

[531] Buchanan, Tyler. "Some voter education programs may be in jeopardy due to new Ohio law." Ohio Capital Journal. July 16, 2021. https://ohiocapitaljournal.com/2021/07/16/some-voter-education-programs-may-be-in-jeopardy-due-to-new-ohio-law/

[532] Stewart, Charles III. "How We Voted in 2020: A First Look at the Survey of the Performance of American Elections." MIT Election Data and Science Lab. December 15, 2020. http://electionlab.mit. edu/sites/default/files/2020-12/How-we-voted-in-2020-v01.pdf

[533] Democracy Docket Staff. "2021 Round-Up: Efforts to Restrict Voting in the States." Democracy Docket. May 21, 2021. https:// www.democracydocket.com/2021/05/voting-round-up-2021/

[534] "Voting Laws Roundup: May 2021." The Brennan Center for Justice. May 28, 2021. https://www.brennancenter.org/our-work/ research-reports/voting-laws-roundup-may-2021

[535] Layne, Nathan. "Explainer: Big changes under Georgia's new election law." Reuters. June 14, 2021. https://www.reuters.com/world/ us/big-changes-under-georgias-new-election-law-2021-06-14/. That 1.3 million represented 26% of the state's electorate. Nick

Corasaniti and Reid J. Epstein "What Georgia's Voting Law Really Does." The New York Times. August 18, 2021. https://www.nytimes.com/2021/04/02/us/politics/georgia-voting-law-annotated.html

[536] Isaiah Poritz, Mark Niesse, Stephen Fowler, and Sarah Kallis. "Drop box use heavy in Democratic areas before Georgia voting law." The Atlanta Journal Constitution. July 12, 2021. https://www.ajc.com/politics/drop-box-use-soared-in-democratic-areas-before-georgia-voting-law/N4ZTGHLWD5BRBOUKBHTUCFVOEU/

[537] Isaiah Poritz, Mark Niesse, Stephen Fowler, and Sarah Kallis. "Drop box use heavy in Democratic areas before Georgia voting law." The Atlanta Journal Constitution. July 12, 2021. https://www.ajc.com/politics/drop-box-use-soared-in-democratic-areas-before-georgia-voting-law/N4ZTGHLWD5BRBOUKBHTUCFVOEU/

[538] Nick Corasaniti and Reid J. Epstein "What Georgia's Voting Law Really Does." The New York Times. August 18, 2021. https://www.nytimes.com/2021/04/02/us/politics/georgia-voting-law-annotated.html

[539] Berman, Ari. "361 Voter Suppression Bills Have Already Been Introduced This Year." Mother Jones. April 1, 2021. https://www.motherjones.com/politics/2021/04/361-voter-suppression-bills-have-already-been-introduced-this-year/

[540] "Voting Laws Roundup: March 2021." The Brennan Center for Justice. April 1, 2021. https://www.brennancenter.org/our-work/research-reports/voting-laws-roundup-march-2021

[541] Acacia Coronado and Nicholas Riccardi. "Explainer: Details of the final version of Texas voting bill." Associated Press. August 31, 2021. https://apnews.com/article/health-texas-voting-coronavirus-pandemic-voting-rights-adeea8570592740b202f9d2bab6e0622. Democracy Docket Staff. "2021 Round-Up: Efforts to Restrict Voting in the States." Democracy Docket. May 21, 2021. https://www.democracydocket.com/2021/05/voting-round-up-2021/; Berman, Ari. "361 Voter Suppression Bills Have Already Been Introduced This Year." Mother Jones Magazine. April 1, 2021. https://www.motherjones.com/politics/2021/04/361-voter-suppression-bills-have-already-been-introduced-this-year/

[542] "Tell Your Legislators to Oppose These Hyper Partisan Anti-Voter Measures." Common Cause Wisconsin. March 29, 2021. https://www.commoncausewisconsin.org/2021/03/tell-your-legislators-to-oppose-these.html

[543] "Voting Laws Roundup: March 2021." The Brennan Center for Justice. April 1, 2021. https://www.brennancenter.org/our-work/research-reports/voting-laws-roundup-march-2021

[544] Mayer, Jane. "The Big money Behind The Big Lie." The New Yorker. August 2, 2021. https://www.newyorker.com/magazine/2021/08/09/the-big-money-behind-the-big-lie

[545] "Voting Laws Roundup: March 2021." The Brennan Center for Justice. April 1, 2021. https://www.brennancenter.org/our-work/research-reports/voting-laws-roundup-march-2021

[546] Beckwith, Ryan Teague. "GOP Risks Purging Eligible Voters in Drive to Cull States' Rolls." Bloomberg. April 30, 2021. https://www.bloomberg.com/news/articles/2021-04-30/gop-risks-purging-eligible-voters-in-drive-to-cull-states-rolls

[547] Democracy Docket Staff. "2021 Round-Up: Efforts to Restrict Voting in the States." Democracy Docket. May 21, 2021. https://www.democracydocket.com/2021/05/voting-round-up-2021/

[548] "Voting Laws Roundup: May 2021." The Brennan Center for Justice. May 28, 2021. https://www.brennancenter.org/our-work/research-reports/voting-laws-roundup-may-2021

[549] Nick Corasaniti and Reid J. Epstein "What Georgia's Voting Law Really Does." The New York Times. August 18, 2021. https://www.nytimes.com/2021/04/02/us/politics/georgia-voting-law-annotated.html

[550] Democracy Docket Staff. "2021 Round-Up: Efforts to Restrict Voting in the States." Democracy Docket. May 21, 2021. https://www.democracydocket.com/2021/05/voting-round-up-2021/

[551] Democracy Docket Staff. "2020 Early Voting in Georgia." Democracy Docket. March 16, 2021. https://www.democracydocket.com/2021/03/2020-early-voting-in-georgia/

[552] Totenberg, Nina. "The Supreme Court Deals A New Blow To Voting Rights, Upholding Arizona Restrictions." NPR.org. July 1, 2021. https://www.npr.org/2021/07/01/998758022/the-supreme-court-upheld-upholds-arizona-measures-that-restrict-voting

[553] Millhiser, Ian. "Georgia Republicans didn't waste any time in using their new voter suppression law." Vox Media. August 5, 2021. https://www.vox.com/22607616/georgia-republicans-fulton-county-atlanta-voter-suppression-sb202-jim-crow; Nathan Layne and Tim Reid. "Republicans trigger review of election officials in Georgia." Reuters. July 30, 2021. https://www.reuters.com/world/us/republicans-trigger-review-election-officials-georgia-2021-07-30/.

[554] Nick Corasaniti and Reid J. Epstein "What Georgia's Voting Law Really Does." The New York Times. August 18, 2021. https://www.nytimes.com/2021/04/02/us/politics/georgia-voting-law-annotated.html

[555] Blake, Aaron. "2 secretaries of state undercut Trump's fraud claims in key, GOP-controlled states. Republicans have now voted to strip both of power." The Washington Post. May 27, 2021. https://www.washingtonpost.com/politics/2021/05/27/gops-brazen-move-strip-power-fraud-narrative-busting-secretary-state-again/

[556] Nathaniel Rakich. "Dozen Other States Are Trying To Take Power Away From Local Election Officials. fivethirtyeight.com April 3, 2021. https://fivethirtyeight.com/features/its-not-just-georgia-more-than-a-dozen-other-states-are-trying-to-take-power-away-from-local-election-officials/

[557] Levine, Sam. "How Trump's big lie has been weaponized since the Capitol attack." The Guardian. July 7, 2021. https://www.theguardian.com/us-news/2021/jul/07/us-capitol-riot-attack-on-democracy; "Voting Laws Roundup: May 2021." The Brennan Center for Justice. May 28, 2021. https://www.brennancenter.org/our-work/research-reports/voting-laws-roundup-may-2021; Alicia Bannon, Douglas Keith, and Patrick Berry. "Legislative Assaults on State Courts—2021." The Brennan Center for Justice. May 19, 2021 https://www.brennancenter.org/our-work/research-reports/legislative-assaults-state-courts-2021.

[558] Alicia Bannon, Douglas Keith, and Patrick Berry. "Legislative Assaults on State Courts—2021." The Brennan Center for Justice. May 19, 2021 https://www.brennancenter.org/our-work/research-reports/legislative-assaults-state-courts-2021

[559] Alicia Bannon, Douglas Keith, and Patrick Berry. "Legislative Assaults on State Courts—2021." The Brennan Center for Justice. May 19, 2021 https://www.brennancenter.org/our-work/research-reports/legislative-assaults-state-courts-2021

[560] Alicia Bannon, Douglas Keith, and Patrick Berry. "Legislative Assaults on State Courts—2021." The Brennan Center for Justice. May 19, 2021 https://www.brennancenter.org/our-work/research-reports/legislative-assaults-state-courts-2021

[561] Alicia Bannon, Douglas Keith, and Patrick Berry. "Legislative Assaults on State Courts—2021." The Brennan Center for Justice. May 19, 2021 https://www.brennancenter.org/our-work/research-reports/legislative-assaults-state-courts-2021

[562] Riccardi, Nicholas. "Experts or 'grifters'? Little-known firm runs Arizona audit." Associated Press. May 23, 2021. https://apnews.com/article/donald-trump-arizona-business-technology-election-recounts-c5948f1d2ecdff9e93d4aa27ba0c1315

[563] Riccardi, Nicholas. "Experts or 'grifters'? Little-known firm runs Arizona audit." Associated Press. May 23, 2021. https://apnews.com/article/donald-trump-arizona-business-technology-election-recounts-c5948f1d2ecdff9e93d4aa27ba0c1315

[564] Cassidy, Christina. "Experts warn of dangers from breach of voter system software." Associated Press. August 28, 2021. https://apnews.com/article/technology-software-election-2020-1341028212960b9b4ed713620d764629

[565] Andrew Oxford and Mary Jo Pitzl. "Arizona Senate to seek more election material from Maricopa County; door-to-door questioning recommended." AZCentral.com. July 15, 2021. https://www.azcentral.com/story/news/politics/elections/2021/07/15/arizona-audit-senate-seek-more-maricopa-county-election-records/7973154002/

[566] Montellaro, Zach. "Trump audit excitement meets with fear from election officials." Politico. June 30, 2021. https://www.politico.com/news/2021/06/30/2020-election-audit-arizona-497049

[567] Layne, Nathan. "Philadelphia sees $40 mln in possible costs from Trump ally's election probe." Reuters. July 12, 2021. https://www.reuters.com/world/us/philadelphia-sees-40-mln-possible-costs-trump-allys-election-probe-2021-07-12/

[568] "Brandtjen, Murphy say they'd like to see Arizona-style audit of Wisconsin's November election." Wispoliticis.com. June 15, 2021. https://www.wispolitics.com/2021/brandtjen-murphy-say-theyd-like-to-see-arizona-style-audit-of-wisconsins-november-election/

[569] Snodgrass, Erin. "With Trump focused on election recounts, here are the ongoing attempts by GOP officials to 'review' the 2020 election results." Business Insider. June 3, 2021. https://www.businessinsider.com/all-the-attempts-by-state-and-local-gop-to-review-2020-election

[570] Montellaro, Zach. "Trump audit excitement meets with fear from election officials." Politico. June 30, 2021. https://www.politico.com/news/2021/06/30/2020-election-audit-arizona-497049

[571] Burris, Sarah K. "Florida Republicans demand 'forensic audit' of election in 5 Democratic counties." Raw Story. July 26, 2021. https://www.rawstory.com/florida-republican-election-audit-democrats/; Sommer, Will. Republicans Now Want to 'Audit' Election Results in States That Trump Won." The Daily Beast. June 15, 2021. https://www.thedailybeast.com/republicans-now-want-to-audit-2020-election-results-in-states-that-donald-trump-won.

[572] Smith, Alex. "Missouri Voters Approve Medicaid Expansion Despite Resistance From Republican Leaders." NPR.org. August 5, 2020. https://www.npr.org/sections/health-shots/2020/08/05/898899246/missouri-voters-approve-medicaid-expansion-despite-resistance-from-republican-le

[573] "Status of State Medicaid Expansion Decisions: Interactive Map." KFF.org. August 10, 2021. https://www.kff.org/medicaid/issue-brief/status-of-state-medicaid-expansion-decisions-interactive-map/

[574] Palmer, Todd. "Missouri voters sign off on Medicaid expansion." KSHB.com. August 4, 2020. https://www.kshb.com/news/election-2020/missouri-voters-sign-off-on-medicaid-expansion

[575] Associated Press. "Missouri lawmakers OK $35B budget without Medicaid expansion." KSHB.com. May 7, 2021. https://www.kshb.com/news/local-news/missouri-lawmakers-ok-35b-budget-without-medicaid-expansion

[576] Lieb, David A. "Missouri governor drops voter-approved Medicaid expansion." Associated Press. May 13, 2021. https://apnews.com/article/mo-state-wire-michael-brown-medicaid-business-health-19125d5b1d59ab6a9cb29ff48769a4e9

[577] Lieb, David A. "Missouri governor drops voter-approved Medicaid expansion." Associated Press. May 13, 2021. https://apnews.com/article/mo-state-wire-michael-brown-medicaid-business-health-19125d5b1d59ab6a9cb29ff48769a4e9

[578] Alicia Bannon, Douglas Keith, and Patrick Berry. "Legislative Assaults on State Courts—2021." The Brennan Center for Justice. May 19, 2021 https://www.brennancenter.org/our-work/research-reports/legislative-assaults-state-courts-2021

[579] Ari Berman and Nick Surgey. "Leaked Video: Dark Money Group Brags About Writing GOP Voter Suppression Bills Across the Country." Mother Jones Magazine. May 13, 2021. https://www.motherjones.com/politics/2021/05/heritage-foundation-dark-money-voter-suppression-laws/

[580] Anthony Izaguirre and Nicholas Riccardi. "Conservative group boasts of secret role in voting laws." Associated Press. May 14, 2021. https://apnews.com/article/politics-donald-trump-laws-voting-government-and-politics-c07c55f7dd3ad5847d31d7a5123bb82c

[581] Ari Berman and Nick Surgey. "Leaked Video: Dark Money Group Brags About Writing GOP Voter Suppression Bills Across the Country." Mother Jones Magazine. May 13, 2021. https://www.motherjones.com/politics/2021/05/heritage-foundation-dark-money-voter-suppression-laws/

[582] Jake Pearson and Mike Spies. "Before limiting ballot drop boxes, top Ohio election official consulted Heritage Foundation promoter of voting fraud fears." Cinncinnati.com. September 24, 2020. https://www.cincinnati.com/story/news/2020/09/24/before-limiting-ballot-drop-boxes-top-ohio-election-official-consulted-heritage-foundation-promoter/3515143001/

[583] Anthony Izaguirre and Nicholas Riccardi. "Conservative group boasts of secret role in voting laws." Associated Press. May 14,2021. https://apnews.com/article/politics-donald-trump-laws-voting-government-and-politics-c07c55f7dd3ad5847d31d7a5123bb82c

[584] "The Facts About Election Integrity and the Need for States to Fix Their Election Systems." The Heritage Foundation. February 1, 2021. https://www.heritage.org/election-integrity-facts

[585] Derysh, Igor. "Conservative groups are writing GOP voter suppression bills—and spending millions to pass them." Salon. March 27, 2021. https://www.salon.com/2021/03/27/conservative-groups-are-writing-gop-voter-suppression-bills---and-spending-millions-to-pass-them/#google_vignette; Nick Corasaniti and Reid J. Epstein. "G.O.P. and Allies Draft 'Best Practices' for Restricting Voting." The New York Times. March 23, 2021. https://www.nytimes.com/2021/03/23/us/politics/republican-voter-laws.html.

[586] Michael Biesecker and Nicholas Riccardi. "An all-hands moment': GOP rallies behind voting." Associated Press. March 19, 2021. limitshttps://apnews.com/article/legislature-voting-rights-ted-cruz-legislation-elections-6270306f67108ac16f4ee7b45a8afdb3

[587] Alex Kotch and Dan Wiener. "ALEC Members Lead Voter Suppression Efforts in 2020 Battleground States." ExpposedbyCMD.org. April 13, 2021. https://www.exposedbycmd.org/2021/04/13/alec-members-lead-voter-suppression-efforts-in-2020-battleground-states/

[588] "Fair Fight Action, and Over 300 Organizations Call on Corporations to Cut Ties with ALEC." Commondreams.org. June 14, 2021. https://www.commondreams.org/newswire/2021/06/14/

common-cause-fair-fight-action-and-over-300-organizations-call-corporations-cut

[589] Ari Berman and Nick Surgey. "Leaked Video: Dark Money Group Brags About Writing GOP Voter Suppression Bills Across the Country." Mother Jones Magazine. May 13, 2021. https://www.motherjones.com/politics/2021/05/heritage-foundation-dark-money-voter-suppression-laws/; Nick Corasaniti and Reid J. Epstein. "G.O.P. and Allies Draft 'Best Practices' for Restricting Voting." The New York Times. March 23, 2021. https://www.nytimes.com/2021/03/23/us/politics/republican-voter-laws.html

[590] Nick Corasaniti and Reid J. Epstein. "G.O.P. and Allies Draft 'Best Practices' for Restricting Voting." The New York Times. March 23, 2021. https://www.nytimes.com/2021/03/23/us/politics/republican-voter-laws.html

[591] Mayer, Jane. "The Big Money Behind the Big Lie." The New Yorker. August 2, 2021. https://www.newyorker.com/magazine/2021/08/09/the-big-money-behind-the-big-lie

[592] Udoma, Ebong. "UConn Study: At Least 96% of Black Lives Matter Protests Were Peaceful." WSHU.org. October 19, 2020. https://www.wshu.org/post/uconn-study-least-96-black-lives-matter-protests-were-peaceful

[593] Isabella Grullón Paz and Nick Corasaniti. "Did the George Floyd Protests Boost Democratic Voter Registration?" The New York Times. August 11, 2020. https://www.nytimes.com/2020/08/11/us/politics/democrats-voter-registration-george-floyd.html; Wise, Alana. "Protests Against Police Brutality Boosted Democratic Voter Registrations." NPR.org. August 11, 2020. https://www.npr.org/2020/08/11/901406969/protests-against-police-brutality-boosted-democratic-voter-registrations

[594] Wise, Alana. "Protests Against Police Brutality Boosted Democratic Voter Registrations." NPR.org. August 11, 2020. https://www.npr.org/2020/08/11/901406969/protests-against-police-brutality-boosted-democratic-voter-registrations

[595] Bump, Philip. "It's not just voting: Legislators have introduced 100 state bills targeting protesting." The Washington Post. May 13, 2021. https://www.washingtonpost.com/politics/2021/05/13/its-not-just-voting-legislators-have-introduced-100-state-bills-targeting-protesting/

[596] Bump, Philip. "It's not just voting: Legislators have introduced 100 state bills targeting protesting." The Washington Post. May 13, 2021. https://www.washingtonpost.com/politics/2021/05/13/its-not-just-voting-legislators-have-introduced-100-state-bills-targeting-protesting/

[597] Patricia Mazzei and Reid J. Epstein. "G.O.P. Bills Target Protesters (and Absolve Motorists Who Hit Them)." The New York Times. April 21, 2021. https://www.nytimes.com/2021/04/21/us/politics/republican-anti-protest-laws.html.

[598] Peters, Cameron. "State-level Republicans are making it easier to run over protestors." Vox Media. April 25, 2021. https://www.vox.com/2021/4/25/22367019/gop-laws-oklahoma-iowa-florida-floyd-blm-protests-police; Alleen Brown, Akela Lacy. "STATE LEGISLATURES MAKE "UNPRECEDENTED" PUSH ON ANTI-PROTEST BILLS." The Intercept. January 21, 2021. https://theintercept.com/2021/01/21/anti-protest-riot-state-laws/

[599] Sweren-Becker, Eliza. "Who Watches the Poll Watchers?" The Brennan Center. April 29, 2021. https://www.brennancenter.org/our-work/research-reports/who-watches-poll-watchers

[600] Ollstein, Alice Miranda. "Texas abortion ban spawns look-alike laws but could be short-lived." Politico. September 2, 2021. https://www.politico.com/news/2021/09/02/texas-abortion-law-private-right-to-sue-509244

[601] Cathryn Stout and Gabrielle LaMarr LeMee. "Efforts to restrict teaching about racism across the U.S." Chalk Beat. July 22, 2021. https://www.chalkbeat.org/22525983/map-critical-race-theory-legislation-teaching-racism

[602] CRT is an academic approach a fraction of students would most likely encounter at law school or post-graduate levels.

[603] Alexandra Gibbons and Rashawn Ray. "Why are states banning critical race theory?" The Brookings Institute. August 2021. https://www.brookings.edu/blog/fixgov/2021/07/02/why-are-states-banning-critical-race-theory/

[604] Chapter 404, House Bill No. 2898. Arizona House of Represen tatives. 2021-2022. https://www.azleg.gov/legtext/55leg/1R/laws/0404.pdf

[605] Senate Bill no. 460. Michigan House of Representatives. 2021-2022. https://www.legislature.mi.gov/documents/2021-2022/billintro duced/Senate/pdf/2021-SIB-0460.pdf

[606] Snyder, Timothy. "The War on History Is a War on Democracy." The New York Times Magazine. June 29, 2021. https://www.nytimes.com/2021/06/29/magazine/memory-laws.html

[607] Snyder, Timothy. "The War on History Is a War on Democracy." The New York Times Magazine. June 29, 2021. https://www.nytimes.com/2021/06/29/magazine/memory-laws.html

[608] Snyder, Timothy. "The War on History Is a War on Democracy." The New York Times Magazine. June 29, 2021. https://www.nytimes.com/2021/06/29/magazine/memory-laws.html

[609] "Debunking the Voter Fraud Myth." The Brennan Center for Justice. January 31, 2017. https://www.brennancenter.org/our-work/research-reports/debunking-voter-fraud-myth

[610] Arendt, Hannah. The Origins of Totalitarianism. (Orlando: Harcourt, Inc. 1973), 382.

[611] Frankovic, Kathy. "Why won't Americans get vaccinated?" YouGov America. July 15, 2021. https://today.yougov.com/topics/politics/articles-reports/2021/07/15/why-wont-americans-get-vaccinated-poll-data

[612] Palma, Sky. "Over half of AZ Republicans think GOP election audit will show Trump won in 2020." Deadstate.org. July 19, 2021. https://deadstate.org/over-half-of-az-republicans-think-gop-election-audit-will-show-trump-won-in-2020/

[613] Marquez, Xavier. "This is why authoritarian leaders use the 'Big Lie'." The Washington Post. January 26, 2017. https://www.washingtonpost.com/news/monkey-cage/wp/2017/01/26/this-is-why-authoritarian-leaders-use-the-big-lie/

[614] Levy, Jacob T. "Authoritarianism and Post-Truth Politics." The Niskanen Center. November 30, 2016. https://www.niskanencenter.org/authoritarianism-post-truth-politics/

[615] Levy, Jacob T. "Authoritarianism and Post-Truth Politics." The Niskanen Center. November 30, 2016. https://www.niskanencenter.org/authoritarianism-post-truth-politics/

[616] Frei, Matt. 'Big lies are part of authoritarian regime changes in history' – Prof Timothy Snyder on Trump election fraud claims." Channel4.com. January 14, 2021. https://www.channel4.com/news/big-lies-are-part-of-authoritarian-regime-changes-in-history-prof-timothy-snyder-on-trump-election-fraud-claims

Chapter 10: What's Next? And to What End?

[617] Daley, David. "How to Get Away With Gerrymandering." Slate. October 2, 2019. https://slate.com/news-and-politics/2019/10/alec-meeting-gerrymandering-audio-recording.html

[618] Alex Keena, Anthony McGann, Charles Anthony Smith, and Michael Latner. "Redistricting might gain Republicans a few seats in Congress. Their real gains will be in state legislatures." The Washington Post. May 4, 2021. https://www.washingtonpost.com/politics/2021/05/04/redistricting-might-gain-republicans-few-seats-congress-their-real-gains-will-be-state-legislatures/

[619] Berman, Ari. "GOP Could Retake the House in 2022 Just by Gerrymandering Four Southern States." Mother Jones Magazine. July 29, 2021. https://www.motherjones.com/politics/2021/07/gop-could-retake-the-house-in-2022-just-by-gerrymandering-four-southern-states/

[620] Berman, Ari. "GOP Could Retake the House in 2022 Just by Gerrymandering Four Southern States." Mother Jones Magazine. July 29, 2021. https://www.motherjones.com/politics/2021/07/gop-

could-retake-the-house-in-2022-just-by-gerrymandering-four-southern-states/

[621] Cox, Chelsey. "Fact check: State legislatures choose electors, but electors vote how state dictates." USA Today. November 10, 2020. https://www.usatoday.com/story/news/factcheck/2020/11/10/fact-check-state-legislators-choose-electors/6204171002/

[622] Ball, Molly. "The GOP Plan to Take the Electoral-Vote-Rigging Scheme National." The Atlantic. January 25, 2013. https://www.theatlantic.com/politics/archive/2013/01/the-gop-plan-to-take-the-electoral-vote-rigging-scheme-national/272523/

[623] Gomez, Henry J. "Secretary of State Jon Husted and other Republicans say Electoral College changes not in store for Ohio." Cleveland.com. January 29, 2013. https://www.cleveland.com/open/2013/01/secretary_of_state_jon_husted_2.html

[624] Ball, Molly. "The GOP Plan to Take the Electoral-Vote-Rigging Scheme National." The Atlantic. January 25, 2013. https://www.theatlantic.com/politics/archive/2013/01/the-gop-plan-to-take-the-electoral-vote-rigging-scheme-national/272523/; Gaskins, Keesha. "Tying Presidential Electors to Gerrymandered Congressional Districts will Sabotage Elections." The Brennan Center for Justice. January 22, 2013. https://www.brennancenter.org/our-work/analysis-opinion/tying-presidential-electors-gerrymandered-congressional-districts-will

[625] Hansen, Richard L. "Trump Is Planning a Much More Respectable Coup Next Time." Slate. August 5, 2021. https://slate.com/news-and-politics/2021/08/trump-2024-coup-federalist-society-doctrine.html

[626] Mayer, Jane. "The Big money Behind The Big Lie." The New Yorker. August 2, 2021. https://www.newyorker.com/magazine/2021/08/09/the-big-money-behind-the-big-lie

[627] Hansen, Richard L. "Trump Is Planning a Much More Respectable Coup Next Time." Slate. August 5, 2021. https://slate.com/news-and-politics/2021/08/trump-2024-coup-federalist-society-doctrine.html

628 Sedensky, Matt. "Conservatives want to bypass usual way to amend Constitution." The Associated Press. November 3, 2018. https://apnews.com/article/constitutions-us-supreme-court-elections-legislation-laws-e84cdca5b568402398eabfcd2b6ada07

629 "ARTICLE V POCKET GUIDE: Beautiful, simple, and to-the-point, the 2020 Pocket Guide is your one-stop-shop for everything Article V." Convention of States.com. 2020. https://conventionofstates.com

630 MacLean, Nancy. *Democracy in Chains.* (New York, New York: Penguin Random House, 2017), xxx-xxxi.

631 Mayer, Jane. *Dark Money.* (New York, New York: Doubleday, 2016), 359.

632 Woodward, C. Vann. *The Strange Career of Jim Crow.* Third Revised Edition. (New York, New York: The Oxford University Press: 2002), 69.

633 Wilkerson, Isabel. *Caste: The Origins of Our Discontents.* (New York, New York: Penguin Random House, 2020), 311.

634 Wilkerson, Isabel. *Caste: The Origins of Our Discontents.* (New York, New York: Penguin Random House, 2020), 318-319.

635 Wilkerson, Isabel. *Caste: The Origins of Our Discontents.* (New York, New York: Penguin Random House, 2020), 328.

636 Montini, EJ. "Arizona Republican lawmaker unwittingly exposes election reform scam." AZCentral.com. April 27, 2021. https://www.azcentral.com/story/opinion/op-ed/ej-montini/2021/04/27/arizona-gop-lawmaker-exposes-election-reform-voter-suppression-scam/7395257002/

637 Daniel Cox, Rachel Lienesch, and Robert P. Jones. "Beyond Economics: Fears of Cultural Displacement Pushed the White Working Class to Trump." American Renaissance. May 16, 2017. https://www.amren.com/news/2017/05/beyond-economics-fears-cultural-displacement-pushed-white-working-class-trump/

⁶³⁸ Bolies, Corbin. "Newt Gingrich Goes Full 'Great Replacement Theory' on Fox." The Daily Beast. August 5, 2021. https://www. thedailybeast.com/newt-gingrich-goes-full-great-replacement-theory-in-maria-bartiromo-interview-on-fox-business

⁶³⁹ Abrams, Stacey. *Our Time is Now.* First Edition. (New York, New York: Henry Holt and Company, 2021), 8-9.

⁶⁴⁰ Wilkerson, Isabel. *Caste: The Origins of Our Discontents.* (New York, New York: Penguin Random House, 2020), 315.

⁶⁴¹ Lucan A. Way and Steven Levitsky. "THE RISE OF COMPETITIVE AUTHORITARIANISM." Journal of Democracy Volume 13, Number 2 April 2002. https://scholar.harvard.edu/levitsky/files/SL_elections.pdf

⁶⁴² Beauchamp, Zack. "Call it Authoritarianism." Vox Media. June 15, 2021. https://www.vox.com/policy-and-politics/2021/6/15/22522504/republicans-authoritarianism-trump-competitive

⁶⁴³ "Statement of Concern: The Threats to American Democracy and the Need for National Voting and Election Administration Standards." NewAmerica.org. June 1, 2021. https://www.newamerica.org/political-reform/statements/statement-of-concern/

⁶⁴⁴ Beauchamp, Zack. "Why it matters that Tucker Carlson is broadcasting from Hungary this week." Vox Media. August 5, 2021. https://www.vox.com/policy-and-politics/2021/8/5/22607465/tucker-carlson-hungary-orban-authoritarianism-democracy-backsliding

⁶⁴⁵ Lucan Ahmad Way and Steven Levitsky. "How autocrats can rig the game and damage democracy." The Washington Post. January 4, 2019. https://www.washingtonpost.com/news/monkey-cage/wp/2019/01/04/how-do-you-know-when-a-democracy-has-slipped-over-into-autocracy/

⁶⁴⁶ Lucan Ahmad Way and Steven Levitsky. "How autocrats can rig the game and damage democracy." The Washington Post. January 4, 2019. https://www.washingtonpost.com/news/monkey-cage/wp/2019/

01/04/how-do-you-know-when-a-democracy-has-slipped-over-into-autocracy/

[647] Beauchamp, Zack. "Why it matters that Tucker Carlson is broadcasting from Hungary this week." Vox Media. August 5, 2021. https://www.vox.com/policy-and-politics/2021/8/5/22607465/tucker-carlson-hungary-orban-authoritarianism-democracy-backsliding

[648] Daniel Cox, Rachel Lienesch, and Robert P. Jones. "Beyond Economics: Fears of Cultural Displacement Pushed the White Working Class to Trump." American Renaissance. May 9, 2017. https://www.amren.com/news/2017/05/beyond-economics-fears-cultural-displacement-pushed-white-working-class-trump/

[649] Heffner, Alexander. "En Route to Autocracy in America." The American Prospect. October 11, 2020. https://prospect.org/politics/en-route-to-autocracy-in-america/

[650] "Statement of Concern: The Threats to American Democracy and the Need for National Voting and Election Administration Standards." NewAmerica.org. June 1, 2021. https://www.newamerica.org/political-reform/statements/statement-of-concern/

[651] "Meet the GOP Enemies of Democracy." RepublicanInsurrectionists.com. 2021. https://www.republicaninsurrectionists.com

Part III

[652] Pamela S. Karlan, Richard H. Pildes, and Samuel Issacharoff. *The Law of Democracy: Legal Structure of the Political Process.* 3rd Edition. (St. Paul, Minnesota: Foundation Press, 2007), 65.

[653] Pamela S. Karlan, Richard H. Pildes, and Samuel Issacharoff. *The Law of Democracy: legal structure of the political process.* 3rd Edition. (St. Paul, Minnesota: Foudation Press, 2007), 65

[654] Alfred A. Moss Jr. and John Hope Franklin. *From Slavery to Freedom: A History of African Americans.* Bob Greiner and Peter Labella. Seventh Edition. (New York, New York: McGraw Hill-Inc., 1994), 261.

[655] Archie E. Allen and John Lewis. "Black Voter Registration Efforts in the South." Notre Dame Law Review. Volume 48, Issue 1. Article 6. October 1, 1972. https://scholarship.law.nd.edu/cgi/viewcontent.cgi?article=2861&context=ndlr

[656] Alfred A. Moss Jr. and John Hope Franklin. *From Slavery to Freedom: A History of African Americans.* Bob Greiner and Peter Labella. Seventh Edition. (New York, New York: McGraw Hill-Inc., 1994), 261.

[657] Archie E. Allen and John Lewis. "Black Voter Registration Efforts in the South." Notre Dame Law Review. Volume 48, Issue 1. Article 6. October 1, 1972. https://scholarship.law.nd.edu/cgi/viewcontent.cgi?article=2861&context=ndlr

[658] Alfred A. Moss Jr. and John Hope Franklin. *From Slavery to Freedom: A History of African Americans.* Bob Greiner and Peter Labella. Seventh Edition. (New York, New York: McGraw Hill-Inc., 1994), 238.

[659] Alfred A. Moss Jr. and John Hope Franklin. *From Slavery to Freedom: A History of African Americans.* Bob Greiner and Peter Labella. Seventh Edition. (New York, New York: McGraw Hill-Inc., 1994), 239- 246.

[660] Woodward, C. Vann. *The Strange Career of Jim Crow.* Third Revised Edition. (New York, New York: The Oxford University Press: 2002), 54.

[661] Alfred A. Moss Jr. and John Hope Franklin. *From Slavery to Freedom: A History of African Americans.* Bob Greiner and Peter Labella. Seventh Edition. (New York, New York: McGraw Hill-Inc., 1994), 239.

[662] Alfred A. Moss Jr. and John Hope Franklin. *From Slavery to Freedom: A History of African Americans.* Bob Greiner and Peter Labella. Seventh Edition. (New York, New York: McGraw Hill-Inc., 1994), 239

[663] Woodward, C. Vann. *The Strange Career of Jim Crow*. Third Revised Edition. (New York, New York: The Oxford University Press: 2002), 54.

[664] Alfred A. Moss Jr. and John Hope Franklin. *From Slavery to Freedom: A History of African Americans*. Bob Greiner and Peter Labella. Seventh Edition. (New York, New York: McGraw Hill-Inc., 1994), 242.

[665] Archie E. Allen and John Lewis. "Black Voter Registration Efforts in the South." Notre Dame Law Review. Volume 48, Issue 1. Article 6. October 1, 1972. https://scholarship.law.nd.edu/cgi/viewcontent.cgi?article=2861&context=ndlr; Alfred A. Moss Jr. and John Hope Franklin. *From Slavery to Freedom: A History of African Americans*. Bob Greiner and Peter Labella. Seventh Edition. (New York, New York: McGraw Hill-Inc., 1994), 239.

[666] Alfred A. Moss Jr. and John Hope Franklin. *From Slavery to Freedom: A History of African Americans*. Bob Greiner and Peter Labella. Seventh Edition. (New York, New York: McGraw Hill-Inc., 1994), 254-263.

[667] Lichtman, Allan J. *The Embattled Vote in America*. (Cambridge, MA: Harvard University Press, 2018), 96.

[668] Wilkerson, Isabel. *Caste: The Origins of Our Discontents*. (New York, New York: Penguin Random House, 2020), 116.

[669] James W. Loewen. *Sundown Towns: A Hidden Dimension of American Racism*. (New York: The New Press, 2018), 39.

[670] Woodward, C. Vann. *The Strange Career of Jim Crow*. Third Revised Edition. (New York, New York: The Oxford University Press: 2002), 65-69.

Chapter 11: Reclaiming Democracy

[671] U.S. Const. art. IV, § 4

[672] Amar, Akhil Reed. *America's Constitution: A Biography*, 1st Edition. (New York, New York: Random House, 2006), 16.

[673] Madison, James. *Federalist No. 39 and 55.*

[674] Madison, James. *Federalist No. 39.*

[675] "Samuel Johnson's 1766 dictionary defined "Republican" as "[p]lacing the government in the people."" Amar, Akhil Reed. *America's Constitution: A Biography*, 1st Edition. (New York, New York: Random House, 2006), 278-79.

[676] Amar, Akhil Reed. "THE CENTRAL MEANING OF REPUBLICAN GOVERNMENT: POPULAR SOVEREIGNTY, MAJORITY RULE, AND THE DENOMINATOR PROBLEM." University of Colorado Law Review. Volume 65. 1993-1994. https://digitalcommons.law. yale.edu/cgi/viewcontent.cgi?article=1969&context=fss_papers.

[677] Chemerinsky, Erwin. "Cases under the Guarantee Clause Should Be Justiciable." University of Colorado Law Review. Volume 65. 1993-1994. https://scholarship.law.duke.edu/cgi/viewcontent.cgi?article=1696&context=faculty_scholarship

[678] Wood, Gordon S. *The Creation of the American Republic, 1776-1787.* (New York, New York: W.W. Norton & Company, 1972), 467.

[679] Amar, Akhil Reed. *America's Constitution: A Biography*, 1st Edition. (New York, New York: Random House, 2006), 70.

[680] Madison, James. Federalist No. 43.

[681] Amar, Akhil Reed. *America's Constitution: A Biography*, 1st Edition. (New York, New York: Random House, 2006), 280.

[682] Lichtman, Allan J. *The Embattled Vote in America.* (Cambridge, MA: Harvard University Press, 2018), 64.

[683] Madison, James. *Federalist No. 43.*

[684] Amar, Akhil Reed. *America's Constitution: A Biography*, 1st Edition. (New York, New York: Random House, 2006), 280.

[685] Madison, James. *Federalist No. 10.*

[686] Broeg, Cormac H. "Waking the Giant: A Role for the Guarantee Clause Exclusion Power in the Twenty-First Century." Iowa Law

Review. Volume 105, Issue 1319, 2020. https://ilr.law.uiowa.edu/print/volume-105-issue-3/waking-the-giant-a-role-for-the-guarantee-clause-exclusion-power-in-the-twenty-first-century/

[687] Luther v. Borden, 48 U.S. 1 (United States Supreme Court, 1849)

[688] Pacific States Tel. & Tel. Co. v. Oregon, 223 U.S. 118 (United States Supreme Court 1849); Luther v. Borden, 48 U.S. 1 (United States Supreme Court, 1849)

[689] Broeg, Cormac H. "Waking the Giant: A Role for the Guarantee Clause Exclusion Power in the Twenty-First Century." Iowa Law Review. Volume 105, Issue 1319, 2020. https://ilr.law.uiowa.edu/print/volume-105-issue-3/waking-the-giant-a-role-for-the-guarantee-clause-exclusion-power-in-the-twenty-first-century/

Chapter 12: Resistance at the National Level

[690] Alfred A. Moss Jr. and John Hope Franklin. *From Slavery to Freedom: A History of African Americans.* Bob Greiner and Peter Labella. Seventh Edition. (New York, New York: McGraw Hill-Inc., 1994), 251.

[691] Woodward, C. Vann. *The Strange Career of Jim Crow.* Third Revised Edition. (New York, New York: The Oxford University Press: 2002), 69.

[692] Daniel I. Weiner, Dominique Erney, and Wendy R. Weiser. "Congress Must Pass the 'For the People Act'." The Brennan Center for Justice. January 29, 2021. https://www.brennancenter.org/our-work/policy-solutions/congress-must-pass-people-act

[693] Ornstein, Norman. "Democrats can't kill the filibuster. But they can gut it." The Washington Post. March 2, 2021. https://www.washingtonpost.com/outlook/2021/03/02/manchin-filibuster-never-sinema/

[694] Lau, Tim. "The Filibuster, Explained." The Brennan Center. April 26, 2021. https://www.brennancenter.org/our-work/research-reports/filibuster-explained

[695] Shepardson, David. "Democrat Abrams urges lifting filibuster for U.S. election reform bill." Reuters. March 14, 2021. https://www.reuters.com/article/us-usa-congress-voting-idUSKBN2B60FK

[696] Ornstein, Norman. "Democrats can't kill the filibuster. But they can gut it." The Washington Post. March 2, 2021. https://www.washingtonpost.com/outlook/2021/03/02/manchin-filibuster-never-sinema/

[697] Ornstein, Norman. "Democrats can't kill the filibuster. But they can gut it." The Washington Post. March 2, 2021. https://www.washingtonpost.com/outlook/2021/03/02/manchin-filibuster-never-sinema/

[698] Siegel, Jim. "Which side is right in political battle over ECOT blame?" The Columbus Dispatch. September 2, 2018. https://www.dispatch.com/news/20180902/which-side-is-right-in-political-battle-over-ecot-blame

[699] Lipton, Eric. "Lobbyists, Bearing Gifts, Pursue Attorneys General." The New York Times. October 29, 2014. https://www.nytimes.com/2014/10/29/us/lobbyists-bearing-gifts-pursue-attorneys-general.html

[700] Wilson, Reid. "GOP attorneys general group in turmoil after Jan. 6 Trump rally." The Hill. April 22, 2021. https://thehill.com/homenews/campaign/549840-gop-attorneys-general-group-in-turmoil-after-jan-6-trump-rally

[701] "The Network." StatePolicyNetwork.org. 2021. https://spn.org/directory/

[702] Abrams, Stacey. Our Time is Now. First Edition. (New York, New York: Henry Holt and Company, 2021), 127.

[703] "2020 election to cost $14 billion, blowing away spending records." OpenSecrets.org. October 28, 2020. https://www.opensecrets.org/news/2020/10/cost-of-2020-election-14billion-update/

Chapter 13: Resistance at the State Level

[704] Ohio Democratic Party vs. Jon Husted. Case No. 16-3561 (United States Court of Appeals, Sixth Circuit, 2016) at 5. https://www.opn. ca6.uscourts.gov/opinions.pdf/16a0204p-06.pdf

[705] Pierce, Charles. "It's Still Hard To Vote In Ohio." Esquire Magazine. February 26, 2014. https://www.esquire.com/news-politics/politics/a27548/ohio-early-voting-022614/

[706] Galloway, Jim. "Stacey Abrams: 'I will not concede because the erosion of our democracy is not right'." The Atlanta Journal Constitution. November 16, 2018. https://www.ajc.com/blog/politics/stacey-abrams-will-not-concede-because-the-erosion-our-democracy-not-right/JQqttbuF09NYkMQbIYx9BM/

[707] Galloway, Jim. "Stacey Abrams: 'I will not concede because the erosion of our democracy is not right'." The Atlanta Journal Constitution. November 16, 2018. https://www.ajc.com/blog/politics/stacey-abrams-will-not-concede-because-the-erosion-our-democracy-not-right/JQqttbuF09NYkMQbIYx9BM/

[708] Galloway, Jim. "Stacey Abrams: 'I will not concede because the erosion of our democracy is not right'." The Atlanta Journal Constitution. November 16, 2018. https://www.ajc.com/blog/politics/stacey-abrams-will-not-concede-because-the-erosion-our-democracy-not-right/JQqttbuF09NYkMQbIYx9BM/

[709] Abrams, Stacey. Our Time is Now. First Edition. (New York, New York: Henry Holt and Company, 2021), 21.

[710] Fair Fight Action Inc. vs. Brad Raffensperger. Case No. 1:18-cv-05391-SCJ. (U.S. District Court for the Northern District of Georgia, Atlanta Division). https://fairfight.com/wp-content/uploads/2021/05/Second-Amended-Complaint.pdf.

[711] Abrams, Stacey. Our Time is Now. First Edition. (New York, New York: Henry Holt and Company, 2021), 12.

[712] Fair Fight Action Inc. vs. Brad Raffensperger. Case No. 1:18-cv-05391-SCJ. (U.S. District Court for the Northern District

of Georgia, Atlanta Division). https://fairfight.com/wp-content/uploads/2021/05/Second-Amended-Complaint.pdf.

[713] Nick Corasaniti and Reid J. Epstein. "Virginia, the Old Confederacy's Heart, Becomes a Voting Rights Bastion." The New York Times. April 2, 2021. https://www.nytimes.com/2021/04/02/us/politics/virginia-voting-rights-northam.html

[714] "Voting Laws Roundup: May 2021." The Brennan Center for Justice. May 28, 2021. https://www.brennancenter.org/our-work/research-reports/voting-laws-roundup-may-2021#footnote32_jnpkjdb

[715] Nick Corasaniti and Reid J. Epstein. "Virginia, the Old Confederacy's Heart, Becomes a Voting Rights Bastion." The New York Times. April 2, 2021. https://www.nytimes.com/2021/04/02/us/politics/virginia-voting-rights-northam.html

[716] "Voting Laws Roundup: May 2021." The Brennan Center for Justice. May 28, 2021. https://www.brennancenter.org/our-work/research-reports/voting-laws-roundup-may-2021#footnote32_jnpkjdb

[717] Nirappil, Fenit. "Democrats make significant gains in Virginia legislature; control of House in play." The Washington Post. November 8, 2017. https://www.washingtonpost.com/local/virginia-politics/democrats-poised-to-make-significant-gains-in-virginia-legislature/2017/11/07/9c2f4d24-c401-11e7-aae0-cb18a8c29c65_story.html

[718] "Virginia House of Delegates elections, 2019." Ballotpedia.com. https://ballotpedia.org/Virginia_House_of_Delegates_elections,_2019

[719] Arthur Laffer, Jonathan Williams, and Stephen Moore. "Rich States, Poor States." 8th Edition. The American Legislative Exchange Council. 2015. https://www.alec.org/app/uploads/2015/10/RSPS_8th_Edition-Final.pdf

[720] Harmon, Michael. "Sam Brownback declares war on Kansas: This is how extremists gut a state -- and democracy." Salon Magazine.

April 12, 2016 https://www.salon.com/2016/04/12/sam_brownback_ declares_war_on_kansas_this_is_how_extremists_gut_a_state_ and_democracy/

[721] Arthur Laffer, Jonathan Williams, and Stephen Moore. "Rich States, Poor States." 11th Edition. The American Legislative Exchange Council. 2021. https://www.richstatespoorstates.org/app/ uploads/2018/04/RSPS-2018-WEB.pdf

[722] Gleckman, Howard. "The Great Kansas Tax Cut Experiment Crashes And Burns." Forbes. June 7, 2017. https://www.forbes.com/ sites/beltway/2017/06/07/the-great-kansas-tax-cut-experiment-crashes-and-burns/?sh=35bb34dd5508

[723] Lee, Trymaine. "Kansas school districts to close early after tax cut 'experiment'." MSNBC.com. April 4, 2015. https://www.msnbc. com/msnbc/kansas-school-districts-close-early-after-tax-cut-experiment-msna566356

[724] Tobias, Suzanne Perez. "Southeast Kansas district implements four-day school week." The Wichita Eagle. April 19, 2016. https:// www.kansas.com/news/local/education/article72631157.html

[725] Leachman, Michael. "Timeline: 5 years of Kansas' Tax-Cut Disaster." Center on Budget and Policy Priorities. May 24, 2017. https://www.cbpp.org/blog/timeline-5-years-of-kansas-tax-cut-disaster

[726] Gale, William G. "The Kansas tax cut experiment." The Brookings Institute. July 11, 2017. https://www.brookings.edu/ blog/unpacked/2017/07/11/the-kansas-tax-cut-experiment/; Gleckman, Howard. "The Great Kansas Tax Cut Experiment Crashes And Burns." Forbes. June 7, 2017. https://www.forbes.com/sites

[727] Greenblatt, Alan. "The Long Road to Recovery After Years of Severe Budget Cuts." Governing.com. July 29, 2019. https://www. governing.com/archive/gov-kansas-governor.html

[728] Arthur Laffer, Jonathan Williams, and Stephen Moore. "Rich States, Poor States." 8th Edition. The American Legislative Exchange Council. 2015. https://www.alec.org/app/uploads/2015/10/RSPS_8th_Edition-Final.pdf

[729] Arthur Laffer, Jonathan Williams, and Stephen Moore. "Rich States, Poor States." 13th Edition. The American Legislative Exchange Council. 2021. https://www.alec.org/app/uploads/2020/08/13th-RSPS-FINAL_WEB.pdf

[730] Smith, Mitch. "Laura Kelly, a Kansas Democrat, Tops Kobach in Governor's Race." The New York Times. November 6, 2018. https://www.nytimes.com/2018/11/06/us/laura-kelly-wins-kansas-governors-race.html; Green, Chris. "Promises matter in the 2018 Kansas governor's race between Kris Kobach, Laura Kelly and Greg Orman." KLC Journal. October 3, 2018. https://klcjournal.com/promises-matter-in-the-2018-kansas-governors-race-between-kris-kobach-laura-kelly-and-greg-orman/

[731] Smith, Mitch. "Laura Kelly, a Kansas Democrat, Tops Kobach in Governor's Race." The New York Times. November 6, 2018. https://www.nytimes.com/2018/11/06/us/laura-kelly-wins-kansas-governors-race.html

[732] "Laura Kelly 2018 Democratic Primary Kansas Governor TV Ad #1." Youtube.com KansasPolitics. July 14, 2018. https://www.youtube.com/watch?v=vL9MwpVwRxI

[733] "Laura Kelly 2018 Democratic Primary Kansas Governor TV Ad #2." Youtube.com KansasPolitics. July 31, 2018. https://www.youtube.com/watch?v=TbOcsLUlV0A

[734] Kelly, Laura. "Gubernatorial Victory Speech - Nov. 6, 2018." Iowa State University Archives of Women's Political Communication. November 6, 2018. https://awpc.cattcenter.iastate.edu/2019/01/10/gubernatorial-victory-speech-nov-6-2018/

[735] "Fix the Roads." Youtube.com. Gretchen Whitmer. July 24, 2018. https://www.youtube.com/watch?v=ud2zh0EkKi4

[736] Sommerhauser, Mark. "What sank Scott Walker? His ambition, his record, Tony Evers, and the Donald Trump backlash." The Associated Press. November 12, 2018. https://apnews.com/article/2ce4043717df4d44b3385e38a611bc50

[737] Kenning, Chris. "Ohio lawmakers approve redistricting reform proposal for voters." Reuters. February 6, 2018. https://www. reuters.com/article/us-ohio-redistricting/ohio-lawmakers-approve-redistricting-reform-proposal-for-voters-idUSKBN1FR00N

[738] Wartman, Scott. "Hamilton County GOP chair deletes tweet on gerrymandering after backlash." Cincinnati Enquirer. August 25, 2021. https://www.cincinnati.com/story/news/politics/2021/08/25/redistricting-hamilton-county-republican-chair-deletes-tweet/5584114001/

[739] Abrams, Stacey. *Our Time is Now*. First Edition. (New York, New York: Henry Holt and Company, 2021), 138.

[740] Eighteen states allow citizens to initiate Constitutional Amendments like we did to reform the districting process. Twenty-one states allow citizens to initiate directed statutes. Twenty-three states allow voters to veto legislation, as Ohio did with Senate Bill 5.

[741] Abrams, Stacey. *Our Time is Now*. First Edition. (New York, New York: Henry Holt and Company, 2021), 6.

[742] "Casey Weinstein." Ballotpedia.com. https://ballotpedia.org/Casey_Weinstein

[743] "Phil Robinson." Ballotpedia.com. https://ballotpedia.org/Phil_Robinson

[744] "Jessica Miranda." Ballotpedia.com. https://ballotpedia.org/Jessica_Miranda

[745] Namigadde, Adora. "Reynoldsburg Makes History With America's First Nepali-Bhutanese Elected Official." WOSU.org. November 7, 2019. https://news.wosu.org/news/2019-11-07/reynoldsburg-makes-history-with-americas-first-nepali-bhutanese-elected-official

[746] Nirappil, Fenit. "Democrats make significant gains in Virginia legislature; control of House in play." The Washington Post. November 8, 2017. https://www.washingtonpost.com/local/virginia-politics/democrats-poised-to-make-significant-gains-in-virginia-legislature/2017/11/07/9c2f4d24-c401-11e7-aae0-cb18a8c29c65_story.html

[747] Abrams, Stacey. *Our Time is Now*. First Edition. (New York, New York: Henry Holt and Company, 2021), 207; Nilsen, Ella. "The women, people of color, and LGBTQ candidates who made history in the 2017 election." Vox Media. November 8, 2017. https://www.vox.com/policy-and-politics/2017/11/8/16622884/women-minorities-lgbtq-candidates-made-history; Trull, Armando. "Northern Virginia's New Delegates Reflect The Diversity Of The Region." WASMU.org. November 10, 2017. https://wamu.org/story/17/11/10/northern-virginias-new-delegates-reflect-diversity-region/.

[748] Lublin, David. "Eight White-Majority Districts Elect black Members of Congress this year. That's a breakthrough." Washington Post. November 9, 2018. https://www.washingtonpost.com/news/monkey-cage/wp/2018/11/19/this-november-eight-mostly-white-districts-elected-black-members-of-congress-thats-a-breakthrough/

[749] Niesse, Mark. "Almost all eligible Georgians are registered to vote, data show." Atlanta Journal Constitution. Aug 19, 2021. https://www.ajc.com/politics/almost-all-eligible-georgians-are-registered-to-vote-data-show/WVN373LTIZAN7IJECDODHRJWLM/

[750] Glaser, Mark. "5 Reasons that 2020 Was the Year of Nonprofit Local News." The Knight Foundation. December 10, 2020. https://knightfoundation.org/articles/5-reasons-that-2020-was-the-year-of-nonprofit-local-news/

[751] "Who We Are." The American Journalism Project. http://www.theajp.org/who-we-are/

[752] "Rise of the Nonprofits." Northwestern Medill School of Journalism. 2019. https://localnewsinitiative.northwestern.edu/research/news-leaders/rise-of-nonprofits/

[753] Allen, Barbara. "The Trib Effect." Poynter.org. https://www.poynter.org/story-of-the-texas-tribune/

[754] Allen, Barbara. "The Trib Effect." Poynter.org. https://www.poynter.org/story-of-the-texas-tribune/

[755] Allen, Barbara. "The Trib Effect." Poynter.org. https://www.poynter.org/story-of-the-texas-tribune/

[756] Buchanan, Tyler. "Sen. Portman heard from 'dozens' of black leaders. Here's what they said." Ohio Capital Journal. June 9, 2020. https://ohiocapitaljournal.com/2020/06/09/sen-portman-heard-from-dozens-of-black-leaders-his-office-wont-name-one/

[757] "Indivisible States: How State Legislatures Work." Indivisble.org. 2021. https://indivisible.org/resource/indivisible-states-how-state-legislatures-work

[758] "Indivisible States: Tactics For State Legislative Advocacy." Indivisble.org. 2021. https://indivisible.org/resource/indivisible-states-tactics-state-legislative-advocacy